READINGS
IN
STRATIFICATIONAL
LINGUISTICS

edited by
Adam Makkai
and
David G. Lockwood

graphics by
Earl M. Herrick

The University of Alabama Press
University, Alabama

CONTENTS

Preface

THE PRESENT VOLUME is a collection of some of the most significant articles on stratificational linguistics which were written over the past several years. It fulfills an urgent need for a representative anthology, consisting of the writings of various authors, which reflects the development of stratificational theory and its applications to specific problems of linguistic descriptions. We hope that this work will answer the frequently heard demand for a single volume which will explain the workings of stratificational linguistics to the uninitiated, and which can serve as a textbook for graduate or advanced undergraduate courses dealing with the comparison of modern linguistic theories and stratificational grammar specifically.

The book is divided into two main sections: I. Aspects of the stratificational view of language, and II. Specific studies in stratificational phonology, grammar, and semology. Section I contains articles dealing with theoretical considerations, while section II illustrates specific applications of the theory.

The evolution of stratificational thinking and the resultant changes in terminology and approach, which are bound to be present in any new theory, have been a source of confusion and criticism in the past. An attempt has been made to resolve this difficulty in the present volume, first by the inclusion of Lamb's recent article 'The Crooked Path of Progress in Cognitive Linguistics,' which discusses the stages in the development of stratificational theory, following a classification originally proposed by Ilah Fleming. Furthermore, articles dealing with the same general area have been arranged chronologically and the stage of the theory which each represents has been specifically indicated.

It is hoped that in this way the reader will be able to follow the development of the theory and to understand the reasons for the changes that have been made.

At the beginning of each section there is an introductory passage written by the editors discussing the import of stratificational theory in that particular aspect of theoretical linguistics and showing the evolution of stratificational thinking as new insights were gained into the workings of language. These introductory passages also contain brief characterizations of each article in the given section in order to put it into its proper perspective with regard to the theory as a whole.

Careful editing of all the articles has been done in order to make them conform as far as it seemed practicable to the style sheet now in use by the Linguistic Society of America, and to make for a fully consistent style throughout this volume. Additionally, some portions of some articles which repeated examples or points previously made in earlier articles have been deleted in order to make the book an integrated whole rather than merely a bound collection of articles. Wherever such deletions or changes in terminology occur, the reader will find an editorial comment in French brackets « » calling attention to the fact that deletion or changing of terminology has occurred.

At the end of the volume there is an integrated bibliography of references from all contributions in this volume, replacing the individual and, hence, often repetitive bibliographies of each article. Bibliographical footnotes have been worked into the text in accordance with the style sheet of the Linguistic Society of America. There is also an index of authors' names, with page number references, at the end of the volume.

For reasons of space, it was not possible to include all the articles we would have liked to. In general, we tried to limit ourselves to those articles which have contributed significantly to the theory or which are particularly effective in demonstrating the validity and applicability of stratificational analysis.

Preference has been given to significant, but previously unpublished articles over those that have appeared in readily available journals, such as *Language*.

WE DID NOT INCLUDE portions of any books, such as Sydney M. Lamb's *Outline of Stratificational Grammar,* since these are easily obtainable elsewhere. We also did not include any articles which are programmatic, whose theoretical orientation is currently being revised by the author, or which deal not with language directly but rather with broader applications of stratificational analysis to such cultural phenomena as music, dancing, and sign language. A future anthology may perhaps specialize in the nonlinguistic applications of stratificational theory.

ADAM MAKKAI
DAVID G. LOCKWOOD

STRATIFICATIONAL LINGUISTICS

ASPECTS
OF THE STRATIFICATIONAL
VIEW OF LANGUAGE

The six papers in this section of the book introduce the reader to the stratificational philosophy of language in general. They do not, however, show the application of the theory to the solution of extensive linguistic problems.

John Algeo's 'Stratificational Grammar' has the distinction of being the most readable account of so complex and difficult a problem. It is thus the logical paper with which to begin such a book. Not only does the author possess a thorough command of the technicalities involved, but he is able to provide the beginner with appropriate analogies from literary history and classical antiquity.

This introduction is followed by an unusually thorough and self-searching account of the evolution and current state of the theory; namely, Lamb's paper 'The Crooked Path of Progress in Cognitive Linguistics.' We cannot overemphasize the importance of careful self-documentation in this respect. A word of comparison might be in order here, in that it is clear in 1972 that it is necessary to distinguish several stages in the development of transformational-generative grammar as well, if indeed we can call modern transformational grammar a single theory. Following the lead of Ilah Flemming (1969) Lamb systematically leads the reader through each step in the development of stratificational theory, comparing the insights provided at each stage with those of both classical Neo-Bloomfieldian and other theories. The stages thus referred to (I-IV) have been used throughout this reader to indicate the vintage of each contribution.

The next two papers by Lamb give an introduction to the theory at two different stages of its development—III and IV. In addition, each article expounds the relation of the theory to a specific research area: namely, machine translation and general cognition.

The first of these articles, 'Stratificational Linguistics as a Basis for Machine Translation,' outlines the theory of Stage III. Further details of the model at this stage are introduced in 'Kinship Terminology and Linguistic Structure' (in Section II). In the version presented here, the tactic systems, considered adjuncts to the main generative mechanism (except in the case of semotactics) in earlier stages, begin to be more fully integrated into the model. The tactics of each stratum is stated in terms of so-called BASIC XEMES. Each of these units is the realization of an XON of the stratum above, and is realized as an actual or realized XEME of its own stratal system. Discrepancies between Xons and basic Xemes involve mainly arrangement, and are indicated by the tactics, while those between basic Xemes and realized Xemes are specified by realization rules. This paper also puts considerable emphasis on Lamb's desire for maximum simplicity, comparing the process of linguistic simplification to factoring in high-school algebra.

'Linguistic and Cognitive Networks' then reasserts the basic concepts of the theory so far developed in terms of a fairly recent version of stage IV. Here the emphasis is on the linguistic system as a network of relationships, and the reader finds the position systematically developed with data from English exemplifying the properties of the various strata. The treatment of some of the examples has been somewhat simplified for the purpose of introductory exposition, and does not represent Lamb's current opinion of their precise analysis. For example, phonological components for types of articulation are now thought to come directly out of the phonotactics, rather than being introduced in the phonemic sign pattern as is done here. A feature of this paper which does reflect a more recent development is the extension of the morphotactics to encompass phrases as well as single words. In the earlier version of stage IV, as in the *Outline of Stratificational Grammar,* morphotactics was considered responsible for the distribution of morphemes only up to the level of words. The concept of DIAMONDS as connections between strata is also systematically introduced in this paper. Most significantly, it also provides an extension of the theory toward a representation of cognitive concepts, such as the structure of a baseball game, animal taxonomy, and the classical syllogism. It is demonstrated that the same kind of relational networks used for linguistic structure can be extended to represent human cognition as well. It is still not absolutely clear, of course, to what extent cognition can be considered a part of linguistics. Lamb tentatively proposes the term GNOSTEMIC STRATUM in this paper for that part of man's competence where 'thinking', the most abstract part of our consciousness, is located.

The remaining three papers in this section are the work of Peter A. Reich. They are somewhat less general than those of Lamb, though each deals with a specific concept within stratificational theory that has broad implications for the theory as a whole.

The first of these papers, 'Competence, Performance, and Relational Networks,' seeks to show the relation of the theory to psycholinguistics. It reviews Fodor and Garrett 1966, which, the author points out, documents the failure of transformational theory to predict psycholinguistic data. It is shown how a relational network model based on Lamb's stratificational grammar (and Reich frequently proposes his own solutions independently of Lamb's work) attempts to avoid this failure by incorporating a distinction between linguistic and problem solving mechanisms, and restrictions which attempt to make relational networks behave in a way similar to the brain.

Reich's 'Symbols, Relations, and Structural Complexity' compares the relational network approach to linguistic description with the rewrite rule approach. It discusses in considerable detail an evaluation procedure for alternate network solutions and proposes new treatments of optionality and AND-OR choices. This article is particularly important because it demonstrates that the algebraic notation used by Chomsky and his followers can be misleading with regard to the matter of 'simplicity'. The Chomsky notation fails to make certain relations explicit, and it allows simplifications which are purely a matter of symbol-manipulation rather than significant generalizations. Both of these points are revealed by the network notation of stratificational grammar. The evaluation procedure developed here provides a stratificational answer to Chomsky's assertion of 1957 that one of the important goals of theoretical linguistics should be the construction of an evaluation procedure to allow the comparison of competing treatments of the same data.

A. M.
D. G. L.

CHAPTER ONE

*Stratificational Grammar**

JOHN ALGEO

HENRY ADAMS seems to have been at least partly right when, in *The Education of Henry Adams,* he postulated a law of acceleration in human life whereby scientific knowledge increases in complexity at an ever increasing rate.[1] At least recent events in American linguistics lend support to the idea of such a law of acceleration. New linguistic theory has been following new linguistic theory with dizzy speed.

However, our recent progress in linguistics differs from Adams's law of acceleration in one respect. In 1905 Henry Adams thought that knowledge was increasing so rapidly that sometime between the 1930's and the 1950's it would reach a zenith from which it would be possible to predict the past and future course of human life as accurately as a mathematician could plot the path of a comet. To be sure, there are those who believe that the perihelion of linguistic knowledge was reached in 1933 or in 1957, thus verifying Adams' prediction, but linguistic theorists as a whole have gone on grinding out one new theory after another as though in general linguistics as in General Electric, progress were our most important product.

In fact, change in linguistic theory is so rapid that nowadays you have to specify not only whose theory you are talking about, but what year's model you have in mind. Chomsky's *Syntactic Structures* of 1957 is already being referred to as 'classical transformational theory,' thus placing it in the same category as *Oedipus Rex* and the Phidian Jove. Acceleration could hardly be greater. Moreover there are signs that Chomsky's 1965 *Aspects*

*From *Journal of English Linguistics* 3.1–7 (1969). An earlier version appeared in the *South Atlantic Bulletin* 23:2.1–4 (1968). Reprinted by permission.

of the Theory of Syntax may soon be thought of as what disc-jockeys call a Golden Oldie, because extensive design changes have been proposed in the theory. Apparently we must get used to trading in our grammar along with our car each year for a newer model. But those who regret the Detroit syndrome in grammar can at least take comfort in the thought that it keeps the linguistic economy moving. In short there seems to be no immediate prospect of our running out of new theories because we have reached final linguistic truth. We can look forward to the law of acceleration continuing to operate in language study for some time to come.

However, talk about acceleration and progress is misleading. It sounds too uniform, too well-directed, and much too harmonious. In fact, a better metaphor for the present state of linguistic theory would be that of a battle. Bloomfieldian and Tragerian Structuralism, which seemed firmly ensconced in the fortress of orthodoxy a scant ten years ago, have been overrun by the armies of Transformationalism. Tagmemic chaplains have set up their tents in the exotic bush. There are rumors of an invasion by Firthian foreigners. Dashing across the empty plains from a distant Danish horizon comes a new band, the troop of Stratificationalism. We need some modern Prudentius to describe this Glossomachia.

This paper will discuss stratificational theory, one of the newer entries in the lists, in a general way, there being in fact hardly any other way in which it can be discussed at present. Consequently these remarks might be more fittingly called the prolegomena to a paper on stratificational theory. The theory itself is far from fully developed and there is as yet no extensive grammar of any language written in stratificational terms. Nevertheless, James Sledd's trenchant observation that stratificational grammar 'at the moment is like posterity—a gleam in its father's eye' is no longer entirely just. Recent meetings of the Linguistic Society have included papers applying stratificational theory to various problems, and there is a small, but growing literature on the subject, as Ilah Fleming's bibliography demonstrates. Although still in a formative stage, stratificational theory has some interesting promises, and if it lives up to them, it will be worth our attention. Before examining its promises, however, we need to consider what the theory is, and it will be convenient to begin by distinguishing three senses in which the term stratificational may be used.

In the most general sense, stratificational theory describes a language as consisting of a limited number of strata or, to speak unmetaphorically, sub-systems. The stratificational view thus contrasts with a grammar that tries to account for the whole of a language as a single system, with a single basic unit combined into complex structures. For example, an unstratified grammar might describe morphemes as composed directly of phonemes. A stratified description instead recognizes two different subsystems, each with its own characteristic unit, morpheme and phoneme. Morphemes are not composed of phonemes, but are indirectly connected to them through a relationship that can be called REALIZATION.

Although some Bloomfieldians (including Bloomfield himself) have at some times spoken as though they held an unstratified view, there is no reason to believe any natural language can be described within such a limited framework. Consequently in practice linguists have used some variety of stratified description, although often an inexplicit one. So it turns out that most grammars are at least partly or at least informally stratified. Their authors are thus in the position of Molière's *bourgeois gentilhomme,* who discovered to his delight that he had been speaking prose all his life without knowing it. Most grammarians have been writing stratificational grammars without knowing it because they have dealt with two or more kinds of units that are related to one another, but not simply as a whole to its parts, or as a class to its members. The question is thus not whether a grammar is stratified, but whether it is explicitly stratified. If the stratification is explicit, the following questions become relevant: How many strata does the grammar recognize? What is the internal structure of each stratum? How are the strata related to one another?

The foregoing questions lead us to the second sense in which the term stratificational grammar may be used: namely, to designate a model of language that is being developed chiefly by Sydney Lamb and H. A. Gleason, Jr. It is an explicitly stratified grammar that recognizes six strata grouped into three major components of two strata each:

> *Linguistic Strata*   communicative content
>   semology: meaning
>   hypersememic
>   sememic smallest integral unit of meaning
>   grammar:
>   lexemic
>   morphemic
>   phonology: sound
>   phonemic   vocal expression
>   hypophonemic

(marginal annotation: stratification)

Collectively, the strata are a system or code for relating communicative content at the 'top' to vocal expression at the 'bottom.'

Each stratum has its characteristic unit or eme. The top and the bottom strata are concerned with distinctive features—of meaning and of sound, respectively. Their emes are the minimal differences in the content and in the expression of a text. The distinctive features of sound, the hypophonemes in Lamb's terminology, are relatively easy to study because there are so few of them—only about twelve to fifteen in most languages. Sample hypophonemes are PLOSION, SPIRANCY, NASALITY, LABIALITY, and UNVOICING. The distinctive features of meaning are much more numerous, and consequently much more difficult to study. They will presumably include items like ENTITY, PROCESS, ANIMATE, ABSTRACT, HUMAN, MALE, and FEMALE. Although several starts have been made, not much has been accomplished for this part of language except for some severely limited areas like kinship terminology, which has been studied if not exhaustively, at least exhaustingly, in the anthropological journals.

The sememic stratum deals in meaning-units of the kind C. F. Hockett called 'idioms' in *A Course in Modern Linguistics* (New York: Macmillan, 1958), p. 172. These idioms or sememes may be realized on lower strata as phrases *(bull in a china shop, put up with)*, as complex words *(refer, housewife)* or as single morphemes *(ox, plural)*. The characteristic of the sememe is that it cannot be divided into segments without losing some or all of its meaning. It is therefore the smallest integral unit of meaning, whether it corresponds to a single morpheme or a combination of them.

The lexemic stratum deals with what has traditionally been called syntax and corresponds roughly to Chomsky's level of surface structure. The eme of this stratum is the smallest unit that forms syntactic combinations. Such lexemes are realized on the next lower stratum as morphemes *(bull, put, with,* the plural-*s)* or as morpheme constructions *(housewife, chinashop, refer)* whose internal structure does not involve syntactic relations.

The Lambian morpheme and phoneme are units of the same size as the familiar neo-Bloomfieldian units, but they differ from their familiar namesakes in significant ways. Lamb's morpheme is approximately the equivalent of what has traditionally been called a morphemically conditioned allomorph such as *go* and the *wen-* of *went* or the noun plural -*s* and the -*en* of *oxen*. Lamb's phoneme shares some of the characteristics of the conventional morphophoneme. For example the *n* of *an,* because it occurs only before vowels and never before consonants, must be a different Lambian phoneme from the *n* of *than,* which has no such limitations on its distribution. Although these two *n*'s differ in phonemic distribution, they have the same realization and thus are identical on the hypophonemic stratum.

Each stratum consists of an inventory of its characteristic units or emes, and a set of tactic rules that specify how the emes combine with one another on that stratum. Finally, strata are connected to one another by realizational rules, which describe how the emes of one stratum are linked to those of another. For example these rules relate the morpheme *blue* to various lexemes above it such as *bluebird, sky-blue, blues* 'melancholia,' and simple *blue,* as well as to the phonemes below it, *b, l,* and *u*. The realizational rules come in three parts: the upper alternation pattern, which connects to a higher stratum and accounts for conditioned alternation; the lower alternation pattern, which accounts for free variation; and the sign pattern, which leads to a lower stratum. At either end, the whole linguistic system is connected to nonlinguistic reality, to experience or thought at the top and to vocal-auditory sound at the bottom.

Any text, for example a sentence, exists on all strata simultaneously. On each stratum, the text will be a structure of emes ordered by the appropriate tactic rules, but on each stratum it will have a different structure. In effect, the strata furnish alternate ways of looking at the texts of a language. In Gleason's view expressed during the summer Linguistic Institute of 1967, the structure on the semological strata is that of a network or reticulum in which a single unit may have multiple connections with other units, as in the Shakespearean text 'Men have died from time to time, and worms have eaten them, but not for love' the same *men* have different connections to the dying and the eating. Grammatically, the text is a tree of the familiar constituent structure sort. Phonologically, it is a chain or a string of elements. And it is all these things—network, tree, and string—at once. Or rather, a text is a complex set of relationships linking some bit of human experience, its meaning, to sound waves in the air. The grammarian describes these relationships as a series of interlocked structures.

Some important consequences follow from the notion that a single text has a number of different but simultaneous structures. One is that two texts may be identical or highly similar on one stratum, while they are significantly different on some other stratum. As a well-known and often cited example we can take the two texts *The sons raise meat* and *The sun's rays meet*. These two texts are distinct on the grammatical strata, but have overlapping phonological realizations. This is the relationship of homonymy, which can be defined for the present purpose as the overlapping on some stratum of texts that are distinct on higher strata.

Bloomfieldian structuralism had no trouble in accounting for homonymy of the kind illustrated by *The sons raise meat* and *The sun's rays meet* because it had, in effect, separated phonology and grammar as distinct strata. But there are other kinds of homonymy, for example that illustrated by the three texts *his picture* 'he possesses it,' *his picture* 'he made it,' and *his picture* 'it is a picture of him.' These three texts are distinct semologically, but overlap grammatically. This kind of homonymy Bloomfieldianism was unable to cope with because it had not stratified the relevant portions of the system. Bloomfieldianism tried to deal with some semological matters as part of its morphemics and syntax. The rest it simply ignored as outside the proper concern of linguistics. The Bloomfieldians were using a ploy common to grammarians of all schools, who regularly conclude that whatever their particular theory cannot handle is outside the proper concern of linguistics or else that it is trivial and uninteresting.

A properly stratified description will, however, have no trouble in handling any kind of homonymy nor its opposite, synonymy, the overlapping on some stratum of texts that are distinct on lower strata. This definition of synonymy, like that of homonymy, is an extension of the common meaning to designate a relationship that includes but is considerably more general than the received use of the term. Bloomfieldianism was able to account for synonyms of the kind *I will miss you* versus *I'll mishya,* which are phonologically different but grammatically alike. However it had no easy way of showing that *his arrival, him to arrive,* and *he arrives* are also synonyms, being grammatically different realizations of the same semological structure.

Because each text exists on six different strata and because two texts can overlap on some strata but not on others, there is no need and indeed no room for process statements in the Lamb-Gleason stratificational grammar, except as descriptions of historical change in a language. A process statement says that *x* becomes, or is changed into, or is replaced by *y*, but in a stratified grammar, *x* never disappears, is never changed into anything. *X* as a unit on one stratum may be realized as *y* on another stratum, but does not thereby disappear. Rather *x* remains as part of the structure of a text in its own stratal system, as unchanged and unchangeable as that breed of marble men and maidens with which Keats' urn was overwrought.

In this regard, it should be recognized that there is nothing inherently wrong with process statements. They are one way of characterizing linguistic structures. The task of the grammarian is to describe that complex set of relationships linking sound and meaning, which has already been mentioned. To carry out his task he may create an imaginary time dimension along which he moves some of the units he is concerned with. He will then describe linguistic relationships as a process in which one thing becomes another. Or to carry out his task he may create an imaginary space dimension (or several imaginary space dimensions) in which he locates the units he is concerned with. He will then describe linguistic relationships as an arrangement of items relative to one another. Both process and arrangement descriptions are metaphors. There may be valid grounds for preferring one metaphor to the other, but these grounds cannot be that either metaphor represents language as it 'really' is. Both are fictions. Lamb, however, while agreeing that a process statement in a synchronic description is sheer fiction, believes that the stratal description he offers as an alternative to it is more than simple metaphor—is, in fact, an analog to structural differences in the brain involved in speech production and perception. If that is correct it would be grounds for preferring imaginary space as less fictional than imaginary time. Nevertheless, the choice between the two forms of statement is probably made most often on aesthetic grounds. It would seem that every little girl and boy that's born into our world alive is not only a little liberal or else a little conservative, but also a little Heraclitean or else a little Parmenidean. If he is a born Heraclitean, he loves Becoming and grows into a Transformationalist. If he is a born Parmenidean, he is enamored with Being and is realized on the adult stratum as Sydney Lamb.

The third sense of stratificational grammar that can be distinguished is really a system of notation, a device for making statements about linguistic relationships. If we want to be quite rigorous in our linguistic statements, and rigor is very much in fashion just now, we need some precise and unambiguous method of expressing ourselves. Here we have several options. We may use quasi-algebraic formulas, which are also very much in fashion just now although this sort of notational device is at least a hundred years old. One style for writing such formulas is the familiar S → NP + VP, which may be read as 'A sentence consists of a noun phrase followed by a verb phrase.' That reading suggests a second option. We can always be rigorous in writing our grammar by using normal English in a rigorous way. Only such 'normal' English will turn out not to be normal at all, but to be an abnormal and highly restricted variety of natural language.

Natural language is unrigorous, ambiguous, and poetry-ridden. That is why it is so adaptable and so useful. The kind of quasi-normal English we can use in writing a rigorous grammar is a sublanguage that needs to be interpreted in exactly the same way a quasi-algebraic formula needs interpretation.

A rigorous stratificational grammar can be written in quasi-normal English or in quasi-algebraic formulas, or it can also be written in another way: with a special sort of diagram Sydney Lamb has invented. These drawings are quasi-circuitry diagrams consisting entirely of lines and nodes of various kinds. The diagrams are equivalent to formulas or 'normal' English as a means of expressing grammatical relationships. And since diagrams, formulas, and 'normal' English are equivalent ways of expressing a grammar, the choice between them depends on convenience and prejudice. The diagrams are useful graphic presentations of linguistic data that make immediately obvious certain relationships between linguistic units which might otherwise be overlooked, but they are not an indispensable part of the Lamb-Gleason model. However, they occupy such a prominent place in Lamb's *Outline of Stratificational Grammar* (1966d) that the casual reader is likely to equate the grammar with the diagrams. And that would be a mistake. The diagram is only one out of several possible ways of making statements about the system of language and the structure of texts.

It was suggested earlier that stratificational grammar holds some promises that will make it worth our attention. Here it is possible only to mention few of them. First, stratificational grammar claims not to be subject to the limitations that have been ascribed to simple phrase structure or 'taxonomic' grammars, and hence it claims to offer a viable alternative to transformational grammar. As long as linguistic theory is in its present unsettled state, those of us concerned with the grammar of English must take care to examine all known approaches to the study of language so that we may arrive at the one that is most useful for our purposes. Second, stratificational grammar aims at accounting not merely for sentences, but also for texts of larger extent: paragraphs, narratives, sonnets, five-act tragedies, epics, and the *Encyclopaedia Britannica,* any text that has formal unity. At a time when many grammarians seem unable to look beyond the sentence, it is instructive to recall that traditionally grammar has been closely linked with rhetoric and literature, studies that require a larger view. Third, and most important, stratificational grammar proposes not only to be a model for the abstract system lying behind the process of language, but to be a model for the very process itself. That is, Lamb is trying to develop an analogical model for the production and the comprehension of speech, a theory that will not only define and describe the texts of a language, but will do so in a way that explains how human beings might themselves produce and understand such texts. Now these are very great and very ambitious claims. They smack of hubris, or at least of chutspah, but if those who are working on stratificational grammar can substantiate any portion of these claims, the results will be well worth the effort, and we will have a new and valuable insight into the workings of human language.

NOTE

1. The author is grateful to Sydney M. Lamb and David C. Bennett for comments on the earlier version; neither, however, is accountable for the mistakes that remain.

CHAPTER TWO

The Crooked Path of Progress in Cognitive Linguistics*

SYDNEY M. LAMB

ABSTRACT. This paper briefly reviews the history of stratificational theory, here called cognitive linguistics since it aims to provide a model of the information system that enables a person to speak his language. The theory began in the mid-fifties with a three-stratum model, and it added a fourth stratum, above the classical morphemic level, in 1961. During the sixties a series of revisions occurred, not all of which involved direct progress. The paper concludes with a brief introduction to the current model, which has three grammatical strata and one phonological stratum for the language proper, plus a conceptual system containing all of the individual's knowledge (other than his language).

ORIENTATION. In the early sixties linguistic theoreticians spent a lot of their energy trying to persuade others that THEY were right. The most vociferous of such persuaders were the transformationalists, and they won quite a few converts. But many remained unpersuaded, or only partly persuaded; and it appears that during the late sixties, as different factions developed within the transformational school, a degree of tolerance—or perhaps it was just resignation—developed, and more and more linguists decided that they could go on living even if others held different points of view. Now for a linguist to allow others to disagree with him doesn't necessarily mean that he has decided to tolerate stubbornness, stupidity, or ignorance. Perhaps some linguists have been realizing that different objectives call

*From *Monograph Series on Languages and Linguistics* 24.99–123. Reprinted by permission.

for different formulations, so that the current variety of linguistic theories is quite acceptable as the reasonable outcome of the variety of objectives being pursued by differently motivated linguists. This point was first brought home to me by Halliday's paper 'Syntax and the consumer', presented at the first Georgetown Round Table in which I participated, in 1964. His point was simply that you will get different syntactic theories for different purposes.

It has been common during the past decade to designate linguistic theories on the basis of some important feature of their descriptive apparatus. We have tagmemics, which makes use of tagmemes, transformational grammar, in which transformational rules play an important role, systemic grammar, which makes use of a device for which the technical term within that theory is 'system', stratificational grammar, which is stratified.

Now if it is correct, as I just suggested, that these different theories have resulted from different aims,[1] then we might alternatively designate them in accordance with these aims in order to clarify the situation and strengthen our tolerance for one another's differing formulations. Thus systemic grammar might be called functional grammar, since its approach was arrived at through a concern with the communicative functions of linguistic choices made by the speaker. Stratificational grammar can be called cognitive linguistics, since it is concerned with representing the speaker's internal information system which makes it possible for him to speak his language and to understand utterances received from others. I leave it to Pike and Smith, respectively, to designate what alternative names might be applied to tagmemics and aspectual theory. For transformational grammar the appropriate alternative term is already in use: It may properly be called generative grammar, or generative linguistics, as its aim is to provide a system of rules which can generate all the sentences of a language and only those.

GENERATIVE LINGUISTICS. A few years ago I would have thought it inappropriate for the term generative to be assigned just to the transformational school because I considered that stratificational theory, among others,[2] also had a generative aim. I did not state the aim in the same way for stratificational theory, since it seemed to me, following Hjelmslev, that the more sensible objective was to generate the texts of the language, including those longer than sentences. But this is of course also a basically generative aim. Since other schools of thought in linguistics have or have had generative aims, one could more accurately characterize transformational generative grammar as that which attempts to generate by the use of a particular notational system of production rules borrowed from symbolic logic. (Gleason has suggested that it be called rescriptive grammar.) But the simple designation 'generative linguistics' is not inappropriate, since this theory more than any of the others tends to let other aims be subordinate to the overriding generative objective.

But I must add to this that for the current version of stratificational theory the term generative would not be correctly applied in any case—that is, the term 'generative-stratificational grammar' suggested by Karl Teeter in a recent talk to the Yale Linguistics Club (entitled 'Generative-Bloomfieldian Grammar') is a misnomer as applied to current stratificational theory. Some time ago I rejected as a practical impossibility the goal of generating all the texts of a language and only those, and I proposed that as an alternative we need a relative aim (Lamb 1966a:541–543). That is, we want a grammar that generates as many texts as possible (rather than all the texts) while generating as few as possible spurious texts. Since the absolute goal is impossible, we would use this relative standard to choose between two competing grammars.

But my current position goes further than this and rejects the generative goal as unrealistic even as a theoretical possibility, since that goal presupposes that there is such a thing as the set of grammatical sentences,[3] as a well-defined set. But such a well-defined set does not exist (cf. Hockett 1968b). In any real language, the boundary between what is grammatical and what is not is constantly shifting. And you can't avoid the problem even by assuming that you are stopping the language at a point in time in order to define the set of sentences at that point, since at any point of time there are semi-grammatical sentences. The constant flux of a real language entails that new grammatical devices are gradually coming into use, along with new idioms and the like, while others are gradually withering; here one is dealing with continuous rather than discrete phenomena. The 'boundary' between grammatical and ungrammatical is a continuum, not a sharp boundary. To try to enumerate the sentences of a language—even at a point in time—is like trying to enumerate the leaves on a tree at a point of time in June. How far formed does a newly forming leaf have to be to count as a leaf? At what point does a bug-eaten leaf cease to be a leaf?

Thus I for one am happy to leave the term generative as an exclusive designation for the transformationalist school. In any case, it appears to be the only school that attaches such overriding importance to the generative aim.

COGNITIVE LINGUISTICS. The other term that calls for comment is 'cognitive linguistics', which I propose as a designation for that branch of linguistic inquiry which aims at characterizing the speaker's internal information system that makes it possible for him to speak his language and to understand utterances received from others. Is it appropriate that this term should apply only to what has been known as stratificational theory? The reason I say 'yes' is that the basic requirement which a linguistic theory must meet to qualify for this term is that it take account of the basic fact about human beings who know a language. That fact is that they are able to speak it. And they are able to understand sentences received from other speakers. In short, they are able to perform. Their knowledge of their language, their internal linguistic information system, is a competence to perform. That knowledge is capable of being used by them for speaking and understanding. Thus any linguistic theory qualifies as cognitive linguistics which aims to provide an account of a language that can be used as a basis for a performance model. As far as I know, stratificational theory is the only one that qualifies at present (cf. Reich 1967); but we would be delighted to welcome linguists from other backgrounds to this fascinating and fertile area, if they can suitably modify their theories so that they can confront the fundamental fact that must be dealt with. My strong suspicion is that any such modifications will inevitably be in the direction of stratificational theory. Indeed, we have already seen moves of some transformationalists in this direction, and we welcome further such revisions.

1. Background and Beginnings.

The developments of the sixties in cognitive linguistics cover almost the entire history of this theory. A preliminary model existed by the end of the fifties, but it had not yet been publicly announced, nor had the term 'stratificational' been used for it, until 1961. Various revisions and additions were made during the sixties, as hypotheses were formulated and tested, and as attempts were made to increase the scope of data accounted for. And one might perhaps be justified in saying that by 1970 the theory was no longer merely programmatic but actually existed, so that as the seventies begin it has finally become sufficiently developed to be proposed seriously as a relatively coherent theory of language.

THE BACKGROUND. This brief review of developments must begin with the acknowledgement that cognitive linguistics did not originate out of the blue but was built upon the admirable work of its predecessors, of whom I should mention particularly Nida, Hockett, Hjelmslev, and Chomsky. These theorists of course in turn built upon earlier work, including that of Bloomfield, Sapir, Saussure, and others (and the list of those who influenced Bloomfield goes all the way back to Pāṇini).

Now the neo-Bloomfieldian model I had been taught as a graduate student in the early fifties had two structural levels, phonemic and morphemic (cf. Nida 1949, Hockett 1954). A morpheme had allomorphs or might have just one morph, and a morph was composed of phonemes. Allomorphs might be either morphologically conditioned or phonologically conditioned and many alternations of the latter type were economically described by means of morphophonemic rules, but such rules were generally not considered to have any structural status, as the structural fact was that the morpheme had allomorphs. The morphophonemic rule was just a descriptive device for summarizing numerous statements specifying phonologically conditioned allomorphs.

STAGE I. My first major disillusionment with this neo-Bloomfieldian model came when I tried to apply it to Monachi, a Utoaztecan language of California I was attempting to describe. Despite what I had been taught, I kept finding evidence indicating that there was another level of structure between the morphemic and phonemic levels. It wasn't economical to go from morphemes to phonemic forms in just one step. Rather, it was evident that there was one level of alternation involving morpheme-sized units, with morphological conditioning environments, and below it a level of phonologically conditioned alternation among phonological units.[4]

I therefore concluded that there was an intermediate level between the morphemic and phonemic levels of neo-Bloomfieldian linguistics. I called it (at this time) the morphophonemic level. (Later it got renamed—see below.) I also rejected the commonly held notion of the morpheme as a class of allomorphs in favor of the concept of the morpheme as an element existing on a different realizational level from that of its allomorphs. In other words, the allomorphs were the realizations of the morpheme rather than its members. These allomorphs were composed of morphophonemes. The conditioning environments for alternations among allomorphs were morphological. Then morphophonemes were realized as phonemes, which were composed of phonological components, and alternations at this level were conditioned by morphophonemic environments. This treatment puts the morphophonemic rule into a different status than it had before, in two ways. First, it was a statement of realization, just like that between morphemes and allomorphs, or between phonemes and allophones, rather than a process statement. Second, it was given a structural status and not just considered a convenient descriptive device for summarizing statements about allomorphs.

TABLE 1. Some Monachi verb stems

Gloss	Singular agent	Plural agent
'to wander'	nywi	moo
'to sit'	qa'ty	jy'k^{w}i
'to stand'	wyny	qo'no
'to lie'	hapi	q^{w}api

This three-level model, departing from the earlier two-level view, might be taken as the beginning of stratificational grammar, since it is hardly fitting to call a system stratified if it has only two strata. The term stratum and the term stratificational were not used in connection with it, however, until the sixties. The three-level model was first proposed at a meeting of the Linguistics Group at Berkeley in 1957, and it was used in my dissertation, completed in the same year. I was not yet ready to present it more publicly.

While it had dealt with one serious defect of neo-Bloomfieldian grammar, this original stratificational model remained less than completely satisfying in that it failed to deal with certain phenomena which suggested that there must be further structure above the morphemic level. For example, Monachi has some verb stems which come in semantically related pairs, one for singular agent, one for plural agent in each pair, otherwise having the same meaning. These are shown in Table 1. They are not to be compared with *go* : *wen*(t) or *good* : *bett*(er) of English, since the Monachi stems are contrastive in identical morphological environments. Other examples pointing to the possible existence of a higher level appeared at about the same time in Chomsky's *Syntactic Structures* (1957), for example *the shooting of the hunters* and the active: passive relationship. But the device which Chomsky, following his teacher Harris, proposed for dealing with these data, namely the now-famous transformational rule, was unacceptable to me since it was a process formulation, involving mutation of forms on the same level; and while such a formulation could apparently account for the primary data it was not realistic as applied to encoding and decoding.

Rather, these and similar data made me suspect that there might be some additional level of structure above the classical morphemic level; but I didn't get around to exploring this possibility until the beginning of the sixties.

2. Developments of the Sixties

Cognitive linguistics entered the sixties with exploration leading to the conclusion that there was indeed a higher level, and it adopted the name stratificational grammar. It then went through a series of refinements and revisions, not all of which, as we can now see, represented actual progress. That is why I call the path a crooked one.

Following Ilah Fleming (1969) we may recognize three stages of development during the sixties, Stages II, III, and IV. Each of these stages worked with a particular cognitive model of language, and minor model changes occurred within each stage. Ignoring these minor model changes we may designate the models as Model II, Model III, and Model IV, using the same numbers as for the stages in which they were used.

STAGE II. Now of course it wouldn't have to be the case that an additional level of structure would be related to its lower neighbor in the same way that the morphemic is to the morphophonemic, and so forth; but examination of the evidence indicated that this was indeed the case, for the essential properties. Thus, for example, calling the higher level the 'sememic', we may say, with reference to Table 1, that Monachi has a sememe 'to wander' which is realized morphemically as either *nywi* or *moo* depending on whether it is occurring with singular or plural agent. Similarly, we can account for the ambiguity in *the shooting of the hunters* by recognizing that *of* is the ambiguous realization of either the agent sememe or the goal sememe, both of which have other, but differing, realizations (Lamb 1964a:72–3).

There is a nice parallel here, between transformations and morphophonemic rewrite rules. The earlier treatments of morphophonemic alternations used process or mutation rules, applying to 'basic' phonemes to yield actually occurring phonemes. Neo-Bloomfieldians rejected the structural validity of such rules because they were process rules applying to units of one level to yield units of the same level in a fictional time span; they therefore lacked what we may now call cognitive reality. Other linguists found these process formulations so useful, since they could summarize in one statement the alternation of indefinitely many allomorphs, that they went ahead and used them and said, in effect, 'let cognitive reality be hanged, I want economy!' Now the stratificational answer is to get both the economy and the cognitive reality, by setting up the morphophonemic rule as a realizational phenomenon rather than a process. Thus instead of saying that *m* is replaced by *w* intervocalically, we say that there is a higher-level element, a morphophoneme, which has alternate realizations /m/ and /w/, of which the latter occurs intervocalically, the former elsewhere.

Now we find a similar situation higher in the linguistic structure. And again the descriptive device which occurred first historically was a process formulation, developed by Harris and adopted by Chomsky, in this case called the transformation. Many linguists rejected the transformation on grounds which we may summarize by saying that it is cognitively unrealistic. Others said, in effect, 'cognitive reality be hanged, look at all the things we can do with transformations!' And again the resolution of the conflict is to recognize that we are actually dealing with a higher level and with alternative realizations of the higher-level entities, the relationship being that of realization rather than transformation. In other words, we can account for the data treated by Chomsky and his followers without giving up cognitive reality.

This second model was the first one I considered ready for public presentation. It was proposed in a paper read at the Christmas meeting of the Linguistic Society in 1961, in which it was argued that we must recognize a stratum between the classical morphemic and phonemic levels as well as a fourth stratum above the classical morphemic. It was further argued that the relationship between different such levels was different from the class-member relationship and the process relationship, with which it had generally been confused; and the term STRATUM was proposed for a realizationally defined level. Hockett (1961) had independently arrived at the same term at about the same time.

A short time later, Chomsky brought forth his revised conception, in which there was a deep structure and which no longer had any optional meaning-bearing transformations. This deep structure (the term is from Hockett 1958:246–52) comes part way toward the sememic stratum, but only part way, for the rules relating deep structure to surface structure were still transformations, process rules which perform operations on some items while leaving others unchanged. The consequence is that a 'deep structure' so formulated is really a selection of various surface features and is not in fact very deep.

An informally published *Outline of Stratificational Grammar* appeared in 1962,[5] but the first formal published presentations did not appear until two years later (Gleason 1964, Lamb 1964a, 1964b). Two of the three papers which then appeared owe their existence to the Georgetown Round Table.

A further step taken during Stage II was an analysis of the relationship of realization into a number of more elementary relationships, which were called diversification, neutralization, zero realization, empty realization, composite realization, portmanteau realization, and anataxis (Lamb 1964a). In fact it was this analysis which was used to establish that the newly added sememic stratum was indeed another stratum, related to the next lower one in the same way that the more familiar strata are related to their lower neighbors.

In the early part of Stage II it was not clear whether each stratum had a tactics, but by 1963 it was apparent that there were indeed four independent tactic patterns. The problem of specifying the details of the interconnection of the tactic patterns with realizational elements, however, remained unsolved.

TERMINOLOGICAL PROBLEMS. It has always seemed wise to me for any terminology to stick as closely as possible to established traditions. Now if the tradition has terms for only two levels, and if some of these are used ambiguously or vaguely, then something must be added, but one does best to add as little as possible, and then in keeping with tradition as much as possible.

FIGURE 1. The Classical Model

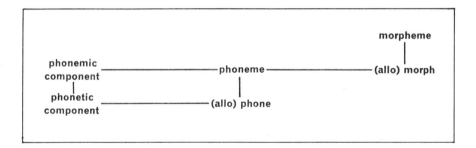

FIGURE 2. Model I
a: Morphologically conditioned alternation.
b, c: Phonologically conditioned alternation, to be described as (c̀) realization of morphophonemes by phonemes.

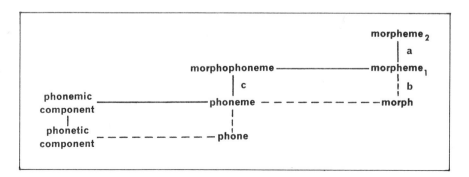

The terminology of the classical structural tradition can be represented as in Figure 1, in which the vertical dimension represents realization while the horizontal represents composition (cf. Hockett 1961).[6] For example, a morph is composed of phonemes and is a realization of a morpheme.

Using the same diagramming conventions, we may represent the relationships among the units of Stage I as in Figure 2. In this figure the dotted lines represent relationships which, while they exist, need not be explicitly described in the grammar, since they are automatically (and more simply) defined by the specification of the 'solid-line' relationships. This model is described as having three strata since the lowest level, the phonetic, was not considered to be part of the linguistic structure.

The terms given as 'morpheme₁' and 'morpheme₂' furnish our first example of a terminological problem. The tradition provides only one term for two structural units which must be distinguished. Of these morpheme₂ is closer to the morpheme of the fifties, but morpheme₁ is closer to Bloomfield's morpheme, which was described as composed of phonemes. Those not familiar with the history of stratificational theory need not be bothered now with a discussion of what was done with the terminology at Stage I since we get a better idea of what is needed if we go directly to Stage II (Figure 3).

FIGURE 3. Model II

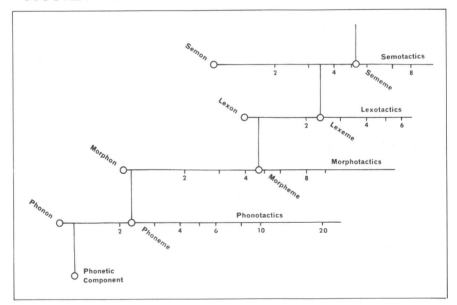

Here we have the term morpheme for 'morpheme₁' of Figure 2, and lexon for 'morpheme₂'. The term lexon is formed with a suffix used for the elementary unit of each stratum, so it means 'elementary unit of the lexemic stratum' or 'component of a lexeme'. Similarly, the morphon is a component of a morpheme; and the term may also be considered a shortening of 'morph(oph)on(eme)'. Thus we add only one suffix to the terminology rather than a series of additional terms. The term lexeme is here used in roughly the sense it already had in the tradition extending from Whorf (1938) to Conklin (1962) (cf. Lamb 1966a:567–9). And the term sememe has an even longer tradition, having been used not only by Bloomfield but also by the Swedish linguist Adolph Noreen, who in the early part of this century proposed that a linguistic structure has three levels, phonemic, morphemic, and sememic, with units which he called the phoneme, the morpheme and the sememe (Noreen 1903–18, Pollak 1923).

In Figure 3 the minimal units (phonon, morphon, etc.) are placed to the left of the top of the appropriate vertical lines rather than right at the intersections as in the earlier figures. This calls attention to the fact that the minimal unit of each stratum does not always coincide with the unit having a realization on the next lower stratum. For example, the morpheme *second* is the realization of the combination of lexons *two* and *-th,* entering into portmanteau realization (Lamb 1964a). The vertical lines are placed to show some average estimated quantitative relationships for a typical language. For example, according to the rough estimate, there are about five morphons in the average morpheme. Semon is placed rather far to the left of the vertical line since it was considered at this time that there was an extensive amount of portmanteau realization at this level (Lamb 1966e[7]).

Another feature of Figure 3 is that the horizontal lines extend to the right of the 'emic' units (e.g. morpheme). The reason is that there are structurally significant combinations of these units, specified by the tactics of each stratum.

STAGE III. The next step was to examine the interconnections among the seven relationships which are collectively involved in the difference between one stratum and the next. Upon such examination it soon became apparent that they are systematically ordered with respect to one another, so that a 'full stratum' of difference, say from lexons to morphons, consists of several little steps rather than just one big one with all the realizational relationships in a single bundle. In part this situation had already been recognized in Stage II, in that morphemes were present at a level intermediate between lexons and morphons; and Figure 3 also separates out portmanteau realization. But in Stage III further separation of the relationships was recognized, resulting in the scheme shown in Figure 4 (Lamb 1965). (Later work showed that this is not exactly the right way to sort them out; but if this was not a step straight ahead, at least the path was moving 'diagonally' forward at this point.) In this scheme there are two intermediate levels between the lexon and the morphon, and again we have a terminological problem in that a distinction is drawn between two units both of which are like the former morpheme. It seemed easiest to call them simply the basic morpheme and the actual or realized morpheme. The simple term MORPHEME could be used for short for the latter.

FIGURE 4. Model III
a: anataxis, zero realization, empty realization
b: diversification, neutralization, portmanteau realization, zero realization
c: composite realization

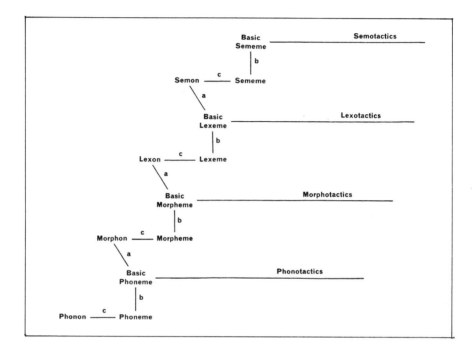

With the recognition of the new intermediate step it was no longer sufficient to say that the linguistic system just consisted of strata together with realizational relationships separating them. Rather, it became necessary to recognize the STRATAL SYSTEM, a complex structure of which the stratum was just one part. Thus the morphemic stratal system included the morphons, morphemes, basic morphemes, together with their interrelationships, plus the morphotactics. The level of the morphons and morphemes could be called the morphemic stratum.

Perhaps the most noteworthy feature of Stage III is that alternation is recognized both above and below the tactic pattern of each stratal system. This meant, among other things, that four layers of alternation were recognized between the lexon and the phoneme, where neo-Bloomfieldian structural linguistics had only one.

Another step taken at this stage was a refinement of the definitions of the realizational relationships, which (except for anataxis) were now analyzed as different combinations of the elementary oppositions AND vs.

OR and UPWARD (toward content) vs. DOWNWARD (toward expression), as follows:

Name	Definition	Example
Diversification	downward or	past ppl. / -en, -ed
Neutralization	upward or	past ppl, past tense / -ed
Composite realization	downward and	second / s e k ǝ n d
Portmanteau realization	upward and	two -th / seɫond
Zero realization	downward or with zero as one choice	pl. / -z, Ø, ...
Empty realization	upward or with zero as one choice	DO, Ø / do

This somewhat neater analysis was accompanied by the development of a graphic notation (here I was influenced by Halliday) and, as its conceptual correlate, the discovery that the whole of the linguistic structure could be represented as a network of relationships, rather than a system of ITEMS AND their relationships (cf. Hjelmslev 1961:22–3). In other words, things like morphons and morphemes are not objects or symbols (although the English language forces us to speak of them in this way) but positions in a network of relationships. But the relational network notation was not used in print till the publications representing Stage IV.

STAGE IV. Stage IV might be said to have begun in November 1965, as I was reworking some material for a lecture, with a revision of the model of the stratal system. The basic revision was to put most of the alternations of a stratal system above the tactics rather than just below the tactic pattern. The only instances of diversification left below the tactics in Model IV were those directly involved in portmanteau realization. The resulting organization of the stratal system may be represented as in Figure 5. Here the morphemic system serves as a typical example and the types of relationships found in each part of the system are indicated by nodes of the relational network notation.

The MORPHEMIC SIGNS of this model correspond to the (realized) morphemes of Stage III, but the morphemes and the morphotactics of Model IV are at a lower level (i.e. closer to expression) than the basic morphemes and morphotactics of Model III, because of their position with relation to the morphological alternation. Similarly, the basic lexemes of Model III are closer to semons of Model IV than to Model IV lexemes.

FIGURE 5. Organization of the Morphemic System in Early Stage IV

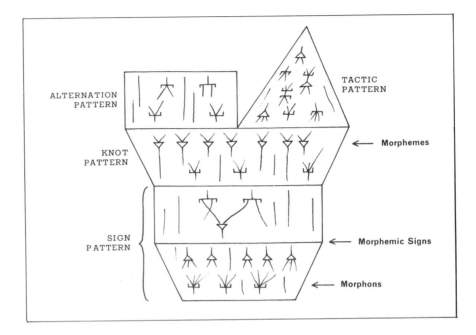

Why this difference in the treatment of alternation? As with most revisions, the basic motivation was economy. Diversification above the tactics has the property that the realization chosen in a given instance is that which fits the tactic environment. In other words, the conditioning environments are given by the associated tactic pattern and therefore need not be stated separately (Lamb 1966b:563; Lamb 1966d:55–6). Previously, the statement of conditioning environment had been a structurally significant part of the realization rule. This appears to be a considerable saving.

When I found for several instances of diversification in different stratal systems that they could apparently be accounted for more simply above than below the tactics, I proceeded to the conclusion that diversification in general should be treated this way. The only exception was that involving portmanteau realization, for which the conditioning environment was at the same time the other participant in the portmanteau realization, as shown in Figure 6, where *-TH* conditions and is conditioned by *TWO*, with the resulting realization *second*.

The other major departure of Model IV was an increase in the number of stratal systems, from four to six. The additions were, very roughly speaking, at the bottom and the top. This feature of the model was perhaps its main target of criticism, and we can now look back at it as an example of the crookedness of the path of progress in cognitive linguistics. For in this instance the critics were right. How, then, did the model get that way? It was largely a consequence of the hypothesis as to how the stratal system was organized. In particular, Model IV allowed only one level of diversification (aside from portmanteau realization) and one level of composite realization in the stratal system. When it became evident that one must recognize two levels of alternation in phonology,[8] and it also appeared that the tactics of consonant clusters conflicted with syllable tactics, requiring two separate tactic patterns, I concluded that one must recognize two stratal systems in phonology, which could be called 'phonemic' and 'hypophonemic' (Lamb 1966b).

FIGURE 6. Portmanteau Realization in Early Stage IV

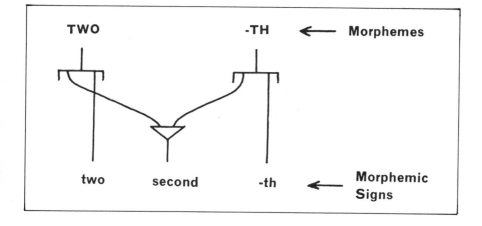

At the semological end of the network also there was evidence for two separate stratal systems. This was not new evidence, since it had already been partly accounted for in the sememic system of Model III, which distinguished basic sememes from realized sememes, with a level of alternation intervening (Lamb 1965b). These basic sememes became the hypersememes of Stage IV, elements of the hypersememic system, which was set up above the sememic.

The resulting six stratal systems could conveniently be grouped as three pairs of systems, two each for semology, grammar, and phonology; but no structural evidence was found for such pairing—it remained a matter of convenience.

This early Stage IV model is the one presented in *Outline of Stratificational Grammar* (Lamb 1966d). Although it was just a preliminary outline, it was published as a small book and was therefore reviewed in the linguistic journals. This occasion provided criticism of the model, some of which was valid, some of which was based on misunderstanding. The most serious defect of the *Outline* was that it was just an outline; it didn't go into detailed explanation or presentation of evidence. Thus the failures of critics to understand some points are largely excusable.

But the most serious defects in the model were those which I became aware of on my own and those which were brought to my attention by my co-worker Peter Reich.

MINOR MODEL CHANGES IN STAGE IV. In 1967 we went through some minor model changes, which corrected some of the more serious defects.

One of the problems involved the interconnection of the tactic pattern with the realizational portion of the stratal system. In the *Outline* the connections took the form of the 'upward ands' of the 'knot pattern' (see Figure 5), on the grounds that a morpheme connected upwards both to the lexemic stratum AND to the morphotactics. The assumption was that the tactic pattern is oriented in the same up-and-down dimension as the realizational portion. But that assumption turns out not to be valid. Rather, the whole of a tactic pattern is on one and the same realizational level, so it occupies a horizontal plane. It specifies the allowable combinations of elements of a single realizational level. Thus the connection of a morpheme to the morphotactics should be sideways rather than upwards. For this type of connection a new node was invented, called the DIAMOND. Four types of diamond node are shown in Figure 7. As the third of these illustrates, it is possible, in the revised conception, for a line from the higher stratum to go into the midst of a tactic pattern, whereas in the earlier version all realizational connections to the tactics were at the bottom of the tactic pattern. (For more on diamonds see Lamb 1970.)

FIGURE 7. Types of Diamond Node

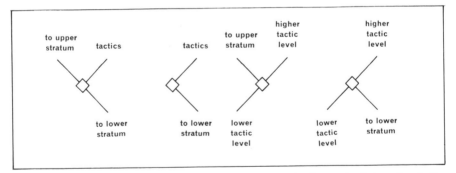

A second infelicity of Model IV (in its original version) involved the sign pattern, which had the form illustrated in Figure 8. It soon became apparent that the limitation to a single level of such patterning within each stratal system was unnecessary and that it entailed uneconomical handling of certain information. The solution was the multi-level sign pattern. Its attractiveness may be illustrated by an example from the lexemic sign pattern for a speaker of English who knows enough about birds to have the lexemes *yellow-bellied sapsucker* and *red-headed woodpecker* alongside of the lexemes *sapsucker* and *woodpecker*. Figure 9 shows the two analyses.

Examples favoring a multi-level sign pattern in the morphemic system are provided by long morphemes such as *lobster, dromedary, encyclopedia.*

FIGURE 8. Basic Form of Sign Pattern

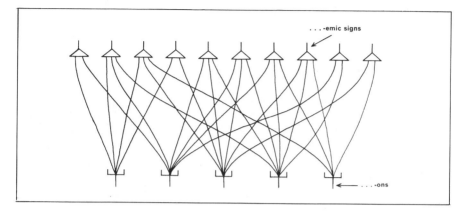

FIGURE 9. Lexemic Sign Patterns

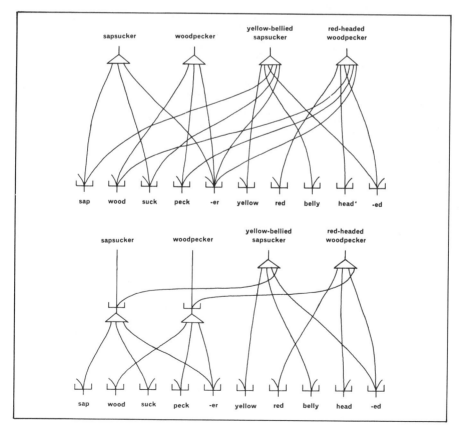

Now the 'and' nodes in a sign pattern generally correspond to 'ands' of an adjacent tactic pattern. The tactic pattern generates new combinations of elements at its level; the sign pattern contains the fixed or prefabricated items that through repeated use have come to be treated as units. Thus the different levels of a multi-level sign pattern should correspond to the different levels of the associated tactic pattern. Because of this correspondence, one gets a more economical picture of the organization of the linguistic network if one places the sign patterns on a horizontal plane along with the tactic patterns.

The treatment of portmanteau realization was also subjected to alternative analysis, primarily in consequence of considerations arising from our work on performance models, in connection with the Linguistic Automation Project. I shall spare you from the details and proceed directly to the punch line, which is Figure 10, an alternative to Figure 6. In this treatment, which is made possible by the conception of the tactic plane as horizontal to the realizational lines and thus intersectable by them in its interior, the portmanteau realization is handled neither below nor above the tactics, but AT the tactic level. Above it (shown as at upper left) we have the two lexons *TWO* and *-TH*; while just below the tactics (shown as at lower right) we have the single morpheme *second,* occurring as realization of these two lexons. The 'and' node in the tactics is the construction for ordinals—the first line leads to numerals, the second to the suffix *-th*. But as the ordered 'or' node provides, if the numeral is *TWO*, the left-hand line is taken instead of the construction, so that the 'prefabricated' ordinal *second* occurs. (For semological examples, see Ikegami 1970.)

FIGURE 10. Portmanteau Realization in Late Stage IV

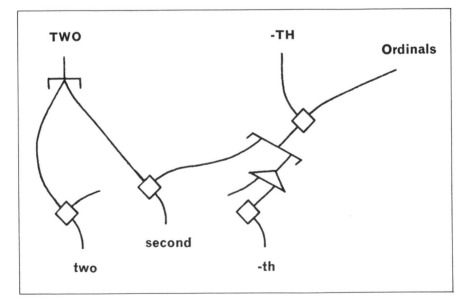

With the removal of portmanteau realization from below the tactic pattern, there would be no occurrence of diversification ('downward or') at this level of the stratal system. But at about the same time our attention was drawn to some examples of free variation, and it was apparent that the model of early Stage IV had not properly provided for this phenomenon. The crucial property of free variation is that the alternants can occur in the same tactic environment. For this reason, it is uneconomical to account for such alternation above the tactics, since this would involve two lines from a 'downward or' connecting to a single tactic location. Elementary simplification procedures (Lamb 1966d:43–7) shift the 'downward or' to below the tactics, in keeping with the fact that the difference between the two alternants is of no tactic significance. Thus we introduced a subtactic alternation pattern into the stratal system (cf. Bennett 1968).

These revisions had been made by the Fall of 1967, and they could well have resulted in a new synthesis, which we might call Model V; but I was at the same time aware of additional problems for which new solutions were not so readily forthcoming, and of others for which there seemed to be several alternative solutions none of which seemed clearly better than the others. Thus from late 1967 till the end of the decade we were without a stable integrated model, since we had no successful synthesis of non-defective hypotheses.

The most perplexing of the problems was that there seemed to be needless repetition of diamond nodes for simple lexemes and simple sememes. A simple lexeme is one which connects to a single lexon rather than to a combination of lexons. For example, English has the morpheme *wood*. But according to Model IV it also must have a lexeme *wood*, since this element participates in the lexotactics right along with complex lexemes like *woodpecker* and *yellow-bellied sapsucker*. Moreover, the model required that we have sememes for these lexemes, since they played a part in semotactics right along with complex sememes like *a stitch in time saves nine*. It seemed clear that this was a case of excess surface information, but it was not clear how to eliminate it without getting into some very messy complications. A number of solutions were attempted, one of which was used in a paper I presented at the annual meeting of the Linguistic Society in 1967. But neither this nor the other attempts were fully satisfactory.

Another problem area, actually a whole dimension of problems, was that of formalizing the processes of encoding and decoding. This area was the primary concern of the Linguistic Automation Project. The work uncovered more questions than answers but contributed greatly to our understanding not only of these processes but of linguistic structure in general.[9]

And then there were suspicions that the model had too many strata. Each of them had been added only when the evidence demanded it; but perhaps some of the evidence could be differently interpreted.

Part of the evidence for stratification comes from alternation, and as we approached the end of the decade we found increasing evidence of alternation other than free variation below the tactic pattern; and it appeared that we might be moving toward a refined version of Model III.[10] This is another illustration of the crookedness of our path, for it became apparent that not all of our earlier revisions had been in the direction of actual progress.

Meanwhile, up at the highest levels of the linguistic structure, Gleason and his students were working out principles of discourse analysis from a stratificational point of view. A number of valuable studies have resulted from this effort (e.g. Gleason 1968, Austin 1966, Cromack 1968, Taber 1966).

3. The Current Model

In late 1970 and early 1971 a new synthesis finally emerged. It resulted from breaking out of some previous conceptions of the organization of the overall network, considered as a series of stratal systems. As mentioned above, the six stratal systems of Stage IV had been grouped into three pairs, and although this pairing had no structural significance, there was a lurking suspicion that the overall structure did somehow consist of three major parts and that future revisions would reveal that the two members of each pair did go together. For example one speculation was that a more complex model of the stratal system would bring the phonemic and hypophonemic systems together into a single stratal system, and that corresponding coalescences could be made for the grammatical and semological pairs. As it turns out, this speculation was partly sound but partly misleading.

Continued study of alternation and its interconnections with the tactics and the sign pattern led to a model of the stratal system which comes rather close to that of Stage III. The stratal system in the new model has an alternation pattern both above and below the tactics. But the lower alternation pattern apparently overlaps with the sign pattern, since some alternations can be most economically accounted for in the midst of the sign pattern rather than above or below it. In the morphemic system, for example, this treatment allows us to deal efficiently with alternations among segments of specific morphemes, such as the vowel in *do* : *did* : *done* and the *V* in *have* : *had* (cf. Reich 1968c).

Now it is indeed possible to coalesce the former phonemic and hypophonemic systems into a single stratal system. This happy simplification is made possible in part by the new model of the stratal system and in part by a reinterpretation of the evidence which was formerly seen as forcing the recognition of two separate tactic patterns in phonology.

One is tempted to suppose that the morphemic and lexemic strata might be similarly coalesced, but this possibility does not work out. The essential property of a stratum is its distinctive tactic pattern. Now linguists have long recognized the obvious fact that languages have syllable structure. That is the essence of phonotactics. And if there is anything that is inescapable about linguistic structure it is that there are such things as prefixes, stems, and suffixes, which combine in characteristic ways to form words.

That is the essence of morphotactics. And it is in clear conflict with phonotactics, in that tactic boundaries and constituent structure are different. So there are clearly two separate tactic patterns here. And if there is anything even more widely recognized by linguists of varying persuasions than stems and affixes, it is that clauses come in subjects and predicates, that subjects are, or contain, noun phrases, and predicates are, or contain, verb phrases. That is the essence of lexotactics. And its independence from morphotactics is shown by such conflicts as that in *the queen of England's hat* and that in English verb phrases, where, for example:

lexemic: 3-sg. perfect   passive   *take*

is realized as

morphemic: have   -z   +   be   -en   +   take   -en   +

with entirely different tactic structure. And I think that most of you in this enlightened audience will agree that there is still another tactic pattern, that at which, instead of subjects and objects, we find agents, goals, instruments, benefactives, datives, and the like. Its independence from lexotactics is clearly shown by such examples as active and passive pairs, which are grossly different at the lexotactic level while almost identical semotactically.

Now, what about the hypersememic stratum of Stage IV? When we explore it we find that this stratum has to contain all of the individual's knowledge of his culture, his personal history, his physical environment, in short everything he knows, save the language itself, which is already represented in the lower strata. In other words one is dealing here with information that lies outside the scope of what is traditionally considered language. And one is dealing with a system of far greater complexity than any of the lower stratal systems—indeed probably more complex than all of them put together. Therefore it seems appropriate to give a special status to this highest level—to consider it as outside the language proper (which does not mean for a moment that the linguist is prohibited from its premises) and to give it a more fitting name than the awkward term 'hypersememic'. Accordingly I now call it the *conceptual system,* or for those who would like another Greek term, the *gnostemic system;* its basic units are the *gnosteme* and the *gnoston.* The gnoston is an elementary unit of knowledge, and this position in the system corresponds well to its Greek meaning, 'something which is known'.

With this revision the linguistic system proper, according to Model V, has the same four strata that were recognized back in Stage II: Sememic, Lexemic, Morphemic, and Phonemic.

But there is one further major revision, which amounts to a partial coalescence of the morphemic, lexemic, and sememic systems. It is a solution to the perplexing problem of repetition of diamond nodes for simple lexemes and simple sememes, mentioned above. Related to this problem is the fact that morphotactic classes which are needed to specify the occurrence of morphemes in derivational constructions are often semantically defined; this situation was left unaccounted for in Stage IV. It suggests that there must somehow be direct links from morphemes to meaning, bypassing the lexemic and sememic strata. Similar considerations at the lexemic stratum indicate that there must be connections from the conceptual system to the lexemic stratum, bypassing the sememic. Thus one arrives at a scheme in which some points of the conceptual network connect to the sememic stratum, some to the lexemic stratum, some to the morphemic stratum.

Now to say only this is not to answer the problem of how we nevertheless account for the participation of morphemes like *wood* in clauses, which are produced in the lexemic and sememic systems. The essence of the solution is a device that may be called the 'representative', since it functions like a representative in a legislature, who acts for the people he represents, at least in theory, so that their interests are served without their having to be present in the legislature. A representative in the lexemic system is a diamond node which connects into the lexotactics and downward to one or more (viz 'downward or') locations in the morphotactics, leading to the morphological forms which it represents, both fixed morphemes and, in some cases, products of productive constructions. Such a representative functions as a single lexeme in the lexotactics, but it connects downward to several or many morphemes, which are distinguished from one another by their different connections to the conceptual system, as well as in part by different morphotactic properties.

Thus the morphemic, lexemic, and sememic strata do achieve a partial coalescence in that they share a common inventory of morphemes (while the lexemic and sememic strata also share a common inventory of lexemes), and in that all three are in part directly connected to the conceptual system.

According to the current model, then, the linguistic system as a whole, which is distinguishable from, but intricately interconnected with, the conceptual system, consists of two main portions, which could be called phonology and grammar; and the phonology consists of a single stratal system, while the grammar consists of three partially independent stratal systems, whose three separate tactic patterns are concerned with morphology, surface syntax, and deep syntax.

Last Spring, at the end of my course on Language and the Brain, in which we had been considering, among other things, various of the uncertainties and unsolved problems of Stage IV, I told my students that I would be happy when I knew as much as I thought I knew in 1966. I am now able to report that I am happy.

NOTES

1. Actually I believe that this is correct only in part, that there are also other reasons for the differences. But let us concentrate on this one for now.

2. As I have previously pointed out (Lamb 1967, 1966a), Hockett, a 'neo-Bloomfieldian', and Hjelmslev had both advocated the generative aim some years before Chomsky appeared on the scene.

3. I shall now just use the term sentence, to make the discussion applicable to transformational-generative grammar as well as, by implication, to any type of generative grammar that would attempt also to generate units of discourse composed of sentences.

4. Cf. Hockett 1961. Hockett considers a solution like that described here, but in the end rejects it.

5. This *Outline* proposed the possibility that languages have five strata, but the four-stratum model was returned to by late 1962.

6. It is true that neo-Bloomfieldians didn't always recognize phonological components, nor did they always systematize the relationships among their units to the degree shown here. But if one performs a logical analysis of their use of the terms and removes inconsistencies, one arrives at this scheme.

7. This paper was published in 1966 but was presented at a conference in 1963 and revised in 1964.

8. Rescriptive phonologists find evidence for more than two levels of alternation in phonology (e.g Chafe 1968), but mutation rules impose their own notational ordering requirements independent of the linguistic structure and therefore cannot be used as a basis for arguing about how much stratificational ordering is needed if one uses a realizational format (Lamb: 1972).

9. Two approaches were followed in this area. Peter Reich attempted to specify the operation of the nodes by defining each as a finite-state machine. A general network processor was constructed for the 7094 computer, using this approach (Reich 1968b). The other approach was to set up models of the internal structure of the nodes, specified by means of more elementary network components. At this more elementary level there are four basic node types, the branching, the 'and' junction, the 'or' junction, and the blocking element; and all lines are one-way. A computer system for testing networks constructed in this system is currently being prepared.

10. In connection with the treatment of alternation, some new network devices, including one-way lines and nodes, have been posited. These and many other matters touched upon here are described in Lockwood (1972b).

CHAPTER THREE

Stratificational Linguistics as a Basis for Machine Translation*

SYDNEY M. LAMB

THE BASIC THEME of this paper is that simplicity is a good thing and that it can be achieved by isolating recurrent partial similarities, which involves separating various things from one another. It is especially the case that a machine translation procedure should be separated into stages in accordance with the stratification of linguistic structure. But I shall also consider briefly a couple of other types of separation whose importance for machine translation has not yet been recognized by all research groups.

Consider the expression

$$abc + abd + abe + ab(f + g)$$

from ninth grade algebra, and compare it with the expression

$$ab(c + d + e + f + g),$$

which conveys exactly the same information. Or at least it conveys exactly the same EFFECTIVE INFORMATION. But I would like to distinguish two kinds of information, namely SURFACE INFORMATION and EFFECTIVE INFORMATION. We may say that these two expressions have exactly the same effective information but that the second has less surface information than the first. This is another way of saying that the second is simpler than the first. In fact, the simplest and most effective way of defining simplicity is in terms of surface information. Given any two linguistic descriptions or partial descriptions which have the same effective information we will prefer that which has less surface information, and we will prefer it because

*Originally presented at the U.S.–Japan seminar on Mechanical translation, Tokyo, April 20–28, 1964, this paper appears in print for the first time in the present volume. This work was supported in part by the National Science Foundation.

of its simplicity. Its greater simplicity resides in the very fact of its smaller amount of surface information.

There is nothing abstruse about the concept of surface information. On the contrary it is a disarmingly simple concept. It can be precisely measured in terms of the number of symbol tokens and the amount of information per symbol token, which can be stated in terms of binary digits and depends on the number of symbols from which it must be distinguished. But it usually is not necessary to consider binary digits because the alternatives which the linguist ordinarily has to consider differ so grossly in simplicity that the very roughest kind of count of surface information clearly reveals a decisive difference. In the example above, it is not necessary to know how many bits of information each of the letters is worth, as long as they are all equal. We may consider the information content of the parentheses and the plus sign to be considerably less than that of letters, so that they may be ignored when comparing the surface information of the two expressions. The number of tokens of them is the same in both expressions anyway.

Now the first expression above has thirteen letter tokens while the second has only seven. It is precisely this difference which makes the second expression simpler than the first. Notice also that the difference between 13 and 7, namely 6, is exactly accounted for by the three repetitions of *ab* in the first expression. Six is the amount of the EXCESS SURFACE INFORMATION. There are six units of excess surface information because *ab* was written a total of four times (for eight units) whereas it was needed only once.

But notice also that the two expressions above do not differ just in simplicity. They also differ in generality and hence in the insight which they provide. The second expression above is more general as well as simpler. It has generalized the fact of the occurrence of *ab* with each of *c, d, e, f,* and *g,* whereas the first expression leaves these as isolated phenomena. Simplicity, then, is desirable not just in itself but because true simplicity goes hand in hand with generality. Simplicity and generality are like the two sides of the same coin. When you achieve one you also automatically get the other.

Now I would like to make the rather extravagant assertion that this same basic type of simplification operation lies at the very heart of all effective linguistic analysis, of all effective work on the design of machine translation systems—even of all science. (And I might also mention that this same operation of simplification is one of the most important aspects of the designing of efficient programs for a computer). To take an example from science, consider the Ptolemaic and Copernican descriptions of the solar system. It would be a mistake to say that the difference between these two descriptions is that one is correct while the other is incorrect, if by correct we mean something about whether or not the facts are correctly accounted for. All of the facts of the movements and positions of the planets can be accounted for with the earth taken as the center of the solar system as in the Ptolemaic model. These two accounts of the solar system are (or can be) equal in effective information. What makes the Copernican description much more attractive, insightful, and informative is simply that it is more simple. It takes less surface information to present the Copernican description. Here we may also note the generality that goes hand in hand with the simplification. The Copernican system is more general in that it ascribes the same basic patterns of motion to all of the planets, including the earth (which of course was entirely different from all of the other planets in the Ptolemaic model). We may also note one other highly significant fact about the simpler, more general description; namely, that the basic concepts used in it turn out to also be capable of accounting for phenomena observed outside of the solar system itself. The rotational and orbital motion, gravitation and centrifugal force and so forth are found also in other astronomical systems. In just the same way, one of the nice things about a simple linguistic analysis of a given corpus as opposed to a less simple one is that the simple one stands a much better chance of being able to account for new, previously unexamined material without the addition of extra rules.

Table I.

Sg.	N	dama	baba
	G	damy	baby
	D	dame	babe
	A	damu	babu
	I	damoj	baboj
	L	dame	babe
Pl.	N	damy	baby
	G	dam	bab
	D	damam	babam
	A	dam	bab
	I	damami	babami
	L	damax	babax

Let us now consider a linguistic example, shown in Table I. Here I show the inflectional paradigms of two Russian nouns. An alternative description of exactly the same material is given in Table II. Here we see what I hope is obviously a startling difference in surface information (but with the same effective information).

If we examine the method by which this simplification (i.e., reduction of excess surface information) was achieved, we see that it involved SEGMENTATION BASED ON THE FINDING OF RECURRENT PARTIAL SIMILARITIES. This is really the same process as that used in the algebraic illustration given above. The elementary algebra student is able to achieve the factorization by discovering a RECURRING PARTIAL SIMILARITY, namely the occurrence of *ab* in the four separate terms. The second expression shows the result of segmenting out this similar part and expressing it in the description only once instead of four separate times. In the same way, the second linguistic description above achieved its simplicity and generality by the segmentation of the inflectional suffixes from the stems, again since they were recurrent partial similarities. All of the forms in the first column of Table I are partially similar, as are all the forms in the second column. Similarly the two forms in each row of Table I are partially similar. Table II shows the result of isolating the partial similarities and generalizing on the basis of them. The repetition found in the first description is excess surface information. (The process is the same, again, as that which Copernicus used when he found that all of the planets are partially similar to one another in their motion).

Table II.

Stems	*Endings*	Sg.	Pl.
dam	N	a	y
bab	G	y	—
	D	e	am
	A	u	—
	I	oj	ami
	L	e	ax

An efficient machine translation system, like a good linguistic analysis, is achieved by separating various things from one another on the basis of recurrent partial similarities. I shall describe now three important types of separation which enable one to get rid of excess baggage in a machine translation system, namely (1) separation of the program from the linguistic information, (2) segmentation of words, and (3) separation of the translation process as a whole into stages in accordance with linguistic stratification. It is this third type of separation, that based on stratification, that most of this paper is devoted to.

First let us consider the separation of the program from the linguistic information. Such separation is advocated by the University of California project as well as those of the University of Grenoble, the Rand Corporation, and the University of Texas. In an unseparated system, the linguistic information is built right into the program. I shall illustrate with an over-simplified illustration of a sequence of program steps with linguistic information built in that might form part of a syntactic decoder:

> Is current item coded *adjective?*
> > if YES, go to A
> > if NO,
> Is current item coded *verb?*
> > if YES, go to V
> > if NO,
> Is current item . . .

Then beginning at A there might be instructions something like the following:

> Is following item coded *noun?*
> if NO, go to AA
> if YES, form constitute and label it *noun.*

Ignoring the irrelevant fact that this illustration is oversimplified, we see that the linguistic information, which the ordinary linguist would be more accustomed to putting into rules or statements of relationships, has been stuck right into instructions telling the computer to follow a particular procedure, and that each part of the procedure is *ad hoc* for the particular information incorporated, rather than general.

In a system which keeps the information separate from the program, it is expressed in rules or formulaic statements, whose form has to be precisely defined, and a program is written which will have the capability of operating with any statement which is in that specified form. The advantages of the separation are: (1) it allows the linguist to write his rules as rules rather than in a flow chart or in some programming language: (2) when the linguist wants to revise some of his statements he can do so very easily, without any need for reprogramming (which is usually very time-consuming); (3) the various basic operations which must be carried out by the machine to perform the process have to be written out only once in the separated program, whereas in the integrated one they must be repeated over and over again with the different units of linguistic information which are subjected to the same basic operations; (4) the program, since it is written to operate with statements of a specified form, can operate on such statements not just for one language but for any language, so that new programs do not have to be written when we decide to translate from a new source language.

Next we may consider the desirability of segmenting words. (For a more detailed treatment see Lamb, 1961a). This type of separation is illustrated above in Tables I and II. It brings about a reduction not only in the number of dictionary entries needed but also in the amount of linguistic information needed per dictionary entry. In the examples above, a dictionary based on the analysis of Table I would require eighteen entries for the material shown, whereas a dictionary based on Table II requires only eleven. The difference between eighteen and eleven does not seem very great, but if we think in terms of 100 nouns of this declension type, then the numbers are 900 and 109. And in general, for b bases and s suffixes each of which can occur with any of the bases, the figures are $b \times s$ and $b + s$.

Let us consider an abstract example, shown in Tables III and IV. Here I show only four bases and two suffixes. The rectangles in the figures enclose the dictionary information for each entry. There is a certain amount of information needed for each base as well as for each suffix, so in the unsegmented dictionary of Table III each entry must be large enough to contain the information for both the base and the suffix. (The translation of, say, the genitive singular suffix depends on factors which are independent of

Table III.

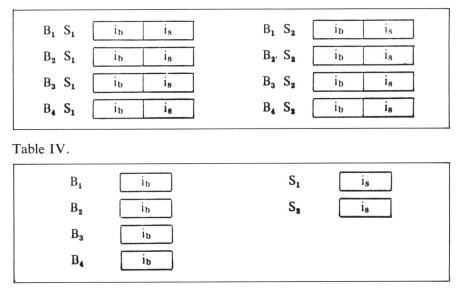

Table IV.

the stem with which it occurs). But in the segmented dictionary of Table IV each entry for a base requires only the information for that base, so each entry is smaller than in the case of Table III. By isolating the recurrent partial similarities of Table III, we achieve a reduction in number of entries from 8 to 6 (4 x 2 reduced to 4 + 2) but a reduction in total VOLUME OF RULES from 16 units to 6 units (considering the dictionary information for each base and suffix to be the same, namely one unit). The formula for volume of information in an unsegmented dictionary, considering only bases and suffixes and allowing only one suffix per word, where b is the number of bases, s is the number of suffixes, i_b is the average amount of information per base, and i_s is the average amount of information per suffix, is

$$b \cdot s \cdot (i_b + i_s),$$

which, if we let $i_b = i_s = i$, is equal to

$$b \cdot s \cdot 2i.$$

But if we segment, then the amount of information is only

$$b \cdot i_b + s \cdot i_s$$

or roughly

$$b \cdot i + s \cdot i = (b + s) \cdot i.$$

Thus the EXCESS SURFACE INFORMATION RATIO is

$$\frac{b \cdot s \cdot 2i}{(b + s)i} = \frac{2bs}{b + s}$$

So if we are dealing with 10,000 bases each of which occurs with each of ten suffixes, the excess surface information ratio is

$$\frac{2 \cdot 10,000 \cdot 10}{10,000 + 10} = \frac{200,000}{10,010} \quad \frac{20}{1}$$

In other words, under these conditions the unsegmented dictionary has about twenty times as much surface information as the segmented one, for the same effective information. But even this ratio is not as high as it would actually be in the more realistic situation which would allow more than one suffix (e.g. both derivational and inflectional) per word.

In the case of the Russian dictionary constructed at the University of California, words were segmented into bases, prefixes, derivational suffixes, and inflectional suffixes. The dictionary has around 20,000 entries (not counting those for the chemical nomenclature, which amount to an additional 2,000 to 3,000); but the number of words that are formable from these units (defining word as a sequence of graphemes that can occur between spaces or punctuation), using only grammatical constructions, is more than 2,000,000. This is a difference of more than one hundred to one in number of entries required. Obviously this difference, particularly when we add to it the consideration of amount of information needed per dictionary entry, is of enormous importance when we consider the question of the amount of storage space needed by a computer, and the amount of time required for obtaining the dictionary information for items in a text.

The third type of separation I would like to consider (and the one which relates to stratification) is that of the translation procedure as a whole into stages. As an illustration of the kind of economy that can be achieved by such separation, consider the bilingual dictionary—say a Russian-English dictionary—and the separated equivalent, which would consist of a Russian dictionary on the one hand and an English dictionary on the other, with addresses in the Russian dictionary identifying locations in the English dictionary. In the unseparated Russian-English dictionary, a given English lexeme might occur over and over again in different dictionary entries because it would be a suitable translation equivalent for several different Russian items. But in the separated version each English lexical item needs to be listed only once. (For further details see Lamb, 1965a).

The general case, as it exists between any two strata, is illustrated in Figures 1 and 2. If A realizes, or is realized by, a and b alternatively, but b is also one of the alternatives in the same relation to B, and so forth; then in the system which does not separate into stages on the basis of the stratification the elements b,c, etc. have to be repeated as in Figure 1. But if one isolates these recurrent similarities and states them only once instead of repeatedly, then one has the situation diagrammed in Figure 2.

The greater simplicity of Figure 2 is of larger proportions than would be apparent if the units shown as a, b, c, and d are taken to be in the midst of a series of strata (rather than at the end), since in that case there is further branching from each of them (to the right in the diagram, if it were extended). Suppose, for example, that we take them to be sememic units which are the realizates of the lexemes A, B, C, and D (for explanations of these concepts, see Lamb 1964a). In one type of translation system, these sememic units (a, b, c, d) would connect, with branching and merging, to lexemic realizations in the target language. This situation amounts to

Figure 1 Figure 2

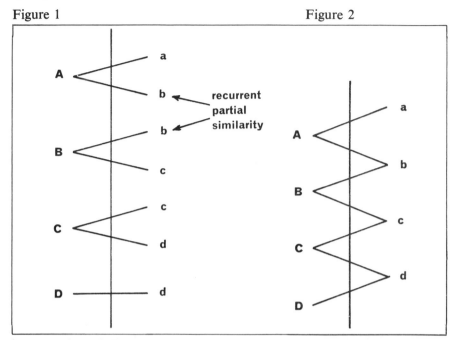

an extension of Figures 1 and 2 two steps beyond what is shown in the diagram, and the extended Figure 1, with its compounding of excess surface information, represents the system which tries to convert directly from lexemes of the source language into lexemes of the target language, while the similarly extended and far simpler Figure 2 may be interpreted as the situation achieved by separating the translation process into stages in accordance with the stratification present. (Some of the statements that have been made about the impossibility of economically high-speed dictionary look-up using existing computers have been fallacious simply because, among other things, the calculations were made in terms of excessively bulky dictionaries in which each entry would have to contain all the information that would be needed if no stratificational separation were made).

A more concrete example and one which is contained within a single language is furnished by the genitive lexeme of Russian, which has several morphemic realizations and is in turn the realization of several different semons. To illustrate with simplified diagrams of the alternative decoding processes, let a, b, c be different realizations of the genitive lexeme G, and let S, T, U be three semons which are realized by G, according to the realization rules, which may be diagrammed as R within a circle.

Then Figure 3 shows the repetition for a system which fails to recognize the lexemic stratum but which tries to convert directly from the morphemic shapes to the sememic realizates; while Figure 4 shows the corresponding situation for a stratified system. In reality, the difference in complexity is much greater than that shown in the diagrams, since (1) there are more than three morphemic realizations of G, (2) all of them are portmanteaus

Figure 3

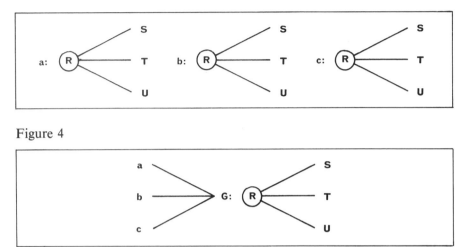

Figure 4

for G combined with singular or plural, and (3) there are not just three but perhaps a dozen or more sememic realizates of G.

To take another example, consider the English lexemes L/go/, L/go crazy/, L/go in for/, L/go through with/, L/undergo/. Each of these lexemes must be treated as a separate unit for economical handling of its sememic and syntactic relations (which is why they are to be analyzed as lexemes), yet if each is treated separately with regard to the past tense, not to mention the past participle, then the rule which provides the correct realizations *went, went crazy, went in for, went through with, underwent* must be given repeatedly. But if the strata are kept separate this statement is needed only once, as a morphological realization rule relating to the single lexon L/go/, a component of each of these five lexemes.

Thus, in short, the identification of recurrent partial similarities in linguistic structure leads to recognition of, among other things, the stratification of language, and in machine translation research the recognition of this stratification leads to the separation of the translation procedure as a whole into several stages. Since proper treatment of stratificational phenomena is so vital to machine translation, and since they have been dealt with so unsystematically in the past, I shall now go into some detail with regard to stratification and the simplicity to be achieved by recognizing it.

A. The stratification of language

The stratification of language has been recognized in varying degrees by many people who have worked with language, both amateurs and professional scientists. Hjelmslev (1943, 1954) and Hockett (1954, 1958, 1961) are prominent among the linguistic scientists who have recognized it, and I (1964a) have attempted to extend their observations to an explicit recognition of four structural strata, the *phonemic, morphemic, lexemic,* and *sememic,* which are apparently present in at least most natural spoken languages.

A language, by its nature, relates sounds (or graphs) to meanings. The relationship is a very complex one which turns out to be analyzable in terms of a series of systems each of which connects two neighboring *strata*. The sememic stratum has units directly related to meaning. These sememes may be thought of as encodable into units of the next lower stratum, which in turn are themselves encodable, and so on, until one comes out with units directly related to speech or writing (i.e. with phonemes or graphemes), which may now be spoken or written as the case may be. In understanding the importance of stratification to machine translation, it is helpful to look at the structure of spoken languages even though machine translation research is currently concerned with written languages, since the latter are based upon spoken languages and derive much of their structural patterning from them.

A few examples will give an indication of the various types of situations dealt with between different pairs of neighboring strata. If we consider the *t* in *eighth* in relation to the *t* of *water* in spoken English, we can see that from one point of view they are quite different. The former is dental, tense, and voiceless; the latter is postalveolar, lax, and voiced. These are phonetically two different entities, but phonemically the same, since the phonetic differences are non-distinctive. A rule can be given to account for the various features that are present in different environments, and those features, thus accounted for, no longer need be considered at the higher stratum. Similarly, but one level higher, if we compare *sane* and *sanity,* or *vain,* and *vanity,* or *nation* and *national,* we see a recurrent variation between two entities which are phonemically different. But in some other sense there is a single unit *sane* underlying both of the units *sane* and *sanity,* and the recurrence of the alternation for *vain* and *nation* indicates that it is not directly a property of *sane* as a whole, but rather a property of one of its components. Similarly, but one level higher, the forms which we represent orthographically as *good* and *better* are altogether different at one level, but at another they are partially the same. That is, the latter, from the lexemic point of view, consists of the former plus the comparative lexeme. Finally, *can,* as in *he can go,* is lexemically different from *be able to,* as in *he will be able to go,* but at another level these are one and the same unit. These examples are all concerned with DIVERSIFICATION, one of the several phenomena which characterize linguistic realization.

The reason for this complexity in linguistic structure is, in part, that sounds and meanings are, by their natures, patterned differently from each other. They each have their own set of structural relationships. Phonemic systems must be adapted to transmittability of speech through the air and to the articulatory and auditory organs, while sememic systems must be adapted to thought and memory patterns and to cultures and the world about which people talk. Speech takes place in time, which is linear; but the brain and the world are three-dimensional. Moreover, the processes of linguistic change affect phonological and semological systems in different ways. Thus a close correspondence between them would be impossible.

The same is true for written languages because writing systems are based upon spoken languages, so that they tend to have close correspondence to phonemic but not to sememic systems. On the other hand, written symbolic systems that have been developed independently of spoken language, such as symbolic logic, mathematics, and programming languages, do not have this property. Here we find a very close correspondence between writing and meaning, and little stratification.

Hjelmslev (1943), influenced by Saussure (1916), recognized the stratification of language, but he did not go far enough. His system has EXPRESSION SUBSTANCE (which corresponds to the phonetic stratum), EXPRESSION FORM (corresponding roughly to phonology, in the sense of that term used in this paper), CONTENT SUBSTANCE (which corresponds to the semantic stratum), and CONTENT FORM. But when one studies the linguistic data more closely, one finds that Hjelmslev's content form ranges over what are really three separate systems. These may be called morphology, lexology, and semology (see below).

On the other hand, American linguists have often tried to get along without any explicit stratification at all, except in separating phonetic and phonemic strata; or else, in some cases they have, like Hjelmslev, recognized separate structural strata, but too few of them.

The stratum is a type of level, but it is a different type of level from others which linguists frequently talk about. It is the type which is concerned with realization,[1] and it must be kept distinct from other kinds of levels, such as combinatory and classificatory levels, with which it has often been confused.

The combinatory or size level is the type of level which is concerned with combinations of linguistic units, the type one is speaking of when one says that the phrase is at a higher level than the word or that the sentence is at a higher level than the clause. Such levels exist within strata. They can be kept distinct from other kinds of levels by being called RANKS, as is done by Halliday (1961). Combinations of linguistic units exist on the same stratum as those units. Thus each stratum has a series of ranks. For example, the syllable is at a higher rank than the phoneme, but on the same stratum. Similarly, lexemes and combinations of lexemes such as clauses and sentences are all on the lexemic stratum.

The stratification hierarchy is also to be distinguished from taxonomic or classificatory hierarchies. The relationship between one stratum and an adjacent one is NOT that units of the one are classes whose members are units of the other. That is, the stratificational view is not the same as that which holds that a morpheme is a class of allomorphs and that a phoneme is a class of allophones. That view is too simple to fit the empirical data. Classes of linguistic units, like combinations, exist on the same stratum as those units. For example, the class of vowel phonemes (which really is a class) is on the phonemic stratum, and the class of nominal lexemes is on the lexemic.

As the concept of stratification is not yet well established in linguistics, the terminology that is appropriate to it is in a state of disarray. Neither I nor anyone else can even make a pretense of presenting the terminology that is standard in linguistics. Instead the terminology used here is presented as my own, with the hopeful assertion that much of it will be found to agree more or less with those of other linguists. The names I use for some principal units and their strata are shown in Figure 5, in which the vertical dimension represents stratification, with higher strata shown higher in the diagram, and the horizontal dimension is used for different ranks, with potentially smaller units on the left, potentially larger ones on the right.

Figure 5

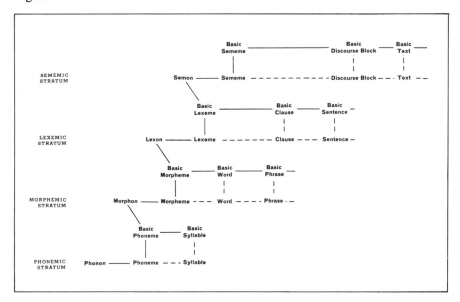

The elementary unit of a stratum is named with the suffix -ON. Thus the elementary units of the phonemic stratum, i.e. the components of phonemes, may be called phonons. The English phoneme P/m/ may be analyzed as composed of the phonons P/Cl/ 'Closed', P/Lb/ 'Labial', and P/Ns/ 'Nasal'. The syllable P/men/ may be written phonically as

Cl	Vo	Cl
Lb	Fr	Ap
Ns		Ns

Phonemes occur not in haphazard combinations but in arrangements having definite patterns (which of course vary from language to language). The patterns of arrangement on any stratum may be accounted for by tactic rules. The basic or elementary unit for purposes of such rules may be named the basic Xeme, where X is phon-, morph-, lex-, or sem-, as the case may be. (A basic phoneme may alternatively be called a morphophoneme, and basic morphemes and basic lexemes may similarly be called lexomorphemes and semolexemes, respectively). These basic emes are set up by the grammarian in such a way that the tactics will be as simple as possible (without being incorrect or incomplete). Basic emes (e.g. basic phonemes) may differ from actual emes (e.g. phonemes) in that a given basic eme may be realized as different actual emes in different environments (diversification) and in that a given actual eme may be the realization of different basic emes in different occurrences (neutralization). For example, the English basic phoneme BP/a/ in combination with another which may be written BP/:/ is realized as P/ey/, as in *sane,* otherwise when stressed as P/a/, as in *sanity,* and when unstressed as P/ə/ (cf. autom*a*tion, autom*a*tic, autom*a*ton; c*a*t*a*strophe, c*a*t*a*strophic).

When the tactics for a given stratum of a given language is made as simple as possible it reveals one or more important types of tactic units of higher rank than the basic eme, i.e. neatly structured combinations of basic emes. Such a unit in the phonology of at least most natural spoken languages is the basic syllable. The realization of a basic syllable, which is defined by the realization rules pertaining to its components, is a syllable. Although Figure 9 does not show any names of larger units than syllable at the phonemic stratum, such larger units exist, since any of the larger units of the upper strata has a phonemic realization.

Basic phonemes can differ from morphons, which are components of morphemes, in arrangement and in certain other ways too technical to be discussed here. An example of difference in arrangement is furnished by certain realizations of the past tense lexon of English, such as the one occurring with *take*. Morphonically, this realization follows *take,* but its realization in terms of basic phonemes (and in terms of actual phonemes) occurs within that of the verb. Such difference in arrangement, which is commonly found between neighboring strata, may be called anataxis.

«For a more recent treatment of the phenomenon referred to in this article as ANATAXIS, See Lockwood 1972c (' "Replacives" without Process') in this volume.»

Whereas phonotactic rules describe the composition of all possible basic syllables for a language in general terms, the composition of the morphemes must be described individually for each one. Morphological realization rules may be used for this purpose as well as for stating the relationships between the actual morphemes and the basic morphemes. For example, the realization rule for the basic morpheme *good* would state that when followed by the comparative suffix *-er* it is realized as M/behd/, when followed by the superlative *-st* it is realized as M/be/, while elsewhere it is realized as M/gud/. Note that this unit M/gud/ as a whole is the morpheme and that its components, M/g/, M/u/, and M/d/, are the morphons.

Morphotactic rules describe how basic morphemes are combined into basic words and basic phrases, thus indirectly describing how morphemes are combined into words and phrases. (Of course, higher-ranking units, such as morphological realizations of sentences and texts, also exist). Whereas such tactic categories as 'obstruent', 'vowel', etc. are relevant to the tactics of the phonology, in the morphology the tactic categories of basic morphemes of a typical Indo-European language would have such labels as 'verbal prefixes', 'noun bases', 'deverbative nominalizing suffixes', 'case suffixes', etc.

Basic morphemes occur in different arrangements from those of lexons, since the latter are components of lexemes, whose patterns of arrangement are governed by lexotactic rules. As an example, the perfect tense lexeme L/have > en/ of English is continuous, like all lexemes, but part of its morphological realization, namely *have*, precedes the morphological realization of the verb while the other part, the past participle suffix, follows.

A lexeme is composed of one or more lexons and is the realization of a basic lexeme. As an example, the past tense lexeme of English and the perfect tense lexeme may be analyzed as alternate realizations of a single basic lexeme since they occur in mutually exclusive environments, when environments are characterized in terms of basic lexemes.[2] The rule for this basic lexeme would state that it has the realization L/have > en/ when occurring in combination with other tenses or in non-finite verb expressions (e.g. *he would like to have gone*), and the realization L/ > ed/ elsewhere. Lexotactic rules characterize the set of basic clauses and that of basic sentences for a given linguistic structure in terms of basic lexemes as the ultimate constituents. The determination as to whether a given combination of lexons composes one lexeme or more than one or less than one is provided by the lexotactics, just as in morphology the determination as to whether a given combination of morphons composes one morpheme or more or less than one is provided by the morphotactics. For example, L/wide th/ *width* is one lexeme, while L/tall ness/ is two since, unlike *width*, it is formed according to a lexotactic construction. The English lexeme L/ness/ occurs freely with adjectives, including polylexemic ones (e.g. 'the *many-sidedness* of the Khrushchev personality', said by a television news commentator), so that the only way to accurately characterize its occurrence is to specify that it occurs with members of a particular distribution class; but the lexon L/th/ occurs with only about a dozen English adjectives, which do not constitute a distribution class on any other grounds and hence must be listed individually (in realization rules) to specify their occurrence with it. Therefore *tallness* is two lexemes, while *width* is one, which is composed of two lexons.

Although they exist on different strata and are therefore not directly commensurate, one may say that there is a rough correspondence in size between lexons and morphemes in that the number of tokens of each in the realization of a given basic sentence is usually about the same. Similarly, there is a rough correspondence in size between the morphon and the phoneme. There is somewhat less correspondence between morphemes and syllables and between lexemes and words. The syllable is a combination of phonemes and the morpheme is a combination of morphons, but they are combinations of different types. The realization of a morpheme is sometimes larger, sometimes smaller, sometimes the same in size as the syllable. Similarly, the lexeme has no necessary correlation in size with the word. The realization of a lexeme may be a word or it may be smaller than a word or larger (in which case it is called an idiom), or it may even be realized as parts of two different words, as is L/have > en/ in *has taken*.

Basic lexemes can differ from semons in arrangement and in certain other ways. Basic lexemes (of at least some languages) may be analyzed as occurring in trees that are something like dependency trees (cf. Tesnière 1959), Hays 1961, 1963), while sememes (which are composed of semons) occur in networks.

« During the subsequent development of the theory dependency trees were abandoned. The reason for this decision was the fact that dependency trees used elements at their nodes, whereas the nodes of the more modern theory, for which the and-or dichotomy has become basic, do not contain any elements but function purely as connecting devices. Thus dependency trees seemed incompatible with this newer approach.»

Thus in the sememic realizate of *a cabinetmaker has mislaid his brace and bit* (Figure 6), S/cabinetmaker/ is both the agent of S/mislay/ and the possessor of S/brace and bit/, and these two sememes in turn are connected to each other through the S/goal/ realation. But on the lexemic stratum there are two separate realizations of s/cabinetmaker/, namely L/cabinet make er/ (a lexeme composed of three lexons) and L/he/, so that the clause has the form of a tree instead of a network with a closed circuit.

Figure 6

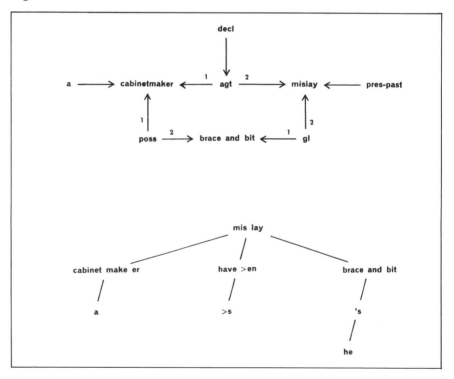

Just as some lexemes are simple (e.g. ᴸ/ > ed/ and ᴸ/find/ in *Joan found her hat*) while others are complex (e.g. ᴸ/be > ing/, ᴸ/look for/, and ᴸ/pocket book/ in *Joan is looking for her pocketbook*), so sememes can be either simple or complex. ˢ/possessive/, as in *her hat*, is a simple sememe, and an example of a complex sememe is the sememic realizate of *may I ask* in *May I ask who's calling?* (said by secretaries on the telephone). If the realizate were taken as polysememic instead of a single sememe, then the appropriate answer would be *yes* or *no*, to which (if it were *yes*) the secretary would respond *Who's calling?* (Cf. the lexeme ᴸ/under stand/ which, if it were polylexemic instead of single lexeme, would mean to stand underneath). Sememes are realizations of basic sememes. For example, *may I ask* is one realization of a basic sememe of politeness occurring with the interrogative basic sememe, of which an alternate realization is *may I tell him*.

Finally, the combinations of sememes which are well-formed according to a given linguistic structure, namely the texts and structured portions of texts, which may be called discourse blocks, may be accounted for (or generated) by means of semotactic rules, which apply to the basic sememes as simple tactic units and which characterize basic discourse blocks and basic texts as complex tactic units.

An illustration which covers all four structural strata is given as Figure 7. In it the lexemes, morphemes, and phonemes are shown in terms of

Figure 7

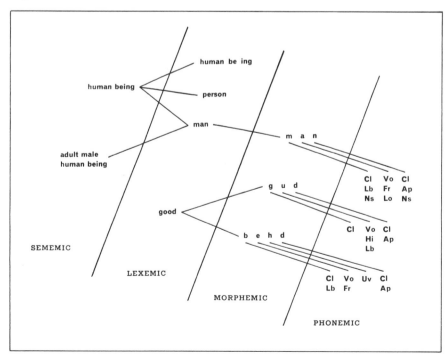

their components, i.e. their lexons, morphons, and phonons, respectively. The sememe S/human being/ is shown with three lexemic realizations; L/human be ing/, L/person/, and L/man/, of which two consist of single lexons while one is composed of three. The lexon L/man/, an indivisible unit, is realized by the morpheme M/man/, which is composed of three morphons, while for L/good/ two of the three morphemic realizations are shown. Phonemic realizations are shown (in terms of phonons) for M/man/, M/gud/, and M/behd/.

A full description of a language, according to stratificational theory, has semological, lexological (in traditional terms, lexical and syntactic), morphological, and phonological components, as well as a phonetics, which relates the structure to actual speech sounds (cf. Figure 8). Each of these components may be divided into two major sections, covering (1) tactics and (2) realizations. (Even the phonetics has a primitive tactics, which deals with the composition of segments). Realization rules are a means of describing the relationships between basic emes and actual emes as well as the componency of the actual emes.[3] Thus phonological realization rules relate basic phonemes, phonemes, and phonons to one another, while morphological realization rules relate basic morphemes, morphemes, and morphons, etc.

Figure 8

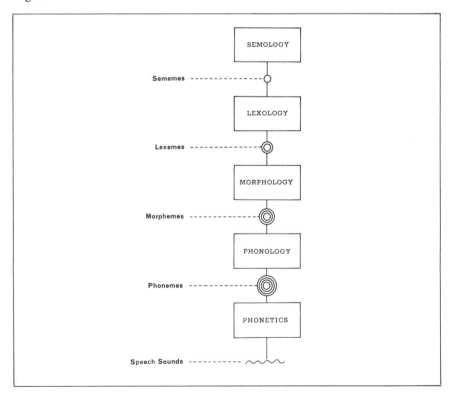

The semology generates or characterizes the (infinite) set of well-formed sememic networks for a language. The lexological component, if left to itself, i.e. if uncontrolled by the semology, generates the (infinite) set of grammatical sentences of a language, including both nonsensical and 'sensical' sentences (i.e. the larger of the two circles under the lexology in Figure 8). The smaller (but still infinite) set of sentences which are both grammatical and sensical is generated by the lexological rules if the choices allowed by them are governed by sememic networks instead of being made at random. A typical sememic network gives rise not to just one sentence but to a sequence of two or three or more (cf. Gleason, 1964:93–95), and the morphological component, which generates words and phrases, commonly provides more than one phrase for each sentence which comes to it from the lexology. In the normal use of language, the morphology operates under the control of the lexology, which in turn is controlled by the semology, thus generating the morphological realizations of the grammatical and sensical lexemic trees (represented by the smallest of the circles under morphology in Figure 8); if controlled by an uncontrolled lexology, the morphology generates a still larger set (the outer circle) which includes ungrammatical sequences (in the outer circle but not the middle one) in addition to the grammatical ones specified by the lexology. Lexological control is exercized by the lexons, which constitute specifications of what choices are to be made at points where there are alternatives. When the need arises, the morphology can provide new lexemes from its generatable stock or morphologically well-formed words and phrases. Similarly, the phonology generates sequences of syllables, normally under control of the controlled morphology, but when not under such control it generates nonsense syllables (as well as sensical ones), and with a certain type of relaxed control the result is jabberwocky, while with control by various esthetic factors in addition to more or less relaxed morphological and lexological control, the result is poetry (or attempted poetry). In addition, the phonology can be called upon, as it were, to provide new morphemes, just as the morphology makes possible the creation of new lexemes.

As there is a tactics associated with each stratum, the patterns of arrangement found on one stratum do not directly correspond to those of neighboring strata. An illustration of the type of difference in arrangement between the sememic stratum and the lexemic is given above in Figure 6, which also provides an indication of the type of difference to be found between the lexemic and morphemic strata, since the morphemic arrangement can be analyzed as a linear chain in which the order of the morphemes can be seen in the written realization *a cabinetmaker has mislaid his brace and bit*. A more striking difference between the lexemic and morphemic arrangements is exhibited by the simple interrogative version of the same clause. For it, the sememic network can be set up with the sememe ^{S}/int/ 'interrogative' in place of the ^{S}/decl/ 'declarative' of Figure 6. This sememe in this environment is realized by a feature which may be symbolized '>' (the same as that which appears in ^{L}/have > en/) attached to the head of the subject phrase. This element specifies to the morphology that whatever it accompanies (including anything under it in the tree) is to be delayed until the following word (cf. *has mislaid* [BM]/have z + mislay en/). Thus the subject phrase *a cabinetmaker* is delayed one word and the interrogative order is *has a cabinetmaker mislaid his brace and bit?*

More striking still is the situation involving word order in German clauses, which has plagued students through the years because of its seeming complexity. But actually what appears to be a very complicated pattern of arrangement when viewed solely at the morphemic stratum (or lower) turns out to be very simple when it is related to the lexology. The basic clause structure is very similar to that of English on the lexemic stratum; but German has a special rule used by its morphology in realizing lexemic trees, to the effect that only the first word of the verb phrase is realized in the expected order, and any remaining words are delayed in a temporary push-down store until the end of the clause; and if it is a subordinate clause, then every word of the verb phrase including the first is delayed in the push-down store. A push-down store has the property that the last item to go in is the first one out while the first in is the last out, etc. Thus the tree of Figure 9 is realized as *der Bauer wird das Entchen umbringen können* 'the farmer will be able to kill the duckling' (with infinitive suffixes supplied

Figure 9

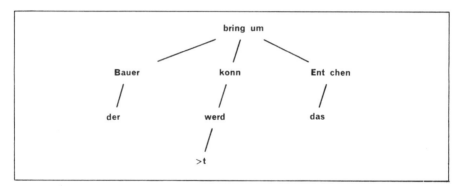

by the morphology as empty morphemes and *wird* as the realization of [BM]/werd t/). Without the pushdown store delay the order would have been *der Bauer wird [können bringen um] das Entchen* (with brackets enclosing the portion that is delayed). If [L]/werd/ is not present, then (without any other difference in the lexemic tree) the order is *der Bauer kann das Entchen umbringen,* and if neither [L]/werd/ nor [L]/könn/ is present then the order is *der Bauer bringt das Entchen um.* And if the clause as shown in Figure 9 is introduced by *dass* 'that', then all words of the verb phrase are delayed, and the order is *dass der Bauer das Entchen umbringen können wird.* Thus the gross differences in linear order seen on the surface are accounted for by a simple delay rule which is merely a matter of morphological realization of a simple and constant pattern of lexemic arrangement.

Since most or all current machine translation research is concerned with written languages, we should now turn to consideration of how their structure relates to that of the spoken languages on which they are based. In the first place the upper strata are generally substantially the same. Written languages differ from their spoken models in that at some point, usually relatively low in the generative hierarchy, the encoding is to rules which will lead to written marks instead of speech sounds. In alphabetic languages, the written characters—i.e. letters—take the place, roughly, of either basic phonemes or phonemes; or more commonly the orthography is of mixed character, reflecting partly phonemes and partly basic phonemes. In syllabaries the characters stand for basic or actual syllables. In Chinese, the characters are the written alternatives to morphemes of the spoken language for representing lexons. Clearly, therefore, the first stages of machine translation systems having Russian and Chinese as source languages will differ from each other. In Chinese there is in fact less to do since the input is already in the form of morphemes.

In the case of Russian, the graphemes, which are to be considered the elementary units in terms of which the input is given to the computer, correspond in several respects more closely to the basic phonemes than to the phonemes of spoken Russian in that they fail to exhibit some of the phonologically conditioned alternation found among the phonemes, e.g. alternation of vowels under varying stress conditions. It is therefore efficient to treat the graphemes of written Russian like basic phonemes in the more general structural model described above, so that with Russian, as with Chinese, we can avoid the stage of phonological decoding. (But the head start is not as great as for Chinese since the input units for the latter are morphemes).

B. Stratificational translation

A machine translation system must have the linguistic information and computer programs necessary for a decoding capability in one language (the source language) and an encoding capability in the other. In other words, most of the machine translation process involves programs and information whose usefulness is not limited to translation. Only that which is in the middle is specifically concerned with translation, while automatic linguistic decoding and encoding have numerous uses. To speak of the process of automatic translation, then, is mainly to speak of automatic decoding and encoding. Decoding is the process of going through the linguistic structure from bottom to top, while encoding is the reverse process. Each may be separated into sections on the basis of stratification (and in fact neither can be efficient if such separation is not made), so that we may speak of phonological decoding, morphological decoding, etc. That is, corresponding to each of the components of a linguistic structure described above (cf. Figure 8) there is a decoding process and an encoding process. Inasmuch as these 'ologies' all have the same type of internal organization (cf. Figure 5 above), each having tactics and realizations, with rules of similar forms, it might be expected that the processes of encoding and decoding are basically the same from one of them to another. And this is indeed the case. That is, the same basic decoding process applies for phonological, morphological, lexological, or semological decoding, and the same is true for encoding. Moreover, the processes of encoding and decoding for any of the 'ologies' are quite similar to each other, and may be regarded as variations on the same basic process; and the linguistic information needed for their execution is the same for either process and can be organized in roughly the same way. This organization of the linguistic information is also basically the same as that which can be used for an economical description of the structure. That is, it is not the case that the linguistic information must be organized in one way for decoding and in another for encoding, and that neither of these is the same as that which would be used for a linguistic description. It is not the case that the organization to be used for efficient description is unsuitable as a basis for production or decoding (as is the case for, e.g., the transformational approach to linguistics).

Encoding with respect to the Xology, where X is phon-, morph-, lex-, or sem-, consists of the formation of a combination of basic Xemes in accordance with the Xotactic rules, and the realization of the basic Xemes as actual Xemes, consisting of Xons, in accordance with the Xemic realization rules. Of course since the Xotactics (as information) generates (in the abstract sense) infinitely many combinations of basic Xemes, the production process must be under some kind of control to enable it to produce just a particular one at a given time. In experiments with computers involving a single stratum, control can be supplied by random numbers, as in the work of Yngve (1962);[4] and under various special circumstances or for special purposes, human language-users may provide various kinds of special control; but for normal speech and writing the control comes from the stratum above, or in the case of semological production it comes from the communicative intentions of the speaker (or writer), the circumstances in which he is speaking, and features of what he is speaking about.

The kind of control which an upper stratum exercises on the tactics of the next lower one is most easily seen in morphemic control of the phonotactics, since phonology is the simplest of the 'ologies'. Wherever a choice is available to the phonology, a morphon specifies which of the alternatives is to be selected. In other words, a morphon is not to be thought of as an object to be replaced or otherwise operated upon but rather as a specifier or selector, whose occurrence consists of activating a particular connection in the phonology. The phonology generates (again in the abstract sense) all well-formed syllables and combinations thereof, and a morpheme consists of the specifications leading to the production of a specific syllable or portion of a syllable or combination of syllables, as opposed to all the others which could be produced. For example, the morpheme which may be transcribed ^{M}/mor/ consists of the specifications leading to the specific syllable ^{P}/mor/ (orthographically, *more*). Although for notational convenience one can use the same letters 'mor' for ^{M}/mor/, ^{BP}/mor/, and ^{P}/mor/, the units symbolized by these letters are quite different. In ᴾ/mor/, each letter stands for a bundle of phonons, while in ᴹ/mor/ each letter stands for a choice specifier, and in ᴮᴾ/mor/ each letter stands for the designation of a specific phonological realization rule selected jointly by the tactics and the corresponding morphon. The ᴹ/m/ specifies not a particular basic phoneme selected from the whole set of basic phonemes, but rather a particular possibility for the onset position of the syllable. Following it, i.e. after a nasal in the onset position, the phonology requires that a vowel come next, and the next morphon specifies a particular vowel as opposed to the others. In other words, what is symbolized as ᴹ/o/ in the notation ᴹ/mor/ selects one possibility from the set of vowels, while ᴮᴾ/o/ designates one member of the whole set of phonemic realization rules, i.e. a set with a larger number of members.

The basic principles of decoding with respect to any of the 'ologies' may be illustrated with morphological decoding, which is the first part of a machine translation system in which Russian is the source language. For the general model discussed above, morphological decoding covers the decoding operations leading from basic phonemes to basic morphemes. As discussed above, the Russian orthography is in large part oriented to the basic phonemes of Russian rather than the actual phonemes, so that it is efficient to treat the input chain of graphemes as composed of basic phonemes, handling what graphological alternation there is as if it were morphological alternation.

Decoding up to actual morphemes may be accomplished by means of a dictionary look-up process. For the most efficient dictionary look-up procedure that has been designed so far, the distinction between morphons and basic phonemes (or graphemes of a language like Russian) is utilized by coding the morphemes (i.e. the realizations in the morphemic realization rules, the strings which appear in them at the right of '/') collectively in a tree structure, which for computational efficiency is stored in two parts, namely (1) the 'letter tables', which can be directly addressed using the first few graphemes of a morpheme successively as addresses, and (2) numerous short 'truncate lists', in which the search for a matching morpheme can be completed. The first letter of a word is used to refer directly to its entry in the first-letter table, the contents of which are the address of the second-letter table for all morphemes beginning with that first letter; and the second letter determines the addressing of an entry in that second-letter table, etc. The procedure was described in an early version by Lamb and Jacobsen (1961) and later by Veillon (1963), who worked out some valuable improvements in certain features of the original technique. A version with further improvements is being programmed by the Machine Translation Project of the University of California, Berkeley, but it has not yet been described in print. It is hundreds of times as fast in its operation as what was said by some a few years ago to be the 'absolute maximum' speed that could be achieved for dictionary look-up by computer.

Of course ambiguities can be encountered in this look-up phase, since some chains of basic phonemes (in at least most languages) have more than one possible segmentation. For example, English *unionized* can be segmented *union-ize-d* or *un-ion-ize-d*. Wherever such alternatives are encountered, all possibilities are to be carried forward. Any phase of the decoding process may encounter ambiguities, in which case multiple possibilities are passed on the next phase, where they can hopefully be resolved. An unresolved ambiguity remaining after the final phase of decoding reflects a true ambiguity in the text, provided that the linguistic information in the decoding system is complete and correct.

Upon finding each morpheme, the program is in effect given a direct reference to every basic morpheme of which that morpheme can be a realization. There may be two or more for which it is a neutralized realization. How then, when there are such multiple possibilities, does the program determine which is the correct one? When a basic morpheme has multiple realizations (i.e. when diversification is present), the realization rules specify which one is correct for any occurrence by giving a conditioning environment for each realization. But such conditioning environments are not directly suitable for 'upward' conversion to basic morphemes from neutralized actual morphemes, because they are expressed in terms of basic morphemes (not actual ones) and because in any case—i.e. even if restated in terms of actual morphemes—they would not in general suffice to resolve all cases of this type of ambiguity, since different realizates do not have to be in complementary distribution. In other words, realization rules are oriented towards encoding but not towards decoding. So there is a two-fold problem here: First, how then is such ambiguity to be resolved? Second, how is the information in realization rules concerning conditioning environments to be utilized in decoding? (Surely it must be necessary in some way, for if not then decoding would require less information than encoding, which hardly seems likely). The answer is that at this stage of the decoding process, the information concerning conditioning environments is simply to be ignored; but it will be used a little later. Bypassing the conditioning environments, then, the program is given directly all possible realizates for each possible morpheme, according to each possible segmentation (since all possible segmentations are carried forward to the next stage, as mentioned above). And what happens next is that each of the possibilities is taken through the morphotactics, which has the effect of rejecting all those that are not morphotactically well-formed (i.e. usually most of the multiple possibilities). The process is illustrated in Figure 10. In part one, it goes directly to all possible realizates of the ambiguous chain that are given by the realization rules. In part two all such possible realizates are tested by the tactics, which (in the usual case) rejects most of them (in the diagram, all but one). The Berkeley MT project has a tactic decoding procedure which allows multiple possibilities to be tested against the tactic rules in parallel, i.e. simultaneously in a single left-to-right pass through the chain, rather than serially (one after another), which would be far more time-consuming.

But then there must come the final phase of morphological decoding, in which whatever possibilities remain are put through the realization rules, but this time in the opposite direction, i.e. in the encoding direction, in

Figure 10

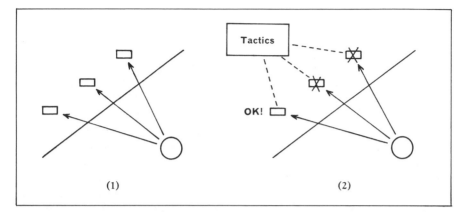

order to see whether the result of such encoding matches the input chain. It is here that the information concerning conditioning environments is used. (And so the morphotactic rules and the realization rules—i.e. the same linguistic information—are used for both encoding and decoding.) Any provisional decoding for which the test encoding fails to match the input is of course rejected. Whatever provisional morphological decodings remain are now no longer provisional but are to be taken as the morphological decodings. They fit the rules and their encodings match the input. If there is more than one morphological decoding for a given chain, that chain is morphologically ambiguous, and both (or all) decodings are passed on to the lexological decoding. Such a system has, of course, the ability to reject an input chain as being morphologically ill-formed—i.e. as having no valid morphological decoding (e.g. a word with a typographical error).

As a simple example consider the word *liven* of written (not spoken) English. The look-up would result in segmentation *live-n* and in references to multiple basic morphemes for each of these two actual morphemes. For *live* we have as basic morphemes a verb *live* and an adjective *live*. For *en*, there are several basic morphemes, including a verbal prefix, as in *endear, enshrine, enslave, entwine,* the past participle suffix of verbs, as in *taken, proven,* and a verbalizing suffix occurring with adjectives, as in *harden, sweeten.* Considering just these possibilities, we have two possible realizates for the first morpheme and three for the second, giving six (two times three) provisional decodings for the sequence. But these are immediately narrowed down to two by the tactic rules, which allow of the six, only the verb followed by the past participle suffix, and the adjective followed by the verbalizing suffix. Running these two remaining possibilities back through the realization rules in the encoding direction, we see that the provisional decoding of verb followed by past participle suffix is disallowed, since the realization rule for the past participle suffix specifies that with *live* it is realized as *d*. Therefore we have the one remaining decoding for the word, i.e. adjective followed by verbalizing suffix. (Note that if the word had been *livens,* the tactics alone would have narrowed the possibilities down to one).

Lexological decoding consists of phases corresponding to those described above for morphological decoding. First there is the look-up, but this time in the lexeme dictionary instead of the morpheme dictionary. Just as the morpheme dictionary provides the information making it possible to segment combinations of basic phonemes (or graphemes) into morphemes, giving references to basic morphemes for each such morpheme, so the lexeme dictionary provides the information making it possible to segment combinations of basic morphemes into lexemes, giving references to basic lexemes for each such lexeme. The combinations of provisional lexological decodings are then tested by the lexotactics, which rejects all that are not lexotactically well-formed, and the remaining provisional lexotactic decodings are further tested by being put through the lexological realization rules in the encoding direction for comparison of the test encodings with the input combination of basic morphemes. Whatever provisional decodings now remain are taken as the lexological decodings, and are ready for semological decoding. There may of course be two or more lexological decodings for a sentence, since there are such things as lexologically ambiguous sentences; in fact such sentences are quite common. So, as before, whenever such multiple decodings exist, all are passed on to the next stage, in this case semological decoding.

Semological decoding is similar in its basic design to morphological and lexological decoding (and in fact the same is true for phonological decoding, which is a necessary stage for spoken languages). A preliminary discussion of the use of semotactic information to resolve ambiguities is given in Lamb 1966c.[5] The linguistic analysis needed for this stage is of overwhelming proportions by comparison with any of the first three stages, and several years of research lie ahead in this area, to provide the computer with the linguistic information needed.

Each language has its own semological structure, but it is quite likely that for a translation system for at least some pairs of languages it will be efficient to set up a single compromise semotactics for them, in which case the results of semological decoding will be immediately ready for encoding in the target language, beginning with the sememic realization rules. Such an approach would seem to be desirable in translating from Russian to English, since these two languages have various similarities in semological structure, possibly reflecting the fact that both are Indo-European languages. But it is possible that for some language pairs, such as English and Chinese, it will be desirable to have separate semotactic systems, in which case there will be a stage of conversion from the one to the other before the encoding stages.

In either case, the remainder of the translation process consists of the stages of encoding, from sememic networks to lexemic trees, and so forth, until strings of target language graphemes are arrived at, at which time, of course, we are ready for output to the printer.

NOTES

1. The relationship of realization is described and illustrated in Lamb, 1964a (where it was originally called representation).

2. The evidence for this analysis was brought to my attention by M.A.K. Halliday.

3. Cf. the description of realization rules in Lamb, 1964b. At the stage of the theory represented by that paper, however, phonological realization rules, for example, would be used to describe all of the features of the phonemic realization of MORPHONS (and the phononic composition of the PHONEMES), whereas in the system represented in this paper they are used only for describing the realization of BASIC PHONEMES, and differences between morphons and basic phonemes are accounted for by the tactic rules of the phonology.

4. This work of Yngve illustrates very well the use of the computer and a random number generator for testing grammatical rules, but is not to be taken as an illustration of encoding for any specific stratum, since the types of grammatical rules used are tactic only and account for a mixture of lexotactic and morphotactic phenomena.

5. That paper, however, is probably in error when it states that the phase of test encoding using realization rules is unnecessary in the semology because of absence of diversification.

CHAPTER FOUR

Linguistic and Cognitive Networks*

SYDNEY M. LAMB

THE TYPE OF NETWORK treated in this paper is a network of relationships, and it is my intent to show how linguistic data and cognitional data can be accounted for by means of such networks. We shall start out by looking at some linguistic data, with a particular concern for identifying the relationships which they exhibit. That is, the emphasis is on their interrelationships rather than directly upon the items of data themselves. As we proceed, we shall observe how the individual relationships are organized into larger configurations forming networks of relationships, and we shall find that the types of relations and configurations of relations to be observed in linguistic data are also present in cognitional data. It then becomes interesting to view such linguistic and cognitive networks as models of the knowledge, or of some of the knowledge, that a typical human being has stored in his brain.

We may begin with the simple case of the adjective *good,* which, as we all know, has the comparative *better.* That is, we say *better,* rather than *gooder.* Now what is the relationship between *good* and *better?* In the first place, *better* is of course a comparative and it ends in *-er,* like other comparatives, *taller, higher, bigger,* etc. Thus the *-er* is evidently an expression for the comparative element of the grammar, and *better* thus consists of two parts *bett-* and *-er.* The remainder *bett-* which is left after identifying the *-er* of *better* is clearly in some very close relationship with *good.* We may say that these two units of expression have the same meaning

*From *Cognition: a Multiple View* (Paul Garvin, ed.) [1971]. Reprinted by permission. This work was supported in part by the National Science Foundation.

or content, since the difference in meaning is entirely accounted for by the *-er,* representing the comparative element, as may be established by the fact that the pairs *tall—taller, big—bigger* show the same difference in meaning and differ only in the presence or absence of *-er.* In other words, there must be some underlying or more abstract entity *GOOD* which has the alternative representations *gud* and *bet.* These alternative expression units may be called alternate realizations of the more abstract entity (Figure 1a).

Now the expression I am referring to here is spoken rather than written expression. English, like many other languages, has both forms of expression available, but the spoken expression system occupies a more basic position in the mind of the individual, since it is learned first and the writing system is learned on the basis of the knowledge of the spoken expression system already present in the child's mind. That is, knowledge of the writing system, as internalized in the brain, is built upon that of the phonological system. Thus in the diagram 'gud' is a symbolization chosen to be consistent with the phonological expression /gud/.

Now we may be more precise about the relationship between *gud* and *bet:* they are in an either-or relationship as expressions for the underlying entity *GOOD.* That is, *GOOD* is realized as either *gud* or *bet,* never as both of these at the same time. The relationship is diagrammed in Figure 1b, in which the quasi-rectangular symbol at the intersection of the lines may be called an 'or' node. The '(er)' identifies the condition for the choice of *bet* as opposed to *gud.* This condition can also be incorporated into a diagram of relationships but I refrain from going into this matter in this brief introductory treatment and instead refer the reader to the more technical account in Lamb 1966d. I also leave *best* out of this example just to keep it simple, since its inclusion would not affect the points under discussion.

Figure 1

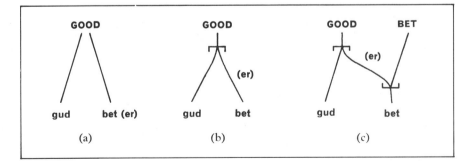

Now this expression unit *bet* is also used as the expression for a particular verb, as in
  I'll bet you that Nixon will not be reelected in 1972.
Here too we have an 'or' relationship, but this one is of opposite direction, since we have a single expression unit as realization of either of two content

units. Figure 1c shows that the abstract element *GOOD* is realized as either *gud* or *bet*, and this *bet* is a realization of either *GOOD* or *BET*.

Now it is already apparent from this very small amount of data that we must distinguish EXPRESSION from CONTENT in the linguistic system as these often fail to correspond to each other in one-to-one relationships—the single content unit *GOOD* is related to two separate expression units *gud* and *bet*, and the single expression unit *bet* is related to two separate content units. (For further discussion of expression and content, see Hjelmslev 1943, Lamb 1966a).

The linguistic system of the speaker's mind is a sort of code, which relates meanings or concepts, at one end, to speech sounds, at the other end. In drawing diagrams of portions of this code, we follow the convention that the upward direction is toward meaning or concepts, while downward is toward speech.

Moving on, let us consider the English word *den*. We can analyze it, on the side of expression, as a sequence of three phonological units, *d, e, n*. This relationship may be represented by the diagram of Figure 2a, in which the triangular node signifies an 'and' relationship, since we have the phonological segments *d* and *e* and *n* rather than one *or* another of these segments. Moreover, the order *d e n* is significant, as represented by the left-to-right ordering of the connections of the lines to the bottom of the triangle, since if the order is reversed, for example, we get an entirely different linguistic unit, *Ned*.

Figure 2

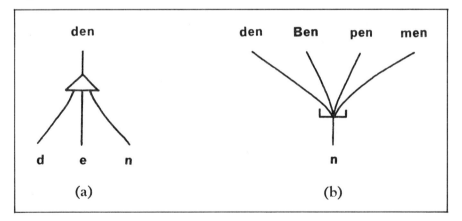

(a)   (b)

Now it is relevant to identify these parts, *d, e, n*, of the expression since, among other things, they are found to recur in the expression of other linguistic units. For example *n* occurs not only as a component of *den*, but also in *Ben, pen, men*, and so forth as represented in Figure 2b in which we may note that an upward 'or' relationship is involved, since a given occurence of *n* is a segment of EITHER *den* OR *Ben* OR *pen* OR *men* (not to mention other possibilities.)

Now if we put these observations together we arrive at a configuration of relationships that may be diagrammed as in Figure 3 for a small sample of data.

Figure 3

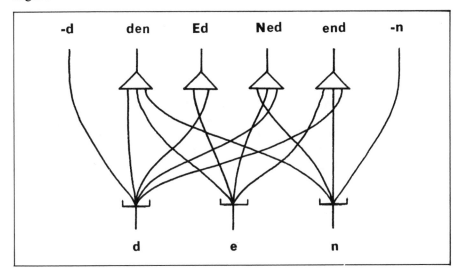

In this diagram *-d* at the upper left is the suffix of *rubbed, bugged,* etc., and *-n* at the upper right is the suffix of *taken, seen,* etc. These units of grammatical level happen to be expressed by single phonological segments and therefore connect downwards to phonological units without any intervening 'and' nodes.

This configuration of relationships may be called a SIGN PATTERN, in keeping with the traditional concept of the linguistic sign (Saussure 1916, Hjelmslev 1943): each of these 'and' nodes, with its connecting lines, represents a sign; the lower lines lead to the SIGNIFIANTS of Saussure, while the upper line leads to the SIGNIFIÉ. A sign pattern is characterized by a row of 'and' nodes with connections downward to a row of upward 'or' nodes. There are more lines at the top of a sign pattern than at the bottom: if the partial sign pattern of Figure 3 were expanded to cover all of the material that a typical speaker of English has at this level in his internalized linguistic system, we would find a few thousand lines at the top and only about forty or fifty at the bottom. As *-d* and *-n* illustrate, some lines at the top of a sign pattern may connect downward to an upward 'or' without any intervening 'and' node. Such lines represent SIMPLE SIGNS. The units at the top of this sign pattern may be called MORPHEMES and those at the bottom may be called MORPHONS. This use of the term morpheme is different from some uses of that term, in which it is applied to the combination of phonological units rather than to the single element which is REALIZED by that combination of units. This difference in the way the terms are used is in keeping with the differences in orientation. The usual practise in linguistics, particularly in the Boas-Sapir-Bloomfield-Harris-Chomsky tradition, is to focus on the data, whereas our concern here is with the network of relationships which is manifested by the data. When one is focusing on data the morpheme is obviously a combination of smaller units; for example, a sequence of phonemes or a matrix of distinctive features. But when we look at the relationships which underlie the data we identify a SINGLE POINT in the network, which is CONNECTED TO the phonological units, rather than being composed of them.

Now if we look a little more closely at the phonological segments of the sign pattern described above, we can see that they are not elementary—further analysis is possible. Notice that *d,* as in *doe* and *n* as in *no* are pronounced with the same tongue position. For both of these segments, the apex of the tongue is against the bony ridge behind the upper teeth. This is also true of *t* as in *toe;* but the *d* differs from the *t* in being voiced. Similarly, *m* as in *Moe, b* as in *beau,* and *p* as in *Poe* are all pronounced with the lips. Moreover, the difference between *m* and *n* is the same as that between *b* and *d,* and the same as that between *p* and *t.* We could represent these relationships by means of a table (Figure 4).

Figure 4

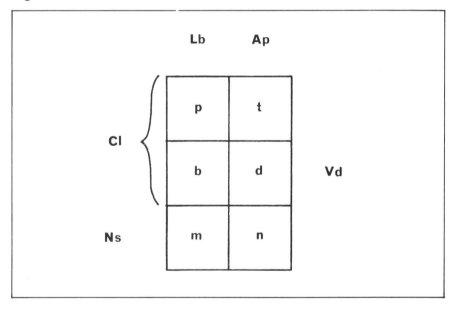

But these same facts can also be completely represented in terms of the basic 'and' and 'or' relationships already identified (Figure 5). Here, however, the 'and' connections are unordered, since the phonological components—e.g. Closure and Labial in the case of *b*—are simultaneous. So we recognize the unordered 'and' in addition to the ordered 'and'.

Here we have another sign pattern—a row of 'and' nodes above a row of upward 'or' nodes. We may distinguish between the sign pattern described above and this one by calling the former the MORPHEMIC SIGN PATTERN and this one the PHONEMIC SIGN PATTERN. The units at the top of the phonemic sign pattern may be called PHONEMES and those at the bottom may be called PHONONS.

Figure 5

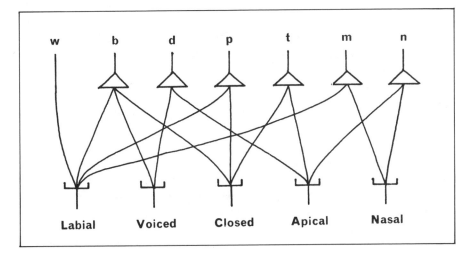

In Figure 5, only those phonons are shown which are DISTINCTIVE—i.e., capable of DISTINGUISHING meaning. Thus *m* and *n* both have closure of the mouth, just as do *b* and *d*, but the closure is predictable with the Nasal component and is therefore non-distinctive. The phoneme *w* may be analyzed as having only one distinctive feature, Labial, so it provides an illustration of a SIMPLE PHONEMIC SIGN, or SIMPLE PHONEME. (Non-distinctive phonological components are supplied at a lower point in the network; cf. Lamb 1966b.)

In the linguistic code the phonemic sign pattern is clearly below the morphemic sign pattern, but if we consider further evidence we can see that it is not directly below the latter and that the morphon and the phoneme cannot be equated. For example, we find downward 'or' relationships at this level similar AS RELATIONSHIPS to that exhibited by *GOOD*, *gud*, and *bet*. Consider the vowel sounds of the first syllables of

> *nation : national*
> *sane : sanity*
> *vain : vanity*

Here we have two different vocalic units but obviously a single higher-level entity, since *nation* and the *nation-* of *national* clearly represent the same morpheme. This alternation is at a lower level of the system than that of *gud* and *bet*, since these two are altogether different phonologically.

We also find evidence of downward 'or' nodes—i.e., of alternation—below the phonemic sign pattern. Consider the *n* of the prefix *in-* as in *inorganic*. Instead of *in-* we find *im-* in *impolite, impatient*. Just as *nation* and *nation-* of national are phonologically the same except for the alternating vocalism, so *m* and *n* are the same except for position of articulation. The alternation is between Apical and Labial, but the Nasal component does not vary.

Thus we seem to have evidence for the recurrence of similar patterns of relationships at different levels of the linguistic system. And we can see further such stratification at a higher level than those considered so far.

It used to be supposed, in linguistics, that morphemes (i.e. units like *good, den*) have a direct relationship to meaning. But what about *understand, undertake, undergo, go in for?* If *understand* consists of the two morphemes *under* and *stand*, then how do we account for its meaning? But if we take *understand* as a single morpheme, as neo-Bloomfieldians are forced to do in keeping with their principle that the morpheme is a minimum meaningful unit, then how do we account for the fact that the past tense of *understand* is *understood?* If *understand* is one morpheme and *stand* is another, then the fact that their respective past tenses are *understood* and *stood* has to be treated as two separate facts, and one can only say, on the side, 'What a remarkable coincidence! ' It becomes even more remarkable when we encounter *withstand* and its past tense *withstood*. We have a similar situation with *go-went, undergo-underwent, go in for-went in for*, and we simply cannot adequately account for the facts except by abandoning the Bloomfield-ian concept of the morpheme as a minimal meaningful unit—i.e., a unit which is not composed of smaller units such that the meaning of the whole is the combination of the meaning of the parts. For *understand* and *undergo* are minimal meaningful units, and yet they may be analyzed into smaller GRAMMATICAL PARTS: *under, stand*, and *go*.

Figure 6

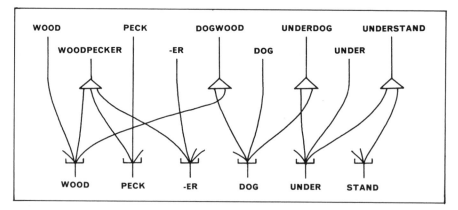

Thus we are dealing with another sign pattern, at a higher level than the morphemic sign pattern (Figure 6). This may be called the LEXEMIC

SIGN PATTERN and the elements at its top and bottom may be called LEXEMES and LEXONS, respectively. (The term LEXEME has a tradition going back to Whorf 1938, but its importance has been recognized by only a minority of linguists, even up to the present time.) With recognition of the lexemic sign pattern, the alternation involving *go-went, undergo-underwent,* etc. can be treated as a single alternation involving the lexon LN/go/. This alternation is at the same level as that of the morphemes M/gud/ and M/bet/, and the higher-level entity *GOOD* of which they are alternate realizations may now be identified as the lexon LN/good/.

Notice that, as with our other sign patterns, there are some simple lexemes in addition to the complex lexemes, and that we recognize complex lexemes for cases in which none of the participating lexons has alternating morphemic realizations, for example *dogwood.* If this were not done we would have to recognize a separate morpheme for *dogwood,* and the morphemic sign pattern would be unnecessarily complex (Figure 7). By recognizing L/dog-wood/ as a complex lexeme we take advantage of the morphemic signs M/dog/ and M/wood/, which are needed in any case (Figure 8).

Another way of looking at this argument is to consider what it is necessary to add to the system when it acquires the new vocabulary item *dogwood,* on the assumption that *dog* and *wood* are already represented in the system. The alternatives may be seen in these diagrams, and that of Figure 8 requires the addition of fewer new lines.

In Figure 8, the diamond-shaped nodes in the middle are for connections to the morphemic syntax or MORPHOTACTICS, the pattern of relationships which accounts for (i.e. generates) the allowable combinations of morphemes (see below). These diamond nodes should be added at the top of Figure

Figure 7

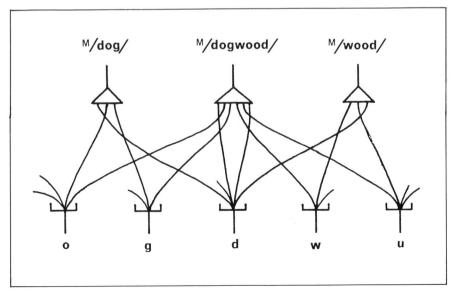

7 to make it comparable to Figure 8 and there would have to be three of them, since M/dogwood/ would also require one.

Notice that *woodpecker* also requires a complex lexeme, even though its meaning is related to the combination of meaning of its parts—but a baby woodpecker is still a woodpecker even though it doesn't peck wood, and a sparrow may occasionally peck at some wood, but that doesn't make it a woodpecker. (For further discussion of this point see Lamb 1966a).

Figure 8

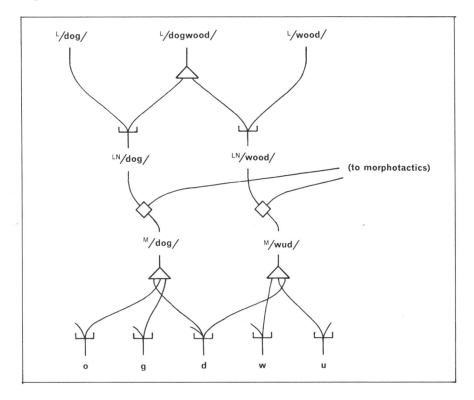

Now we are ready to consider the status of the morpheme. What is it? Up to now I have referred to morphemes as elements and have identified them by means of symbols, e.g. M/wud/ *(wood)*. But what do these symbols stand for? Well, what are the properties of the morpheme M/wud/? It has a phonological expression, a connection upwards to the lexemes L/wood/, L/woodpecker/, L/dogwood/, etc., (which in turn are connected to meanings) and a connection to a certain point in the morphotactic pattern (representing the fact that it functions as a noun, perhaps a certain subtype of noun). And that's all—it is nothing other than the point which has those connections. That is, it is nothing more than a position in a network of relationships. Thus the symbol M/wud/ is merely a label for that position—it is not some kind of chunk of stuff, some kind of object which the network has in addition to its lines and nodes. Thus we could draw it just as accurately—or rather, more accurately—redraw the diagram as in Figure 9, with the symbols for the lexons and morphemes omitted since they do not constitute part of the structure of the linguistic system. In this diagram the symbols for the lexemes (at the top) and for the morphons (at the bottom) are written at the sides of the lines which they label, rather than at the ends. They are merely labels, not part of the structure, by the same type of argument that applies in the case of morphemes. And similarly, the entire linguistic system consists just of relationships—not symbols and relationships, just relationships, which may be diagrammed in a network of lines and nodes. Symbols are needed only at the end points of a diagram. In a network diagram of the whole of a linguistic structure (which would take far too big a sheet of paper to be a feasible undertaking), symbols would be needed only for phonetic features, at the bottom, and concepts, at the top. On the other hand, diagrams are in general much easier to read if we sprinkle labels around rather liberally; but from now on the labels will be at the sides of lines.

Figure 9

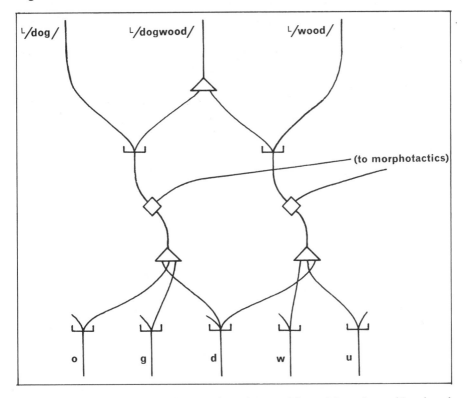

This point has been so widely misunderstood by critics of stratificational theory that one must conclude that it is rather difficult to understand; or at least it is difficult for those who are accustomed to the type of thinking that has prevailed in the Boas-Sapir-Bloomfield-Harris-Chomsky tradition. In this tradition there have been two tendencies in description, called 'item-and-arrangement' and 'item-and-process' (Hockett 1954). In the former, to give a grossly oversimplified account, one has linguistic items together with rules or other statements specifying how these items are arranged, while in the item-and-process approach one has items together with rules or other statements specifying operations performed upon these items. Now there has often been controversy between these two approaches, but they are really just two versions of the same basic tradition. Just as the New Left of politics opposes itself to both the Old Left and the Old Right, which it considers to be two varieties of the same basic mistake, so the relational approach in linguistics, which stems from Hjelmslev (1943; cf. Lamb 1966a), must be distinguished from both varieties of the item-and- (process/arrangement) approach, since linguistic structure, in its view, DOES NOT HAVE ITEMS AT ALL, nor does it have rules.

Now if we look further we find still another sign pattern, for there are 'crystallized' combinations of lexemes which must be considered as units for their meanings to be understood: *he'll never get to first base, he's got two strikes against him, don't take any wooden nickels, he put his foot in his mouth, as far as ... is/are concerned.* This one may be called the SEMEMIC SIGN PATTERN, and the lines at the top and bottom of it may be called SEMEMES and SEMONS, respectively. (The term SEMEME was first used by Noreen 1903–1918). We also find alternation (i.e. downward 'or' relationships) among lexemes as realizations of semons, just as at lower strata. The semon SN/future-tense/ is realized as L/will/ in *John will be late* but as L/be-going-to/ (a complex lexeme) in *John was going to be late* in which S/future/ functions within the context of S/past/. Similarly, SN/can/ is realized as L/can/ in *Archibald can understand Hjelmslev* but in the future it is realized as L/be-able-to/ (a complex lexeme), as in *Noah will be able to understand Hjelmslev.* Another example (borrowed from D. Bennett 1968) is furnished by SN/although/, which is realized in three different ways in:

They left *although* it was raining.
They left *in spite of* the rain.
It was raining. *Nevertheless* they left.

Now there are a number of other relationships to be found among lexemes and between lexemes and sememes. Some of them have been recognized for years by the man on the street (who, by the way, is not necessarily on the street); but it has not generally been realized how simple they are when analyzed into elementary relationships. Some of the more commonly noted phenomena are these:

First, a lexeme can have more than one meaning. An example is the English word *table,* which can designate either a piece of furniture or a type of display of information on the page of a book.

Second, different lexemes can have the same meaning, for example *big* and *large*.

Third, the meanings of some lexemes can be analyzed into components of meaning. For example, the English word *mare* can be analyzed into the components *female* and *horse;* similarly, *doe* has the components *female* and *deer,* and *hen* has the components *female* and *chicken.*

A fourth observation is that some pairs of lexemes have opposite meanings. An example is the pair *big* and *little.*

Fifth, there are combinations of lexemes which have meanings different from the combinations of their separate meanings. These are often called idioms. We have already taken care of them by means of the sememic sign pattern. (And some of the things commonly called idioms are accounted for by the lexemic sign pattern.)

«The question as to whether there are two idiomaticity areas (lexemic and sememic) in most natural languages, and whether there is also a third one (hypersememic or gnostemic) is taken up in A. Makkai 1972.»

Let us take a look at the other four of these commonly observed phenomena.

The first was that a lexeme may be connected to more than one sememe, for example *the table in the book* as opposed to *the book on the table.* This is simply an upward 'or' (Figure 10).

The second observation was that different lexemes may be connected to a single sememic unit, for example *big* and *large.* This is merely a downward 'or' relationship, and further examples are already given above. Note that *big* and *large* are not completely synonymous (and indeed complete synonymy is doubtless impossible), since *large* is not substitutable for *big* in *he's a big fool, he's a big man on campus,* etc. This fact in no way destroys our recognition of *big* and *large* as synonyms. It only means that L/big/ is a realization of other semons besides the one that may alternatively be realized as L/large/ (Figure 11).

Figure 10   Figure 11

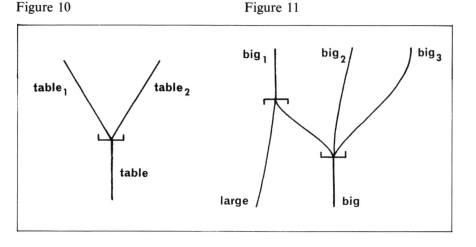

The third of our semantic observations was that some lexemes connect to combinations of sememes. The lexeme *mare* is connected to two sememes, which we may label *horse* and *female*. Now this is simply an upward 'and' relationship (Figure 12). Thus, as with the 'or' relationship, we must recognize two directions, upward and downward.

Figure 12

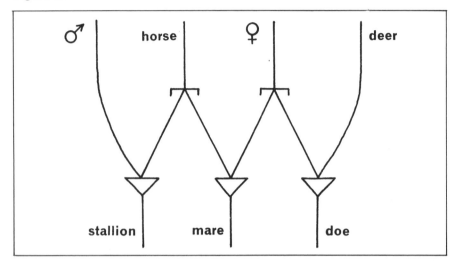

The next observation was that some pairs of lexemes have opposite meanings. As examples we have *big* and *little, high* and *low*. The name ANTONYMY has often been used for this type of relationship, and the items of opposite meaning are called ANTONYMS. But actually there is more than one way in which linguistic units can be opposite in meaning. In the case of such pairs as *big* and *little, large* and *small, tall* and *short,* the second member of each pair is a negative of the first; *little* means not big, *small* means not large, *short* means not tall, and so forth. But the same is not true for *come* and *go*. To not come is not the same as to go. Rather, the difference between these two is one of direction: to come is to move toward the speaker or his point of reference, to go is to move otherwise. One says *come here* and *come to my party,* but *I will go there* and *I will go to Mary's party.* Another pair showing this same relationship is *bring* and *take*. One says *bring it here* but *take it away*. But *go* and *take* are used not only for movement away from the speaker; they are also more general terms, which cover movement without a specific directional orientation. We may say that *go* is the unmarked member of the pair, while *come* is marked for direction towards the speaker or his point of reference. In the same way, *bring* is marked while *take* is unmarked. In providing the structural analysis for these pairs, we say that the marked member of each pair has an additional sememic component; let us call it S/hither/. Thus the sememic sign *bring* leads upward to two sememes, S/take/ and S/hither/ (Figure 13).

Figure 13

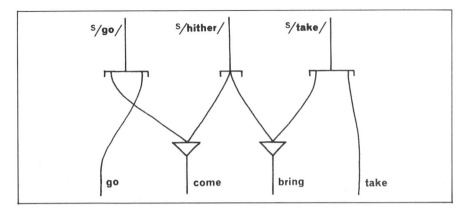

Let us now return to the pairs *high* and *low, big* and *little, large* and *small*. Here one also observes that in each pair one member is marked while the other is unmarked. *Little* means specifically not big; and *big,* while it covers the opposite of *little,* is also a more general term. If the speaker of English asks about the size of an object and does not know whether it is big or little he says, 'how big is it?' not, 'how little is it?' He does not say 'how little is it?' unless he already knows that it is little. In other words, *little* is the marked term, while *big* is unmarked. By applying the same test we may determine that *small* is marked while *large* is unmarked, *low* is marked while *high* is unmarked, *near* is marked while *far* is unmarked; and so forth. As before, the marked terms are those which have the additional component; and in this case that additional component means 'un-'. In other words, *little* is to be analyzed as 'unbig', *near* as 'unfar', and so forth (cf. happy-unhappy, funny-unfunny.) These relations are diagrammed in Figure 14.

Figure 14

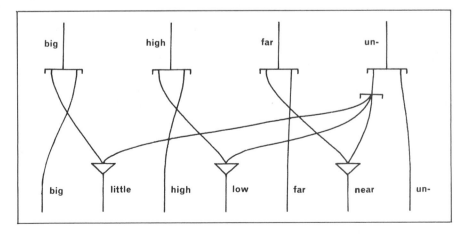

Here, as in the preceding diagram, I have used a new variety of 'or' node, in which the lower lines connect at different points. This node may be called an ordered 'or', but in this case the ordering is a matter of precedence rather than temporal ordering: the left connection is chosen where possible—that is, we don't have a free choice between *little* and **unbig;* the former takes precedence.

Let us now turn to *male* and *female,* a pair which exemplifies still another relationship. In this case, unlike the others, we do not find that one member of the pair is complex relative to the other. It is not correct that *female* is merely the negative of *male.* Inanimate objects are not male, but they are not therefore female. The actual relationship of these terms lies just in the fact that they are members of a class which has only two members. This class is in the cognitive system, and it is also present in the semotactics, i.e. the syntax of sememes.

Figure 15

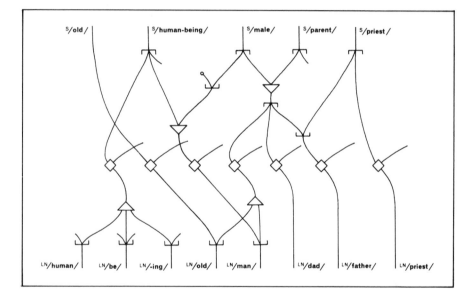

To further illustrate how semantic relationships may be diagrammed in the stratificational network notation, let us consider the following observations: *old man* is ambiguous, since in addition to its literal meaning (for which *old* and *man* represent separate lexemes) it is a designation for 'father', which may also be realized as L/father/ or L/dad/. But L/father/ is also an alternative to L/priest/ as a designation for the sememe S/priest/. Now L/man/ is ambiguously a designation for a human being or a male human being. That is, it realizes S/human-being/ and optionally also the sememe S/male/. In the diagram below, the optionality is indicated by the upward 'or' with one line connecting to a small circle which means zero or nothing—that is, the upward connection at this point is either to S/male/ or to nothing.

And S/human-being/ may alternatively be realized as the lexeme L/ human-being/, a complex lexeme connecting to the lexons LN/human/, LN/be/, and LN/-ing/. All of these observations are incorporated in Figure 15. This diagram also shows the points of connection to the lexotactics, i.e. the syntax of lexemes. These are the diamond-shaped nodes in the middle.

I have now mentioned in passing the existence of three syntactic patterns, at the sememic, lexemic, and morphemic strata. It will come as no surprise that one also finds evidence for syntax of phonemes, i.e. a PHONOTACTICS. To give some idea of what a tactic pattern looks like, I provide in Figure 16 a partial morphotactics for a simple quasi-language that bears some resemblance to English but is much simpler.

Figure 16

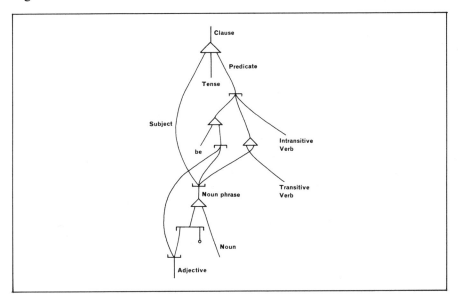

Notice that this pattern is made up of the same relationships that we have previously identified. This diagram indicates that a clause consists of a noun phrase followed by a tense followed by a predicate. There are three types of predicates: *be* followed by an adjective or a noun phrase, a transitive verb followed by a noun phrase, or an intransitive verb. The upward 'or' above the noun phrase construction indicates that the noun phrase can serve in any of three tactic functions, and similarly an adjective can serve in either of two tactic functions. Finally, a noun phrase consists of a noun optionally preceded by an adjective (that is, the downward 'or' provides a choice between nothing and an adjective).

Now I have already mentioned that the points at which a tactic pattern connects to the rest of the network (which may be called the REALIZATIONAL portion) are diagrammed as diamond-shaped nodes. They may be called diamonds. The diamond is something like an 'and' node, but it is more

complicated than those considered so far. The usual type of diamond has
three connections, as shown in Figure 17a.

Figure 17b shows a less common type of diamond, which provides a
connection of a line from the higher stratum to the middle of a tactic line
rather than the end. This type of diamond is used for higher-stratum elements
which are realized by features of arrangement. Figure 17c shows another
type of diamond, which provides for determined elements, i.e. elements
whose presence is determined by the tactics and which therefore have no
connection to the higher stratum. This is not really a node at all, since
it has only two connecting lines; but it is a convenient notational convention
which makes possible a clear boundary between the tactic pattern and the
realizational lines.

Figure 17

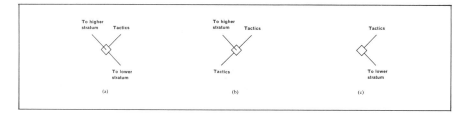

It is convenient to visualize a tactic pattern as occupying a horizontal
plane which intersects the vertical lines of the realizational portion of the
linguistic network. The points of intersection are the diamonds. Since we
find several tactic patterns (see below), the linguistic network has a series
of parallel horizontal planes, the tactic patterns, intersecting the vertical
lines at several strata from top to bottom. In visualizing the overall network
it should further be kept in mind that the lower strata have relatively fewer
lines and nodes than the upper since a sign pattern has more lines at its
top than at its bottom. That is, the network is much larger at the top than
at the bottom.

To see how the diamonds function, let us first consider the question of
how a tactic pattern chooses among alternative elements of the realizational
portion. We may take the case of a morphotactics and the choice between
alternative morphemes, say noun stems. (In this oversimplified morphotactics, derivation and inflection have been omitted.) If the simple morphotactic
pattern diagrammed above is viewed as a generating device, then at the
point 'Noun' we encounter a problem of choosing between the available
nouns. Now what the network has at that point is (let us say for this simple
quasi-language) shown in Figure 18.

When the 'Noun' line of the morphotactics is activated, we may say
that each of the lines coming down from the 'or' node is activated, since
although it is an 'or' node, there is no way of knowing at just that point
which line to choose. The choice is determined by the next higher stratum,
which activates one of the lines going into these diamonds from above.

Here the diamond acts like an 'and' node. If the semantic element for 'house' has been activated, then we may say that the line marked by a star is activated; and when the two connections to diamond 'x' are activated, the third line, leading down to the morpheme M/house/, is activated.

Figure 18

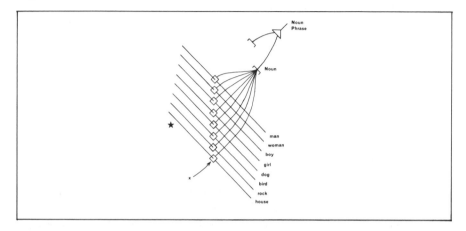

Now in this same way the tactics determines the choice between alternative realizations in many of the cases where downward 'or' nodes are present in the realizational portion. In the example of L/although/, L/in-spite-of/, and L/nevertheless/, mentioned above, the three realizations occur in three different lexotactic environments: L/in-spite-of/ is a preposition, occurring with noun phrases in prepositional phrases; L/nevertheless/ is a clause introducer; and L/although/ is a clause linker, occurring with two clauses (unlike L/nevertheless/, which occurs with single clauses). The situation is diagrammed in Figure 19.

Figure 19

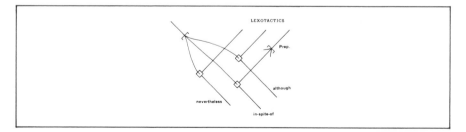

Here too we may say that at the downward 'or', in this case in the realizational portion, all of the downward lines are activated when the upper one is, and the tactics will determine the choice since in any instance only one of the three lines, which connect to three different positions in the tactic network, will be active. Only that diamond which has both of its upper lines activated will activate the lower line, leading to one of the realizations. Here we see the tactic pattern operating as a sort of filter, filtering out unwanted possibilities during the encoding process. A tactics also serves, in encoding, to provide for the temporal ordering of line activations at its level, resulting in the sequencing of the expressions which are put out from the bottom of the network.

In decoding, i.e. in moving upwards through the network from expression to content, the diamond also functions as an 'and' node, but one of different direction. Consider the morpheme M/wel/ *well*, which has five different meanings in:

> *John swims very well*
> *Well, I guess so*
> *They dug a deep well*
> *Last week he was sick but today he is well*
> *I can feel tears well up in my eyes*

Although *well* is quinquiguous (5-ways ambiguous) the context provides a resolution so that only one meaning comes through in each of the five examples above. We may account for this fact by means of the function of the diamonds in the diagram of Figure 20. These five meanings are correlated with five different morphotactic functions, which we may label ADVERB, CONJUNCTION, NOUN, ADJECTIVE, VERB. This means that the five diamonds are connected to five different positions in the morphotactics. In decoding, the upward signal from the line M/wel/ is transmitted along all five lines to all five diamonds, since of course each is a possibility if no context is taken into consideration. But the tactics, in any of these five sentences, is in a position to accept only one of the possibilities. That is, only one of the five lines from the tactics is activated, and that one determines the choice. The diamond is thus functioning as a type of 'and' node, but one of different direction from that involved in encoding. Thus the tactic

Figure 20

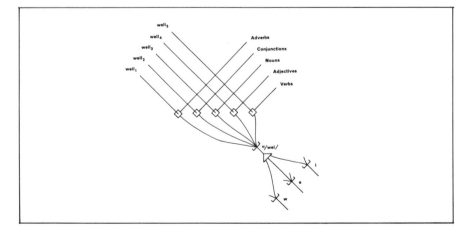

pattern, through the use of the diamonds, acts as a filter also in the decoding process, in this case for filtering out the tactic misfits, so that ambiguities are automatically resolved.

Let us now consider an example of this phenomenon at the next higher stratum. The sentence *John found a book on Broadway* is ambiguous: John might have found a book whose subject matter is the street named Broadway, or it might be that it was on this street that he found the book. But now consider these two related sentences:

John found a bracelet on Broadway.
John found a book on yoga.

These two sentences are unambiguous. Yet their syntactic structure according to the morphotactics is identical to that of the ambiguous sentence. The three sentences are equally ambiguous according to the morphotactics alone, because in all three cases it allows the prepositional phrase to modify either the preceding noun or the verb phrase. But only the first of these three sentences is really ambiguous because for it the lexotactics also allows two interpretations. The ambiguity involves not primarily the two possible morphotactic interpretations but the lexeme *on,* which connects upward to two different semons, ^{SN}/on$_1$/ for location on a concrete object, as in *on the floor* (or temporal location on a day, as in *on Tuesday*) and ^{SN}/on$_2$/ as in *a book on yoga.* The lexotactics of English specifies that the locational /on$_1$/ can occur only with members of the categories of concrete objects and certain time periods, while /on$_2$/ can occur only with members of the category of types of discourse. This category includes objects such as books and speeches and actions like talking, as in *a book on yoga* and *he spoke on yoga.* The sentence *John found a book on Broadway* is ambiguous because both of these interpretations for the lexeme ^{L}/on/ are accepted by the lexotactics: *book* is a type of discourse and *Broadway* is a concrete object. But the sentence *John found a bracelet on Broadway* is unambiguous because the lexotactics rejects one of the interpretations offered by the morphotactics, since bracelet is not a type of discourse. Similarly, *John found a book on yoga* is unambiguous since yoga does not belong to the category of concrete objects in the lexotactics. And notice further that in the sentence *John found a bracelet on yoga* both /on$_1$/ and /on$_2$/ are filtered out by the lexotactics, since neither of them finds a suitable tactic environment. (For further discussion see Lamb 1966c.)

We have now seen some evidence for the existence of both a lexotactics and a morphotactics. That the morphotactics is independent of lexotactics is indicated also by the fact that it generates a larger set of combinations of morphemes when taken by itself than when it operates under control of the lexotactics. For example, *underwhelm, *underhold, *retroduce are morphotactically well-formed but they don't have any lexemic decodings. This property of the morphotactics enables it to supply new combinations of morphemes for new lexemes when the occasion demands: *acid-head, transistor, video-tape, over-kill, credibility-gap, moon-shot.*

Likewise, the phonotactics generates a larger set of combinations than the set of phonemic realizations of morphotactic conbinations. The phonotactics generates the set of all well-formed combinations of phonemes, including many which are known as nonsense syllables—i.e., combinations of phonemes which are phonotactically well-formed but which are not decodable in the morphemic system. Thus a facility is also available for the formation of new morphemes.

Figure 21

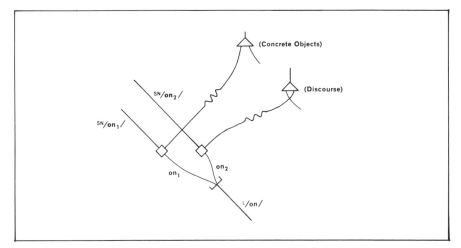

Now I mentioned above that in a diagram of a complete linguistic network, symbols would be needed only at the top and the bottom, for concepts and phonetic features, respectively. We are now ready to consider the question: what are these concepts, or cognitive elements? If we look at cognitive data with a view to their relationships, in the way that linguistic data have been examined in this paper, we find that they too give rise to a network of relationships, and concepts turn out to be representable as positions whose properties are entirely given by what they are connected to in that network. Thus the points at the top of the linguistic network are positions in another network, and the linguistic network and cognitive network are two parts of one large relational network. Now that the elementary relationships and diagramming notation are familiar it will not be necessary to go through such a painstaking account as that given above for the linguistic system, and we can move directly to some examples of the representation of non-linguistic information.

In the game of baseball, there are three quite different types of phenomena which serve the same function, that of the strike—or at least they are almost the same in function: the swing-and-miss and the called strike can serve as any of the three strikes allowed a batter, but a foul ball can only function as the first or second strike; otherwise it has zero function. Three strikes make an out, but this is only one type of out; my cognitive system contains three others, as shown in the diagram. Upon receiving three outs the side at bat is retired. There are two sides, known as the visitors and the home team, of which the visitors are up first. When the visitors and the home-team have both been retired the first time, the first inning is over, and there are then eight additional innings like the first, after which the game is complete. All of these facts, which form a part of my cognitive system, are represented in Figure 22.

Figure 22

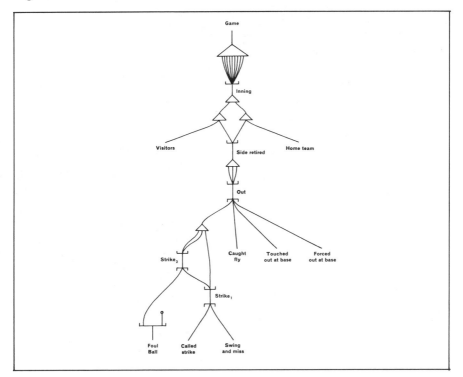

My knowledge of animal taxonomy provides another illustration. Figure 23 shows part of the taxonomy I happen to have acquired and retained in memory. Notice that the position *mammals,* for example, connects downward to types of mammals (extension) and upwards to properties of mammals (intension). The fact that cats, for example, have fur is represented by virtue of the fact that from the line *Cats* there is a path upwards to the property *Fur,* which is given just once for mammals in general. Other features of the diagram I leave to the reader's unguided examination. Here, the upward and downward directions do not have the same significance as in the linguistic network. Upward is toward fewer more general concepts, while downward is toward a larger number of more specific concepts. Not shown in the diagram are connections which some (but by no means all) of the lines have to the linguistic network.

Figure 23

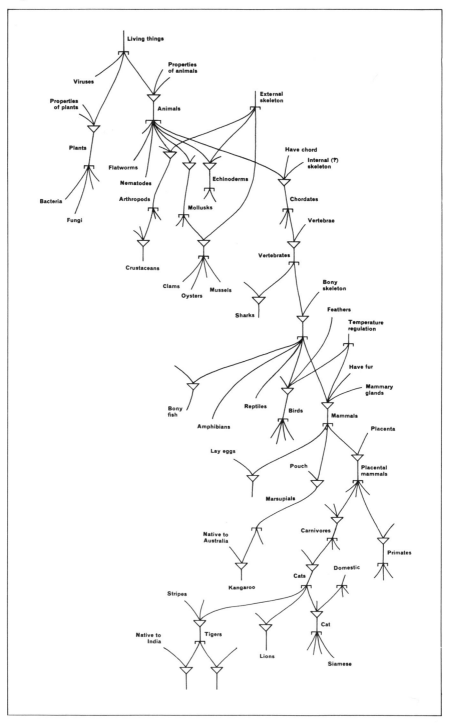

Many further examples are possible, but let us consider just one more: the network representation of 'All men are mortal; Socrates is a man; therefore Socrates is mortal.' The first premise, upon decoding, provides the property of mortality to everything in the set of men, as indicated in Figure 24a. The second premise puts Socrates into that set, as shown in Figure 24b.

Figure 24

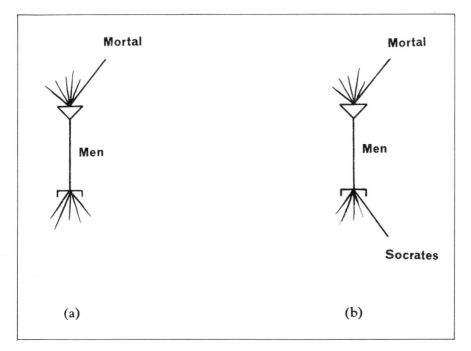

(a)   (b)

We may now, by the universal rules of following paths in relational networks, connect Socrates with mortality as one of his properties, which means that the conclusion of the syllogism is shown as implicit in the knowledge presented by the two premises.

CHAPTER FIVE

Competence, Performance, and Relational Networks*

PETER A. REICH

IN THE PAPER, 'Some Reflections on Competence and Performance,' given at the 1966 Edinburgh University Conference on Psycholinguistics, M.I.T. professors Fodor and Garrett (1966) gave what I feel is a very important critical review of psycholinguistic theorizing over the last decade. While the authors consider Chomsky's insistence upon the competence/performance distinction a 'major methodological clarification', they reject as overly simplistic the interpretation of many psycholinguists that a performance model ought to consist of a model of linguistic competence (that is, a transformational grammar) plus some further component or components at present unknown. The use of competence by the listener is more 'abstract' than the simple but impractical analysis-by-synthesis model. They note in a brief mention of linguistic automation work the impossibility of reversing transformations for sentence parsing. The authors then review the recent work on testing the psychological reality of some of the formal features of transformational theory—in particular the psychological reality of transformations themselves. Initial experiments, involving interrogative, negative, and passive, although not controlled as to length of sentence or meaning, seemed to confirm the simple model that recall of sentences or amount of immediate memory was related in a simple way to 'derivational history' as described by transformational history. However, further experiments by Miller and McKean (1964) and by Mehler (1963), which tested

*Presented at the Annual Meeting of the Linguistic Society of America, December 1967 and reproduced in mimeographed form by the Linguistic Automation Project of Yale University. Reprinted by permission. This work was supported in part by the National Institutes of Health and in part by the National Science Foundation.

the transformations involved in expansion of the auxilliary, FAILED to confirm predictions based on either structure or length. Transformational history FAILED to predict the results obtained by Fodor, Jenkins, and Saporta (undated) in studies of the comparative. Transformational history FAILED to predict behavior with respect to displaced particles and adverbs (Bever, Fodor, Garrett, and Mehler, 1966), and so on (Savin and Perchonok, 1965). The inescapable conclusion of the authors is that while transformational history predicts performance complexity in the special case of PASSIVE, NEGATIVE, INTERROGATIVE and EMPHATIC, corresponding results are not forthcoming for other syntactic relations. These authors conclude that it is a mistake to claim psychological reality for the operations whereby transformational grammars generate structural descriptions.

What should one do when theory fails to match psychological reality? There are two possible ways to resolve the conflict. Fodor and Garrett demonstrate the technique of retreat in the face of the data. They conclude, 'In showing that a predicted complexity order fails to obtain, one has not shown that the grammar is disconfirmed. . . . The internal evidence in favor of the structural descriptions modern grammars generate is so strong that it is difficult to imagine their succumbing to any purely experimental disconfirmation. Rather one would best interpret negative data as showing that an acceptable theory of the relation between competence and performance models will have to represent that relation as abstract, the degree of abstractness being proportioned to the failure of formal features of derivations to correspond to performance variables.' (Fodor and Garrett, 1966:152)

Many find this attitude disturbing. Chafe (1967:89) writes, 'Transformational linguists have pretended that the uncertain applicability of their theory in this last area [language production and reception] is not a shortcoming, but one may still wonder whether a theory that explains the use of language in a more straightforward manner is not, from that standpoint at least, more adequate.' Kay (1967:4. See also Hays and Kay, forthcoming) puts it more strongly: 'There are several objections to . . . these formulations of generative grammar. Most important is the objection that they provide the worst possible basis for an attack on the problems of what Chomsky calls PERFORMANCE.'

Chomsky's theory specifically excludes performance axioms, so one should not be surprised at the lack of correspondence between theory and behavior. There is, however, an alternate resolution to the conflict between theory and data: Advance the theory to meet the data. Ferguson (1966:249) states it this way: 'I . . . suggest that linguists should make predictions directed toward correlation of linguistic analysis with nonlinguistic phenomena. If the nonlinguistic phenomena should not correlate too well, perhaps the linguists should go back and change their theory.'

Fodor and Garrett fail to conceive of the possibility that there might exist a theory which accounts for BOTH the structural descriptions AND the psycholinguistic data. This is precisely what Lamb (1966b, 1966d, see also Gleason, 1964) is attempting to formulate in his Stratificational Theory.

Lamb's theory is one instance of a wide class of theories in which information is stored by means of networks of relationships. Halliday's (1964, 1966, 1967–68) 'systemic' description of grammar is another.

In psychology, many theories utilize network storage of information. Quillian (1966) organizes dictionary information into networks which are convenient for certain kinds of searches. Reitman (1965:203–226. See also 1966) considers cognitive structure as a network of active semantic elements in his ARGUS simulation. Abelson (1963; Abelson and Carroll, 1965; Abelson and Kanouse, 1966, 1967) utilizes network structures in a hierarchical storage of concepts, which he uses in a system simulating people's acceptance of generic assertions. And so on.

This paper suggests certain concepts which could be built into a linguistic theory from the start. The model which we shall build up is compatible with stratificational theory. Although one should not assume that Lamb agrees with all the points discussed, it is hoped that this paper will offer insights into why I feel he is on the right track.

First, I feel one must make a distinction between the LINGUISTIC MECHANISM on the one hand, and the GENERAL PROBLEM SOLVING MECHANISM on the other. I define the LINGUISTIC MECHANISM as that mechanism which allows a speaker to speak, and a listener to listen and understand another speaker, without pencil and paper, diagrams, counting or any other conscious introspective thinking about the structure of the utterance. I do not disagree that a linguist with a pencil and paper will be able to determine the truth value of a deeply embedded sentence. I simply claim he is utilizing different abilities and mechanisms from the person who simply listens to such an utterance, and who, of course, fails to understand it. The ability to analyze consciously is a part of a much more complex GENERAL PROBLEM SOLVING MECHANISM, which, though a fascinating area of research, should be kept separate from the problem of modeling the linguistic mechanism. (Narasimhan, 1967:37 also makes this point.) Simple introspection tells one they are quite different.

Second, although what we know about the brain is very limited, if we build our linguistic model so that it is compatible with some of the properties we believe the brain may have, we may be more able to produce model behavior that agrees with observed behavior. This is based on a reductionist philosophy of science. This means that because I believe that in the real world there is a close relationship between language behavior and the brain, I believe that ULTIMATELY the neurological model of the brain will have a close relationship to the model of linguistic behavior, thus satisfying Narasimhan's 'realizability' criterion. (Narasimhan, 1967:22). Perhaps ULTIMATELY, but why now? By referring to neurological information about which neurophysiologists themselves may not agree, isn't one opening oneself to needless attack? This is perhaps true, but the point is that in building a theory of language behavior one must make SOME assumptions, in any case. Often these assumptions are made without even realizing it. For example, psycholinguists who try to apply transformational theory often are making the assumption that addition, deletion, and rearrangement of strings are basic psychological processes. The fact is that the range of possible systems for describing linguistic information is rich indeed, for there are not just the three or four different systems you may see today in the literature, but rather there is potentially an infinite number of different linguistic systems available, each with its own set of postulates, or unproved assertions.

The ultimate test of a model must be the degree to which it describes the data, rather than the motivation behind the postulates. However, it is useful to state these fundamental assumptions and the reasons they were made, so that when a model becomes inadequate, as the simplistic interpretation of transformational theory has become, the axioms are explicit, and thus available for reevaluation.

Let us consider some of the properties of the brain which we shall employ in the construction of a model of both competence and performance.

PROPERTY (1) The brain consists of a network of interconnected neurons which communicate with each other by means of discrete impulses. Therefore,

Requirement (1) Linguistic behavior shall be modeled by building networks out of a few types of formally defined elements.

Requirement (2) These elements shall communicate with each other by means of a few different types of signals.

PROPERTY (2) The best guess of scientists to date is that long term information is completely stored in the connectivity of the network.[1] One need not go to the biochemistry of the individual neuron to explain the existence of a linguistic (or any other) fact in the brain.[2] Therefore,

Requirement (3) Permanent information is not stored within the logical elements themselves, but only indirectly through their connectivity.

Thus permanent information can be described by logical elements which are finite. If we take into account the well known finiteness of immediate memory (e.g. Miller, 1956), we can conclude that all linguistic information can be represented by finite devices, which can be defined by finite-state diagrams.[3]

PROPERTY (3) The distinction between a passive store of knowledge and a separate 'program' operating upon the passive data commonly made in computing machine theories has not been found useful in modeling the neurology of the brain.[4] Perhaps the knowledge of grammar (i.e. competence) is NOT separate from a performance mechanism. Rather the mechanism of language behavior would be precisely the activity that occurs in the neurological network. It is my belief that the distinction between 'program' and 'data' so useful in computer programming may be detrimental to the progress of psychological and psycholinguistic theory. It is probably a mistake for a psycholinguist to try to study one independently of the other; at least in the past this seems to have led to difficulty.

PROPERTY (4) The activity taking place within the brain does NOT consist of a single event happening at any one time, as is the case in a computer (as seen by a programmer), but rather many neurons are firing at once. Therefore,

> *Requirement* (4) The model of linguistic behavior shall be able to handle parallel processing, in which more than one event may occur at the same time.

PROPERTY (5) The brain is an asynchronous processor. Although more than one thing may happen at the same time, these things may not take the same amount of time, nor need they be in step with one another. Therefore,

> *Requirement* (5) The model shall be asynchronous. In the model I currently favor, all timing requirements are handled by feedback signaling.

PROPERTY (6) It takes about 5/10 of a millisecond for a neural impulse to cross a synapse (Ochs, 1965:303–6). Taking into account the time it takes for an impulse to travel the length of a neuron, a reasonable upper bound on the number of neurons in linear sequence an impulse can pass through in a second is 1800. One cannot utter more than 9 syllables/ sec.[5] If we make the assumption that the minimum number of neurons needed to accomplish a logical operation is one, we arrive at

> *Requirement* (6) The length of the longest sequence of logical operations required to produce or comprehend an utterance shall not exceed 200 logical operations per syllable in the utterance. Borrowing from computer terminology, I refer to this as the REAL TIME requirement.[6] The logical model should require no longer sequence of LOGICAL steps than the brain seems to need NEUROLOGICAL steps to produce or comprehend an utterance.

The real time property is very important. It immediately excludes many possible theories, such as those needing recursive application of large sets of grammatical rules, such as the 'transformational cycle'.[7]

PROPERTY (7) Many biochemists, neurologists, and psychologists have found Hebb's distinction between short term and long term memory a useful one (Hebb, 1966:121–5). Short term memory is envisioned as impulse activity within the neural network of the brain. Sustained neural activity in a particular region leads to permanent changes in the structure of the network in that region, and this structural change is long term memory. Electrical or chemical shock which alters activity but not structure in the brain results in forgetting all that has happened for the previous 15 minutes to an hour or so (Hebb, 1966:123). This concept of a period of consolidation leads to some psycholinguistically interesting predictions. Let us consider a speaker imparting information to a listener. As he speaks, he uses syntactically similar structures. If we assume that this implies the use of neurologically overlapping structures, then one would predict interference with the process of consolidation in the listener. On the other hand, provided the speaker's thoughts were reasonably well organized, the semantic content of his utterances would tend to be distinct from sentence to sentence, and where they did overlap, they would tend to be complementary and supportive, rather than unrelated. We would predict that consolidation would be less interfered with, perhaps even supported. Thus we could predict that people would tend to remember the semantic content of an utterance more readily than they would the syntactic structure. This conclusion is obviously true. But experiments based on carefully controlled syntax and semantics could be used to test the psycho-neural relatedness assumptions and the proposed organization of the grammar.

The model I propose will NOT contain a mechanism which converts short term memory to long term memory. Rather it will contain the SIMPLIFYING ASSUMPTION that all linguistic activity below the semantic level consists only of short term activation, as does semantic activity upon receipt of previously acquired knowledge. But new knowledge results in additions or changes to the network. Network modification activity is a very interesting and important area of research, closely related to verbal learning and language acquisition phenomena, but we shall not consider it further here. Thus we have

> *Requirement* (7) Language behavior below the semantic level should be describable purely in terms of network activation, as opposed to network modification.

This requirement is an attempt to closely model short term events. It is realized that it is inadequate to account for longer term events such as new vocabulary or grammar acquisition.

In addition to the neurologically motivated requirements discussed here are many logically motivated requirements such as the requirement that any element containing more than three connections to other elements may be broken down into networks of basic elements containing only three connections. These are treated in detail in Reich, 1968a.

The basic requirements define a subset of relational network theories. In order to compare different models within this subset, we need simplicity criteria. I propose three measures of complexity for this purpose: structural complexity, behavioral complexity, and definitional complexity.

The measure of structural complexity is well known to people who keep up with stratificational linguistics. It is roughly a count of one for each element with three connections to other elements.[8] That grammar is preferred which has the lowest complexity count, assuming you are comparing grammars which describe the same linguistic information. This measure is designed to quantify the linguist's notions of best grammar.

The second measure, behavioral complexity, is the length of the longest serial sequence of logical steps performed in producing a sentence. It is used to compare complexities of different sentences. This is one measure that I hope will describe some of the data reviewed by Fodor and Garrett which gave others so much trouble. The computer program which simulates parallel processing relational network activity (Reich, 1968b) automatically computes this number. However, we are only just now implementing a grammar of linguistic complexity great enough to investigate its psychological reality. Another interesting possible measure is one based on the finiteness of immediate memory. Depending upon how you conceive of immediate memory, you get different measures, which result in different experimental predictions.

The third measure, definitional complexity, has to do with the definition of the nodes. It turns out that there may well be a whole class of sets of definitions which describe the behavior of the linguistic operations we are concerned with. That set of definitions is best which requires the fewest defining state-transitions, assuming that the theories in question are equivalent with respect to structural and behavioral complexity.

Given the above restrictions, one can formulate a number of important hypotheses which researchers interested in relational networks are actively exploring. Let us consider two:

HYPOTHESIS (1) There exists a relational network model which satisfies the above restrictions and in which all linguistic data can be represented. While we have made simplifying assumptions which limit the applicability of the model proposed in this paper to some psychological phenomena, we have not intended to place any limits on the model which would prevent any LINGUISTIC phenomenon from being described. We do make the distinction between linguistic and problem solving mechanism, you will recall, so that it should be realized that our definition of linguistic phenomena differs to a certain extent from that of the transformationalist. This hypothesis is far from being convincingly demonstrated. It is definitely not a trivial task to represent many linguistic phenomena in a relational framework. Many problems will have to be surmounted before this approach will be convincing to everyone.

HYPOTHESIS (2) A relational network model consistent with the above restrictions will offer insights into behavioral areas, such as psycholinguistics, language acquisition and aphasia. This hypothesis is less tested than hypothesis 1. It is clear that transformational theory has led to some interesting psycholinguistic experiments, which, unfortunately, disproved some of the assumptions on which they were based. Relational network advocates are just beginning to put their toes in these waters. It remains to be seen how well they can avoid the sharks. The relational network approach has yet to offer any substantive insights into language acquisition. However, it is my impression that transformational theory has not offered much either (See Narasimhan, 1967:4–19). Ilah Fleming (1967) has looked into aphasia to explore what insights the major linguistic theories might offer. She has found several concepts of stratificational theory useful in categorizing aphasic difficulties. Because relational network models can be set up to behave consistent with the way we think the brain works, it is in the behavioral area that advocates claim their greatest superiority over competing models; thus it may well be this area that determines whether or not they have a lasting impact on psychology or linguistics.

Let me conclude with the warning that one should NOT interpret the relational network approach as a neurological theory of language. Relational networks differ from neurological networks in many ways. For example, neurons conduct impulses in only one direction, while relational elements transmit in either direction. A given neuron produces only one type of signal, whereas a relational element may produce any of several types, and so on. A relational element should be considered a larger, BEHAVIORALLY defined element rather than a NEUROLOGICALLY defined element. A relational element can be rigorously, mathematically defined, whereas neurons are much more complex. Thus one should interpret the relational network approach as a formal system within which a few neurologically motivated restrictions can be incorporated, but which must stand or fall entirely on its ability to handle linguistic and psycholinguistic data. It is our hope that these requirements will cast linguistic knowledge in a form that will produce heretofore unattainable insights into psycholinguistic data, but much time and work is needed before we will be able to determine whether these hopes are to be realized.

NOTES

1. This is the only formulation I know about which is explicit enough to permit testing of its implications using mathematical or computer simulation models. For references, see Minsky (1963) on 'neural networks' and 'allegedly brainlike computers'.

2. One almost certainly needs to go to the biochemistry of the neuron to account for learning—the act of storing new information. However, reduction to the biochemical level is probably more than a psycholinguist would need in his work.

3. This finiteness deserves further attention, in light of some well-known 'proofs' to the contrary (Chomsky, 1957:18–25, 1956; Postal, 1964). I hope to treat these in a future paper, but the basic principle which makes these 'proofs' inapplicable is the already mentioned distinction between the linguistic and the problem solving mechanism. [See now Reich 1969].

4. One can split simulation and artificial intelligence models into two distinct categories: the neurologically motivated active network models, generally designed to learn some relatively simple discrimination; and problem solving systems, which play bridge, checkers, chess, prove theorems, write music or poetry, etc., and which have always had a sharp distinction between program and data. The lone exception is Reitman's ARGUS (1965:203–26, 247) and even this is a 'mixed' system.

5. This is a generous upper bound. Normal speech seems to have a rate more on the order of 3.6 syllables per second. The speech of radio newscasts has been measured at 6 syllables per second, and Lenneberg estimates an upper bound of 8.3 syllables per second (Lenneberg, 1967:90–3).

6. Narasimhan (1967:appendix p. 6) also uses this term. Lieman (1967:31–2) also suggests efficiency as a requirement in his discussion of 'computational adequacy'. Even Chomsky (1967a:125) has stated, 'It is not unreasonable to suppose that this [the amount of processing involved in production or perception of speech] should be a subsidiary consideration in the selection of a grammar.' He goes on to state in a footnote that he has not been able to make much use of this consideration working within his formal framework.

7. This is not an argument against the use by linguists of the concept of transformational cycle as a formal device (e.g. Chomsky, 1967a:115–8). My objection is to these linguists proposing the transformational cycle as a reasonable psychological model (e.g. Chomsky, 1967a:117, footnote 15).

8. Further considerations lead me to prefer a count of lines rather than nodes to measure structural complexity. See Reich, 1968a.

CHAPTER SIX

Symbols, Relations, and Structural Complexity*

PETER A. REICH

MODERN LINGUISTS often describe their data with a system of rules of the form:

a *is rewritten as* b *in the environment of* c___d

where a and b are strings of symbols. These symbols may represent a tree structure collapsed into a string by means of phrase markers (labelled parentheses). Within the tree structure the symbols may stand for columns of plusses and minuses. The rules are linearly ordered, or perhaps quasilinearly ordered (Chomsky, 1967; Chomsky and Halle, 1968). This means that in producing a particular utterance, one applies, or attempts to apply, rules to the string one is building up one at a time, in linear sequence. After applying all of the rules, or perhaps a subset of them, one may have to reapply the rules or a subset of them again and again until no further changes can be made to the string. If at the end of this process the string consists solely of terminal symbols, one has produced a grammatical utterance. Basically such systems consist of symbols and a few operations on these symbols, including match, copy, concatenate, and replace. This system grew out of a union of the item-and-process approach to linguistics with automata theory, an area of mathematics, which grew out of the development of computers. This system can be shown to be equivalent to a type of computer called a Turing machine (Markov, 1954), and certain more limited systems can be shown to be equivalent to more limited types of automata (Chomsky, 1963b).

*Prepared as a report of the Linguistic Automation Project of Yale University (May 1968). Reprinted by permission. Reich 1970a is a substantially altered version of this paper. We reprint the original.

In sharp contrast to this approach is the theory developed by Lamb (1966b, 1966d), in which the system underlying natural language behavior is formalized as a network of logical elements, or relationships, which communicate with one another using a small set of discrete signals. There are no rules in a stratificational grammar, nor are there symbols in the usual sense of the term. One can, of course, describe the network of relationships in terms of a set of formulas consisting of symbols, which stand for lines in the network, and operators, which stand for nodes in the network. In fact we do this in order to input networks to the computer. However the basic form is the network form. The first operation performed by the Relational Network Simulator (Reich, 1968b) is conversion of the formulas back into networks. One insight of Lamb's formulation is that the use of symbols and rules specifying operations on these symbols is not necessary to the description of the system underlying natural language data. This insight is important, because it brings us a small step closer to understanding how the system underlying language might be stored and used in the brain (Reich, 1967).

Recently published criticism (Chomsky, 1967a; Postal, 1968) of Lamb's theory shows considerable misunderstanding of his basically different system.[1] This is one of a series of papers designed to alleviate this misunderstanding by clarifying the relational network approach. The concern of this paper is with the relational network equivalent of context-free phrase structure grammars (Chomsky and Schutzenberger, 1963). We shall show that if such grammars are made completely explicit, they are equivalent to symmetric list structures, and are representable as network diagrams. We shall discuss structural complexity in this framework, and consider various formal properties of the relations defined. We shall conclude with a discussion of the implications of these properties for language acquisition.

Consider the grammar given in Figure 1. The arrow stands for 'rewrite as', and a space between two symbols represents concatenation.

Figure 1: A Simple Context-Free Phrase Structure Grammar

Initial symbol: S
(1.1)   S → NP VP
(1.2)   NP → A N
(1.3)   VP → V NP
(1.4)   A → a
(1.5)   A → the
(1.6)   N → boy
(1.7)   N → girl
(1.8)   V → hit
(1.9)   V → kissed

Thus rule 1.1 can be read, 'S is rewritten as NP followed by VP'. These are considered unordered rules (the initial numbers are inserted merely for reference). Depending on the order the rules are applied, any of eight different sentences result. Thus if the rules are applied in the order (1.1 1.2 1.4 1.6 1.3 1.8 1.2 1.5 1.7) the result is 'a boy hit the girl', whereas if they are applied in the order (1.1 1.2 1.5 1.7 1.3 1.8 1.2 1.4 1.6) the result is 'the girl hit a boy'. I suggest that the concept of ordering as described above represents a confusion of two concepts—ordering and disjunction.

When we suggest that these rules are unordered, we are not saying all we know about the sequence in which these rules must be applied. We know that rule 1.1 must be the first rule executed. We know that rule 1.2 must be executed after rule 1.1, and that rule 1.3 must also follow rule 1.1 We know that after (not necessarily immediately after) rule 1.2 is executed we must execute either rule 1.4 or rule 1.5, and we must also execute either rule 1.6 or 1.7 We know that every occurrence of the execution of rule 1.2 must have been preceded (not necessarily immediately preceded) either by 1.1 or by 1.3. And so on. What we are doing, of course, is looking at the relationship of the symbols on the right side of the rules to the symbols on the left side.

Figure 2: the C-F Grammar of Figure 1 in Explicit Form

$$\begin{aligned}
&(2.1) \quad S \rightarrow NP_1 \ VP_1 \\
&(2.2) \quad NP_1 \rightarrow A_1 \ N_1 \\
&(2.3) \quad VP_2 \rightarrow V_1 \ NP_3 \\
&(2.4) \quad A_2 \rightarrow a \\
&(2.5) \quad A_3 \rightarrow the \\
&(2.6) \quad N_2 \rightarrow boy \\
&(2.7) \quad N_3 \rightarrow girl \\
&(2.8) \quad V_2 \rightarrow hit \\
&(2.9) \quad V_3 \rightarrow kissed \\[6pt]
&(2.10) \quad A_1 \rightarrow A_2, \ A_3 \\
&(2.11) \quad N_1 \rightarrow N_2, \ N_3 \\
&(2.12) \quad V_1 \rightarrow V_2, \ V_2 \\
&(2.13) \quad NP_1, \ NP_3 \rightarrow NP_2 \\
&(2.14) \quad VP_1 \rightarrow VP_2
\end{aligned}$$

Consider the occurrence of the symbol A in rule 1.2. There are two occurrences of A on the left side of rules—in 1.4 and in 1.5. Thus we can say that rule 1.2 will be followed by either rule 1.4 or rule 1.5. If we subscript occurrences of each symbol in the grammar as shown in Figure 2, we can express this statement as an additional rule, namely rule 2.10, in which the comma stands for the operation of disjunction. We can produce similar rules for the symbols N and V as given in 2.11 and 2.12 respectively. The distribution of NP is just the reverse of the distribution of A, N, and V. In the case of NP there is one occurrence on the left side of a rule (in 2.2) and there are two occurrences on the right side of rules (in 2.1 and 2.3). Here we can say that every occurrence of the execution of rule 1.2 must have been preceeded either by 1.1 or by 1.3. Again we have disjunction, but this time in the other direction. We express this fact in rule 2.13.

In the case of VP there is one occurrence of the symbol on both the right and the left sides, so we simply indicate this in rule 2.14.

Rules 2.10 through 2.14 make explicit the implicit ordering in the grammar of Figure 1. Obviously we have the same relationship in rules 2.10 through 2.12 as we have in rule 2.13, namely disjunction, but with direction reversed. One of the counter-intuitive artifacts of transformational theory is that (following earlier practice in mathematics and logic) a notation was developed to explicitly express disjunction of the type given in rule 2.10, but none was developed to express disjunction of the type given in rule 2.13.[2] In the transformational framework, rules 1.4 and 1.5 would be written A → a, the. However, disjunction does not seem to have the same status as the operation of concatenation. Rather it is simply an 'abbreviatative notation' (Bach, 1964:17) which represents two separate rules (Chomsky, 1957:110; 1963a:288). It does, however, seem to have higher status than the use of symbols like [p] as abbreviations for the appropriate column of distinctive features (Chomsky, 1965:213 footnote 14). In the case of the former, the abbreviated rule is used in the count of symbols as a measure of complexity (Chomsky, 1965:42ff), whereas in the latter case, one must substitute the distinctive features before counting symbols (see Householder, 1965:16–26).

The purpose of calling disjunction an abbreviation seems to be to keep the system mathematically simple. This reasoning is beyond me. If disjunction is in the system, whether implicitly or explicitly, it is there, and giving it the epithet 'abbreviation' does not make it go away. Since one of the purposes of building a formal system is to make the relationships as explicit as possible, the transformational notation may be said to be deficient with respect to disjunction of the type given in rule 2.13. This lack of explicitness seems to have been vaguely perceived by Bach (1964:51–52) when he wrote, 'It is annoying to have to skim through a long lexical list which turns out not to have the symbol you are looking for, and then to be forced to look through numerous rules to see what happens to the item (sometimes hidden in a complex set of contexts). . . . It would be worthwhile practice to list the transformations in which a general symbol is mentioned at the first introduction of the item.' The correction of this deficiency has certain rewards, which we shall now explore.

Notice that when a grammar is given in explicit form as in Figure 2, each nonterminal, noninitial symbol has exactly two occurrences—once on the left side of a rule, and once on the right side. Thus a symbol on the right side of a rule serves as a pointer, or link, to the next rule to be executed, and a symbol on the left side of a rule serves as a pointer or link, back to the previous rule executed. A linked structure in which every forward link has a corresponding backward link is known as a symmetric list (Weizenbaum, 1963). Such a structure suggests that one might represent the information in the form of a graphical network in which the rules are nodes, and the symbols, which are really links, are lines connecting the nodes.

Let us produce such a graph for our sample grammar. First let us simplify the form of our grammar given in Figure 2. We can eliminate all rules of the form x → y where x and y are single symbols without loss of information. We simply eliminate the rule, and replace the other occurrence of x with y. This simplification leads to Figure 3. (We have renamed NP₁ SUBJ and have replaced NP₃ by OBJ. This allows us to drop all subscripts.) We see that we now have in our grammar three types of rules—one type expressing concatenation (rules 3.1 through 3.3), one type expressing disjunction (rules 3.4 through 3.6), and one type expressing reverse disjunction (rule 3.7). We shall express each of these three types of rules with a different node, as shown in Figure 4.[3] The obvious relationship between disjunction and reverse disjunction is expressed by using the same shaped node turned upside down. Using the appropriate node for each of the rules on Figure 3, we connect the links as the rules instruct us, and we arrive at the network shown in Figure 5.

Figure 3: Explicit Form of C-F Grammar Simplified

(3.1)		S	→ SUBJ VP
(3.2)		NP	→ A N
(3.3)		VP	→ V OBJ
(3.4)		A	→ a, the
(3.5)		N	→ boy, girl
(3.6)		V	→ hit, kissed
(3.7)	SUBJ, OBJ		→ NP

Figure 4: The Three Nodes Needed for C-F Grammar

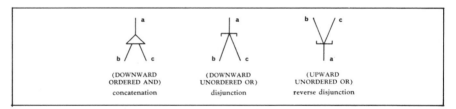

Figure 5: The Grammar of Figure 3 Expressed Graphically

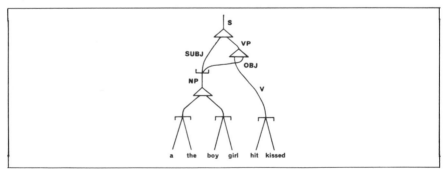

If we allow parenthesis notation in our algebraic formulas, by applying substitution to the seven rules of Figure 3, we see that we can express the same grammar using only two rules, as shown in Figure 6. We now have three sets of rules, all explicitly describing the same linguistic structure. In the set given in Figure 3, each line of the network has a symbolic name in the algebraic form; in the version of Figure 2, some lines have more than one name (for example, VP_1 and VP_2 name the same line); in the version of Figure 6, some lines are not named at all. Is one version to be preferred to another? From the point of view of linguistic structure, the answer is no! They all describe the same structure. Figure 6 has fewer rules and fewer symbols, but that is just a notational artifact.[4] Consider the grammar of Figure 7. It generates the same set of sentences as the grammar of Figure 3.

Figure 6: Representation of Grammar Using Parentheses.

(6.1)	S	→	SUBJ ((hit, kissed) OBJ)
(6.2)	SUBJ, OBJ	→	((a, the) (boy, girl))

Figure 7

S	→	SUBJ ((hit, kissed) OBJ)
SUBJ OBJ	→	(aX), (the Y)
X, Y	→	boy, girl

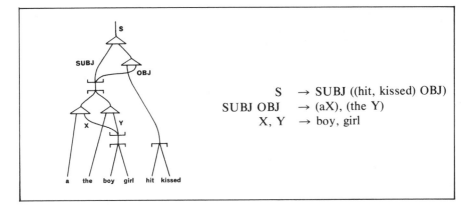

It is described algebraically with the three rules using 31 symbols. Is it to be preferred to the grammar of Figure 3, which has seven rules using 32 symbols? In order to answer this in a way that is linguistically interesting, one must go to networks which each of the algebraic formulations represent. If we compare the network in Figure 5 to the network in Figure 7, we find that the network in Figure 7 is MORE complicated than that of Figure 5. We see that in Figure 5 the lines labelled *a* and *the* immediately come together in a disjunction. In other words, they both belong to the same class. This generalization is not made explicit in the structure of Figure 7. Thus even using the trivial grammars of our examples we find counterexamples to the notion that complexity can be measured by counting symbols. A symbol count measures cleverness at algebraic manipulation rather than linguistic complexity. It would seem to be much better to base a complexity count on the network formulation, regardless of how it is described algebraically.

Two ways to measure the complexity of a network immediately come to mind. One is a count of the number of nodes and the other is a count of the number of lines. If all nodes have exactly three lines coming out of them, it does not matter which we choose, because the number of lines equals the number of nodes times $3/2$ plus the number of lines which lead out from the network (i.e. connect to only one node) times $1/2$. Since we only compare two grammars if they are equivalent in effective information—that is, if they encode and decode the same set of structures (Lamb, 1966d:41–46)—the number of lines which lead out from two networks we are legitimately comparing will always be identical, and thus the one measure is a linear mapping of the other. Since we are only interested in complexity as an ordinal scale (McGinnis, 1965:274–290), the two measures would be equivalent. However, since we do not want to constrain our network to nodes with exactly three lines coming out of them, we must either use the count of the number of lines[5], or modify our node count to take into account the cases where more or less than three lines connect to a node. One way to take these cases into account is to count nodes connected by three lines as 1, and to add 1 to the count for each extra line. Thus a node connecting four lines would have a count of 2, a node connecting five lines would have a count of 3, and so on. A node connecting two lines would have a count of zero. These two counts do not give the same results in all cases. We shall return to this issue later.

Once we express a grammar in terms of a relational network, intermediate symbols become superfluous. What has become of the concept of the rewrite rule? We find that we can replace it with the notion of signals moving through the network. In the case of a grammar utilizing only the three nodes already discussed, the behavior of the signals moving throughout the network is relatively straightforward.[6] We start by sending a signal down from the top of the network. When the signal comes in the a wire of the concatenation node (see Figure 4), the signal continues down the b wire. Thus in Figure 5 a signal moving down from S would move down to SUBJ. When a signal comes in the b wire of reverse disjunction, it continues down the a wire. Thus the signal at SUBJ would reach NP, and by the instruction already given, would continue to A. When a signal comes in the a wire of disjunction, there are two possibilities. Either the signal may continue down the b wire, or it may continue down the c wire. If one is thinking in terms of generating sentences at random, each such choice can be made at random. If one is interested in the set of all sentences, each such choice doubles the number of potential sentences. Let us follow the a wire. This leads to the edge of the network labelled 'the', and we say that 'the' has been output from the grammar. Timing in this model is handled by feedback signalling, so a signal moves up from the line marked 'the'. A signal coming in on the c wire to a disjunction continues up the a wire. In this case the signal comes to A. A signal coming in the *b* wire of concatenation results in a signal being sent down the *c* wire. We have arrived at another disjunction. Let us say that this time the *b* wire is chosen. 'Boy' is output, and feedback is sent up to N. A signal coming in the *c* wire of concatenation continues up the *a* wire, in this case up to NP, and from there up to SUBJ, then down to VP, then to V, then a random selection, let us say to 'kissed'. Feedback travels up to V, then down to OBJ.

Here a further specification is needed. When a signal moves from OBJ down to NP, the node must 'remember' the fact, so that when feedback comes up to NP, the signal will return to OBJ rather than to SUBJ. We say that as the signal passes through the reverse disjunction node from the *c* wire to the *a* wire, the node changes state, and stays in that state until a signal comes in from the *b* wire, whereupon the node returns to its original state.

Thus word by word, a sentence such as 'the boy kissed the girl' is produced. We have replaced the process of rewriting symbols by a process of moving signals through the networks. The instructions concerning how the signals move through the networks are given in terms of state-transition definitions of the nodes. These definitions are summarized in Figure 8. As we build grammars to handle more complicated linguistic information, these definitions become more complex, and we find that we need many different types of nodes not yet discussed, but the basic idea of signals moving through networks remains unchanged. One hypothesis we are exploring is that each of the nodes is finite. We shall not explore this question further here, since it is covered in some detail elsewhere (Reich, 1969).

Figure 8: State Transition Definitions

concatenation

disjunction

reverse disjunction

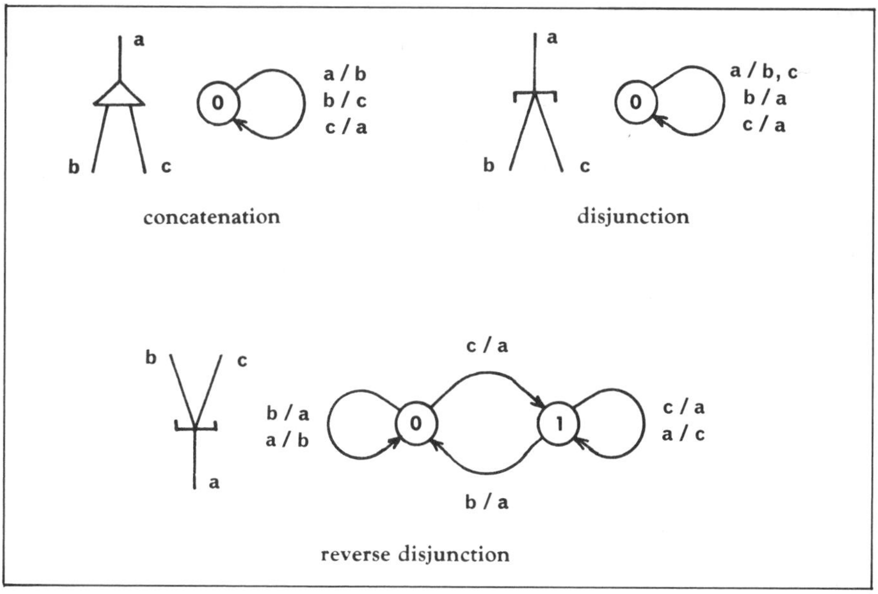

Let us turn now to some formal properties of our relations. One such property is COMMUTATIVITY. A relation R is commutative if b R c is equivalent to c R b. In other words, one could replace b by c, and c by b in the algebraic expression without changing the relationship of b and c to each other. In terms of state transition definitions, the definition must be symmetric with respect to b and c. We see that this is true in the case of disjunction as defined in Figure 8. In our diagrammatic notation we represent commutativity by connecting the b and c wires to the node at the same point. Thus it is always obvious at a glance whether or not a particular node is commutative.

Another formal property is ASSOCIATIVITY. A relation R is associative if b R (c R d) is equivalent to (b R c) R d. All the relations in our system are associative. This means that when two identical relations are connected to one another as shown in part (1) of each of the three triads of Figure 9, the behavior of that portion of the network will be exactly the same as seen from outside the construction as the corresponding relations in part (2), and vice versa. Since the choice of one over the other would be arbitrary, we express the construction as a three-way relation, as shown in parts (3) of the figure.

The associativity requirement has a clear implication for the definition of processing in terms of signals moving through the network. No timing requirements can be based on the number of nodes the signal passes through, since the behavior of networks (1) is defined to be equivalent to the corresponding networks (2).

We have introduced the notion of an n-ary relation, where n is greater than 2. Do we allow arbitrarily large n-ary relations defined arbitrarily, or do we limit them? Our current policy, based on a desire for definitional simplicity (Reich, 1967) is this: The only n-ary relations we define are those which arise from associativity of directly connected identical relations (such as those shown in Figure 9), and these are defined to behave identically to an associative construction of binary relations. Thus we need only define binary and unary relations.

We also require, of course, that the grammar be finite, so that the number of wires leading from any one node must be finite. While this policy is based on formal considerations, is it possible to justify it on psychological or neurophysiological grounds? That is, is it possible that the formal principle may have some underlying psychological foundation? While it is highly speculative at this time, the possibility should not be overlooked. There is a principle in biochemistry that a molecule formed from three or more molecules is always formed in binary stages. The probability is too small that the three molecules will collide simultaneously in the proper orientation. Is it unreasonable to assume that the child learning his language builds up the underlying neural structure step by step in very small units? This intuitively appealing idea poses a problem for the developmental psycholinguist trying to analyze his data within a transformational framework, since transformations are intrinsically more complex. 'To discover the exact point at which a child's grammar contains transformational rules is a difficult, obscure problem,' writes David McNeill (1966:54). He characterizes the process as the building of a system of cumbersome and inelegant phrase structure rules, which are then junked in favor of transformations. 'The pressure—or, if you prefer, the motivation—to devise transformation rules may come from the cognitive clutter that results from not having them (1966:61).' We see that McNeill retreated from an incremental approach to the synoptic concept of 'cognitive clutter.'[7]

To return to associativity, if concatenation is associative, what is the meaning of immediate constituent analysis or phrase structure parenthesization? Why do we prefer 10.1 over 10.2 (Lamb, 1966d:54), 10.3 over 10.4 (Wells, 1947:187–191), 10.7 over 10.8 (Nida, 1949:87), and why do we associate 10.5 with one interpretation of the sentence and 10.6 with another (Chomsky, 1956:118; Chomsky and Schutzenberger, 1963:122)? The answer in terms of relational networks is quite simple. Two identical elements connected as shown in Figure 9(1) can be reassociated to (2) if and only if there is no intervening element on line *a*. Similarly two identical elements connected as shown in (2) can be redistributed if and only if there is no intervening element on line *b*. Thus a particular phrase structure parenthesization means that the concatenation elements are separated by other nodes in such a way that no other associations are possible without making the structure more complex. We shall discuss this in more detail after we have concluded our discussion of formal properties.

Figure 9: Associativity of Relations

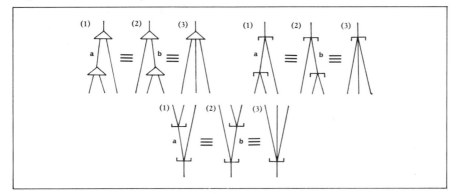

Figure 10: Phase Structure Parenthesization

(10.1) ((un true) ly)
(10.2) (un (true ly))
(10.3) (the (king (of England))) ((open ed) Parliament)
(10.4) (the (king of)) (England ((open ed) Parliament))
(10.5) (they (are (flying planes)))
(10.6) (they ((are flying) planes))
(10.7) (peasants (throughout China)) (work (very hard))
(10.8) ((peasants throughout) (China work)) (very hard)

A third formal property is DISTRIBUTIVITY. In arithmetic this means that (a + b)·c is equivalent to a·c + b·c. We say that multiplication distributes over addition. In our system, concatenation distributes over disjunction. This property is shown in Figure 11.

Figure 11. Distributivity.

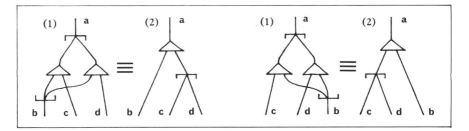

In (2) concatenation is expressed once for the set of elements (c,d). In (1) concatenation has been distributed over the disjunction. It is expressed once for each element in the set. Since concatenation is not commutative, we must state the distributive rule in two forms—left distributivity (Figure 11, left), and right distributivity (Figure 11, right). Notice that the difference between the grammar of Figure 5 and that of Figure 7 is that Figure 7 is the result of distributing the concatenation element below NP in Figure 5 over the disjunction below A.

The next formal property is COINCIDENCE. The lines leading down from a disjunction are said to be elements of that disjunctive set. Two sets are coincident if they contain the same elements. We see in Figure 12 that one need never state the same set twice, as is done in (1).

Figure 12. Coincidence.

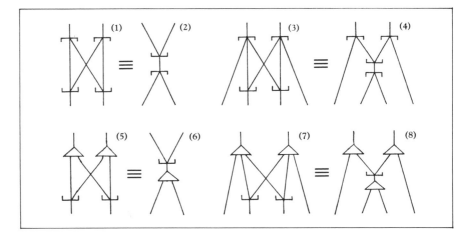

Rather, the same effective information can be expressed once as in (2), and the fact that the set is useful in two places in grammar is represented by reverse disjunction. The simplification of set overlap shown in (3) to structure (4) follows by application of associativity and/or commutativity combined with set coincidence. Concatenative coincidence, in which a particular concatenation is expressed twice, as in (5), can be simplified in the same way, as shown in (6). Similarly, concatenative overlap is the application of associativity (but *not* commutativity) combined with concatenative coincidence, converting structures like (7) to (8).

An additional, rather trivial, formal operation one can perform in simplifying networks is SET REDUCTION. If two elements of a set lead to identical structures, one of the elements is redundant, and can be eliminated. Thus in Figure 13, (1) can be replaced by (2), and (3) can be replaced by (4).

Figure 13. Set Reduction.

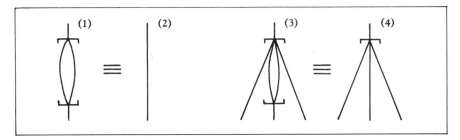

Let us now turn to the surprisingly thorny issue of optionality. Consider the case where a particular wire in linguistic structure is to be realized as either b c d or c d, as occurs, for example, in *un friend ly* vs. *friend ly*. Using the notation we have developed thus far, this can be expressed either as shown in Figure 14(1) or as in 14(2). Given no other information, there is no reason to choose (1) over (2) or vice versa. One of our goals in constructing a formal theory is to develop a third way of expressing the structure, neutral with respect to the artificial distinction which differentiates the other two. When this question arose earlier in this paper, it was a case of associativity, and the problem was resolved by introduction of the n-ary relation. Can this problem be solved by reducing it to the already solved problem? The answer turns out to be yes. In (1) and (2), if that portion of the structure which appears within the rectangle of dashed lines is considered to be a single node, (1) is derivable from (2) by reassociating the two nodes. Do we need to consider this a case of associativity of two different types of nodes? No. Consider the alternate formalism of indicating the optionality by putting an 'optional' element òn that line. If the optional element is a small circle, we arrive at 15(1). Notice that 15(1) has an alternate description in 15(2), but since we now have two contiguous concatenation elements, we can apply our already established associativity rule to arrive at 15(3). This expresses the same relationships, while being neutral with respect to the artificial distinction. In Lamb 1966d, optionality was expressed by using a zero element attached to a disjunction. However, considerations resulting from experiments with various models of performance indicate that this representation is inappropriate, and that it is best to represent optionality as a separate element. There is one thing wrong with this formalism. The particular case in which wire *a* is realizable as *b*, or *c*, or *b c*, but not Ø (nothing), cannot be represented in this notation. One must return to the awkward format of a bypassing line, as shown in Figure 16(1). The structure shown in 16(4) allows *b, c,* or *b c,* but also Ø.

Figure 14

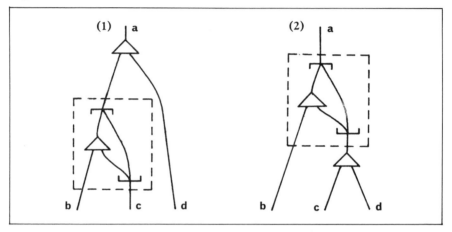

Figure 15

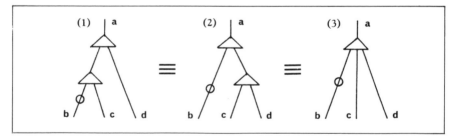

Figure 16

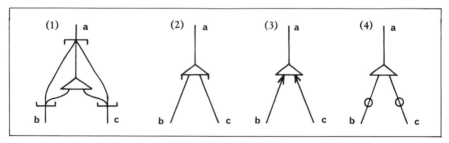

One solution is simply to define a new node to fill the gap. This is the AND-OR, shown in 16(2), and defined to be identical to 16(1). It would be nice if we could get along without inventing a new node. One attempt was the arrowhead notation used in Sampson (1967). An arrowhead on a line meant that that line was independent, and could essentially bypass the concatenation element immediately above it. Thus in Figure 17(1) *a* could be realized as *b c d* or *c d*. This notation has the advantage that an arrowhead on both lines leading down from a concatenation element, as shown in 16(3), would have the same meaning as our missing case, 16(1), namely, that *b* can be an independent realization, that *c* can be an independent realization, or that *b c* can be a realization. In order to allow the possibility of nothing as a realization, one would have to put another arrowhead on the next concatenation element up, as shown in 18(1). If reverse disjunction occurs first, this fact would have to be expressed more than once, as shown in 18(2). Worse yet, this notation has exactly the same fault as the original bypassing line notation. Figure 17(1) is equivalent to Figure 17(2), and there is no way to neutralize the artificial distinction between the two.

Figure 17

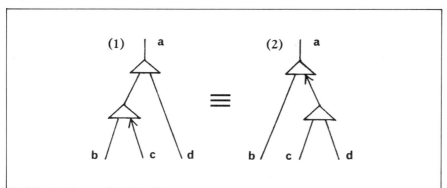

Figure 18

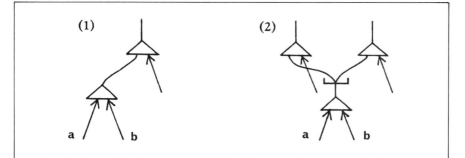

I suggested another possibility—simply define the optional elements so that when one occurs on both lines leading down from concatenation, as in 19(1), its meaning is by definition equivalent to the missing case, namely 19(2). In order to allow the option of realization as nothing, one puts an optional element on the wire leading up from the concatenation element, as shown in 19(3). This neutralizes the artificial distinction between 20(1) and 20(2) by the representation 20(3). Unfortunately, this solution is not without problems. 20(1) looks more complicated than 20(2) since it requires one more optionality element. But this is purely a notational artifact.

Figure 19

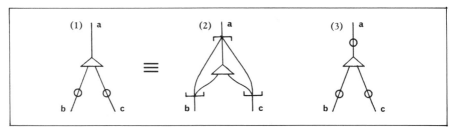

Figure 20

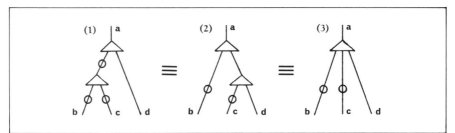

The two concatenation elements in 20(1) can be associated, in spite of the fact that there is an element on the line between them. Thus we would have an exception to our rule about when to apply associativity. Worse yet is the exception to the associativity applicability rule that would result from Figure 21. This structure would allow *b d,* or *c d,* or *b c d.* In spite of the fact that the two concatenation elements are contiguous, they cannot be collapsed to a three way concatenation, nor is there an equivalent structure in which the association goes the other way.

Figure 21

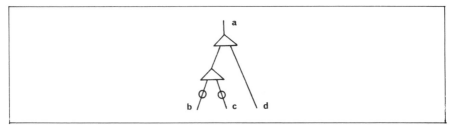

Because of these problems, I have reluctantly concluded that the best solution to the problem of optionality is the one that was originally suggested; namely, mark the optional line with an optionality element, and introduce a new element, the AND-OR, to take care of the missing case.[8] Thus the structure represented in 20(1) would be represented by 22(1), and the associativity can once again be expressed in a straightforward way, 22(1) and 22(2) being equivalent to the preferred 22(3). The problematic structure (Figure 21) is represented using the new node, as shown in 22(4), and thus there is no problem. The AND-OR is not associative with concatenation. Equivalence of effective information is preserved under associativity, right and left distributivity, and coincidence. The optional element shows equivalence under the properties of bypass representation, distributivity, coincidence, and reduction. The formal properties of all nodes thus far discussed are summarized in Figure 23.

Figure 22

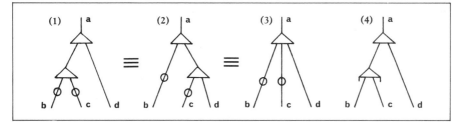

What is gained by this somewhat involved discussion of formal properties of nodes? Formalization is not a goal in itself, but is only meaningful if it leads to insights into the data being studied. Our goal in doing this is to increase the relevance of stratificational theory to the problems of grammatical discovery and language acquisition. The next section of the paper is devoted to a discussion of how we make use of the formal properties of nodes.

In our discussions of grammatical discovery, it seems useful to distinguish among at least three logically distinct operations. They are association, simplification, and extrapolation. Association may be thought of as being either unimodal or bimodal. An example of unimodal association would be the child's learning that *b* followed by ɔ followed by *l* was a word in English, *ball*. Bimodal association would be associating the word *ball* with an object the child is looking at, or with a set of objects the child knows about. Given a grammar which describes the set of utterances the child has heard and understood, extrapolation would be the process of producing a grammar which goes beyond the data, in the sense that it is capable of producing not only the data already given, but also utterances that the child might reasonably expect to run across in the future. In order for association and extrapolation to be possible, a process of simplification must also occur.

In this section we shall concern ourselves exclusively with simplification. We shall use as an example Lamb's exercise of determining the constituent

Figure 23

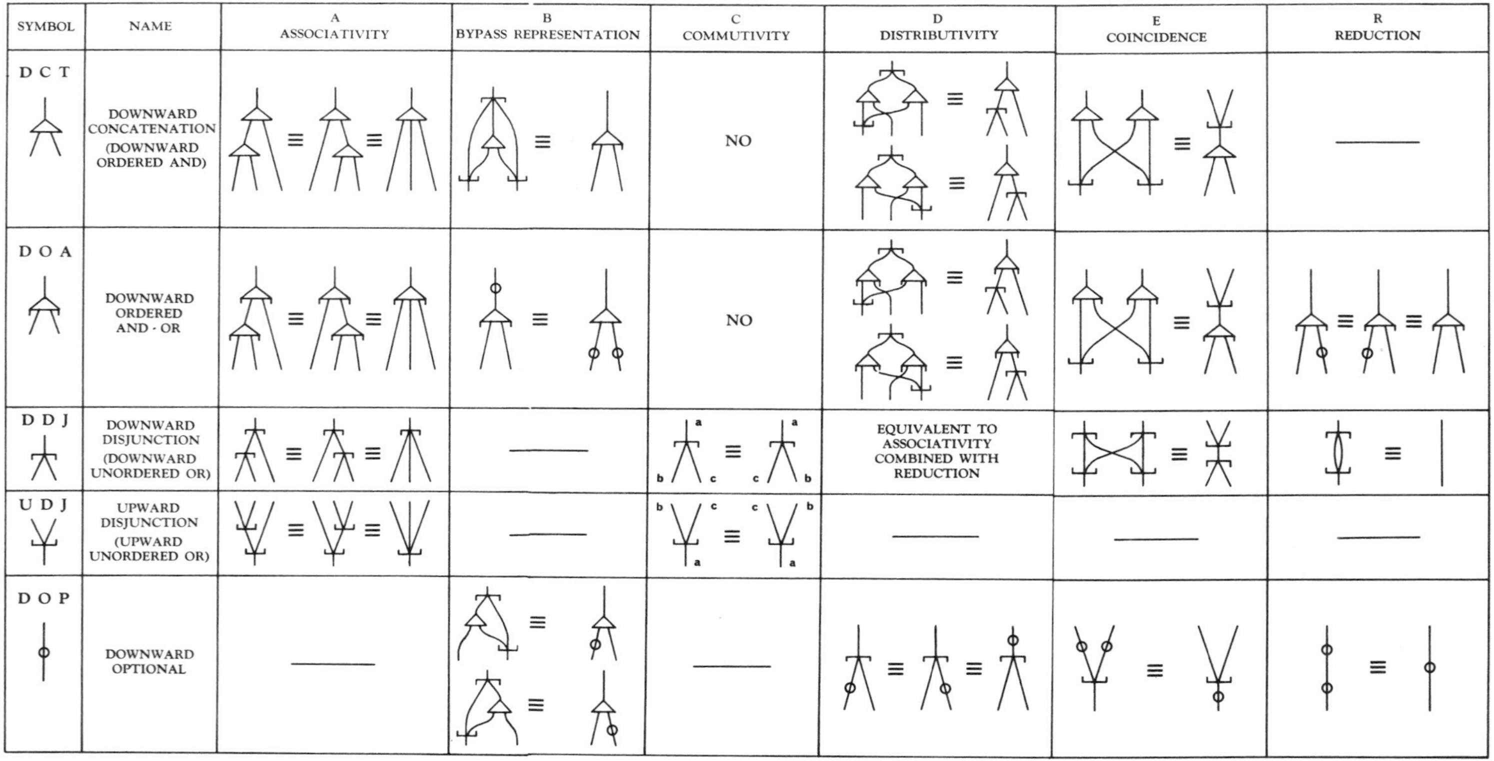
SYMBOL
NAME
A
ASSOCIATIVITY
B
BYPASS REPRESENTATION
C
COMMUTIVITY
D
DISTRIBUTIVITY
E
COINCIDENCE
R
REDUCTION
D C T
DOWNWARD CONCATENATION (DOWNWARD ORDERED AND)
NO
D O A
DOWNWARD ORDERED AND - OR
NO
D D J
DOWNWARD DISJUNCTION (DOWNWARD UNORDERED OR)
EQUIVALENT TO ASSOCIATIVITY COMBINED WITH REDUCTION
U D J
UPWARD DISJUNCTION (UPWARD UNORDERED OR)
D O P
DOWNWARD OPTIONAL

structure of (un true ly) (1966d:54). Considered by itself, of course, we have no reason to prefer one association over the other. Therefore we look at related data from English. Let us consider first the four adverbs (un true ly), (un wise ly), (true ly), and (wise ly).We say that they all occur in English, which we can express in network terms by simply listing them as members of the disjunctive set of adverbs, as shown in Figure 24(1). We shall call this form the disjunctive form of a network. The grammar which consists of merely listing the data is, of course, trivial and uninteresting. However, by utilizing the formal properties given in Figure 23, we can convert a network to other networks which are equivalent in terms of effective information. Our goal is to convert the given network to the simplest possible network which is equivalent in effective information. We see that by application of associativity of downward concatenation (A(DCT)) twice to 24(1) we arrive at 24(2). Then by applying associativity of downward disjunction (A(DDJ)) and distributivity of downward concatenation (D(DCT)) we arrive at 24(3), and so on, step by step until we arrive at 24(8), which is the simplest representation. We see that given only the information about the four adverbs, there is no reason to parenthesize (un true ly) any further. We therefore consider some additional information about English; namely, that it contains the four adjectives (true), (un true), (wise), and (un wise). In other words, we know that a structure equivalent to 25(1) is also a part of the structure of English. First we simplify 25(1) by making use of the appropriate formal properties, as shown in the figure, finally arriving at 25(5). Next we combine the adverb structure of 24(8) with the adjective structure of 25(5), resulting in the structure of 26(1). Utilizing the formal properties again, we discover we can reduce the network to 26(5) without affecting the information in the network. We see that in our final network there is a node between the two concatenation elements, so that one constituent analysis is to be preferred, namely ((un true) ly).

Let us step back and take a look at what we are doing. Consider the set of all possible networks. We can partition this set into a set of mutually exclusive subsets such that two networks are in the same subset if and only if they are equivalent in effective information. Let us look at one particular subset, say the subset of all networks which are equivalent to 24(1). If we think of each network as a point, we can consider the equivalences stated as formal properties as lines connecting points. One of my goals is to identify enough equivalence relations such that all points in the subset (all equivalent networks) are connected to one another so that there is at least one path of logical operations from any one network to any other. The value of such a goal should be obvious. Consider a computer program whose task is to find the simplest network equivalent to 24(1). One way it could go about its task would be to generate, one by one, the set of all possible networks with complexity less than 24(1), then test each one to determine if it is equivalent to 24(1). It would be much easier if the machine had a way of generating all equivalent networks directly, which it would have if it had a complete set of equivalence relations.

Let us assume that we have succeeded in connecting all equivalent networks by means of a network of equivalence relations. What can we say about a procedure for finding the simplest network?[9] Consider the points representing networks to be located in a plane. Now consider the number

Figure 24

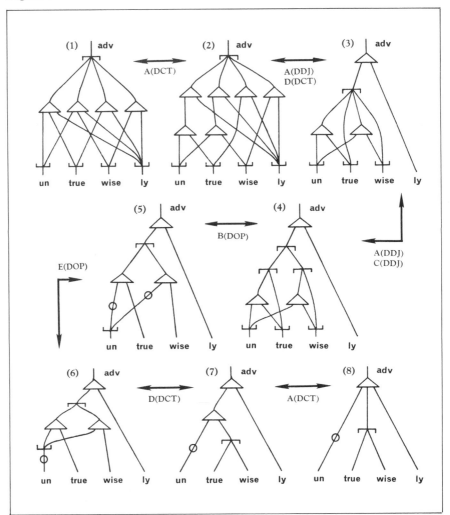

which we use as a measure of complexity to represent a height above the plane immediately above each point. A surface could be made to pass over each of the points at the height given by the measure of complexity. We might picture this surface as hilly countryside. Our problem, stated in these terms, is that, starting from a given point on this countryside, we must explore the countryside by following the given paths, searching for the deepest valley (lowest complexity count). One technique is, of course, exhaustive search, in which all points are looked at, after which the least complex is chosen. This technique is almost never reasonable, and our problem is no exception. Each of our equivalence subsets contains an infinite number of points, which would mean the search would take a very long time indeed. Another technique is to move down the paths in such a way that you are almost always going downhill. That is, at almost every step you take, the

Figure 25

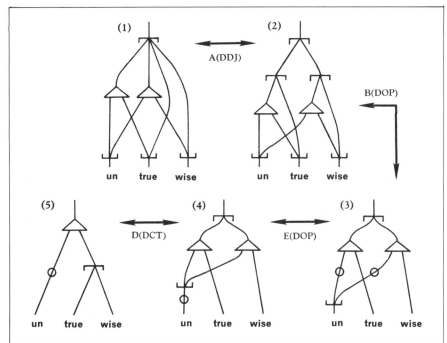

Figure 26

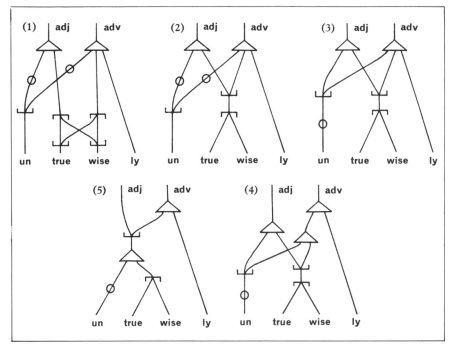

complexity count afterward is less than it was before. This technique is known as hill climbing (Minsky, 1961:409–411). The successfulness of this technique depends upon the ruggedness of the problem terrain. If there is more than one isolated valley, then our walk downward may take us to the wrong place, from which vantage point it will not be at all obvious that there is an alternate, better solution. The ruggedness of the problem terrain depends importantly on the complexity measure used. We have considered two measures in this paper—a count of the number of lines, and a count of the number of nodes plus extra lines. Let us look at the ruggedness of the terrain in the equivalence space of Figure 24 using each of the two complexity counts. In the case of the line count, the step from (2) to (3) is downhill, the step from (3) to (4) is uphill, and the rest of the steps from (4) to (8) are downhill all the way. In the case of the node plus extra line count, the step from (1) to (2) is level (no change in the complexity count), the step from (2) to (3) is downhill, the step from (3) to (4) is level, (4) to (5) is downhill, (5) to (6) is level, (6) to (7) is downhill, and (7) to (8) is level. If we try out our two measures on an alternate simplification path for the same example, shown in Figure 27, the result

Figure 27

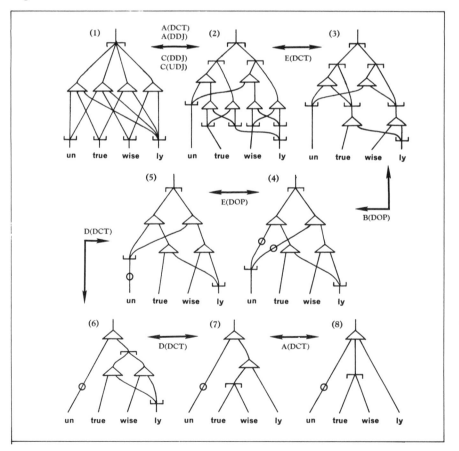

is the same. Similarly, the result is the same in the different problem spaces represented in Figures 25 and 26. Based on these examples, we would prefer the node plus extra line count, since it leads to a less rugged problem space. Before we eliminate the line count from our consideration, we should explore the difference between the two counts more fully. The two measures are strongly nonequivalent, which means that there exist pairs of equivalent constructions for which the two measures give opposing results. One such example is given in Figure 28. The line count prefers 28(2) at 8 lines to 28(1) at 9 lines, while the node plus extra line count prefers 28(1) at 4 to 28(2) at 6. The node plus extra line count corresponds to our intuition that 28(1) is the simpler. Examples such as these give us additional reasons to prefer the node plus extra line count. However, we do prefer Figure 24(8) to 24(7) and 27(8) to 27(7), which the line count expresses while the node plus extra line count is neutral. While the line count does handle associativity preferences, it fails to handle other preferences, such as distributivity of downward optional (Figure 23). The diagram on the right is preferred to the other two, since it neutralizes the artifactual distinction between the other two structures. In Figure 23 the preferred structure of each of the equivalent parts or triples is the one on the right.

Figure 28

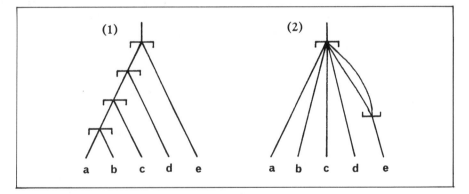

I have found no single number which selects all of the finer distinctions shown in the figure. Therefore I suggest the following two-part algorithm to arrive at the preferred diagram: Starting at the disjunctive form, hill climb by applying the equivalence relations utilizing the node plus extra line count as the measure of complexity. At any step, where more than one possible simplification is possible, each must be tried. When no further simplifications can be made, the simplest structure should then be fine tuned by applying equivalences which do not affect the complexity count, so that all parts of the final structure correspond to that shown on the right in each of the equivalences shown in Figure 23. These equivalences are all local in nature, and thus can be applied in any order, independent of one another. The resulting diagram will be the simplest possible structure. This will be true if and only if the following conjecture is true: Given the node plus extra line count as the measure of complexity, there exists a sequence of equivalence operations which convert a network in disjunctive form to the simplest network which describes the same effective information such that the complexity of each step is less than or equal to the complexity of the preceeding step.

What this conjecture implies is that one may not need to postulate complex special purpose mechanisms to explain how children can learn language so rapidly. Instead, it suggests that the linguistic system may, if formulated properly, be much simpler than most theoreticians have realized, such that relatively simple learning mechanisms suffice to accomplish the seemingly herculean task of discovering the structure of language. This conjecture would be considerably stronger if one could state that no matter what sequence of equivalence operations was performed on the disjunctive form of a network, the resulting network would ultimately be in its maximally simplest form. To put it another way, it would be nice if all paths down the mountain lead to the same valley. While this seems to be true in the equivalence space used in Figures 24 and 26, it is in general not true with the notation we are currently using. This does not preclude the possibility from being true in some other notational system. Although a heuristic program which chose an arbitrary sequence of simplifying equivalence operations would not necessarily end up with an optimal solution, this does not mean that it would not be a reasonable model of the simplification part of language acquisition. One need not assume that each child learning his native language necessarily finds the optimal solution. This area is discussed further in Reich, Forthcoming.

We have tried to show in this paper that if a grammar is stated completely explicitly, it can be represented in the form of a relational network of the type proposed by Lamb. We have discussed some formal properties of such networks, and have made some revisions to Lamb's formulation which allow us to keep the formal properties and the structural complexity count as simple as possible. We have introduced the notion of hill-climbing on equivalence spaces defined by the formal properties and the complexity count as a model of the simplification part of language acquisition. We have suggested that using the complexity count we proposed, the process of simplification of a grammar in disjunctive form is non-uphill all the way. However, we have done all these things only with reference to a system of relationships equivalent to a context-free phrase structure grammar. In other papers in this series we extend these results to networks capable of handling those features of language which cannot be handled by context-free phrase structure grammars. Thus we find that the network approach not only gives a simpler overall system, but one which has the added benefit of starting us along the path of developing a detailed model of the process of language acquisition.

NOTES

1. Part of the misunderstanding probably results from the fact that Lamb is continually changing his theory, so that it is difficult to obtain a coherent picture by reading articles written several years apart. In order to alleviate this problem, Ilah Fleming has written an annotated bibliography of the stratificational literature [1969].

2. At least not until recently. In Chomsky (1967b:424) a rule of this type is used. Like regular disjunction, this type of rule has the status of an abbreviation. As far as I can tell, Chomsky has not yet realized the full import of adding this relation to his system.

3. Throughout this paper I have tried to use Chomsky's terminology wherever possible, on the assumption that more readers have read and understood Chomsky than have read and understood Lamb. In the diagrams, Lamb's terminology is indicated in parentheses. The change in terminology is only an attempt to increase understanding. It has no theoretical significance.

4. Lamb (1966d:54–56) refers to this as superficial information.

5. This was suggested by Lamb (1966b:555) early in 1966. Later Lamb (1966d:46–54) went to a more complicated measure, because the measure gave incorrect results with respect to his treatment of optionality. In June 1966, I discovered a counterexample to this measure and proposed still another measure, the node plus extra line count which has been in use up to now (Lockwood 1967; Sampson 1967). Independent considerations have led us to modify our treatment of optionality, and since the new treatment negated Lamb's 1966 objections to the line count, we shall reconsider it here.

6. The highly simplified model described in this section is not adequate to handle looping, which transformationalists refer to as recursion. Because of this, the simplified signal model is not equivalent to a context-free phrase structure grammar. If one allows push-down storage of states of the nodes, one can build a system that is strictly equivalent to such a grammar. As this topic is covered in detail in Reich, 1969, it will not be discussed here.

7. One can criticize McNeill's proposal on other grounds. The proposal assumes that the concept of a transformation has some psychological validity. Recent experiments have raised serious doubts about this assumption (Fodor and Garrett, 1966; Reich, 1967). McNeill's measure of cognitive grammatical structure in terms of a count of the number of rules is also questionable. For a more careful approach to psychological complexity within the transformational framework, see Brown and Honlon (1968).

8. Gleason (personal communication) has suggested that concatenation, AND-OR, and disjunction can all be thought of as the same function of two variables—the minimum number of successful downward outputs, and the maximum number of same. In concatenation the minimum and the maximum are both 2. In AND-OR, the minimum is 1 and the maximum is 2. In disjunction the minimum and maximum are both 1. This is an insightful way of understanding the nodes. However, I prefer to represent the nodes with different symbols, to emphasize the differences in their formal properties.

9. This problem looks suspiciously like some problems for solving which mathematicians have proved there exists no algorithm (Trakhtenbrot, 1963:92–101). This sort of proof need not concern us, since it refers to an algorithm for solving the general class of problems, rather than any particular problem.

SPECIFIC STUDIES IN STRATIFICATIONAL PHONOLOGY, GRAMMAR, AND SEMOLOGY

PHONOLOGY AND GRAMMAR in a statificational system cover approximately the same ground as would normally be covered in a complete structuralist treatment: phonemics, morphophonemics, morphology, and syntax. Bloomfieldian structural treatments, however, were organized on one, or at the most two, strata. Various papers in Section I, particularly those by Lamb, show the need for more strata in dealing with this area.

One might question the apparent complexity of a conceptual apparatus which requires so many strata, each replete with its own special units and their tactics. In comparison with the Bloomfieldian apparatus, which involves only phonemes and morphemes and various combinations of these, the stratificational model may, at first glance, seem indeed cumbersome. Its innovations have all been advanced, however, in a quest for maximum generality in the treatment of linguistic phenomena. It turns out that a superficially simpler conceptual apparatus can, up to a point, result in treatments that are actually less simple and general than others which are superficially more complex. As stratificationalists are truly interested in the explanatory function of a grammar in addition to its observational and descriptive adequacies, we can say that what actually counts is the number of distinct relational network connections that are necessary to account for a given linguistic phenomenon or set of phenomena. When these are measured and understood as intended, it emerges that a system with more strata can result in 'simpler' treatments than one with too few.

An alternative to the recognition of separate strata is, of course, the use of ordered rewrite rules of the type advocated by Chomsky and his followers. According to their conception, there may exist between two given discrete levels an indefinite number of distinct intermediate levels defined by ordered blocks of one or more rewrite rules. One of these discrete levels, termed 'systematic phonemic', corresponds to the stratificationalist's MORPHONIC level. A second, termed 'systematic phonetic' corresponds roughly to the level of Lamb's HYPOPHONEMIC SIGNS (cf. Lamb's 'Prolegomena' below). The stratificational system recognizes three intermediate levels between these, namely those of the PHONEME, PHONON, and HYPOPHONEME. Advocates of Chomsky's system, on the other hand, have customarily refrained from granting an official status to such intermediate levels, BUT THEY NEVERTHELESS RECOGNIZE SEVERAL INTERMEDIATE LEVELS OF THEIR OWN by their insistence that rules must be ordered with respect to one another. In such a system, languages may vary widely as to the number of such distinct levels they must have, as may closely similar dialects of the same language. In the stratificational view, however, the number of distinct levels may be thought of as varying only within a very narrow range. These 'levels', it should be noted, include not only differences over a full stratum, but also levels WITHIN a single stratal system.

The basis for the differences between these two views of grammatical and phonological structure lies in the basically different notations and outlooks of the two theories. Transformationalists have observed that certain linguistic facts seem to require that rules of the type they use be ordered. Consequently, they have taken ordering to be a fundamental part of their system, and they make use of this feature whenever possible. When the same data are considered from a relational viewpoint, such as that taken by stratificational theory, however, it turns out that much of the ordering of rules is a consequence of the fact that the rules are conceived of as defining processes performed upon combinations of symbols rather than specifying a relationship. In some cases, the relational system uses a network feature which corresponds to the rule ordering, such as the use of the DOWNWARD ORDERED OR node, or the vertical ordering of successive nodes in the network. But in other cases the ordering of the rewriting rule system turns out to be a spurious result of the application to linguistic data of a concept essentially inappropriate to its treatment.

It cannot be overemphasized that the major difference between the modern version of stratificational theory and the transformational view is NOT that stratificational linguistics uses unordered rules while the transformationalists use ordered ones. Rather it is the case that STRATIFICATIONAL THEORY DOES NOT USE ANY RULES AT ALL, BUT VIEWS LINGUISTIC STRUCTURE AS CONSISTING ENTIRELY OF RELATIONSHIPS, SO THAT THE NOTION OF A 'RULE' DOES NOT HAVE ANY MEANING WITHIN IT.

Within the realm of grammar, it should be noted that stratificational theory is particularly well-adapted to the treatment of morphological phenomena, which is a major function of the morphemic system. The traditional notion of 'syntax' corresponds to TACTICS in stratificational linguistics, but there is a separate tactic pattern for each of its strata. Matters treated as 'syntactic' in other theoretical views may belong on the sememic, lexemic, or morphemic stratum in a stratificational description.

It may seem to those unfamiliar with the theory that stratificational tactics is essentially a syntax of the constituent structure type. What, one may ask, is the stratificational answer to the claim advanced by Chomsky that such a phrase-structure model of syntax is inadequate? Consider, for example, an active sentence such as *Paul knifed Martin in the back,* and its passive equivalent, *Martin was knifed in the back by Paul.* It has been claimed that constituent-structure syntax is inadequate because it fails to relate sentences such as these. In a stratificational account, however, such pairs of sentences will be related in the following way: any active-passive pair will have a single SEMEMIC structure which, depending on further sememic factors, will have alternate lexemic realizations, one active, the other passive. The common sememic structure does not resemble either of its realizations (or any other one it might have) any more closely than the other. Thus the relationship of such pairs of sentences is in no sense a matter of the 'derivation' of one from the other (as it has been treated in some of the earlier versions of transformational theory). Rather it is an instance of the phenomenon known in stratificational theory as DIVERSIFICATION—the existence of alternate realizations of a single higher element or structure on a lower stratum.

Consider also the sentence *Visiting linguists can often be a problem.* Sentences such as this have two distinct sememic representations which have a neutralized realization. NEUTRALIZATION is the situation in which distinct elements or structures have identical realizations on a lower stratum—the converse of diversification.

Since all such problematic phenomena can be handled by systematic inter-relations of different strata, a tactic pattern has nothing to be ashamed of for resembling a phrase-structure grammar, for it is indeed quite adequate for the limited problems which are its proper function to handle.

The degree of correspondence of the various strata to the levels called 'deep structure' and 'surface structure' in 'standard' transformational theory varies from one stage of the theory to the other. According to Stage IV, during which most of the contributions to this section were written, the sememic stratum corresponds most closely to the deep structure, while the lexemic stratum deals with the closest equivalent of surface structure. The morphemic stratum at this stage is concerned primarily with the structure of words. In stage III, on the other hand, it is the lexemic stratum which most closely resembles deep structure, including constructions larger than words. In Lamb's most recent research (reflected in the 'The Crooked Path of Progress in Cognitive Linguistics'), developments seem to lead to a stage which resembles Stage III more closely than early Stage IV in these particulars.

Even though the lexotactics of stage IV bears a close resemblance to a phrase-structure syntax, there are a number of points of significant difference. In general terms, the units with which such a lexotactics deals are of a greater degree of abstraction than the 'morpheme' of the Bloomfieldian structuralists. In addition, a lexotactics may provide for unordered combinations (DOWNWARD UNORDERED ANDS) as well as ordered ones. Also many lexemes are complex, consisting of two or more lexons, in order to account for certain kinds of idioms and other combinations behaving as a unit with reference to their connection to meaning.

Probably no other part of linguistic structure was more neglected by the Bloomfieldian structuralists than meaning. In view of the particular socio-historical and scientific setting in which he had to function, however, Bloomfield can perhaps be deemed more 'right' than 'wrong' in his reluctance to deal with meaning. 'Psychologism', 'mentalism', and 'teleology' were taboos in an America whose scholars and scientists, writing under the influence of Watkins's behaviorism, had more in common with the Russian Ivan Pavlov than with the American pragmatist William James. In addition to being behavioristic, the Bloomfieldian anti-mentalist position was also a consequence of the positivism of the 1890's, under whose intellectual influence the German Neogrammarians, Bloomfield's philosophical ancestors, and in some cases his teachers, were examining language. Bloomfieldian mechanism was to a large extent a healthy and unavoidable reaction to Wundt, Humboldt, and such notions as 'volition', 'intention', 'the mind', 'Volksgeist', 'Sprachgeist', and even Sapir's 'genius of a language'. Bloomfield was being cautious rather than dogmatic in advancing the proposal that linguists should, wherever possible, avoid meaning. As several contemporary scholars have demonstrated (especially Karl Teeter of Harvard), Bloomfield, in his *Language* (1933), his description of Menomini, and other writings, showed great sophistication and full awareness of the role of meaning. The culmination of antimentalism was actually reached in the work of Harris (e.g. 1951), frequently referred to nowadays as 'distributionalism'.

Chomsky, a student of Harris, inherited at least as much from his former teacher as he rebelled against in Harris's work. As Lamb suggests in his 'Linguistic and cognitive networks' (pp. 60–83 in this volume), the Boas-Sapir-Bloomfield-Harris-Chomsky tradition may be viewed as a single continuum of development, moving from data-gathering through data-distribution, to the manipulation of abstracted representations of data via process rules termed 'transformations'. In all of these, the units dealt with are treated as actual objects or entities, despite Chomsky's declared intention of treating the UNDERLYING SYSTEM, which must be distinguished from his actual practice.

Stratificational grammar has had a different orientation from the very outset. Saussure observed that 'dans la langue il n'y a que des différences', that is to say, it is the relationship of one item to the other alone that defines that item, and not conversely. This was taken literally by Hjelmslev, who in his *Prolegomena* (1943, 1961) carried forward Saussure's point of view to a logical conclusion. Thus in Hjelmslevian glossematics language was conceived of as a system of relationships connecting CONTENT SUBSTANCE with EXPRESSION SUBSTANCE, i.e. meaning with speech sound. The total system was further organized into subsystems, comparable to the strata of a modern stratificational account.

Modern stratificational linguistics, as developed by Lamb beginning in the late 1950's, has to a considerable extent blended the terms and concepts of Hjelmslevian glossematics with those of some of the best Neo-Bloomfieldian work. Its basic outlook, however, comes more from the former than from the latter, in that the notion expressed by Hjelmslev's dictum 'a totality does not consist of things, but of relationships' is fundamental to its modern conception.

In considering the organization of a stratificational semology, we can perhaps begin by considering the unit through which semology connects to the lower strata, namely the LEXEME. This term has a considerable history, especially among anthropological linguists, beginning with Whorf. Perhaps the most cogent statement about this unit comes from Harold C. Conklin, who in his 'Lexicographical treatment of folk taxonomies' demonstrates that the lexicographer has the task of separating SEMANTICALLY ENDOCENTRIC constructions from SEMANTICALLY EXOCENTRIC ones. Thus *long pink strand, large brown table,* and *angry black bull* are all semantically endocentric, (that is, their meanings add up cumulatively from the listed lexical meanings of the components), whereas *black-eyed Susan* (a kind of daisy rather than a girl who has had a fight with her fiancé) and *Jack-in-the-pulpit* (a kind of flower rather than a preacher named Jack situated in a pulpit) are semantically exocentric, in that their meanings are outside or beyond the meanings of their components. Hockett (1958) proposed the term IDIOM for such units, and this term is essentially appropriate for units which consist of more than one word. (Cf. Makkai 1965, 1972).

In terms of its function in sentences, the lexeme has been defined by stratificational usage as the ultimate constituent in the lexotactics. If we use it in this way, however, we will have to recognize higher-stratum units which can account for the alternation among certain lexemes. The English lexeme *can,* for example, has the peculiarity of not having a future—*will can,* or *shall can* are impossible (except if one is using the verb *can* meaning 'to put in cans'). Its future is supplied, however, by the phrase *will be able to.* We can account for this fact by positing a single SEMEME which has the lexemes *can* and *be able to* as alternate realizations, their distribution being accounted for by the lexotactics.

As conceived of in Stage IV of stratificational theory, however, not even the sememes are the ultimate components of meaning. Consider the following sentences, which would normally be judged to have the same cognitive meaning:

Aunt Hermione died yesterday.
Aunt Hermione passed away yesterday.

So the expressions *die* and *pass away* seem to be substitutable for each other without change of meaning. But we can also use *die* with the same basic meaning (something like 'cease to function') in the following sentences:

Gaston's pet goldfish died last week.
My African violet died while I was on vacation.
The motor keeps dying when I step on the gas.

But the following sentences, substituting *pass away* for *die*, all seem absurd:

*Gaston's pet goldfish passed away last week.
*My African violet passed away while I was on vacation.
*The motor keeps passing away when I step on the gas.

The reason for this, of course, is that the expression *pass away* is substitutable for *die* only with reference to humans, while *die* has a wider range. But in contrast to the situation described for *can* and *be able*, the conditioning factors involved are not the grammatical categories which belong on the lexemic stratum, but semological categories, specifically the category HUMAN as opposed to others. In order to handle such situations, stratificational theory of stage IV has postulated a hypersememic stratum, on which there will be a single entity of which both *die* and *pass away* will be alternate realizations, conditioned (on the sememic stratum) by the category *human* (which allows either, versus other categories which allow only *die*.)

General cognition is another area which takes us above the sememic stratum. Consider the following case: A man, Oliver Quasimodo Yesteryear by name, aged 33, resides in Apartment 33-A at 757 Sunset Boulevard in Hilo, Hawaii. Under the appropriate circumstances, this man may be referred to as *my neighbor, my boss, my landlord, my brother-in-law, he, you* (if addressed), *I* (when he talks about himself), *you lucky dog* (when he wins too much at poker), *Mr. Yesteryear, Sir, loverboy, Honey, Baby, Mack, Hey, you there!, O.Q.* (by associates if he is a management director or tycoon), *Oliver, Ollie, son, Darling, Oliver Quasimodo Yesteryear*, or, if there is more than one by this name, *that Oliver Quasimodo Yesteryear who lives on Sunset Boulevard in Hilo, Hawaii*, and so forth.

In some sense all of these appellations may be thought of as alternate realizations of a single element representing a speaker's internal representation of the person of O. Q. Y. This element may also belong on the hypersememic (or gnostemic) stratum, but research has not yet advanced to the point where it is clear whether this stratum is distinct from general cognition, and to what extent either is properly to be termed linguistic. Terminology has also varied in different stages of stratificational theory on this point. In stage III, for example, many notions termed hypersememic in stage IV were called BASIC SEMEMES, whose realizations were termed REALIZED SEMEMES.

Whatever terminology is used, however, the understanding that the cognitive system is above and feeds into the sememic stratum opens up a vast new area for semological research. The cognitive system (whether or not it is a part of the hypersememic stratum) is envisaged as the depository of elements of general cognition in which, for example, concepts such as 'true' or 'false' would be registered. So if one were to hear the sentence *M.I.T. is in London, England*, there is no objection one can make to it on linguistic grounds. It is well-formed in every respect. One may, of course, object that it is false, i.e. it fails to fit with other knowledge stored in the cognitive system.

At this point what may be called the CONTEXTUAL ADJUSTABILITY PRINCI-

PLE becomes relevant. This principle has been widely used in recent years by transformationally oriented semanticists in making up complex examples, e.g. in recent papers of George Lakoff and James D. McCawley. If it should happen that Chomsky, Fodor, Katz, and Halle all went to London to teach in some particular year, it would not be strange for a linguist to say *M.I.T. is in London, England.*

Particularly popular nowadays in transformationally-based semantics papers are various examples that have to do with the separation of the speaker's experience into a 'real world' and an 'imaginary world'. Such examples as

The Nazi dreamt that he was a kind soul.
I dreamt I was Brigitte Bardot and that I kissed me.
I dreamt that I was two little kittens and that I played with one another.
    (sic!)

have been cited as sentences whose peculiarities cannot be explained by any syntactic features of the 'deep structure'. Characteristically, such examples have been advanced by Lakoff, McCawley and others who advocate the abolition of deep structure as a separate level in a transformational grammar, or more drastically, the abolition of the difference between syntax and semantics and the elevation of the generative aspect of linguistic behavior to the sphere of semantics. While it is still impossible to predict where this new movement within transformational-generative grammar will lead, it is becoming increasingly clear that there is a need to recognize an area feeding into the sememic stratum in order to handle such phenomena successfully.

Among other things, the postulation of such an area enables stratificational linguistics to handle the analysis of complicated literary passages, as in the following example.[1] A writer assumes that each reader brings more to the reading of a given work than just a knowledge of the language. It is quite possible for a foreign student in an American university, for example, to have a good working command of English and still not fully grasp certain English literary works. If such a student were to read Ambrose Bierce's *Devil's Dictionary* (1958), the author's scathing indictment of human nature might well go unappreciated if the reader is unsophisticated enough to take its content literally.

The Devil's Dictionary becomes truly meaningful only if the reader shares certain cultural and intellectual experience which can only be found in the cognitive system, which has been neglected by linguists until recently. Lamb's treatment of cognitive data such as the structure of a baseball game and animal taxonomy (1971, in Part I of this volume) suggests a particularly useful approach to comprehending how we understand Bierce. By mapping the relationships between the cognitive system and language proper, we can account for the multiplicity of levels of meaning in literary works.

Since Bierce is playing several games at once, it is possible and necessary to analyze his work from a number of valid points of departure. Consider the following entries:

ABSURDITY	A statement or belief manifestly inconsistent with one's own opinion.
ADMIRATION	Our polite recognition of another's resemblance to ourselves.
BIGOT	One person who is obstinately and zealously attached to an opinion that you do not entertain.
BORE	A person who talks when you wish him to listen.
COMMENDATION	The tribute that we pay to achievements that resemble, but do not equal, our own.
IMPIETY	Your irreverence toward my deity.
LOQUACITY	A disorder which renders the sufferer unable to curb his tongue when you wish to talk.
RASH	Insensible to the value of our advice.

Bierce is telling us that it is human nature to define as faults the inability of others to recognize our obvious superiority. Meaning is defined by the ego, and the reference is human foible.

Bierce has rewritten the English lexicon within the cognitive system. The reader juxtaposes Bierce's cognitive network for human nature alongside the less subjective network which defines the entries more traditionally. The interplay between what represents sheer exaggeration, on the one hand, and a valid observation of human foible, on the other, is what generates humor AND the real meaning of Bierce's lexicon.

Bierce views each individual as structuring 'reality' within his cognitive system so that he alone is defined by 'positive qualities'. Others are defined by 'faults', most of which are the inability to recognize the superiority of ego.

In literature, particularly poetry, syntax clearly plays a subservient role to meaning. Only a theory which explores the semantic relationships within the cognitive system can lend real insights into meaning. At present, more work is going on at the sememic stratum than in the hypersememic cognitive system, since there is a vast amount of unexplored territory on this lower stratum as well. This fact, however, must not preclude first attempts at tackling the problems of hypersemology-cognition, which will necessarily be enlarged and refined as research in adjacent areas develops corroborating findings or forces appropriate modifications of them.

The first stratificational paper to deal with phonological problems was Lamb's 'On Alternation, Transformation, Realization, and Stratification' (1964). This paper was based on the insights of Stage II, but has not been included here. No phonological study has appeared based on the insights of Stage III, therefore the first paper of this section, Lamb's 'Prolegomena to a Theory of Phonology' is one based on Stage IV. This article, in fact, was the first contribution of this stage to become available. It is clearly the most important work on stratificational phonology which has appeared to date, but as the 'prolegomena' to the theory rather than the theory itself, it requires considerable amplification in order for all of its implications to be fully understood. In this paper Lamb first mentions the types of phenomena which are of concern to phonological theory and then discusses classical phonemics. He defends classical phonemics against the attacks that have been levelled by Chomsky and Halle, showing in particular that the inefficiency of the traditional phonemic analysis of Russian can be remedied without departing from the classical principles of phonemics. He then goes on, however, to point out some deficiencies which are REALLY present in classical phonemics, and develops the outlines of a new theory of phonology. This was the first work to employ the graphic notation in its modern form, and the first to divide phonological (morphophonemic) alternations into two types. Morphonic alternations are those which can be more economically treated between the morphemic and the phonemic strata, and phononic alternations are those whose treatment is achieved the most economically between the phonemic and the hypophonemic strata, in terms of componential units also referred to in the literature as 'unary' or 'singulary' distinctive features.

Lockwood's paper ' "Replacives" without Process' deals with an aspect of the interrelation between English morphology and phonology, specifically the phonotactics, in the sense of stage IV. The problem of the so-called 'replacives', as in the example *sing, sang, sung,* has been handled by structural linguists primarily as a matter of morphology. This paper compares stratificational interpretations of some of these earlier analyses with the author's own solution, demonstrating the superiority of the latter from the point of view of an evaluation procedure made possible by the network notation, showing how this system can be used for comparing alternate analyses of the same problem. The relative simplicity of the competing solutions can then be measured.

'Economy' is the main theme of the paper by Valerie Becker Makkai 'On the Correlation of Morphemes and Lexemes.' Data from French, Italian, and Spanish verb paradigms are used to demonstrate the necessity of separating the morphemic stratum from the lexemic, in order to avoid needlessly repeating the same information.

In his paper 'The Problem of Inflectional Morphemes,' Lockwood treats a notoriously recalictrant problem from the stratificational point of view. It is shown that neither a formalist approach, nor a functionalist approach, is really adequate for accounting for the inflectional systems of Indo-European and other similarly inflected languages. By a 'formalist approach' is meant the tradition which bases morpheme identification on phonemic shape correlated with meaning. The 'functionalist approach', on the other hand, bases its morphemic analysis primarily on syntactic function. The stratificational approach proposed in this paper takes BOTH functional AND formal properties into account, but each on its own proper stratum. It emerges that neither the functionalist nor the formalist approach is adequate by itself, and that the stratificational reallocation of their respective findings on the appropriate strata is the most satisfactory solution. Data from Classical Latin are used to illustrate the solutions presented.

The first selection dealing with semology, Lamb's 'The Sememic Approach to Structural Semantics,' provides one of the earliest outlines of the stratificational view in general, and has particular reference to problems of semology. At this stage, only one stratum above the grammatical (lexemic) was posited, while by stage IV a division into a sememic and a hypersememic stratum was proposed. Another point at which this article differs from both stage III and stage IV is in its use of the term SEMON for a semantic component—the upward component of a sememe, whereas the ONS of lower strata were downward components of their respective EMES. Various semantic problems are discussed in this paper, including some matters which have been treated as syntactic by followers of the transformational-generative view. The notion emerges that many phenomena for which the followers of Chomsky are forced to use syntactic transformations can be handled as matters of discrepancy between the lexemic and the sememic stratum.

In his 'Kinship Terminology and Linguistic Structure,' Lamb applies stratificational linguistics to one of the most extensively discussed problems within the anthropologically oriented tradition of structural semantics. The model presented here is that of stage III, as in 'Stratificational Linguistics as a Basis for Machine Translation' (in Part I of this volume). The principal data treated is from Omaha Type III kinship systems, which were earlier described by Lounsbury in terms of 'reduction rules' applied to the various kinship types. Lamb makes the point that there is actually a specific semotactic construction underlying such rules, and once the construction in question is isolated and identified, Lounsbury's otherwise quite accurate rules are automatically derivable from it. The rule is, therefore, considered the 'symptom' and the construction the 'disease'. The same point, it seems, could be extended to linguistic systems in general: when viewed from the standpoint of stratificational theory, rules, even those involving a considerable abstraction from the data, are only preliminary statements. What the stratificational linguist is trying to do is to discover the system of relationships underlying the 'rules'.

The next contribution, Gleason's Contrastive Analysis in Discourse Structure,' represents a very important trend within the stratificational view, to which Gleason and his students have devoted particular attention. This is the analysis of discourse structure, treated on the sememic stratum, or in some cases on the hypersememic. Similar work has been done by Taber, Cromack, Stennes, and others. Their studies are too long, however, to be included in this volume. Here Gleason presents a stratificational model for discourse structures, applying it to data from English, Kâte, and Adamawa Fulani. Particular attention is paid to such problems as the organization of events, and the identification of participants, including anaphora, within a particular discourse. This system is further related to the more general theme of contrastive analysis. We refrain from assigning this paper to a specific stage of development, since Gleason's work, though basically stratificational in its orientation, is developing along lines which are essentially independent of Lamb's research.

Bennett's article on 'English Prepositions' provides a stratificational interpretation of several aspects of semology. His main topic is synonymy, but he treats polysemy, idiomaticity, and componency as well. This article was also the first to incorporate some innovations within Stage IV after the publication of Lamb's *Outline* (1966d): it uses DIAMONDS in place of the former upward ANDS for the connection of the tactics to the realizational patterns, so that both encoding and decoding can be handled. The paper also introduced an additional alternation pattern BELOW the diamonds, in which unconditioned diversification can be handled more economically than in the upper alternation pattern, where it was treated in earlier versions of stage IV.

Bennett's second article 'A Stratificational View of Polysemy' presents further amplification of his views on polysemy, expressed in part in the preceding article. Here the major part of the discussion centers around the meanings of the English preposition *over*. Bennett's inclination is basically to the 'Gesamtbedeutung' approach also advocated by Jakobson and many anthropological linguists. He reduces, as far as possible, the apparent meanings of *over* by isolating their common core of semantic features. The paper departs from a strict interpretation of the 'Gesamtbedeutung' approach, however, in that it also allows the possibility that a lexeme may have multiple meanings when necessary.

The final paper, Adam Makkai's 'The Transformation of a Turkish Pasha into a Big Fat Dummy,' discusses the application of the stratificational model (of whatever stage) to problems of translation of both prose and formal verse. It points out that only a theory which can formally account for transduction both from meaning to sound and from sound to meaning can begin to account for translation which cannot be viewed solely as a matter of 'performance' as opposed to 'competence'. It is further suggested that cultural institutions in the hypersememic (or gnostemic) system of both the speaker and the hearer play an integral part in all types of translation.

A. M.
D. G. L.

NOTE

1. Grateful acknowledgment is made to Mr. Terry Shor, formerly of the University of Illinois at Chicago Circle, for the examples and suggested analysis of Bierce's redefinitions.

CHAPTER SEVEN

Prolegomena to a
Theory of Phonology*

SYDNEY M. LAMB

*Since different writers do not in fact agree in the phonemic
treatment of the same language, there arise then frequent
controversies over the 'correctness' or 'incorrectness' in
the use of phonemes.*
YUEN-REN CHAO (1934)

THIS PAPER discusses various types of phonological phenomena, some
of the concepts that linguists have employed in dealing with them, and
certain questions to which previous work in phonological theory has not
provided satisfactory answers. These considerations lead to the recognition
of some distinctions heretofore overlooked and to a new theory of phonology,
certain features of which are outlined.

Certain fairly conspicuous features of phonological patterning have long
been recognized. It is probably beyond dispute that at least the following
types of phenomena (described for the present in relatively vague terms)
are characteristic of all spoken languages and hence must be accounted
for:

1. UNITS. Perhaps the fundamental fact about phonology is that (in all
spoken languages) the phonological entities corresponding to minimal elements of the grammatical system (i.e. morphemes in the terminology of
some linguists) are in general not minimal but are divisible into smaller
phonological entities. In somewhat looser phraseology it might be said the
morphemes (or minimal grammatical signs) have phonological 'parts' which

---

*From *Language* 42.536–573. Reprinted by permission.

recur as parts of other morphemes. That amounts to stating that there exist such things as phonological units independently of grammatical units. Accordingly the term 'units' may be used as a short label for this property. It has commonly also been observed that the number of such phonological units is smaller than the number of morphemes.

This fundamental property is the basis of Hjelmslev's distinction (1961:46) between expression and content: '... a description in accordance with our principles must analyze content and expression separately, with each of the two analyses eventually yielding a restricted number of entities, which are not necessarily susceptible of one-to-one matching with entities in the opposite plane.' Bloomfield (1926) described the property as follows: 'Different morphemes may be alike or partly alike as to vocal features... A minimum same of vocal feature is a phoneme or distinctive sound. As, for instance, English [b, s, t], the English normal word-stress, the Chinese tones.... The number of different phonemes in a language is a small submultiple of the number of forms.'

2. ALTERNATION. The combination of phonological units corresponding to a morpheme may vary from one occurrence of the morpheme to another. It is generally agreed that the indefinitely discriminable variation in acoustic features of a unit within a fixed linguistic context is outside of linguistic structure, hence not to be counted as phonological alternation. Otherwise the number of phonological entities in the linguistic structure would be indefinitely large and continually growing with the occurrence of new utterances. Beyond this rather inescapable point there is very little general agreement, despite decades of work on phonological theory. According to one widespread view there are two quite distinct types of alternation and, accordingly, three clearly distinguishable types of phonological units. Although terminology varies somewhat, the terms morphophoneme, phoneme, and allophone are often used for the three types of units, and the two types of alternation are sometimes referred to as morphophonemic (i.e. alternation among phonemes corresponding to a single morphophoneme) and phonemic (alternation among allophones corresponding to a single phoneme). A conflicting view has been proposed by Halle and Chomsky.[1] It has a lower level bearing some resemblance to that of the allophones of conventional practice and an upper level somewhat higher than that of the conventional morphophonemes; but between these two no structural level is recognized. There is in any specific linguistic structure a sequence of rewrite rules, but no intervening level exists except in the sense that a level may be said to exist between each pair of ordered rewrite rules. The number of such levels is of course rather large and varies from one language to another, even from one dialect of the same language to another. The phonological units of this view differ from those of the other also in that they are binary distinctive features. Various additional ways of treating phonological alternation have been proposed, but they need not be described here, since this introductory statement is not intended as a historical survey.

3. TACTICS. Phonological units occur in definite patterns of arrangement

which are independent of the grammatical patterns and meanings of the morphemes which they represent. That is, there is in every language a set of relationships concerned with the composition of syllables and other combinations of phonological units.[2] The term phonotactics has often been used in this connection.

4. COMPONENTS. There exist in any language a small number of phonological features which are components of phonological segments. The term phonological unit used above is intentionally quite vague, since different theories recognize different phonological units, and there may be different kinds of phonological units recognized within a single theory. It is to be noted, however, that phonological units of two different size levels have generally been recognized. That is, it has been common to distinguish phonological segments and components of such segments. One is concerned here with a different type of level from that which relates to alternation. The morphophonemes, phonemes, and allophones mentioned above are all phonological segments, and any of them may have components according to one type of phonological theory, while another type would assert that phonemes and allophones have components but morphophonemes do not. Much of the literature dealing with components is not explicit about such matters, however. The Chomsky-Halle approach follows Jakobson in recognizing phonological components of a special two-valued type, i.e. binary distinctive features.[3] This school is also unusual in not granting any structural status to phonological units of a higher size level than these distinctive features, i.e. in not recognizing phonological segments as elements in a linguistic structure.[4] The phonological side of this school's morpheme is a distinctive feature matrix rather than a chain of phonological segments.[5] (This matter is discussed below).

Although these four types of phonological phenomena are quite generally recognized in one way or another, very little explicit detail concerning them is well established. A particularly noteworthy gap, often overlooked, is the absence of an acceptable specification of how these various types of phenomena are related to one another within a linguistic structure. For example, the following questions have not received fully satisfactory answers: (1) What are the ultimate constituents[6] of the phonotactics—phonemes, morphophonemes, components of phonemes? (2) Do morphophonemes (as well as phonemes) have components; and if so what is their relationship to components of phonemes? (3) How (in detail) do we relate to each other the two ways of specifying arrangements of phonologic units, i.e. (a) by the phonotactics, (b) by morphology plus the specification of composition of morphemes? (4) What is the proper role of phonological components in the description of alternation among phonological segments? (5) If the phoneme is not elementary but has components, then what is its structural status, if any? (This question seems particularly pertinent if the components are taken as the ultimate constituents of the tactics.)

In connection with phonological alternation there may be raised several additional questions, some of which have met with widely varying answers during the past several years. Conventional phonemics, the best known approach to phonological phenomena, provides a good orientation for further investigation into some of these questions, even though it is a bit vague on certain points and variable on others. It may be designated C-phonemics for short; if the reader prefers he may take the C as standing for 'Classical'.

The Phonemic Principle

The outstanding characteristic of C-phonemics is its insistence that there is such a thing as a phonemic level. That is, it holds that some features of speech sound or of articulation are distinctive while others are not. The former are phonemic, the latter subphonemic. Another version of the principle is that contrastive phonetic differences must be distinguished from those differences which are non-contrastive. In this connection the well known concept of complementary distribution[7] and Hjelmslev's commutation (1961) are important concepts. This same phonemic level is specified by the very closely related distinction, mentioned above, between alternation among allophones of a phoneme on the one hand and alternation among phonemes on the other.

Since the term phonemics has usually been used for an area which excludes treatment of morphophonemic alternation, various quite different ways of treating morphophonemic alternation have accompanied C-phonemics at different times and places. C-phonemics itself says nothing about how morphophonemic alternation is to be handled, except that it is to be sharply distinguished from alternation among allophones.

C-phonemic treatment of phonemic components has often been haphazard, indirect, or incidental, but explicit recognition to components as structural elements has been granted by, for example, Harris (1944), Bloch (1948, 1950), Martin (1951), and Hockett (1947b, c). Implicit recognition has quite generally been given to components by C-phonemicists when they have displayed phonemic inventories in charts organized according to manners and positions of articulation. Perhaps it did not occur to some of them, however, to ponder the structural significance of such arrangement.

With regard to phonotactics C-phonemics has had no explicit or consistent policy. Some treatments have taken phonemes to be the ultimate constituents,[8] but Hockett, in his *Manual of phonology* (1955), took the position that the ultimate constituents are the phonemic components and that the phoneme is no more than a constitute at a particular size level of the phonotactics. He thus proposed to answer one of the long-standing problems of C-phonemics by relegating it to the status of pseudoproblem, to which there is not and should not be a single fixed answer. This is the problem involved in such questions as: Unit phoneme or cluster?, one phoneme or two?, tš or č?

C-phonemics should not be confused with the fictitious framework which Chomsky calls taxonomic phonemics (T-phonemics), a system apparently created by him to serve as the helpless victim of a dramatic onslaught.[9] Chomsky characterizes T-phonemics in terms of four conditions which he calls linearity, invariance, biuniqueness, and local determinacy. The biuniqueness condition, of which the local determinacy condition is a part, is the basic requirement stated above which distinguishes alternation among phonemes from alternation among allophones. The invariance condition, which would require that all components of a phoneme have a phonetic realization in every occurrence of the phoneme, is present for some versions of C-phonemics but not for others;[10] and C-phonemics has no linearity requirement. Chomsky's fictitious linearity condition 'requires that each occurrence of a phoneme in the phonemic representation of an utterance be associated with a particular succession of (one or more) consecutive phones... as its 'member' or 'realization'; and, furthermore, that if A precedes B in the phonemic representation, then the phone sequence associated with A precedes... that associated with B...' (1964:78).[11]

That such a requirement is not a part of C-phonemics is clear from the theoretical writings as well as from the phonological descriptions of C-phonemicists. For example, no C-phonemicist ever proposed analyzing a tone language as having a separate set of vowel phonemes for each tone. As an example on the theoretical side, Bloch's 'Postulates for phonemic analysis', a standard theoretical work on C-phonemics, contains several statements explicitly indicating that he accepted no such requirement. (1948:sections 48.2, 52.4, 53.2, 53.6, 56.1, 56.2, 57.2).[12]

An important part of Chomsky's attack on T-phonemics is directed against what he calls the biuniqueness condition. Since that condition, in one form or another, is shared by C-phonemics, and is in fact one of its most cherished principles, it is appropriate to consider it in some detail before going on to other matters.

The Biuniqueness of Phonemic Solutions of Phonetic Systems

As Chomsky states it (1964:80), 'the biuniqueness condition... asserts that each sequence of phones is represented by a unique sequence of phonemes and that each sequence of phonemes represents a unique sequence of phones.' He clarifies in a footnote that 'In this form, the condition is of course rarely met. What is intended, rather, is that each sequence of phonemes represents a sequence of phones that is unique up to free variation.' The use of the term biuniqueness in this connection stems from a statement made by Hockett (1951:340).[13]

Several points of clarification are needed if this principle is to be properly understood. First, it is important to distinguish it from the ways in which it has been used. Chomsky and Halle are correct in their criticism of the attempts of C-phonemicists to define rigorous procedures of analysis by means of principles such as that of biuniqueness and that of complementary distribution. That is to say, the C-phonemicists were surely mistaken in their supposition that it was necessary and feasible to specify such procedures.[14] But the type of use to which the principles were put must be distinguished from the principles themselves. This criticism is concerned only with basic methodology, not with the criteria which were used to implement it. The same criteria may be applicable in a different methodological orientation. Thus the so-called biuniqueness condition should be considered as one of the properties of an acceptable C-phonemic solution, not as a procedural device. Note that this statement makes no commitment as to whether the property is an independent criterion of acceptability or an automatic consequence of one or more other properties. In either case it remains interesting and useful (for reasons indicated below).

By the same token, the statement of the biuniqueness requirement should refer to linguistic structure or to the phonemic description, rather than to the raw or partially analyzed linguistic data.

A good example of the considerations involved is provided by Monachi, a Uto-Aztecan language of California. In the dialect of Bishop, California, [m] alternates with [w̃] (nasalized [w]); the latter occurs after vowels, while the former never occurs after vowels (both segments are always followed by a vowel). In the dialect of North Fork, the corresponding alternation is between [m] and [w] (non-nasalized). To the C-phonemicist this description fails to give a clear picture of the situation, since it lacks certain essential information (whose absence would not disturb Chomsky or Halle). The relevant further fact is that there is also (in both dialects) a [w] (non-nasalized) which does not participate in the alternation and which contrasts with [m]. Now the structural relationships are clear to the C-phonemicist. In North Fork there is neutralization, and [w] after vowels is phonologically ambiguous, but in Bishop [w̃] and [w] are in contrast. According to C-phonemics the alternation in Bishop is subphonemic, i.e. [m] and [w̃] are allophones of one phoneme; but in North Fork it is a morphophonemic alternation, even though the conditioning environments are the same in the two dialects. Thus the C-phonemic transcription of the forms 'will go' and 'our future going' is /miyawai/, /tawiyawai'na/ in North Fork, /miyawai/, /tamiyawai'na/ in Bishop. And the transcription /wiya/ 'acorns', /tawiya/ 'our acorns' applies for both dialects.

Consider further a hypothetical dialect just like that of North Fork except that it lacks a [w] contrasting with [m], i.e. it has no forms like /wiya/ 'acorns'. In this case [m] and [w] would be considered allophones of the same phoneme. Note that the well trained C-phonemicist would analyze the components of this phoneme differently from those of the Bishop /m/. In the hypothetical dialect, the feature labial is distinctive for this phoneme but nasality is non-distinctive. In Bishop, on the other hand, the components labial and nasal are both distinctive; i.e. nasality is distinctive because of the contrast between [w̃] and [w]. Closure is not distinctive in either phoneme; when present (i.e. in environments other than intervocalic) it is determined.

What is the motivation for this principle that requires the C-phonemicist to write /tawiyawai'na/? A preliminary answer may be found by considering the concept of distinctiveness.

Any communication system must have a way to express meaning, i.e. an expression system. In general, whatever physical medium is used for expression (speech, writing, DNA, etc.) must have diversity, i.e. divergence from uniformity. Otherwise information could not be expressed. In natural spoken language, this diversity is in the speech. But speech, even of a single language, exhibits innumerably many different sound features, and only some of these differences are distinctive, i.e. are able to distinguish different meanings. It is of fundamental importance to identify these distinctive features of difference and to distinguish them from those which are not distinctive. This is the reason for separating the C-phonemic level from the phonetic in describing spoken languages. It allows the description to distinguish those features of the diversity in the medium of expression which have communicative significance from those which do not.

Perhaps an illustration from outside of language will provide perspective to help make the principle more obvious. Consider a familiar communicative device used by certain unprincipled gamblers: marked cards. Those who have seen a deck of marked cards or have heard them described by experts are familiar with the fact that the distinctive markings, which serve to distinguish kings from tens, etc., are extremely difficult to detect, since they are embedded in the design on the backs of the cards, a medium which has a great deal of non-distinctive diversity. A 'phonetic' description of the backs of these cards would describe all of the diversity of the design in detail; and it would be useless to anyone wanting to know what the system was. In considering the backs of these cards from the point of view of their communicative function it is precisely the distinctive markings which are relevant. Only these are of interest to one concerned with the system. The difference between distinctive and nondistinctive, between contrastive and noncontrastive, between 'emic' and 'etic', is crucial.

To those who have the experience of hearing an unfamiliar language for the first time, or who see a page of unfamiliar phonetic transcription, there is a comparable situation. The speech is a bewildering variety of sound, a patterned but unfathomable diversity. Yet to one who knows the phonemic system of the language, as to the gambler who knows the 'emic' system of the marked cards, recognition of the meaning encoded in the medium is immediate and effortless. Like the gambler with his cards, the linguist who is given a description of a language to read will find it relatively useless if it does not separate the distinctive from the nondistinctive. Without such separation the basis of expression—that which makes the communication system communicative—is left hidden.

The principle of differentiating the distinctive from the nondistinctive by means of phonemic as opposed to phonetic transcription means that although the phonetic transcription should show all the detail that is practically feasible, the phonemic transcription should show all those features which are distinctive, and no others. In other words, the phonemic transcription should differentiate units which have a distinctive difference, but it should not differentiate where there are nondistinctive or nonexistent differences. More precisely, the distinctiveness principle is that a correct C-phonemic solution treats two units (i.e. segments, syllables, or the like) as phonemically different if and only if there is a distinctive phonetic difference between them. By distinctive phonetic difference I mean a difference in at least one distinctive phonetic feature; a phonetic feature is distinctive if its presence is not determined by its immediate environment. (A more precise specification is given below.)

Thus (1) Bishop [m] and [w̃] are not phonemically different because the difference between them is not distinctive; (2) North Fork [w]₁ which alternates with [m] and [w]₂ which does not (corresponding to Bishop [w̃] and [w] respectively) are not phonemically different, since there is no distinctive phonetic difference between them, since there is no phonetic difference at all between them; (3) the North Fork alternants [m] and [w]₁ are phonemically different, since [w]₁ and [w]₂ are phonemically alike and [m] and [w]₂ are distinctively different (since [m] has the feature of nasality, which is not determined since it may be either present or absent in the environment in question).

The biuniqueness condition is a corollary of the distinctiveness principle. It follows from the distinctiveness principle; the reverse is not true, since the distinctiveness principle is more stringent: it allows only those features which are distinctive to be considered phonemic. The biuniqueness principle by itself would accept uneconomical solutions that failed to make use of complementary distribution, e.g. a description of the Bishop dialect in which [m] and [w̃] were treated as 'phonemically' different.

The question of whether the distinctiveness principle is an independent criterion for acceptability of a phonemic solution or is merely a consequence of some other more basic principle is considered below. At this point it need be observed only that a description is relatively uninformative to the extent that it violates this principle.

On the other hand, the biuniqueness condition has been criticized on the grounds that it requires uneconomical descriptions in certain situations. The argument has been presented by Halle, using as an example the Russian obstruents (1959:22–23):

> In Russian, voicing is distinctive for all obstruents except /c/, /č/ and /x/, which do not possess voiced cognates. These three obstruents are voiceless unless followed by a voiced obstruent, in which case they are voiced. At the end of the word, however, this is true of all Russian obstruents: they are voiceless, unless the following word begins with a voiced obstruent, in which case they are voiced. E.g. [m'ok 1,i] 'was (he) getting wet?', but [m'og bɨ] 'were (he) getting wet'; [ž'eč 1,i] 'should one burn?', but [ž'eǯ bɨ] 'were one to burn'.
>
> In a phonological representation which satisfies [the biuniqueness condition] the quoted utterances would be symbolized as follows: /m'ok 1,i/, /m'og bi/, /ž'eč 1,i/ /ž'eč bi/. Moreover, a rule would be required stating that obstruents lacking voiced cognates—i.e. /c/ /č/ and /x/—are voiced in position before voiced obstruents. Since this, however, is true of all obstruents, the net effect of [the biuniqueness condition] would be a splitting up of the obstruents into two classes and the addition of a special rule. If [the biuniqueness condition] is dropped, the four utterances would be symbolized as follows: {m'ok 1,i} {m'ok bi} {ž'eč 1,i} {ž'eč bi}, and the above rule could be generalized to cover all obstruents,

instead of only {č} {c} and {x}. It is evident that [the biuniqueness condition] involves a significant increase in the complexity of the representation.

The phonemic analysis which Halle criticizes is the traditional one. He claims that it is a consequence of the biuniqueness condition. If so it would also be a consequence of the distinctiveness principle. The question that must be considered here is whether it really does follow from that principle or whether this is merely an instance of the argument post hoc ergo propter hoc.[15]

If one looks closely at the Russian obstruent clusters from the point of view of the distinctiveness principle, one finds that voicing or lack of it is not a distinctive property of the individual segments. Voicing is present or absent for the whole cluster, except that /v/ can be preceded by a voiceless obstruent, as in *svjet* 'light'. Therefore, to assign voicing or unvoicing to individual segments in a cluster is to violate the principle of distinctiveness. That is, it is uneconomical from the standpoint of C-phonemics. It is assigning phonemic status to phonetic features which in fact are not distinctive. The traditional phonemicization results not from the distinctiveness principle (or from its biuniqueness corollary) but, on the contrary, from a failure fully to apply that principle.

This situation may be compared with one in which, for some language, there are vowel clusters and contrastive pitch. Any vowel cluster, let us say, has either high pitch or low pitch, for the whole cluster. How does the C-phonemicist analyze this situation? He does not set up two sets of vowel phonemes, i.e. one set of high-pitched vowels and one of low-pitched vowels. Instead he sets up just one set of vowels and separates pitch from them. In the typical situation of this type (if not in all of them) one of the pitch levels will be in some sense neutral or unmarked by comparison with the other. Suppose, for example, that the high pitch is accompanied by stress and occurs only once per word while low pitched vowels occur in all other syllables. The analyst would set up one accent phoneme, represented phonetically by high pitch plus stress on the entire vowel cluster with which it occurs. Low pitch, in other words, is taken as the neutral condition. Notice what he does not do: (1) he does not set up two sets of vowels, one with high pitch, the other with low; (2) he does not have two accent phonemes, since only one is necessary; (3) he does not say that the accent phoneme occurs separately with each vowel phoneme in a vowel cluster, but only once per cluster.

Similarly, in the case of the Russian obstruents, we observe that: (1) voicing is not distinctive for the individual segments in an obstruent cluster;[16] (2) (as indicated by morphophonemic alternations) the voicing of the whole cluster is determined by its last member, or by the next to last if the last is [v]; (3) the voiced non-obstruents, for which there is no contrast of voicing, the normal condition is voiced.[17] Therefore, the solution is to set up a phoneme of 'devoicing', whose phonetic applicability extends from the beginning of an obstruent cluster to the point of its occurrence; that is, the devoicing phoneme is to be written at the end of the sequence which its phonetic realization accompanies. It may be symbolized as /h/.

Neither voice nor lack of it is to be assigned to individual segments. The voiced condition is the normal one, a determined feature automatically present when the speech mechanism is in operation, unless it is turned off by the devoicing phoneme, which has effect for a whole cluster rather than a single segment.

In the example concerning vowels, the corresponding statement would be that neither low pitch nor high pitch is to be assigned to individual segments, but rather that low pitch is the normal condition automatically present where vowels and other resonants occur, unless the high pitch phoneme is present, and this phoneme applies to a whole vowel cluster.

The general principle involved here relates quite closely to the statements above concerning the expression side of a communication system. An expression system must have a physical medium in which information can be encoded, in terms of consistent divergences from uniformity. It is helpful to distinguish not just two but three aspects of the physical or 'etic' side of the expression system: (1) the distinctive differences, (2) the nondistinctive differences which accompany them, and (3) the background features or automatically present features of the physical medium. Naturally, just as the C-phonemicist does not set up structural elements on the 'emic' level for the nondistinctive differences, so also he should refrain from setting up elements to account for the features of the medium. Instead, these features may be accounted for by the very fact that the medium is there. The medium, since it is the medium, cannot express meaning and is therefore nondistinctive; rather, meaning is expressed by things done to the medium. In the case of the marked cards, if the information is expressed by divergences in the spokes of wheels in the design, then the wheels and their normal spokes do not require structural elements on the 'emic' stratum. In the case of printing on paper, one does not have to set up any graphemes for the paper. If one describes the realization of the grapheme G/o/ as a closed circle (where the closure is distinctive because of the contrast with G/c/) then one does not also need an element to account for the white disc inside the circle.

Similarly, some of the sound features present in speech are to be accounted for as features of the medium, automatically present by virtue of the fact that the speech-producing mechanism is in operation; and the structural elements of the phonemic level represent various types of diversity put into this medium. Since Russian has a contrast of voicing only in the obstruents, one may look to the non-obstruents for the normal, background condition; and one finds that presence of voice is the normal condition there. To say that voicing is the positive structural feature because it is louder, i.e. physically more positive, is no more cogent than to say that the disc inside the printed G/o/ is positive rather than the enclosing circle, on the grounds that the disc is brighter. For printed expression in general the white brightness is there automatically unless it is masked out by ink; and similarly, for Russian speech, voice is automatically there unless it is counteracted by the devoicing phoneme or by final position.

Thus phonemic analysis may be viewed as part of a process of accounting for articulation. Some of the articulatory features are to be accounted for as normally present when the speech production mechanism is in operation. These can, by the way, be divided into two types: (1) those which are universal for human spoken language; and (2) those which are automatically present when a specific language is being spoken but are not accounted for by (1). Of the remaining articulatory features, some are distinctive, others non-distinctive. Those which are non-distinctive are to be described as automatic accompaniments of distinctive features in various environments. For all those features which cannot be accounted for as any of the above it is necessary to set up phonemic elements. Thus one way to loosely define the set of elements of the phonemic level is to say that they are the entities set up to account, as economically as possible, for the features of the phonetic substance that cannot otherwise be accounted for.

Voicing in Russian is to be accounted for by a general rule (either for Russian or perhaps for human spoken language in general), and it is a condition that can be counteracted by the phonemic devoicing element. Moreover, lack of voicing for an obstruent cluster is accounted for by a single occurrence of the devoicing element. This analysis is consistent with the principles of C-phonemics (in particular, with the biuniqueness condition) but it is more economical than the traditional phonemic analysis of Russian obstruents. In fact it is more economical simply because the distinctiveness principle has been more thoroughly applied than in the case of the former analysis.

But with this more efficient C-phonemicization, motivated independently of morphophonemic considerations, Halle's argument no longer applies. The 'assimilation' in voicing can be accounted for by a single rule stating that the devoicing morphophoneme is realized phonemically as zero (i.e. has no phonemic realization) whenever it is followed by an obstruent other than /v/. This one rule accounts for the 'assimilation' of voiceless obstruents to following voiced ones, while the 'assimilation' of voiced obstruents to following voiceless ones requires no morphophonemic rule because it is taken care of automatically by the revised phonemicization. Halle's examples would be written according to this analysis as follows (first in morphophonemic transcription, then in phonemic): M/m'ogh l,i/, M/m'ogh bi/, M/ž'ežh l,i/, M/ž'ežh bi/; and P/m'ogh l,i/, P/m'og bi/, P/ž'ežh l,i/, P/ž'ež/ bi/. What is unusual about the three obstruents in question, according to the new analysis, is that they have a limited distribution. They occur only followed by /h/ or by obstruents; other obstruents occur also before resonants.

Thus the inefficiency which Halle correctly finds in the traditional phonemic analysis of Russian has nothing to do with biuniqueness. It is the result not of a basic defect in the C-phonemic principles, but of an incomplete and therefore inadequate separation of the nondistinctive features from the distinctive ones. It is therefore hard to understand why Chomsky responded to this argument[18] by asserting that my position agrees with Halle's (Chomsky:1966:80–82)! Evidently it is necessary to point out that there is a difference between (1) rejecting a specific analysis for a particular language and (2) rejecting a general principle of phonological analysis.

Although the foregoing pages defend the distinctiveness principle of C-phonemics, they are not to be taken as asserting that C-phonemics is altogether acceptable, for it is not. While the biuniqueness principle is not one of them, there do exist weaknesses in C-phonemics, and the system does not prove adequate to handle the problems posed below.

Sound Patterns in Language

As indicated above, C-phonemics is vague on some points and variable on others. To certain questions about phonological relationships it has provided no clear answers. The next step is to look at some of these relationships more closely. The orientation at the outset of this examination is provided by C-phonemics, but it will be necessary to go beyond that formulation, to replace its vaguenesses with precision, and to introduce new distinctions where they are needed to provide more economical accounts of phonological phenomena.

It is appropriate to begin with the four generally recognized types of phonological patterning listed at the beginning of this paper. My aim is to identify and describe the relationships involved (rather than the objects which are manifestations of them or rewrite rules which generate such manifestations) as accurately and simply as possible. In doing so it is helpful, if not essential, to employ some system of precise notation. A graphic notation is used here.

1. UNITS. The morphemes of a language are not altogether different from one another with regard to their expression (or phonological realization), but have recurrent partial similarities. In other words, they are, in general, phonologically complex. Moreover, the number of phonological units which occur as their components is in every language smaller than the number of morphemes. This configuration of relationships may be called a sign pattern. The example involving the morphemes *end, Ned, den, and, Dan, d, n, Ed, Nan,* and *Dad* is diagrammed in Figure 1.

Diagrams of this type are made up of lines and nodes. The sole function of the lines is to show connections between nodes (except in the special cases at the boundaries of linguistic structure, where a line connects a node to something outside the structure). Thus the length or curvature of a line is of no significance. The diagrams have two directions: upward (toward meaning) and downward (toward expression). In Figure 1 there are two types of nodes. The triangular ones show a left to right ordering of the lines connecting at the lower side, depicting the ordering of phonological elements within (the representation of) a morpheme.

Figure 1

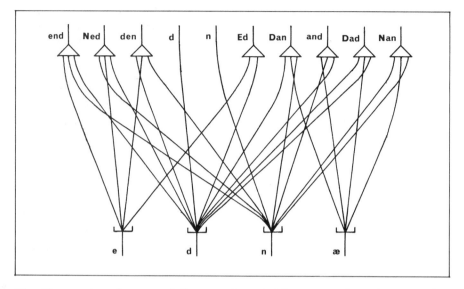

The lines going downward from *end* go to the same three lower nodes as those from *Ned,* but the order is different. On the upper side of each triangular node is a single line, corresponding to the morpheme viewed as an elementary unit. The lower side corresponds to the morpheme viewed as a combination of phonological units. Whether one considers the morpheme to be simple or complex is just a matter of terminology; that is, it depends upon what part of the diagram one chooses to apply the label 'morpheme' to. For example, one might choose to apply it to the upper line, to the combination of lower lines, or to the node itself (still further possibilities exist if the diagram is extended upward). Those who consider the morpheme to be a combination of phonological units must nevertheless accept the single line extending upward from the node, since the morpheme is universally recognized as minimal in one sense or another (for example, as a minimal meaningful element or a minimal grammatical element). The labels 'end', 'Ned', etc. in the diagram are merely aids to the reader and are in no way part of the structure. It is, naturally, of no significance whatever that a combination of three letters is used as a label for a single line. What matters is that it is a single line.

Two simple morphemes are shown, *d* and *n* (as in *showed* and *shown*), and since they are treated as phonologically simple, they require no triangular node.

The nodes at the lower part of the diagram are of a different type. Any single occurrence of *e,* as part of the representation of one of the morphemes shown, 'belongs' to only one of them; i.e. to *end,* OR to *Ned* OR to *den,* etc. Accordingly, this type of node may be called an 'or' node. The triangular ones may be called 'and' nodes, since, for example, when *end* occurs, then *e* AND *n* AND *d* occur (together, in that order).

The fact that morphemes tend to be phonologically complex is of course depicted by the multiple lines going downward from the 'and' nodes; and the fact that phonological components are recurrent, as components of multiple morphemes, is shown by the multiple lines leading upward from the 'or' nodes. Note also that the diagram distinguishes *e* as a component of *end* from the general *e* as abstracted from the various forms of which it is a component.

2. ALTERNATION. Phonological units may alternate with other phonological units in representations of morphemes. Figure 2 shows an abstract example of some but not all of the relationships to be identified in this type of phenomenon. It is consistent with C-phonemics in distinguishing alternation involving neutralization from that among units not distinctively different; the latter are below the former.

This diagram introduces a partly new type of node, namely an 'or' node of opposite direction from those in Figure 1. This type may be called a 'downward or', and the other an 'upward or'. The morphophoneme *A* leads DOWNWARD to either phoneme *p* OR to phoneme *q*. The neutralized phoneme *q* leads UPWARD either to morphophoneme *A* OR to *B*.[19] Also present in Figure 2 are lines connecting to small circles, signifying zero. The morphophoneme *C* leads downward either to phoneme *r* or to nothing (i.e. is realized as zero). The phoneme *s* leads upward either to morphophoneme *D* or to nothing (i.e. no morphophoneme); in the latter case it is empty, like the second vowel in *boxes*. The diagram is incomplete in that it fails to show conditioning environments for the alternations and in that it ignores phonotactics and phonemic components. These matters are taken up below.

Figure 2

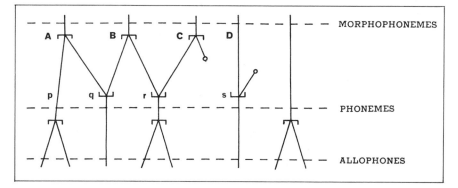

The formulation depicted in Figure 2 is one in which morphophonemes are granted structural status. It thus disagrees with the view which rejects morphophonemes and instead treats all morphophonemic alternation as alternation among allomorphs of morphemes, each allomorph being a combination of phonemes. The graphic notation shows the difference between these two formulations very clearly. The view which treats all morphophonemic alternation as alternation among allomorphs requires a much more complicated diagram than that for the formulation using morphophonemes. Consider, for example, the alternation in Monachi between the phonemes P/m/ and P/w/, described above. The two formulations are diagrammed in Figures 3 and 4 for the morphemes meaning 'go' and 'hand'. With morphophonemes as structural elements there is a single downward 'or' for the alternation; but for the view that denies structural status to morphophonemes there is a separate downward 'or' as well as an additional 'and' node for every morpheme exhibiting this alternation. Moreover, the diagram does not show the further complication that would be required in specifying the conditioning environment. The difference between the two diagrams would of course be greatly magnified if additional morphemes exhibiting the alternation were included.

The objection to morphophonemes seems to have been the erroneous notion that they require process description. This mistake has been made quite commonly by both opponents and supporters of morphophonemic rules. The process or rewriting formulation, which crept into morphophonemic description from diachronic linguistics, would recognize only two elements for the alternation shown in Figure 4, namely P/m/ and P/w/, instead of three (M/m/, P/m/, and P/w/) and would use a rewrite rule which would replace P/m/ by P/w/ in intervocalic position. But Figure 4 portrays a quite different conception of morphophonemic alternation, since the line labelled M/m/ is a different line from either of those labelled P/m/ and P/w/. One must not be misled by the fact that the same letter *m* is used in the label for both M/m/ and P/m/. Labels are chosen for mnemonic convenience and are not part of the structure. There is no replacement of P/m/ by P/w/. Rather, either P/m/ or P/w/ occurs as realization of M/m/.[20] Many of those who have supposed that morphophonemic rules are necessarily process or rewrite rules have at the same time described allophones of phonemes and allomorphs of morphemes without supposing that process is involved in these relationships. But as Figures 2 and 3 show, there is no structural basis for supposing that the situations differ in this way. All involve downward 'or' relationships, in which the line above the 'or' node is a different element from each of those below. (Although the analysis shown in Figure 3 is clearly inefficient for the alternation shown, this type of treatment, i.e. with the downward 'or' above the downward 'and' of the sign pattern, is clearly indicated in some situations, e.g. the alternation of *good* and *bett-*.) That synchronic morphophonemic alternation is quite different from diachronic phonological change (which really is a process) may be seen by comparing Figures 14 and 15 below. Since the structure shown for the Bishop dialect coincides with that of an earlier stage of North Fork, the change from Figure 15 to Figure 14, which involves moving certain lines and nodes, represents the diachronic phonological change in which pre-North Fork *P/m/ *[w̃] between vowels became modern North Fork P/w/. But the synchronic morphophonemic alternation, and likewise the processes of normal production and decoding of speech, involve no changes of lines or nodes.

Figure 3

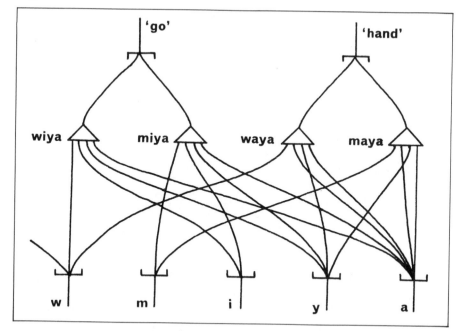

Figure 4

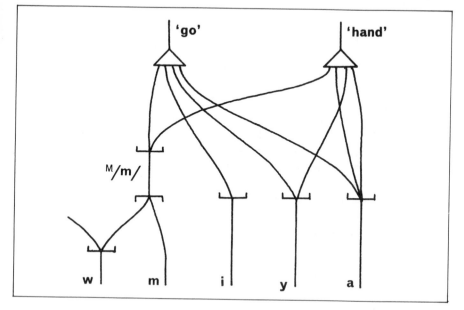

3. TACTICS. Combinations of phonological units conform to definite patterns of arrangement. Figure 5 shows part of the phonotactic pattern of the North Fork dialect of Monachi. The 'and' labelled S is the syllable construction. It leads downward first to a consonant (p, t, ...), then to

a vowel (e, a, . . .), then to either /i/ or /·/ (vowel length) or nothing, then to /h/ or /ʔ/ or /'/ or nothing. (/'/ is realized as length and fortis articulation of the following consonant.) Examples of syllables generated by this tactics are: *pa, teʔ, pu', ta·, ʔai, pe·ʔ, ʔui.*

Figure 5

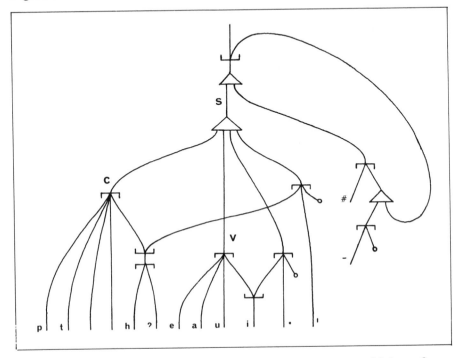

4. COMPONENTS. Phonemes have recurrent components, which are fewer in number than they. This pattern is of the same basic type as that shown in Figure 1 and described above. It differs (other than quantitatively) only in that here the components tend to be simultaneous instead of successive. Thus the lines come down from the same point of each triangular node in Figure 6 rather than in left to right order. The example diagrammed in Figure 6 may be taken as applying to English or to Monachi or to various other languages. The labels for components stand for 'apical', 'closed', 'nasal', and 'labial'.

These phonemic components, or PHONONS for short, are singulary, not binary. Binary features have two values, plus and minus. To specify the presence of a binary feature would require not only identification of the feature but also indication of whether its value is plus or minus. Thus the use of binary features would require the addition of some new ad hoc device to the system of graphic notation, representing an additional type of conceptual equipment needed in a linguistic theory which would use them. Note also that the phonemes in Figure 6 have only two phonons each (some phonemes have three phonons, some only one), whereas with binary features of the type advocated by Chomsky and Halle each segment has some eleven features after the redundancy rules and about half a dozen before them.

Figure 6

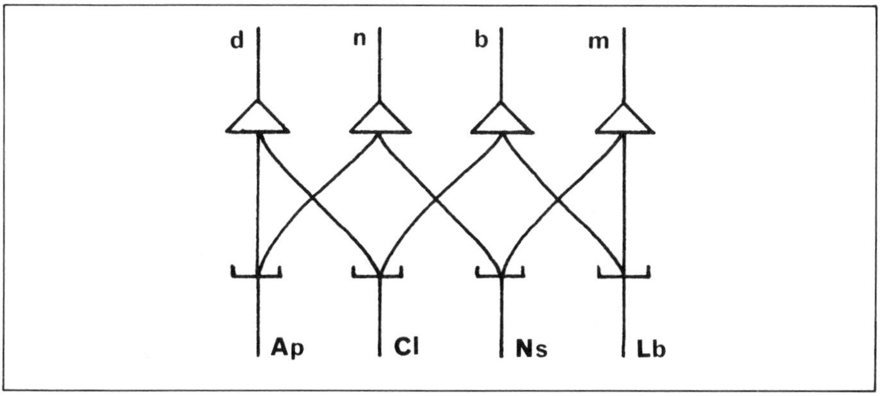

Another question concerning distinctive features is: Why recognize two sign patterns (Figure 1 and Figure 6)? Why not 'divide' morphemes directly into distinctive features, bypassing the phonemes? This is, roughly, the recommendation of Chomsky and Halle, except that they would go even further: not morphemes but lexical items (many of which, in any language, are morphemically complex) are to be represented in the dictionary by binary distinctive feature matrices.[21]

As in the alternative treatment for morphophonemic alternation discussed above with reference to Figures 3 and 4, it is the criterion of simplicity (or, equivalently, of economy, parsimony, or generalization) which provides the answer to this question. This criterion, in its proper use, is based upon considerations which are not specific to linguistics but are generally applicable (and are continually applied subconsciously) to scientific work.

Suppose that there are two descriptions or parts of descriptions (of anything at all) which are equivalent in effective information, i.e. in the data (real or abstract) which they account for, and which differ only in that the first states a certain relationship repeatedly, i.e. two or more times for separate entities exhibiting it, while the second, by abstracting the relationship, states it only once. Then the second is to be preferred. It describes the same effective information with less surface information, since it states the relationship only once instead of repeatedly. At the same time the statement of that relationship is more general in that it accounts once for information stated repeatedly in the first description. That is, the second description is simpler because it contains a generalization absent from the first. Generalization and simplicity are two aspects of the same property. One might almost say that the second description is closer to the truth than the first, since the first describes the relationship as if it were several different relationships rather than one, i.e. in a way that would be appropriate if they were different.

For the sake of precision the simplicity principle may be implemented concretely for any of various systems of notation. Its implementation for an algebraic notation has been discussed in a preliminary way elsewhere.[22] Here the implementation for graphic notation may be considered.[23] The two graphs shown in Figure 7 are identical in effective information. The set of all possible combinations of entities to which X leads at the bottom is the same for both: *ab, ac, ad.*

Figure 7

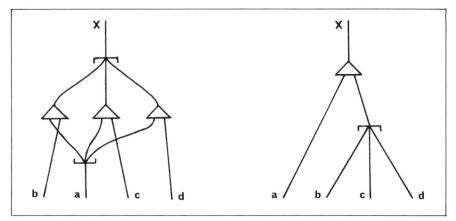

The first says 'X leads down to *ab* or *ac* or *ad.*' The second says 'X leads down to *a* and (*b* or *c* or *d*).' The description at right states this effective information with less surface information: It uses only six lines, while the one at left uses eleven.[24] The description at right includes a generalization absent from the first, namely that every combination has the same first member, *a*. The description at the right has stated the occurrence of *a* only once, while that at the left has stated it three separate times. The one line for *a* at the right is doing the work of four lines at the left, and the 'and' node at right is doing the work of three 'ands' at left. In the left hand description, the occurrence of *a* in the three combinations is stated in a way that would be appropriate if it were three separate entities. Thus this description is perhaps to be regarded as not actually revealing the whole truth about the situation. These considerations are of course quite independent of the kind of phenomena which the diagram may be describing. A configuration of the type shown could appear in a tactic pattern at any stratum of a language, but it could also appear in systems other than natural languages. The implementation of the simplicity principle for this notation is applicable to the description of any phenomena to which notation of this type is appropriate.

Figures 3 and 4 are equal in effective information but Figure 3 has twenty-eight lines while Figure 4 has only eighteen. This difference is easily correlated with generalizations in Figure 4 which Figure 3 lacks; that is, with repetitions in Figure 3 of information stated once in Figure 4. Thus for the morpheme 'go' Figure 3 says two separate times that the last three segments are *iya*.

Figure 8 illustrates the proposal that morphemes be described as leading directly to phonons in a single sign pattern. It uses 56 lines. Figure 9, using two sign patterns, has the same effective information, but only 40 lines. The difference between 40 and 56 may not seem great, but the eight lines at the top and the six at the bottom correspond exactly in the two descriptions. Subtracting this constant gives a comparison for the different part: 42 lines as opposed to 26. As with Figures 3 and 4, the difference grows greater as more morphemes are added to the description. The difference in surface information is of course directly related to generalizations in Figure 9 which are absent from Figure 8. In fact each upward 'or' represents a generalization, since it brings together several lines from above and allows their downward componency to be stated once instead of repeatedly. That is, the value of the phoneme-sized unit is precisely that it represents a generalization missing from the description which fails to recognize it. In the formulation of Figure 8, the componency of a given segment is stated separately for each morpheme of which it is a part, instead of once. (Needless to say, if binary distinctive features were used instead of phonons the amount of excess surface information would be even greater.)

Figure 8

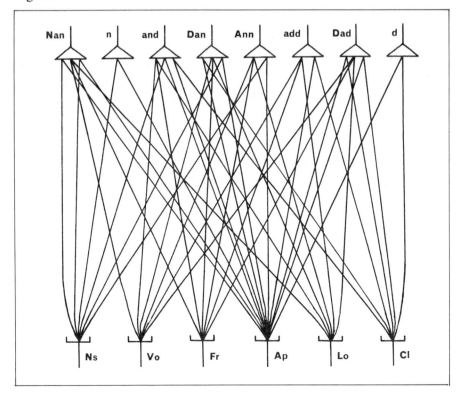

Figure 9

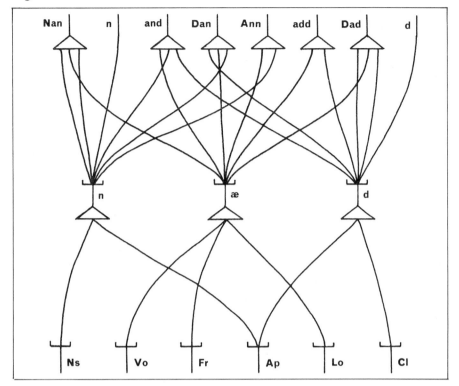

Actually, the proposal of Chomsky and Halle is even more extravagant than the foregoing comparison reveals, for they recommend that lexical items (rather than morphemes) be given in the dictionary as distinctive feature matrices. That is, they propose to use a single sign pattern in place of three (phonemic, morphemic, and lexemic), not just two. Lexemes like *woodpecker, tightwad, crawfish, understand, New York,* etc. are to be directly provided with distinctive feature matrices. Thus if *pro-* is a component of 100 lexemes (e.g. *propose, produce, proclaim, profess*) then the column of distinctive features for *p* is to be given 100 separate times solely for *p* as a component of *pro-*, i.e. apart from *p* as component of *pre-, per-, -pose,* etc.

A System of Descriptive Phonology

Three types of phonological pattern have been identified above: the sign pattern, the alternation pattern, and the tactic pattern. The next problem is to determine how these patterns are related to one another, how they fit together to form a phonological system as a whole. In terms of the graphic notation, this is a question of how the diagrams of the patterns are to be connected to one another.

Two of the above figures show connections of one pattern directly to another of the same type without any intermediate relationships. In Figure

2 the morphophonemic alternation pattern leads directly to an allophonic alternation pattern, and Figure 9 shows the morphemic sign pattern connecting directly to the phonemic sign pattern. It thus omits the distinction between morphophonemes and phonemes. It is evident that the proper position of the morphophonemic alternation pattern is between the morphemic sign pattern and the phonemic sign pattern, as suggested by Figure 4. (The specific example depicted in Figure 4, however, requires refinement in another way, as indicated below.)

The integration of patterns arrived at so far, then, is the one depicted in Figure 10. A new type of node is introduced in this figure, namely the downward ordered 'or'. Ordering in an 'or' node means that the left branch takes precedence over the right one when it is possible to take either. This type of ordering in the graphic notation corresponds to ordering of subrules of realization rules in algebraic notation.[25]

Figure 10

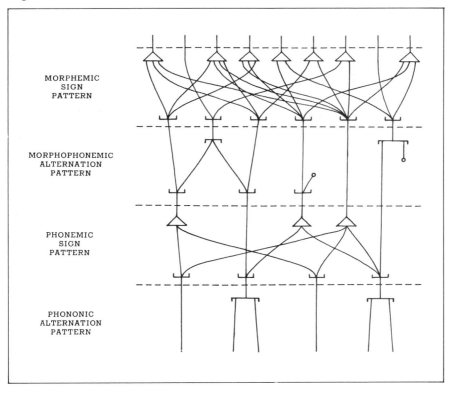

A problem left unsolved by the scheme of Figure 10 is that it appears not to take account of the fact that some (but by no means all) cases of morphophonemic alternation are more simply describable in terms of components than segments. The figure also fails to show (1) how conditioning environments relate to the alternations and (2) tactics.

It has commonly been assumed that phonemes are the ultimate constituents of phonotactics. For this conception, the lines at the bottom of a tactic pattern (cf. Figure 5) would be phonemes. But the lines at the top of the phonemic sign pattern and the bottom of the morphophonemic alternation pattern are also phonemes. There is, however, no conflict here: a phoneme has both a tactic function (according to the common assumption) AND a connection upward to one or more morphophonemes. Thus for each phoneme there must be an upward 'and' node, as shown in Figure 11.

On the other hand, it has been suggested, e.g. Hockett 1955, that the ultimate constituents of the phonotactics are the phonemic components. For this view the row of upward 'ands' would fit in below the phonemic sign pattern. Perhaps also to be considered is the possibility that the connections to tactics belong at the top of the morphophonemic alternation pattern, i.e. that morphophonemes are the ultimate constituents.

The way to answer such a question is not to speculate but to refer to linguistic data and to determine which conception reveals the tactic patterning most elegantly.

Figure 11

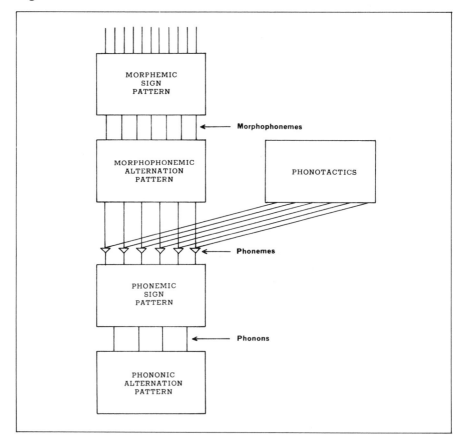

Figure 5 above shows a very neat picture of syllable structure. It has one drawback, however, if it is taken to be a tactics of C-phonemes; although it is tantalizingly close, it does not accurately fit the data. Moreover, there is no simple way to adjust it so that it will agree with the data. There are certain clearly specifiable, hence regular and structurally relevant, discrepancies from what the tactic pattern generates; yet it cannot readily be adjusted to take account of them, since they involve restrictions on what can occur at or across syllable boundaries. For example, a syllable with initial P/m/ never occurs after a syllable with a final vowel. But this fact correlates with the alternation discussed above, between P/m/ and P/w/. The realization rule for this alternation states that the alternant P/w/ occurs after vowel, P/m/ elsewhere. Now it happens that there is also a morphophonemic alternation corresponding to each of the other cooccurrence restrictions. For each of the sequences which does not occur, there is something else which occurs instead. In the (incomplete) list below, the non-occurring sequences are at left, and at the right of each is shown the sequence which occurs where the one at the left would be expected. (V stands for vowel, B for obstruent.)

(1) Vm	Vw
(2) ?B, hB	'B
(3) hm, hn	'm, 'n
(4) '#	#[26]
(5) Vs, Vx	V's, V'x
(6) hh, ?h, 'h	h
(7) h?, ??, '?	?
(8) 'y	't
(9) 'w	'k^w

Two closely related facts are crucial here: (1) the description of the tactic pattern would be greatly complicated by including specification of these restrictions; (2) such specification would be redundant anyway, since it is already given by the description of the morphophonemic alternations.

Thus it appears that the phonotactics is really the tactics of the morphophonemes and that the simplest way to account for the occurring combinations of phonemes is to describe the tactics of the morphophonemes and the morphophonemic alternations.

In English there is evidence pointing in the same direction. Syllable-initial consonant clusters ending in P/y/ occur only when P/uw/ follows, e.g. *Cupid, punitive, music.* This circumstance presents a problem in phonotactics as applied to phonemes, since it involves a cooccurrence restriction across a tactic boundary (i.e. the boundary between consonant cluster and vocalic nucleus). But the problem disappears if the phonotactics is taken as applying to morphophonemes, since P/yuw/ is the realization of morphophonemic M/u:/, a vocalic entity (cf. the morphophonemic alternation in *punitive, punish.*

It turns out, however, that an attempt to apply a simple tactics of syllable structure to combinations of morphophonemes encounters complications just as serious as those described above, if by morphophoneme is meant an element at the bottom of the morphemic sign pattern, i.e. a downward component of a morpheme. The term morphophoneme has not always been used for just these entities,[27] however, so it will enhance precision if we use from here on a term defined to have specifically that meaning. Just as the downward component of a phoneme may be called a phonon, so the downward component of a morpheme may be called a morphon.[28] Then we can say that the simply statable tactic pattern fails to fit morphon combinations (just as it fails to fit phoneme combinations). In this case also, however, the discrepancies between the actual combinations of Monachi morphons and the simple tactics of Figure 5 are all related to morphophonemic alternation. Some examples are presented below. At the left are shown some sequences of morphons (with spaces at morpheme boundaries) and at the right the phonemic combinations which occur as their realizations. (C stands for consonant, V for vowel, B for obstruent, R for resonant.)[29]

(10) VBV <?, V'BV <?   V'BV
(11) VRV <?, V'BV <?   V?RV
(12) Ca <i   Ci
(13) #'C   #C
(14) ' 'C   'C

There are also various morphophonemes of the type conventionally called 'special morphophonemes' and written with capital letters. Thus M/N/ is realized as P/n/ in some environments, as zero in others; it contrasts (at this level) with M/n/, which is realized as P/n/ in all environments.

This situation differs from the preceding one in one significant respect: here it is the sequences in the right hand column, i.e. the realizations, which fit the syllable structure tactics, whereas in examples (1) to (9) it is those at the left, i.e. the realizates.[30]

Similarly in English the morphonic representations of words like *boxes* and *waited* do not fit the syllable structure tactics, since they lack the (empty) vowel of the second syllable. Note also that the presence of the vowel in the phonemic representation seems to be somehow determined by the tactics.

It appears, then, that the tactic pattern of syllable structure, if it is to be economically describable, applies neither to phonemes nor to morphons as the ultimate constituents, but to elements intermediate between them; i.e. to elements which are realizations of morphons and realizates of phonemes. In other words, there seem to be two separate alternation patterns between morphons and phonemes, and the syllable structure tactics fits between them. These intermediate units to which the tactics applies may be called BASIC PHONEMES for the time being.

Moreover it turns out that this separation of morphophonemic alternations into two types corresponds remarkably well to a differently motivated separation hinted at above: some morphophonemic alternations are more easily described in terms of components than segments, while others are more easily described in terms of segments. In particular, the alternations involved in (1) through (9) are economically describable in terms of components and those of (10) through (14) are not. Thus it is apparent that a sign pattern intervenes between the two alternation patterns.

It must also be observed that there are definite tactic patterns involving phonological components as ultimate constituents. Conventional displays of phonemic inventories in charts are not only implicit analyses of C-phonemes into components, as mentioned above; they are also implicit descriptions of some features of the tactic patterning of such components. Thus in various languages the different positions of articulation recognized in such charts are mutually exclusive, hence members of the same distribution class. On the other hand, in some African languages, the features labial, velar, and closed are permitted to cooccur. That is, such a combination is well formed according to the feature tactics of some languages, ill formed according to that of others. Consider also the P/y/ of English consonant clusters, discussed above. At the level of the syllable structure tactics it is not present, since BP/u:/ is present instead; yet it fits neatly into the tactic pattern of English initial consonant clusters, along with P/w/, P/r/, and P/l/. The tactics of phonemic components, then, seems to be concerned primarily with the structure of clusters, including simple clusters, i.e. segments.

In Monachi the feature tactics imposes strict limitations upon what consonant clusters can occur; the permissible clusters are P/'/ plus obstruent or nasal, P/?/ plus resonant, P/h/ plus semivowel, and P/nt/ in a few Spanish loan words. These clusters are fewer than the clusters of basic phonemes, and the differences are accounted for by alternations (2), (3), and (5) to (9) of the lower morphophonemic alternation pattern. That is, there is a simpler cluster structure at the C-phonemic level than at the level of the basic phonemes. Moreover, in each of the clusters the two members belong to separate syllables; i.e. the tactic boundaries of the cluster structure do not correspond to those of the syllable structure. This type of discrepancy between different tactic patterns of the same language is also observed at higher strata.

In Russian the tactic pattern at this level specifies that an obstruent cluster may optionally have a single occurrence of the devoicing element.

Thus the picture which emerges is one of two alternation patterns and, quite closely related to them, two separate tactic patterns, as shown in Figure 12. The row of upward 'ands' at the bottom of the lower alternation pattern corresponds to the C-phonemic level. But the C-phoneme is not present as a structural element. Rather, it is a combination of elements. The structural elements of this stratum are phonon-sized, not phoneme-sized. This refined view of the C-phonemic stratum was in part anticipated by the version of C-phonemics presented in Hockett 1955, discussed above.

A question left in abeyance above is the relationship of alternations to conditioning environments. What must be added to the diagrams as developed so far to make them include the specification of conditioning environments? The answer is: nothing! The conditioning environments are already specified

Figure 12

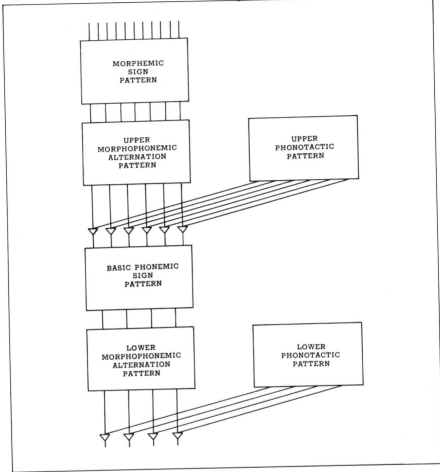

in the tactic pattern associated with each alternation pattern. As noted above, the realizations of the upper alternation pattern fit the upper tactics, while the realizates do not; and the same is true for the lower tactics. In other words, it is conditions within the tactic structure which control the alternation (except in the case of free variation). Of a given pair of alternants, the one which occurs in a given combination is that which fits the tactic pattern. If both fit the tactic pattern, then the occurrence of one of them is specified by ordering in the downward 'or' from which they lead; if this 'or' is unordered, there is free variation.[31]

An example for the upper morphophonemic alternation pattern and upper phonotactics of North Fork Monachi is shown in Figure 13. This is the alternation, noted above as (13) and (14), between BP/'/ and zero as realizations of M/'/. The alternant BP/'/ appears after vowels, i.e. in syllable final position, but initially in words M/'/ has no realization, and when there are two successive occurrences of M/' / only one token of BP/'/ occurs. Thus

M/nohi 'muuʔa'ci/ BP/nohi'mu:ʔa'ci/ 'a very long time ago'; but M/#'muu ʔa'ci/ BP/#mu:ʔa'ci/ 'a long time ago'. Figure 13 shows part of the same tactic pattern illustrated in Figure 5. This pattern allows BP/'/ to occur only in syllable final position, and there only once (per syllable). If there is an occurrence of M/'/ when the tactics is at that position, BP/'/ will occur, since the path from the left side of the ordered 'or' takes precedence. Under any other circumstance this path is blocked by the upward 'and', and the path at right, leading to nothing, must be taken.

Figure 13

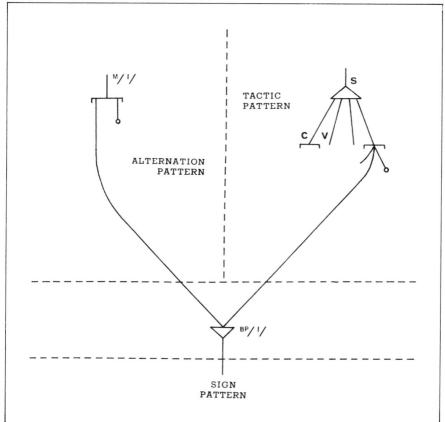

An example for the lower alternation pattern is shown in Figure 14. This is the alternation of C-phonemic CP/m/ (labial and nasal) and CP/w/ (labial) as realizations of BP/m/. More precisely (since this alternation is below the basic phonemic sign pattern) it is an alternation of CP/Ns/ (nasal) with zero as realizations of BP/Ns/. The portion of the tactic pattern shown in the figure accounts for all resonants and resonant clusters except CP/hw/, CP/hy/, CP/'m/, and CP/'n/, which are not essential to the example. It accommodates CP/Ns/ in the combinations CP/#m/, CP/#n/, CP/ʔm/, CP and CP/ʔn/ (intervocalic); but it does not provide for the occurrence of CP/Ns/ together with CP/Lb/

except when CP/#/ or CP/ʔ/ precedes. When BP/m/ occurs after a vowel, CP/Ns/ cannot be accommodated; in this environment the tactic pattern allows CP/Ns/ only in combination with CP/Ap/. It allows CP/Lb/, but for BP/Ns/ the path leading to nothing must be taken since the preferred path is blocked by the upward 'and'. Thus CP/w/ appears as the realization of BP/m/.

Figure 14. The Alternation of [m] and [w] in North Fork.

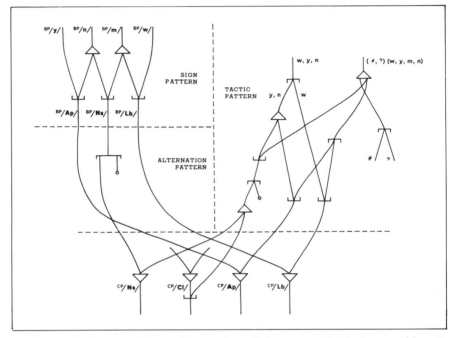

Figure 14 also provides an illustration of the next point to be considered. The tactic pattern at this level can account very simply for non-distinctive features. The component Cl (closed) is determined when Ns occurs (in North Fork, but not in Bishop) as shown by the downward 'and' at the lower left corner of the tactic pattern. The line for this Cl goes down to an upward 'or' below the row of upward 'ands'; i.e. it does not lead down to an upward 'and' like the other lines going down from the tactic pattern. The others have upward 'ands' simply because for each of them there is a connection to the next higher stratum. In other words, they are capable of distinguishing meaning, i.e. distinctive. But the occurrence of Cl with Ns is determined and therefore cannot carry any information. In this connection it is important to observe that the analysis shown is motivated purely by considerations of economy, not by the distinctiveness principle as an independent criterion. If this feature were treated like the others, i.e. if a line were to lead up through the alternation pattern for Cl as a partner of Ns, then it would be necessary to add two additional lines to the sign pattern, since BP/m/ and BP/n/ would each now have BP/Cl/ as an additional component.

As noted above, the Bishop dialect of Monachi has an alternation which is quite similar in some ways. In both dialects there is absence of closure for the intervocalic alternant, and the conditioning environment is the same. But the intervocalic alternant in Bishop contrasts with [w] because it is nasalized, while in North Fork there is neutralization with [w]. This difference, unimportant to Chomsky and Halle, is crucial to the C-phonemicist, who insists that the alternation in North Fork must be distinguished as morphophonemic, while that in Bishop is subphonemic. Why? The structural difference may be seen by comparing Figure 14 with Figure 15, which shows the situation in Bishop. Since Ns is present in both [m] and [w̃] there is no 'or' in the Bishop alternation pattern corresponding to that for North Fork. Instead, Bishop has, for Ns, an upward 'or' within the tactics. Bishop's tactic pattern allows Ns to occur without Cl in one construction; in the other it is accompanied by the nondistinctive Cl. At the C-phonemic level, i.e. at the level of the upward 'ands', BP/m/ always has the same realization, unlike the cognate in North Fork.

Figure 15. The Alternation of [m] and [w̃] in Bishop.

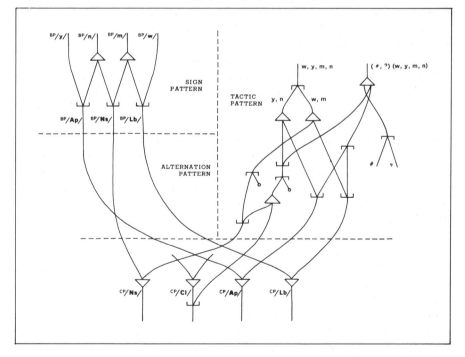

Another comparison may be made with the hypothetical dialect in which the intervocalic alternant is phonetically identical to that of North Fork but in which there is no neutralization, since there is no [w] contrasting with [m]. In all other respects the hypothetical dialect may be taken as identical to North Fork, so that the only difference is whether or not the alternation involves neutralization, a difference which is either important or inconsequential depending upon one's point of view with regard to biuniqueness. The hypothetical dialect is described by three alternative graphs in Figure 16. In the first, the tactic pattern differs from that of North Fork only in accordance with the different facts of the situation; to wit, occurrence of w after # or ʔ is ruled out. But the sign and alternation patterns are the same as for North Fork. This graph, however, has excess surface information. Unlike the North Fork graph, it can be simplified. The two circled nodes of the first graph may be replaced by a single upward 'or', circled in the second graph, and the sign pattern is thus simplified by the removal of two lines. This step is possible without loss of effective information precisely because there is no neutralization; Lb of this dialect, unlike that of North Fork, occurs alone only as realization of ^{BP}/m/. Therefore the additional component ^{BP}/Ns/ is not needed for distinguishing ^{BP}/m/ from other basic phonemes, so the line from ^{BP}/m/ to ^{BP}/Ns/ may be eliminated, and with it the downward 'and'. The label ^{BP}/m/ for this dialect can appropriately be changed to ^{BP}/w/, but this is of course only a change of label. In the second graph the two upward 'ors' above the upward 'and' for Ns can be replaced by a single 'or' below the 'and', resulting in the third graph. This graph shows Ns (along with Cl) as a determined feature when in combination with Lb after # or ʔ. This manipulation of lines and nodes amounts to an explication and justification of the well-trained C-phonemicist's observation upon encountering such an alternation, which he regards as obvious and inescapable: that nasality is nondistinctive in this segment, and hence the situation is structurally different from that of North Fork.

The foregoing demonstration indicates that a phonological description (as long as it is accurate) automatically adheres to the distinctiveness principle (hence to the biuniquenes principle) if it is free from excess surface information. The distinctiveness principle, then, is not needed as an independent criterion of acceptability of phonological solutions. The value which it imparts to a description is automatically provided by the simplicity principle. The status of the distinctiveness principle is therefore that of a practical device, a tool which can aid the linguist in arriving at the simplest possible description of a phonological system.

I remarked above in the discussion of distinctiveness that information can be expressed only by things done to a medium which allows diversity and that, generally, some of the diversity in expression is nondistinctive, i.e. determined by the medium, while the rest is of communicative significance, i.e. distinctive. It is only by allowing nondetermined divergence that a medium of expression can be communicative. Any tactic pattern is such a medium, in particular the lower phonotactic pattern, with which the classical problem of phonemic analysis was centrally concerned. Whenever a tactic pattern has a downward 'or' it is providing for nondetermined diversity. A downward 'or' allows a choice: any of the possibilities is permitted, but none is determined, and so the choice of one as opposed to another can be of communicative significance. In a properly constructed diagram, the paths coming down from an 'or' lead, either directly or indirectly, to

Figure 16. The Alternation of [m] and [w] in the Hypothetical Dialect.

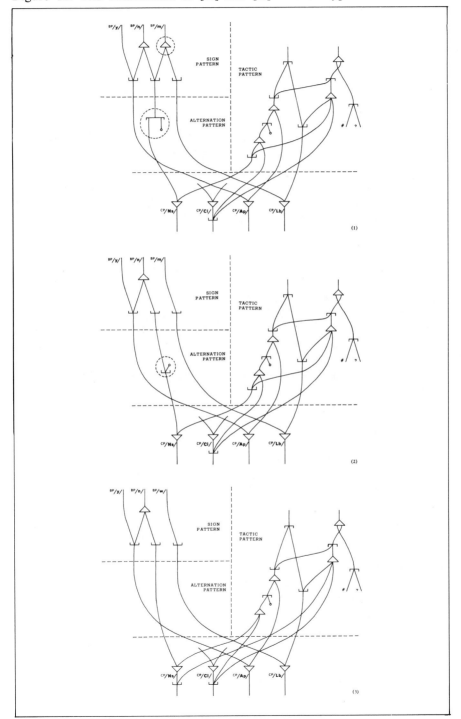

the upward 'ands' below the tactic pattern. The path chosen at the 'or' depends upon which upward 'and' is not blocked, and that depends upon which of the lines leading down from the alternation pattern is 'active'. Occurrence of a linguistic element corresponds to 'activation' of the line or node representing that element in a graph. That is, each line and node represents a type, and any instance of activation of it represents a token (i.e. occurrence) of that type. An upward 'and' node (since it is an 'and', not an 'or) can be activated from above only if both (or all three, etc.) lines leading down to it are active. Hence one of the distinctive elements of the C-phonemic level can occur only when it is 'called for' by both the tactics and the line leading down from the higher stratum. Thus choices, when allowed by the tactics, are made by the higher stratum. In Bishop (Figure 15) when Lb occurs in the tactics (in either tactic environment) it may optionally be accompanied by Ns (note the downward 'or' with one line leading to nothing, the other to CP/Ns/). It will be accompanied by Ns if (and only if) BP/Ns/ is present.

The lines leading upward into the alternation pattern from the upward 'ands' represent the possibilities of 'doing things to the medium'; each one can determine a choice at one or more points at which the tactics has a downward 'or'; hence each represents the possibility of having some communicative significance. Some features, on the other hand, are determined by the tactics. They are properties of the medium and cannot have communicative significance; they do not lead down to upward 'ands', but go on past them.

Just as lines coming down from the alternation pattern control the selection of alternatives in the tactics, so the lines coming down from the tactic pattern control the selection of alternatives in the alternation pattern. This is how environmental conditioning operates.

These considerations apply at every stratum. Choices in the lower tactics are controlled by (lines coming down from) the basic phonemic system. But that system's operation is controlled by the morphemic system, which also has a tactics, one which allows choices to be made by the lexemic system; and so forth.

On redefining the phoneme

The foregoing considerations lead to a conception of phonological structure somewhat different from earlier ones. C-phonemics recognized a phonemic level. Chomsky and Halle put forth the alternative view that there is no structural level between their types of morphophonemic and phonetic levels.[32] But the present investigation finds not only that the C-phonemic level has a sound structural basis after all, but also that there is another level not previously distinguished as a separate entity—that referred to above as the basic phonemic. In one sense the present recognition of the basic phonemic level is not new, since various of its properties have long been recognized. Its 'eme' is the same size as the C-phoneme, its tactics is that of syllable structure; some of its properties have been ascribed to previously recognized morphophonemic levels, which in other respects are higher than it. In short, it has been conflated both with lower levels (primarily by C-phonemicists) and with higher levels (by Chomsky, Halle, myself, and many others). What is new in this study is the separation of this level from the others.

In particular, the present findings split the C-phonemic level into two distinct phonemic levels. What happens to the C-phoneme in this process? It corresponds in size to the basic phoneme, i.e. the 'eme' of the upper phonemic level. But its realizational level is that of the lower one. The C-phoneme turns out not to be a structural element, but a sort of compromise which, as it were, helped to hide the distinction between these two levels from the eyes of phonological theorists; it is a unit on the lower phonemic stratum whose size is that of the basic phoneme. It is a combination of elements of the lower stratum and a realization of the 'eme' of the upper one.

These findings present a terminological problem. What names shall be applied to the entities resulting from the distinctions that have been drawn? In such a situation one may either use an old term in a new meaning or invent a new term. Either choice inevitably draws criticism. Indeed there are those who would like to do away with terminology altogether; unfortunately they have not yet discovered a means of enabling people to communicate without it. Perhaps it is particularly foolhardy to tamper with a term so fraught with emotion as 'phoneme'. One who dares to do such a thing is sure to have his sanity questioned, perhaps even his morals. But the alternative is even worse: to leave the term phoneme in its no longer important C-phonemic meaning and thus to be forced to invent a set of new terms for the two phonological strata.

If one is to redefine the phoneme one may either retain its size and move it up one stratum or retain its realizational level and apply it to those elements which used to be called its components. The former alternative is perhaps the less unsettling, and it leaves fewer problems of finding terms for the other entities to be named. I therefore offer the suggestion that the basic phoneme be called simply the PHONEME. Then the basic phonon, its downward component, may be called the PHONON. A simple means is thus provided for naming the lower phonemic stratum, for it can be called the HYPOPHONEMIC. Its 'eme' (the phonemic component of C-phonemics) is thus the HYPOPHONEME.

It is convenient to identify the 'emes' of a stratal system as the upward 'ands' which lead upward to the tactic and alternation patterns and downward to the sign pattern. The 'ons' are the upward 'ors' at the bottom of the sign pattern or, equivalently, the lines leading down from these 'ors' to the next lower alternation pattern. The alternation pattern between the morphons and the (basic) phonemes (i.e. the upper morphophonemic alternation pattern in Figure 12) may be called the MORPHONIC ALTERNATION

PATTERN; and the 'lower morphophonemic alternation pattern', i.e. that between the (basic) phonons and the hypophonemes, may be called the PHONONIC ALTERNATION PATTERN.

Figure 12 fails to show an important relationship that is found above sign patterns. The 'emes' of a stratal system are not generally in a one to one correspondence with the lines at the top of the sign pattern, since upward 'ors' often intervene; i.e. lines from the upward 'ands' often go down to upward 'ors', as does the line going down from hypophonemic H/Cl/ in Figure 15. In that instance the other line going into the 'or' is a nondistinctive feature, and this type of relationship is evidently to be found at all strata. There are also instances in which two or more 'emes' (i.e. upward 'ands') lead downward to an upward 'or', hence to the same line of the sign pattern. For example, the English morphemes M/well₁/ as in *well, I guess so* and M/well₂/ as in *they dug a deep well* are separate morphemes since they lead upward to different lexemes and to different morphotactic categories; but they lead downward to the same combination of morphons. Thus they meet in an upward 'or' just above the sign pattern. The lines at the top of the morphemic sign pattern may be distinguished from the morphemes by being called MORPHEMIC SIGNS. Thus M/well₁/ and M/well₂/ are different morphemes, but they correspond to the same morphemic sign M/wel/.

Below the hypophonemes there appears not to be a sign pattern, at least not one of the same simple type as those found at higher strata. There is, however, a need to distinguish hypophonemes from the lines below the upward 'ors' into which they lead (e.g. *Cl* in Figure 15); and it is easy to do so by calling the latter HYPOPHONEMIC SIGNS. This is of course the distinction which the C-phonemicist prizes most highly, the boundary between C-phonemic and C-phonetic. The hypophonemic sign *Cl* leads upward either to the hypophoneme H/Cl/ or directly to the hypophonotactics. In the latter case (i.e. when it is occurring with *Ns*) it is nondistinctive.

The subphonemic or allophonic alternation of C-phonemics covers two separate areas: (1) the difference between hypophonemes and hypophonemic signs (e.g. [m] and [w] as C-allophones of CP/m/ in Bishop), (2) variation below the level of the hypophonemic signs. Both types of information are of course important in a phonological description, but as the two areas are structurally different, their descriptions should be separated.

Below the hypophonemic signs it is likely, but not certain, that the type of structure to be dealt with differs from that above; i.e. it appears that the regular succession of pattern types found from hypophonemic signs upward does not continue below them into a hypophonemic sign pattern, etc. If so, this level marks a boundary between one type of structure and another. Below this level one may speak of phonetic manifestation of the hypophonemic material. The primary manifestation is articulatory; it consists of articulatory features. For example, *Cl* is manifested as oral closure. The position of closure, when *Cl* occurs, is determined by another hypophonemic sign, e.g. *Ap* (apical). An occurrence of a hypophonemic sign is a specification to a part of the articulatory apparatus to perform its function. The labels used in this paper for hypophonemes are of course chosen in accordance with these primary manifestations. At the next lower level is the secondary manifestation, which consists of acoustic features, and below this is the tertiary manifestation, consisting of auditory features. Various displaced manifestations are also possible, such as symbols on paper or operations in an artificial speech production machine.

To specify what a phonemic or morphemic sign leads down to requires only the identification of the components and their ordering; but there is at present no simple way to specify how much and what kind of description of the manifestation of a hypophonemic sign is desirable. A minimal specification for Ap would be 'with the apex'. Beyond that, varying kinds and degrees of detail are possible. For Ap in combination with Cl a more detailed specification, applicable to many languages, would be 'close with that part of the apex which is closest to the alveolar ridge at the time.' It will be different parts of the apex depending on the language and the environment. Thus North Fork Monachi has five positions of closure in five different environments (after front vowel, initial, after non-front vowel before front vowel, etc.). Such variation is not a property of Ap or Cl but is mainly the incidental result of where the tongue happens to be at the time the closure takes place. Therefore, the primary value of the description of such positions of closure is that it gives information about the articulation of the vowels, the neutral tongue position, and the timing of the movements from one vowel position to another. Thus in North Fork the position of apical closure is influenced more by the preceding environment than the following. The variation in position differs markedly from that in English, in that the distance from the farthest forward to the farthest back is much greater. The same is true for velar closure. But it is also of interest that the pattern of vocalic environments which determines position of apical closure differs from that for velar. After more detailed information of this and other kinds has been obtained and analyzed for a variety of languages it should be possible to determine what properties of articulation are assignable to human speech in general and what properties are to be accounted for by a specific articulatory system (of a given language or dialect or geographic area) as a whole. The remaining articulatory properties of speech produced in the system—those not accounted for by these two means—are the manifestations of the hypophonemic signs. It is these which are capable of distinguishing meaning, of having communicative significance, within that medium... Could it be another stratum?

NOTES

1. See, for example, Halle 1959, 1962, Chomsky 1964, Chomsky & Halle 1965.

2. There may be some doubt as to whether this point is universally accepted, since one school of phonological thought, that of Chomsky and Halle (cf. footnote 1), has provided no direct means of accounting for such patterns of arrangement. An indirect account of some phonotactic features is to be provided by 'redundancy rules', which add features to individual segments, but it has not been shown how or whether the facts of the phonotactics of a language

in general (e.g. the structure of the English syllable) could be described by such means. Nevertheless it is clear from various remarks in their discussions of redundancy rules that they would like to be able to account for such facts.

3. Cf. Jakobson, Fant, & Halle 1952.

4. Chomsky & Halle 1965:119–   'We conclude . . . that only feature notation has linguistic significance, and that segments are simply to be regarded as conventional abbreviations, utilized to cope with the exigencies of printing but having no linguistic significance in themselves.'

5. Chomsky 1965:84–   ' . . . the lexicon is a set of lexical entries, each lexical entry being a pair *(D,C)*, where *D* is a phonological distinctive feature matrix "spelling" a certain lexical formative and *C* is a collection of specified syntactic features . . .'

6. That is, the items which are treated by the tactics as atomic, items whose combinations are accounted for by it but whose composition, if any, is not.

7. Cf. Swadesh 1934, and numerous other articles. This principle, which follows from the distinctiveness principle discussed below, has been critized by Chomsky and Halle (e.g. 1965:128–130) on the grounds that if it is applied as the sole criterion in phonemic analysis, absurd solutions will result. It should be obvious that the principle was not intended to be applied in isolation from all others.

8. Cf., for example, the treatments of English in Bloomfield 1933:130–135 and in Whorf 1956:223–230.

9. Cf. Chomsky 1964:75ff.

10. Chomsky makes the surprising assertion, for which he offers no support, that 'the invariance condition has no clear meaning unless the linearity condition is also met', (1964:78).

11. Evidently it is also to be understood that, according to this condition, phonemes and phones may occur only in linear sequences. Chomsky incorrectly asserts that the linearity condition follows from definitions of the phoneme as a bundle of distinctive features. It would follow only if there were requirements that (1) features occurring simultaneously may not belong to different bundles, and (2) no bundle can be discontinuous.

12. Note also the following statements from Bloch 1950: 'The order of phones in a phrase is successive, simultaneous, or overlapping: segments occur only in succession; but spans, which are coextensive with qualities common to a train of several segments, occur simultaneously with the segments that compose the train, and may overlap with other spans.' 'Each phoneme is defined by the quality or combination of qualities present in all its members and absent from all other phones of the dialect; and every phone that contains such a quality or combination belongs to the phoneme which is defined by it. A phone that contains two or more such qualities or combinations accordingly belongs to two or more phonemes at once.'

13. The example chosen by Hockett in his discussion is a hypothetical one which is perhaps unrealistic in that it assumes no phonetic difference between prejunctural and postjunctural [t].

14. This statement in no way denies the value of working out and teaching practical procedures of analysis. The point is that such procedures should be distinguished from expositions of linguistic theory and from criteria for evaluating proposed descriptions. Linguistic theory and practical linguistic analysis both benefit from such separation.

15. For a more transparent example of this argument than Halle's Russian one, see Chomsky's discussion of the analysis of the centering offglide of English (1964:104–105).

16. In other words, if a provisional solution had an element of voicing or unvoicing with each segment, we would find it possible to eliminate it on all but one of them.

17. Also, it would be more difficult to handle the fact that *v* may follow voiceless obstruents if the voiceless condition were taken as neutral.

18. Previously presented in Lamb 1963.

19. The graphic notation and associated terminology used in Lamb 1964a are related to the present version as follows: 'vertical' there corresponds to 'or' here, 'horizontal' to 'and'; since these two types of relationship were distinguished by the two dimensions in the earlier notation, diagonally upward was used for what is here simply upward. Figure 1 illustrates composite realization; Figure 2 shows diversification, neutralization, zero realization, and empty realization.

20. For a fuller discussion of the differences between process and realization, see Lamb 1964b.

21. Cf. footnote 5.

22. In Lamb 1962, 1964c, 1965b, See also the discussion of simplicity and related concepts in Lamb 1966a.

23. Graphic and algebraic notations may be designed to be mechanically interconvertible (cf. graphs of conic sections and the associated quadratic equations), so that they differ only as alternative notational implementations of the same underlying set of descriptive concepts. The implementation of the simplicity principle, which must yield comparable results for the alternative notations, is easier for the graphic notation than for the algebraic, since with algebraic notation it is necessary to provide for ignoring nonsignificant differences that result from mechanical limitations of algebraic notation, such as its essentially linear character. In fact the easiest way to implement the simplicity principle for the algebraic notation of stratificational theory is to specify the implementation for the graphic notation plus the rules for converting from the algebraic to the graphic.

24. It might be supposed that nodes should be counted rather than (or in addition to) lines, but nodes are not mutually comparable in a simple way since they can differ from one another in complexity: a node with six lines leading out of one side is more complex than one with only two.

25. Cf. Lamb 1964b. Ordering of subrules of a realization rule often makes it possible to state conditioning environments more simply than if they were unordered, but not always. Nevertheless, as a matter of purely practical convenience, I have used the convention of always writing the subrules of a rule in some order (i.e. even when simplification does not result). In the graphic notation, however, ordering in an 'or' is specified only where relevant.

Realization rules as described in that paper have been simplified considerably as a result of work done since it was written, particularly that reported here.

26. The listing omits various additional alternations related to juncture.

27. For example, in my dissertation on North Fork Monachi, the anataxis of (10) and (11) was described as having effect between morpheme combinations and morphophoneme combinations. Thus the term morphophonemic was applied to the sequences VʔBV (10), VʔRV (11). Then the morphophonemic realization rule corresponding to (2) was applicable to (10). That treatment thus anticipates in part the formulation arrived at here.

28. Downward components must be distinguished from upward components. For example, the morpheme M/worse/ has morphons (M/w/ etc.) as downward components, but has the lexons L/bad/ and L/er/ as upward components. On the suffix -ON, see Lamb 1964a.

29. The morphophoneme M/</ is realized as a specification that the realization of the following morphon occur in the immediately preceding syllable (in the position specified for it by the syllable structure tactics). Examples are: (10) M/yaka<ʔ'ki/ ᴮᴾ/yaʔka'ki/ ᶜᴾ/ya'ka'ki/ 'to cry intermittently', (11) M/miya<ʔ'ki/ ᴮᴾ/miʔya'ki/ ᶜᴾ/miʔya'ki/ 'to go little by little', M/ki'ma <ʔ'ki/ ᴮᴾ/kiʔma'ki/ ᶜᴾ/kiʔma'ki/ 'to come little by little'; (12) M/yaka<i/ ᴮᴾ/yaki/ ᶜᴾ/yaki/ 'to cry at'.

«This device has been abandoned in more recent versions of the theory. Cf. Lockwood's ' "Replacives" without process' elsewhere in this volume for a more recent way of handling the material in example 12.»

30. A realizate is that which is realized—that which a realization is a realization of. Cf. Lamb 1964b.

31. Thus the statement of conditioning environment in a realization rule is actually only a repetition of part of the information already present in the associated tactic pattern; it is, however, a nonsignificant repetition of information stated only once in the graphic description.

32. Chomsky 1964:68–69— 'So far as I can see, there is no other significant level that can be isolated in the phonological component.... the existence of an additional level is highly dubious...'

There is no simple definition possible of just where 'their type of morphophonemic level' is, since it is characterized by them in several different and mutually contradictory ways. In one sense it is a conflation of everything from basic phononic to lexemic.

CHAPTER EIGHT

'Replacives' without Process*

DAVID G. LOCKWOOD

LAMB'S REPEATED ASSERTION that process description is inappropriate in synchronic linguistics[1] has met with as strong criticism from certain quarters[2] as the opposite assertion would have met in the 1940's. One reason for this opposition is surely the fact that certain synchronic phenomena have seemed to the minds of many to require the use of process. Among the phenomena which have seemed most difficult to handle without recourse to process description are the ablauting phenomena of English and other Germanic languages, in which a grammatical category seems to be expressed by the replacement of one vowel by another.

It is the purpose of this paper to indicate how stratificational grammar, without going beyond its basic assumption that a language is a system of relationships, can handle such replacive phenomena.

1. Classic Treatments.

A good example of the phenomenon of 'replacement' in English is the set *sing—sang—sung*. The traditional analysis would say that the past of *sing* is formed by changing the *i* to *a*, or in phonemic terms, the /i/ to /æ/; and the past participle is formed by changing *i* to *u* (/i/ to /ə/).

During the 1940's a controversy existed in American linguistics over the treatment of such phenomena. Bloch's analysis (1947) viewed *sing, sang,* and *sung* as allomorphs, with the last two forms conditioned by the presence of additional morphemes which themselves had zero allomorphs in this environment. We may label these suffixal morphemes {Pt} 'past' and {PP} 'past

---

*This paper appears in print for the first time in this volume.

participle'. So *sing* was considered a simple morpheme, *sang* as another allomorph of this morpheme followed by a zero allomorph of {Pt}, and *sung* a third allomorph together with a zero allomorph of {PP}.[3]

The principal alternate analysis viewed *sang* and *sung* as consisting of *sing* plus replacive allomorphs of {Pt} and {PP}, respectively, so that the manifestation of {Pt} and {PP} was seen as the replacement of the basic vowel of the stem by a different one. This approach, it has been argued, provides a more natural account of the relations involved than does Bloch's analysis, which took covert zero allomorphs over the overt phonemic differences between the contrasting forms. So those linguists willing to accept this kind of analysis in this and similar cases would claim that an allomorph could be (1) an overt sequence of phonemes, (2) zero, or (3) a REPLACIVE—the replacement of one phoneme or phoneme sequence by another.[4] Still the replacive seemed out of place in the item-and-arrangement framework found in the Post-Bloomfieldian linguistics of the late 1940's and the early 1950's. It did not seem capable of formalization within the general approach, and therefore seemed to be an anomaly calling for an apology, perhaps based on the simple fact that it is needed to readily and reasonably account for such cases as that cited.

2. Formalization of Earlier Analyses.

From the standpoint of stratificational theory, a particular linguistic analysis is formalized when it is described in terms of a network of relationships such as those set forth in Lamb's *Outline of Stratificational Grammar* (1966d). Such a formal analysis may be presented either in the form of a graphic notation depicting the relationships and their interconnections directly, or in an algebraic form which provides a secondary description of these graphs. The latter notation is necessary when it comes to handling large amounts of data. However, it is my conviction that, despite the effort required to learn the graphic notation, it is easier to use and follow for limited problems than any form of algebraic notation. Furthermore, graphic notation captures the relational essence of stratificational theory more thoroughly than algebraic, and the simplicity measure used by the theory may be applied more readily to a graphic account than to an algebraic one.[5]

Therefore, all formalizations attempted here will be given in the graphic form, but an attempt will be made to explain the conventions as the exposition progresses, as an aid to those not fully familiar with the system.

It so happens that the graphic notation developed in connection with stratificational theory may be used to present formalizations not only of properly stratificational accounts, but of others as well. The set of all theoretically possible grammars which this notation is capable of handling may be termed the set of NETWORK GRAMMARS, of which stratificational grammars form a subset. A system of grammar which depends on process, however, is not a network grammar. Process is the one widely-used device, fundamental to certain views of language structure, which network notation is inherently incapable of handling. It is the claim of stratificational theory, however, that process is not appropriate to synchronic description, and that all synchronic phenomena which seem to require the postulation of synchronic processes can be handled in other ways which are compatible with the network formalization.

For diachronic linguistics, of course, the case is quite different. Here a process actually is involved, because the structure itself clearly changes in the course of the historical development of a language. Such phenomena can be represented as a change in relational networks—in the number and kind of nodes and the nature of their interconnections—over a period of time.

Bloch's analysis of *sing-sang-sung* is easily representable in network notation, and in fact it might be viewed as one possible tentative stratificational solution to the problem. Let us consider, therefore, its graphic representation, as given in Figure 1. The diamond-shaped nodes[6] near the bottom of this

Figure 1. Bloch's Analysis (1947) in Stratificational Terms.

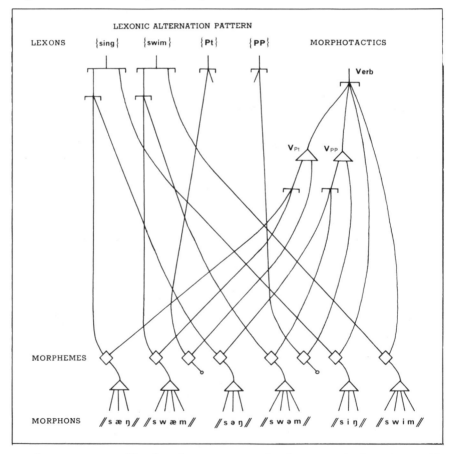

graph represent stratificational MORPHEMES, the closest equivalents in stratificational theory to Bloch's morpheme alternants (later allomorphs).[7] Each diamond shows three connections which define the morpheme: one downward to its realization in terms of morphons (morphophonemes); a second (left upward connection) to the stratum above, where they connect to LEXONS, equivalent to Bloch's morphemes; and a third to the MORPHOTACTICS, a pattern of relationships whose task it is to indicate the possible distributions of morphemes relative to each other (at least up to phrase-sized constructions). The squared nodes below each lexon label are downward ORS, which indicate the presence of alternations. For the lexons {sing} and {swim}, the alternants for past and past participle forms are shown to take precedence over the unmarked forms //siŋ//[8] and //swim// by the ordered OR. (The ordering is shown by the fact that the lines come out of the node in a definite sequence rather than simultaneously.) This node means that where there is more than one possibility, the leftmost possible branch will be taken. The diamonds then further allow the ALTERNATION PATTERN containing these downward ORS to interact with the morphotactics. This very simple tactics generates only six overt morphemes, but following the Bloch analysis, two covert (zero) morphemes are used to assure the proper distribution of these six, so that //sæŋ// and //swæm// will occur only in the past, //səŋ// and //swəm// only in the past participle, and //siŋ// and //swim// only elsewhere. Therefore the alternation pattern controls the operation of the tactics, so that it will select only those morphemes which are signalled from the upper stratum, and at the same time the tactics provides the conditioning environments for the alternations treated in the alternation pattern.[9]

In addition to Nida's classic objection to this analysis (1948:415)—that it ignores overt distinctions in favor of covert ones—there is another obvious deficiency in this treatment: it makes it seem a mere coincidence that *sing, sang,* and *sung* have the same consonants in the same position, and that *sang* and *swam,* both being past forms, have the same vowel. An analysis that fails to capture these obvious generalizations must certainly be deemed less desirable than one which can capture them. This failure is also reflected in the number of relations which must be used to express this analysis in the network form. We must have completely separate diamonds for each supposed alternate form of {sing} and {swim}, and the same would apply to the forms of {sink}, {drink}, {shrink}, {ring}, and all other verbs of the same behavior. And each of these diamonds in turn connects to a completely separate downward AND (the triangular nodes) which specifies its morphonic form. An analysis which does not require this kind of repetition would clearly be preferable.

Another approach to the analysis of these same forms has been suggested by Hockett (1947a:339). This analysis, which like Bloch's might be viewed as a tentative stratificational solution to the problem, would make the assertion that //sæŋ// is a portmanteau involving {sing} and {Pt}, while //səŋ// is similarly a portmanteau involving {sing} and {PP}. Figure 2 graphs this analysis for the sample verbs *sing* and *swim.* This treatment would escape Nida's criticism, since it asserts quite straightforwardly that //səŋ// encompasses the lexons {sing} and {Pt} at the same time and likewise for the other examples. Each such portmanteau is shown by an upward AND in the alternation pattern.[10]

Figure 2. Hockett's Portmanteau Analysis in Stratificational Terms.

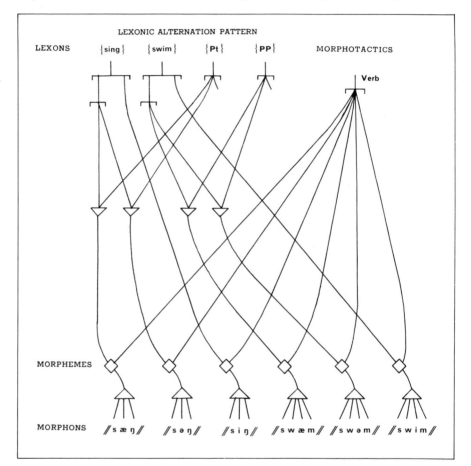

Aside from Nida's criticism, however, this solution is subject to the same criticism as Bloch's analysis, in that it fails to make the similarities between *sing-sang-sung* and likewise *sang-swam-rang-sank,* etc., fully explicit. Hockett clearly recognized that this is a problem when he presented the analysis, but he offered the following answer (1947:339):

> The portmanteau interpretation of such bimorphemic forms need not obscure the phonemic resemblance of which we are speaking. In our morphophonemics we have to mention all portmanteaus. By assembling, in one section of our description, all portmanteaus which have this feature of partial phonemic identity with one of the constituent morphemes and by organizing them into groups on the basis of the specific phonemic difference, we give ample attention to the matter.

Obviously this could not be deemed a suitable answer today. Hockett has directed his remarks to the practical organization and presentation of a grammar, not the generalizing power of an analysis within a formal theory. The criticism is properly directed at the inadequacy of the latter, but Hockett phrases his answer in terms of the former. Therefore, although we clearly do need portmanteaus to handle certain linguistic phenomena reasonably, they do not form the basis for a thoroughly satisfying treatment of the problem at hand.

3. Another Possibility.

Numerous articles in contemporary linguistic journals have been devoted to exposing the morphophonemic regularity of phenomena which earlier linguists have treated as highly irregular. In a considerable number of cases it has been shown that a more thorough and penetrating morphophonemic analysis shows the essential regularity of a number of these phenomena. Most of these exposés have been written within the framework of the transformational-generative approach to phonology, but most of them are not in their essence incompatible with other points of view, such as stratificational theory. Therefore, we might explore the possibility that a similar kind of solution is possible here.

One kind of analysis which is not to be ruled out *a priori* in the stratificational approach is one which shows a special morphon suffixed to *sing*, etc. as the realization of {Pt}, and a different such morphon as the realization of {PP}. These special morphons would have the function of conditioning an alternate form of the stem vowel, but each would itself be realized as zero. Thus there would be two different morphons, but each could be used with all verbs following the *sing-sang-sung* pattern. For the sake of providing each of these morphons with a label, we may call them //q// and //x//. So we can say that the lexonic combination {sing Pt} is realized as morphonic //siŋq//, while {sing PP} is realized as //siŋx//. Then //q, x// would indicate to the phonotactics that the stem vowel is to be realized as |æ| or |ə|, respectively. Figure 3 graphs the morphemic portion of this analysis.

This analysis allows one desirable feature: it treats *sing, swim*, etc. in precisely the same way, obviating the need for parallel but separate accounts for the forms of each verb. This is an advantage over both Bloch's analysis and the portmanteau interpretation. On the other hand, it could be criticized for merely carrying Bloch's covert-over-overt analysis one level lower. It postulates morphons which will never have an overt realization on the lower stratum, but would affect preceding morphons belonging to a separate morpheme. So, in effect, it still says that {Pt} and {PP} are realized as zero, but the zero does not come up until the stratum below.

Formally, the difficulties with this analysis come in showing precisely how the phonotactics is able to condition the supposed morphophonemic alternation of |i|, |æ|, and |ə|. There is no doubt that a phonotactics could be set up to do this, but it seems clear that considerable complication of the tactics would be involved, and the same kind of complication would

Figure 3. The //q, x// Analysis, Morphemic Portion.

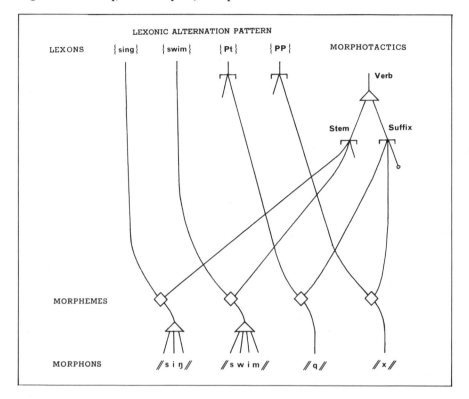

have to be repeated for a considerable number of other ablaut alternations in English.

Therefore, it seems quite clear that what is needed is an analysis which, like the //q, x// analysis, captures the generalization that *sing, swim, sink, ring,* etc. belong to the same class, while not asserting at the same time that *sang, swam,* etc. involve a stem alternation with a zero suffix, as do both Bloch's analysis and the //q, x// analysis. The replacive analysis is one which will allow this, so the problem can be solved if we are able to give a formal representation to this analysis within the stratificational system.

4. The Replacive Analysis.

Until now, it has been the general opinion that a replacive analysis is not capable of formalization within a view of language such as stratificational theory, which does not permit process description. In actuality, it is fairly easy to provide a formalization of this concept within the theory, without any change in the basic principles of the theory itself.[11]

The formal treatment of this solution, like that of the //q, x// solution, involves an interaction between the morphemic and the phonemic strata. The results, however, are much simpler and more readily generalizable to all the replacive phenomena of English than would be the //q, x// solution. The latter fact justifies our preference for this approach. Figure 4 shows the morphemic portion of this solution. The pattern shown here is quite similar to that for the //q, x// solution (Figure 3), except that the AND in the morphotactics is unordered instead of ordered. This indicates that the past and past participle morphemes shown here, realizations of {Pt} and {PP}, are neither prefixes nor suffixes, but what we may call SIMULFIXES. Morphemically, a simulfix is simultaneous with the stem. In other occurrences of the same lexons, of course, they may be realized as suffixes, such as //d// in *sagged* for {Pt}, and //n// in *taken* for {PP}. But for *sang* the tactics provides for //siŋ// and a simultaneous //æ+//.

Figure 4. The Simulfix Analysis Morphemic Portion.

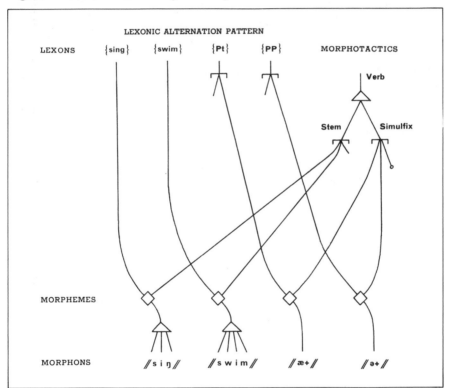

This simultaneity of stem and simulfix obviously cannot be allowed by the phonology. Suprasegmental phonemes are the only kind which can occur simultaneously with vowels and consonants, and two truly simultaneous vowels would never be allowed, in English or any other language. Therefore, the phonotactics of English and other languages will have to resolve this conflict. The relevant portion of English phonotactics is shown in Figure 5. This portion shows a part of the syllable nucleus construction, specifically a downward ordered OR dominating the whole nucleus construction. In general, the function of the ordering of such an OR is to indicate which of two (or more) choices possible at a given point will have precedence. This OR will be set up in such a way that the simulfixed vowels will always connect to the left-hand branch of the OR, the one which has precedence, and all other vowels will connect to the right-hand branch, to be realized only in the absence of a simulfix. Therefore the morphons //æ⁺// and //ə⁺// will have to be separate morphons from the ordinary //æ// and //ə// of such words as *can* and *fun,* as will all other ablaut vowels with respect to the corresponding 'ordinary' vowel. They must be separate in view of their different connection to the phonotactics. We may follow the convention of transcribing all morphons with a similar property with a superscript ⁺, as we have done with these.

Now if we combine the mechanisms shown in Figures 4 and 5, we find that for the past of *sing* the morphotactics tells us to take //siŋ// with the simulfix //æ⁺//. So both //i// and //æ⁺// will be signalled to the phonotactics at the same time. But since a syllable can have only a single nucleus, as shown by the OR, only one of these may be chosen. The ordering of the OR indicates that we will choose to realize //æ⁺//, and //i// will therefore have to go to zero in the alternation pattern.[12] Because of its separate connections to the upper stratum |æ⁺| will still have to be recognized as a separate

Figure 5. The Simulfix Analysis Phonemic Portion.

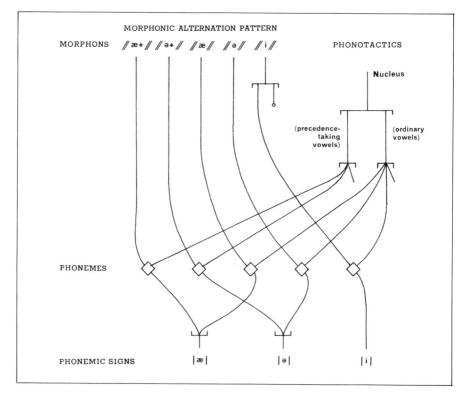

phoneme (in Lamb's sense) from the Iæl of *can, ban*, etc., but below this point the two will be neutralized to the phonemic sign Iæl, as shown by the upward ORs in the diagram. The same applies to other ablauting vowels. When one reaches the phonon level, therefore, they will be treated as the same, since it is properly speaking the phonemic signs, not the phonemes as such, that are 'spelled out' in terms of phonons by the phonemic sign pattern (Lamb 1966d).

Furthermore, the single ordered OR to which $//æ^+//$ and $//ə^+//$ connect can handle all ablauting vowels. No further phonological mechanism will be necessary to handle other types of ablaut in the English verb system, such as that of *take-took, speak-spoke*, as well as the replacive (i.e. simulfixal) realizations of the plural lexon, as in *feet, teeth, geese, mice, lice*, etc.[13]

A further result of this analysis is that verbs need to be classified only according to the vowels of the simulfix. The vowel of the 'basic' form is irrelevant for the purpose of this classification. So all verbs with $//æ^+//$ in the past and $//ə^+//$ in the past participle, like *sing*, and *swim*, are put into the same class, regardless of the stem vowel of the 'basic' form. Most verbs of this class, of course, have the $//i//$ anyway, but one does not: *run*. Usually, of course, this verb is considered to have simply a zero suffix in the past participle, but there is no further basis for establishing a class of verbs with $//æ^+//$ and zero. Such evidence might be, for example, the existence of a verb *zin*, with past *zan* but past participle *zin*. In the absence of any such thing, it is simpler to place *run* in the *sing* class.

Another interesting problem in the English verb system which can be handled along the same lines as those already considered is the treatment of the *-ought* verbs: those whose {Pt, PP} forms have the 'replacive' /ɔt/ for the nucleus and coda of the 'basic' form. The nuclei and codas of these forms show considerable variation, as illustrated by such examples as *seek, teach, bring, think, buy, catch, fight*.

All of these may be handled in the same morphotactic class, using the same devices already outlined for the *sing* class and other similar ones: the stems will be shown by the morphotactics to occur with the suffix $//ɔ^+t^+//$, connecting upward to either {Pt} or {PP}. The morphon $//ɔ^+//$ is another ablauting vowel, connecting in the same way as the others already discussed, while $//t^+//$ is a precedence-taking consonant morphon feeding into the phonotactic coda construction. It will be realized in place of any other possible coda, or, in the case of *buy*, in place of zero coda. So only an additional ordered OR for the coda construction in the phonotactics will be required to handle this phenomenon, together with some ordered ORs in the morphonic alternation pattern allowing the consonants of the various codas to go to zero when the tactics does not allow them.

5. On the Nature of the Stratificational System.

The criticism might be offered that, despite my claims to the contrary, the analysis I have offered is essentially a process treatment, since the phonotactics 'performs an operation' upon the output of the morphology.

It might further be argued that since it has been said that the EMES and ONS of each stratum constitute separate elements, every move from one stratum to another involves CHANGE, and therefore a PROCESS. Behind this sort of interpretation is a fundamental misconception of the nature of the stratificational system, which is found in a number of recent discussions of Lamb's work by linguists of diverse schools.[14] I am convinced that until this misunderstanding is cleared up, it will be impossible for one who holds it to grasp the essence of the stratificational view of language. This section is my attempt to provide this needed clarification.

Most contemporary schools of linguistics depend fundamentally on the concept of the LINGUISTIC UNIT. By a linguistic unit, I mean some sort of 'item' or 'abstract object' which is seen as existing within a' linguistic system as known by the speaker. In some schools, the concept of the unit has played a more important role than in others. It was of extreme importance in conventional structural linguistics, in which phonemes, morphemes, and their combinations and realizations were seen as the central aspect of language design.[15]

In transformational linguistics, the notion of a linguistic RULE occupies a more central position than that of a linguistic unit. The number of units has been reduced to a minimum, but it has not been possible to eliminate them entirely. A rule, as the transformationalists conceive of it, has to have some sort of 'objects' to operate upon, so no such rule-based system could get along without postulating some sort of 'abstract objects'. In contemporary transformational theory, the 'objects' are essentially the features—phonological, syntactic, semantic, morphological, and exception (Postal 1968). An attempt is made to reduce the number of different features to a minimum, and to use as few as possible in a given lexical entry, but there is no way that one can, within the transformational view, get along without positing a large number of such features as abstract realities. Therefore, transformational grammar is a variety of item-and-process linguistics. Its items are abstract features, and its processes are expressed by transformational rules, operating upon complexes of such features generated by the base component. Conventional American structural linguistics, on the other hand, is a variety of item-and-arrangement linguistics. Its items are phonemes and morphemes (and perhaps others, such as morphophonemes, tagmemes, and sememes, in some versions), and it uses various means to describe the arrangements of these abstract objects.

Current stratificational theory—and this is the main point I am trying to make—cannot be properly described as either item-and-arrangement or item-and-process, because the existence of items—abstract objects within the linguistic system—is NOT essential to the operation of its system. In this feature it is unlike any other well-known theoretical framework, except for Hjelmslev's glossematics, to which Lamb (1966a) has already acknowledge his debt on this point. So the terms lexon, morpheme, morphemic sign, morphon, phoneme, phonemic sign, and the rest do not refer to any sort of abstract objects with which stratificational theory operates. Rather, they are convenient labels for certain points in the network of relationships of which the totality of linguistic structure consists. Within language, relations connect only to other relations, never to anything else except across the interfaces connecting language to experience on the one hand, and to articulation on the other. Everything between these interfaces is a series of relationships.

The postulation of 'objects' within language, while not necessary for the workings of the theory itself, is very convenient for purposes of the exposition of analyses. 'Objects' or 'units' are therefore conveniences which allow us to talk more readily about the complex networks of which a linguistic system is seen by the theory to consist. This is what Lamb was referring to when he said (1966d:40):

> In a stratificational framework . . . the decisions leading to the form that will finally appear are made before any form is produced. In the various alternation patterns, tactic patterns, etc. there are no linguistic forms at all; the linguistic structure consists entirely of relationships, and only at its 'lower' end are objects produced, after all the decisions have been made as to what these objects will be.

A whole series of recent criticisms of stratificational theory run astray on the fallacy that stratificational linguistics, like so many other theories, deals with abstract objects. Take, for example, Postal's statement (1968:202):

> The reader should try to imagine what it means, under stratificational assumptions, to say that a person learns a new lexical item, say 'gargoyle'. In a reasonable theory one would say that what has taken place is the addition of a single new set of semantic, syntactic, and phonological properties to the lexicon of the relevant speaker. But in stratificational grammar, the claims are that the speaker has had to learn a new basic sememe, a rule to realize this as a sememe (combination of semons), a rule to map this onto the new basic lexeme which has also been learned, and a new rule to map this onto a lexeme, a new rule to map this lexeme onto the new basic morpheme which has been learned, and finally a rule to map this onto a new morpheme (combination of morphons).

Postal is surely correct in his contention that any theory which made such a claim as this would be absurd, but the point is, of course, that no such claim is made by stratificational theory. The supposed claim is simply the result of Postal's misinterpretation of the theory as one in which, as in transformational theory, the postulation of abstract objects is necessary. It is probably true that among theories requiring such objects, transformational theory is the best proposed to date. But any comparison of this theory with a pseudo-stratificational straw man depending on such objects is bound to be ludicrous.

Therefore, I repeat, it is not the intention of stratificational theory to map whole series of arbitrary symbols one onto the other, as Postal maintains, but to connect one relationship to another and another, forming a network which can ultimately be related to experience and to articulation. The use of arbitrary symbols is merely an aid to the reader trying to follow the relations involved in such a network.[16]

At the same time, the points at which labels are added to diagrams to aid the reader are not wholly arbitrary: they correspond to points of structural relevance in the system, between which various nodes may intervene. The important point is that all labels (except those referring to elements of articulation or experience outside of language) may be removed, but the system will continue to operate in the same way. It will only be somewhat more difficult for the linguist to read, which is clearly a secondary consideration from the theoretical point of view.

Also, without such convenient labels it would always be necessary to show a portion of structure on all the strata in a given diagram. The use of conventional symbols enables us to avoid working out and representing more of the network than we have chosen to focus upon for a given problem.

At any rate, the stratificational claim about the learning of a new lexical item could be phrased as Postal gives it only if it is understood that we are speaking metaphorically. In actuality what one learns is some new connections to the various strata: sememic, lexemic, and morphemic, plus the morphonic shape(s) (a set of connections in the morphemic sign pattern).[17] This set of connections is not extremely different from what Postal sees as a set of PROPERTIES, except for the fact that Postal is forced by his conceptual framework to objectivize as properties what stratificational theory sees as a set of relationships connecting to various strata, and for the fact that when these relationships are organized in a stratified network many of them may be expressed much more succinctly than in a lexical component of a transformational grammar.[18]

The understanding that 'objects' are not essential in the stratificational view will also clear up Palmer's misunderstanding, which prompted his statement (1968:294):

> Indeed, a great deal of repetition is inevitable if one has distinct strata, for a great deal will pass through unchanged...

When a one-to-one correspondence exists between 'elements' of different strata, there will in fact be no necessity to use superfluous 'rules' to realize one 'object' always as another. Rather, the line for the 'unchanged' element will encounter no nodes other than the connections to the tactics of each successive stratum. Therefore the treatment of such an 'element' will be a great deal less complicated than that of one which has many complex and alternate realizations, necessitating various nodes. So any interpretation which requires 'changes' of labels for every different stratum (and for various sublevels within a stratum) will at best be an indirect description of a stratificational grammar, like the algebraic descriptions which Lamb speaks of (1966d:8) as 'a means of describing structural diagrams, and thus only indirectly a means of describing linguistic structures'. And the economy of any stratificational description is not properly measured in terms of the indirect algebraic representation.[19]

NOTES

1. E.g. Lamb 1964a; 1966c:35–40; 1967:411–2.

2. E.g. Chafe 1968:594–9; Palmer 1968:293–4; Postal 1968, ch. 7.

3. Tagmemics would consider that there is an unfilled slot here. I would consider this essentially a variant of Bloch's analysis. I wish to thank Ruth Brend for pointing this out to me. In addition, I am indebted to the following people, whose suggestions and comments have led to various improvements in earlier versions of the paper: Ilah Fleming, Earl Herrick, Sydney M. Lamb, Adam Makkai, and Helen Ullrich.

4. The term 'replacive' was introduced by Nida 1948. Harris (1942:171) treated it as a negative-additive morpheme alternant. Hockett (1947:340) treated it as an 'alternation morph'. Hockett 1954 provides further discussion of alternate solutions to this problem.

5. See Reich 1968a for a discussion of the simplicity measure currently in use, and a demonstration of the impreciseness of algebraic notations in indicating relative simplicity.

6. This device was introduced to overcome definitional difficulties presented by the upward ANDs used to connect strata in Lamb 1966b, 1966d. It was first used in print in D. Bennett 1968.

7. In actuality, Bloch's morpheme alternants were on the classical phonemic stratum. Therefore stratificational morphemes correspond in size to them, but are on a higher level of abstraction (stratum).

8. In this paper, the following notational conventions will be used to identify the stratum on which a given unit belongs: {lexemic}; //morphemic//; |phonemic| (a partly morphophonemic segment, as in Lamb 1966b); and /hypophonemic/ (classical phonemic, but expressed formally in terms of component-sized entities).

9. Lockwood (1972c) gives a further outline of the relations between the lexemic and morphemic strata, with particular reference to inflected languages.

10. In Lamb 1966d, such portmanteaus are treated in the sign pattern of the morphemic stratum. The possibility of treating them in the tactics of this stratum has also been suggested.

11. That is, no change beyond what is indicated in Lamb 1966d, with the replacement of the upward ANDs in the knot pattern by diamonds, as in Bennett (cf. n. 6 above). The basic outline of this analysis was suggested to me by Lamb in personal communication, but the diagrams shown represent my own interpretation. Lamb 1966b:561, n. 42 approximated this sort of treatment with a morphon //<//, 'realized as a specification that the realization of the following morphon occurs in the immediately preceding syllable (in the position specified by the syllable tactics)'. I do not believe that this precise analysis can be formalized within the present stratificational system, however. Newell 1966:97–100 postulates various ablaut morphemes for English without specifying how their ultimate realization is to be accounted for.

12. It is also conceivable that the diamond may be so defined that an impulse from the upper stratum will die if the tactics does not allow it to be realized. This idea was suggested to me by Ilah Fleming.

13. In cases in which a replacive seems to occur on one syllable of a polysyllabic morpheme, it may be necessary to distinguish various nuclei in the phonotactics—those which take replacives as opposed to those which do not. In most cases, however, it seems likely that they would occur in positions which would be definable in terms of stress, position of the syllable in a phonological word or some other feature.

14. Cf. the references in n. 2 above, also Hockett 1968.

15. Some structuralists have expressed the opinion that phonemes and morphemes are real rather than abstract, since they occur in speech. But this notion is based on the view that a phoneme is a class of sounds, and a morpheme, in turn, a class of phoneme sequences. Lamb has shown that the class concept is inadequate for defining such emic units (1966d:33).

16. This misconception is partly the result of the fact that Lamb himself has altered his theory since 1964, while Postal based his criticisms primarily upon Gleason 1964, Lamb 1964a, b and 1965b. Lamb 1964b, however, does suggest that even then he viewed elements in a different way from other theorists, when he says (p.115) '... the realizate could be considered the name of the rule.' Replacing 'rule' with 'relation' or 'complex of relations', we can see

the source of the later conception described here. Also in Lamb 1966e, a paper written earlier than 1964b despite its date of publication, the idea of considering a linguistic 'item' as a point to which a line connects is compared with alternative views taking it as a symbol or as the location of a rule. Furthermore, Postal does offer brief comments on Lamb 1966b, an article based on the newer version of the theory. In this discussion Postal says (1968:52) 'I do not see that it in any substantive way necessitates modification of the fundamental criticisms of earlier statements of stratificational phonemics found in this book above and below.' He is surely incorrect in this judgment.

17. In the case of complex lexemes or complex sememes, which include most new vocabulary items learned beyond early childhood, additional nodes in the lexemic or sememic sign pattern would be required, but in such a case no new phonological connections would be required.

18. In a stratificational grammar, for example, the combination voiced labial stop would be stated only once. In the format proposed by Chomsky, Halle, Postal, and others, the individual components (distinctive features) would have to be represented separately every time a particular combination, such as /b/, would occur. The same goes for every other recurrent combination of phonological components. This is only one of the many generalizations which can be made if information included in a transformational lexicon is stratificationally organized. The principal reason that the transformationalists reject this sort of analysis, I would claim, is that in their rule format such a generalization may be expressed only by introducing a new rule, such as (schematically)

b →   Voiced
           Labial
           Stop

and a similar one for every other distinct segment. It seems to me that this is an artifice of their particular format, which is not shared by the network format of stratificational theory.

19. An algebraic description which gives a rule for each node of the network can be evaluated in the same manner as the corresponding graph. Often an algebraic description, considered by itself, however, can be subjected to spurious simplifications which relate only to algebraic symbols, and not to the structural relations which they describe. Lamb (1966d:54–5) has termed this SUPERFICIAL INFORMATION. See Reich 1968a for further comment on this point.

CHAPTER NINE

On the Correlation of
Morphemes and Lexemes in
the Romance Languages*

VALERIE BECKER MAKKAI

LINGUISTS have long argued about how to treat sets of forms such as English *stand-stood, understand-understood, withstand-withstood*—that is, sets of forms which exhibit some sort of formal patterning but which, synchronically at least, bear very little if any semantic relationship to one another. (See Hockett 1947a, Bloch 1947, Nida 1948.)

Since, according to the tenets of Bloomfieldian descriptive linguistics, the members of a morpheme must mean the same thing, most descriptivists have insisted that *understand* and *withstand* cannot be segmented into *under* and *with* plus *stand-stood*, in spite of the formal identity which exists among the forms. Those who have gone ahead and segmented them anyway have either had to ignore one of their own basic tenets, saying that formal criteria are more important than meaning, or else they have had to resort to the expressed or implicit diachronic argument that segmentation is justified because historically the parts meant the same thing. But such mixing of synchronic and diachronic information has been regarded by most as highly undesirable. Thus everyone agreed that none of the solutions was entirely satisfactory, but there seemed to be no other choice.

For English the problem is a relatively minor one since the number of morphological variants to be listed for any one verb or noun is quite small, and thus one could not be accused of being too uneconomical if one chose not to segment it. But the consequences are far more serious if one does

*Reprinted, with slight revisions, from: *Papers From the Fifth Regional Meeting of the Chicago Linguistic Society*, Robert I. Binnick, Alice Davison, Georgia M. Green, and Jerry L. Morgan, eds. Reprinted by permission.

not segment doubtful forms in languages with more complex inflectional systems. The description of one irregular verb, for example, may easily involve the listing of a half a dozen or more morphological variants, and if several verbs contain this same set of variants it becomes highly wasteful to ignore the identity and repeat the same listing for each verb.

The Romance languages provide a striking example of the problem. In Italian there are at least ten verbs formed on the irregular verb *venire* with various prefixes,[1] most of them with meanings sufficiently divergent to prevent them from being segmented into a prefix plus the morpheme *venire* meaning 'to come'. Yet all of these verbs contain the same formal variants that *venire* has, many of them irregular and thus unpredictable. Each irregularity must be listed for each verb.

In fact, not only do the so-called 'prefixed' verbs not contain the meaning 'come', but in many cases they contain no meanings at all which can be easily componentialized into prefix-meaning and base-meaning. That is, in spite of the fact that formally they appear to be made up of prefix plus verb, in terms of meaning they can only be regarded as single indivisible units. Take, for example, Italian *prevenire* 'to warn', *divenire* 'to become', or *svenire* 'to faint'. We could perhaps impose an artifically devised componentialization on these verbs. For example, we could argue that *prevenire* really means 'to come before'—that is to arrive before the danger arrives and thus alert one to it. But we should not fool ourselves into thinking that we are not using diachronic and formal information in order to reach our conclusions. If the verb meaning 'to warn' were **tapere* or **vadere*, for example, we would not think of componentializing it in this way.

This same type of problem is repeated again and again: Italian *tenere* 'to hold', with eight other verbs which pattern exactly like it, *mettere* 'to put' with twelve, *correre* 'to run' with nine; or take French *venir* 'to come' with seventeen verbs which pattern like it, *tenir* 'to hold' with nine, and *conduire* 'to conduct' with eleven; or take Spanish *poner* 'to put' with at least six other verbs like it, *tener* 'to have' with six, and *conducir* 'to conduct' with six.

No matter whether we choose to segment all these verbs or not, we put ourselves in an awkward position. If we do not segment them we are faced with the necessity of repeating the same morphological information again and again. If we do segment them we must twist the semantic facts in order to justify our act.

The root of the problem lies in the way the morpheme has traditionally been defined. If we attribute to the morpheme both semantic and formal properties, then we must be prepared to pay the price when semantics and form do not coincide. If a morpheme is to be considered as a minimal MEANINGFUL unit, then even though there may be formally definable smaller units, we must ignore them. Likewise, when we have a so-called 'portmanteau'—a FORMALLY indivisible unit which is not minimal meaningfully—such as French *au* 'to the', we must regard it as being a simultaneous occurrence of two morphemes, again ignoring the fact that FORMALLY it consists of one and only one unit. The alternative approach, equally undesirable if not more so, gives form precedence over meaning whenever the two fail to coincide.

The best solution to the dilemma appears to be a redefinition of the morpheme—or rather, a division of the old morpheme into two separate layers, the one dealing with minimal meaningful units, the other with minimal formally definable units. This in fact is what has been done by stratificational linguists in their lexemic versus morphemic strata. (See Conklin 1962, Householder 1959, Lamb 1964a and 1966a, and Lockwood 1972b.)

The various approaches can best be illustrated in diagram form using, as examples, the French verbs *venir* 'to come', *convenir* 'to suit, agree', and *prévenir* 'to warn'.[2] The structuralist who places primary emphasis on meaning might treat these verbs as in Figure 1, where the similarity in form and conditions of occurrence of the allomorphs of each verb is totally ignored. Thus all the allomorphic variations must be listed separately for each verb.

Figure 1

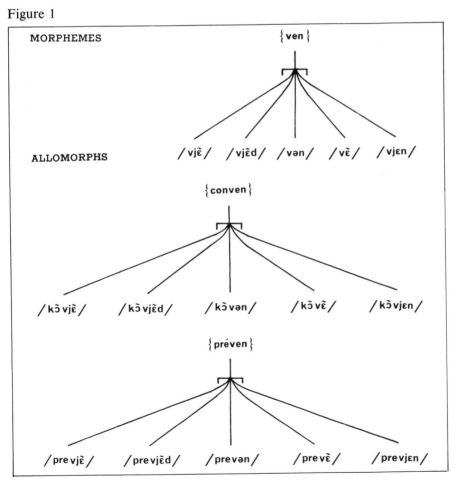

The structuralist who places primary emphasis on form might treat the verbs as in Figure 2, with a great simplification in the statement of form and conditions of occurrence, but completely obliterating the fact that {ven} when preceded by {con} or {pré} not only does not mean the same thing as does {ven} standing alone, but in fact has no independent meaning at all. There is no point at which *conven* and *préven* are treated as units, to which one may add various inflectional affixes.

Figure 2

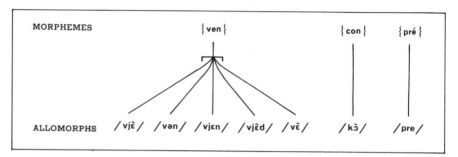

Strangely enough the traditional grammarian perhaps deals with the problem more logically than either of the structuralists by listing each verb as a separate lexical entry with its own unitary meaning, giving the principal parts for *venir,* and then stating for *convenir* and *prévenir* 'conjugated like venir'. This method can be illustrated as in Figure 3.

Figure 3

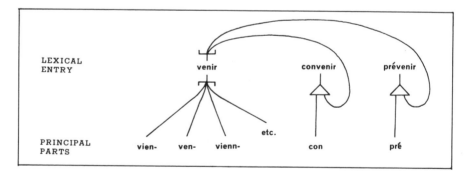

Thus this approach admits the semantic independence of *convenir* and *prévenir*, while at the same time recognizing their formal connection with *venir.*

But it treats *convenir* and *prévenir* as if they are created from *venir* —formally even if not semantically. Although this is, of course, true historically, it is not necessarily so from a synchronic point of view. And if one considers verbs like *conduire, déduire,* and so on, where no independent verb **duire* exists, then there is even less justification for choosing at random one verb and saying that all the others are formed from it. A better way is to regard all the verbs as being based on a formal abstraction, which then yields the various morphological variants. This is what the stratificationalist does, as is shown in simplified form in Figure 4.

Figure 4

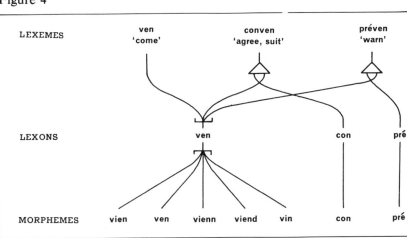

The LEXEMES are the minimal meaningful units, as is indicated in the figure by the inclusion of English translations. These correspond more or less to the morphemes of the conservative structuralist of Figure 1. The LEXONS are abstractions representing the minimal formally definable units, and correspond more or less to the morphemes of the structuralist of Figure 2. The lexons are realized by MORPHEMES, which correspond roughly to the structural linguist's morphemically conditioned allomorphs. The structuralist's phonemically conditioned allomorphs are dealt with on the level where the conditioning actually occurs—namely, the phonemic level. As a result the morphemes of the stratificationalist are not represented in phonemic symbols as allomorphs are, since they may yield more than one sequence of phonemes. The distinction does not show up, however, in the examples at hand, since the allomorphs are all morphemically conditioned. Also not shown in this figure is the fact that other verbs, such as *tenir* and all its derivatives, are conjugated just like *venir*. In a complete treatment all these verbs would be tied together for an even further economy of statement.[3] In a full representation of the system, the choices such as between the morphemes M/vien/, M/ven/, and so on would be controlled by lines leading in from the tactic patterns—the syntax of each level.

The separation of minimal meaningful units and minimal formal units also allows easy handling of portmanteau situations, where what can be segmented on the basis of meaning cannot be segmented in form. This shows up in the morpheme M/vien/, for example, which is not only a realization of the lexon LN/ven/ but also simultaneously represents first, second, and third persons, singular, present, and indicative, or alternatively imperative and singular. If we consider present, indicative, and singular to be the unmarked tense, mood, and number, then the complete pattern for the morpheme M/vien/ will look as in Figure 5.

Figure 5

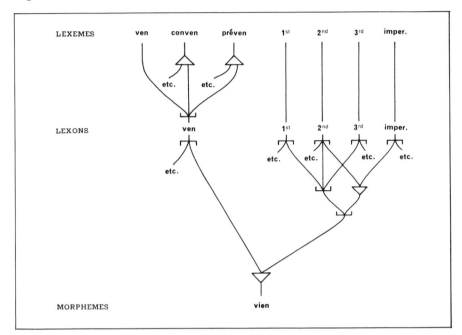

Note that the upward 'or' above the morpheme M/vien/ leads, on the one hand, to imperative and second person (with singular understood since it is not specifically marked as plural), or on the other hand to first, second, or third person, thus illustrating the ambiguity of the form with regard to person. If this path is followed then the form is understood to be singular, present, and indicative since it is not specifically marked as plural nor as any other tense or mood. In a complete diagram the morphemes M/vienn/ and M/vin/ of Figure 4 would also tie into person, tense, number and mood lexons.

One further advantage of this sort of approach is that it neatly handles the problem, which has plagued structuralists, of how to deal with differences such as *cactuses* versus *cacti*, or the past participles *shown* versus *showed*, and so on—that is, differences in form between two units which seem to mean the same thing. Structuralists were forced to conclude that they must not mean the same thing—otherwise they could not account for the formal difference. But then came the problem of deciding which unit carries the meaning difference—are there two different verbs *show*, one of which takes the /n/ allomorph of the past participle while the other takes the /d/ allomorph? Or are there two past participle morphemes? Are the /əz/ of *cactuses*, and the /ay/ of *cacti* one morpheme or two? And so on. Stratificational linguistics, with its separation of meaning and form, takes care of all of these quite easily. If one sees a meaning difference between *showed* and *shown,* then the two would be separated on the lexeme level, with, according to one's decision on the matter, either two lexemes *show* or else two past participle lexemes. However, if one feels that the difference is a purely formal one, he has the option, which the structuralist does not have, of saying that there is only one lexeme *show* and one past participle lexeme. The past participle, then, splits up on the morphemic level into *n* and *ed,* thus alleviating the necessity of attributing a meaning difference where perhaps there is none.

To sum up the advantages of the stratificationalist's separation of lexemic and morphemic strata—he is able to handle with ease:

first, forms such as *conven-* which are unitary in meaning but not in form;

second, forms such as *vien* which are unitary in form but not in meaning;

and third, forms such as past participle *n* and *ed* which apparently mean the same thing but whose conditions of occurrence are not wholly predictable.

The stratificational method can handle all three of these troublesome phenomena, and it appears to handle them better than any other method proposed to date. Whether one wishes to embrace the whole of stratificational theory or not, one cannot deny the appeal of such an approach to the morpheme problem in terms of the simplicity, accuracy, and ease with which it reflects the facts of language.

Appendix of verbs

Note: This list is intended to be a representative sampling of verbs which are conjugated alike and does not pretend to be complete.

Italian:

venire 'to come'
  avvenire 'to happen'
  convenire 'to agree'
  divenire 'to become'
  intervenire 'to intervene'
  pervenire 'to arrive at'
  prevenire 'to warn'
  provenire 'to originate'
  rinvenire 'to find again'
  sovvenire 'to aid'
  svenire 'to faint'

tenere 'to hold'
  appartenere 'to belong'
  astenersi 'to abstain'
  contenere 'to contain'
  mantenere 'to maintain'
  ottenere 'to obtain'
  ritenere 'to retain'
  sostenere 'to support'
  trattenere 'to detain'

correre 'to run'
  accorrere 'to run up'
  concorrere 'to concur'
  discorrere 'to converse'
  incorrere 'to incur'
  occorrere 'to be necessary'
  percorrere 'to run through'
  scorrere 'to flow'
  soccorrere 'to assist'
  transcorrere 'to pass over'

mettere 'to put'
  ammettere 'to admit'
  commettere 'to commit'
  frammettere 'to interpose'
  omettere 'to omit'
  permettere 'to permit'

promettere 'to promise'
rimettere 'to replace'
rimettere 'to reset'
rimettere 'to put off'

scommettere 'to bet, wager'
smettere 'to stop'
transmettere 'to transmit'

French:
venir 'to come'
  avenir 'to happen'
  advenir 'to happen'
  convenir 'to agree, suit'
  contrevenir 'to violate'
  circonvenir 'to circumvent'
  devenir 'to become'
  disconvenir 'to be discordant'
  intervenir 'to intervene'
  parvenir 'to attain'
  prévenir 'to warn; prevent'
  provenir 'to proceed'
  revenir 'to come back'
  redevenir 'to become again'
  se souvenir 'to recollect'
  subvenir 'to aid'
  survenir 'to occur'
  se ressouvenir 'to recollect'

tenir 'to hold'
  s'abstenir 'to abstain'

appartenir 'to belong'
contenir 'to contain'
détenir 'to detain'
entretenir 'to entertain'
maintenir 'to maintain'
obtenir 'to obtain'
retenir 'to retain'
soutenir 'to sustain'

conduire 'to conduct'
  éconduire 'to show out, dismiss'
  reconduire 'to lead back'
  déduire 'to deduct'
  enduire 'to coat'
  induire 'to induce'
  introduire 'to introduce'
  produire 'to produce'
  réduire 'to reduce'
  reproduire 'to reproduce'
  séduire 'to seduce'
  traduire 'to translate'

Spanish:
poner 'to put, place'
  disponer 'to dispose'
  exponer 'to expose'
  imponer 'to impose'
  oponer 'to oppose'
  proponer 'to propose'
  suponer 'to suppose'

conducir 'to conduct'
  aducir 'to adduce'
  deducir 'to deduce'
  inducir 'to induce'

producir 'to produce'
reducir 'to limit; reduce'
traducir 'to translate'

tener 'to have'
  contener 'to contain'
  detener 'to stop'
  obtener 'to obtain'
  mantener 'to support, maintain'
  retener 'to retain, withhold'
  sostener 'to support'

NOTES

1. See appendix for sample lists of the verbs referred to.

2. Note that, in the stratificational notation used here, the square brackets pointing up or down are 'ors' indicating choices—that is, of the several items leading into the one side of the bracket, only one at a time is realized by, or is a realization of, the one item on the other side of the bracket. Triangles represent 'ands'—that is, all items leading into one side

of the triangle are realized by, or are realizations of, the one item on the other side of the triangle.

3. When a complete stratificational treatment of the phonology of French is worked out it will probably turn out that at least some of the morphological variations shown here can be handled instead as phonological alternations, occurring not only in *tenir* and *venir* and their derivatives but also in all other verbs which show these same variations.

CHAPTER TEN

The Problem of
Inflectional Morphemes*

DAVID G. LOCKWOOD

STRUCTURAL LINGUISTS have viewed the morpheme on the basis of some combination of the following fundamental assumptions:

(1) The morpheme has a formal unity—its allomorphs have a close relation in phonetic form.

(2) The morpheme has a functional unity—each morpheme fulfills a definable function in the syntax of the language.

(3) The morpheme has a semantic unity—each morpheme has a fundamental meaning, which is present in all its occurrences.[1]

These three assumptions have played different roles in the thought of different linguists, such that each person considering the problems posed by the morpheme has arrived at his own particular combination of assumptions, placing more or less emphasis on each of the three cited above. Most linguists approaching the problem, however, have sought to emphasize either assumption (1) or assumption (2), the latter sometimes being combined with assumption (3), if function is not distinguished from meaning, as it frequently was not in Post-Bloomfieldian linguistics.[2]

1. The Formalist Position.

Any linguist whose view of the morpheme places primary emphasis on assumption (1) may be said to espouse the FORMALIST position. Among the clearest followers of this position were American linguists of the late 1930's who operated primarily under the influence of Bloomfield's *Language*, which defined the morpheme as 'a linguistic form which bears no partial

---

*This paper appears in print for the first time in this volume.

phonetic-semantic resemblance to any other form.' (1933:161) To a linguist following this tradition, a morpheme had to have a single phonemic shape, or a number of similar phonemic shapes (termed alternants by Bloomfield, later allomorphs) whose occurrence is in some way predictable.[3]

The position of linguists of this persuasion can be most fully contrasted with others if we consider their treatment of inflectional paradigms. For this purpose, let us consider the Latin paradigms in Table I.

	'forest'	'eye'	'ship'
NOMINATIVE SINGULAR	silv-a	ocul-us	nāv-is
GENITIVE SINGULAR	silv-æ	ocul-ī	nāv-is
DATIVE SINGULAR	silv-æ	ocul-ō	nāv-ī
ACCUSATIVE SINGULAR	silv-am	ocul-um	nāv-em
ABLATIVE SINGULAR	silv-ā	ocul-ō	nāv-e
NOMINATIVE PLURAL	silv-æ	ocul-ī	nāv-ēs
GENITIVE PLURAL	silv-ārum	ocul-ōrum	nāv-ium
DATIVE PLURAL	silv-īs	ocul-īs	nāv-ibus
ACCUSATIVE PLURAL	silv-ās	ocul-ōs	nāv-ēs
ABLATIVE PLURAL	silv-īs	ocul-īs	nāv-ibus

Table I. Three Latin Paradigms in Traditional Orthography (Vocative case forms are not considered in these examples.)

In the view of the formalist, the items in these paradigms would be divided into morphemes as indicated by the hyphens, and the endings would be considered morphemically different to the extent that they differ either formally or functionally-semantically. By this criterion the *īs* of the dative plural in the declension of *silva* and *oculus* may be considered a single morpheme, and the *īs* of the ablative plural of the same declensions may likewise be considered a single morpheme. But the dative *īs* and the ablative *īs* may not be combined, in view of the difference in their function. All other endings in the given data differ either in form or in function, and are therefore not to be combined according to this view.

Some linguists have viewed morphemes identical in function but different in form and associated with different inflectional classes as 'complementary morphemes' (Nida 1949:110). It would be reasoned that while within the noun system the genitive singular endings æ and *ī*, for example, do not contrast,[4] they would contrast in the adjective, where the forms of different genders would differ only in these suffixes:

magnæ 'of the large one (fem.)'
magnī 'of the large one (masc. or neut.)'

Others have taken the same view of suppletive stems such as those English *go, went; be, is, am* or Latin *ferō, tulī, lātus* (forms of 'to bear'). More widespread later, of course, was the idea that such stems are morphologically conditioned allomorphs in view of the parallel *amō, amāvī, amātus* (forms of 'to love'), grammatically corresponding forms showing the same stem.

The essential feature of what I call the formalist position, however, is a reluctance to consider formally different morphs of identical function as allomorphs of a single morpheme unless at least one of the following conditions is met: (1) their distribution is phonologically conditioned, (2) their distribution is paralleled by that of morphemes with only one allomorph or phonologically conditioned allomorphs, or (3) their shape is so obviously similar that the conclusion is inescapable.

In the case of paradigmatic sets such as those we have been considering, criterion (2) often failed to allow grouping into a single morpheme, because we seldom find an instance in which the same ending is used in a given function for all classes, though some particular endings of the same function were separated morphemically. They were considered separate morphemes in many instances where another point of view would have treated them as the same morpheme. The fact that the same endings were used in the same functions for adjectives in the classical languages, with the addition of gender distinctions, moreover, tended to reinforce the conclusion of linguists of the formalist position that endings belonging to different classes could not be considered co-allomorphs.

Formalist morphemic analysis is by no means confined to the older period of American linguistics, however, as evidenced by the position of Aronson in his very recent work on Bulgarian, where he says in reference to English:

> We regard the alternation /s/-/z/ in the English plural as automatic, and such desinences as -n as INDEPENDENT MORPHEMES (emphasis mine—DGL) with limited distribution, rather than as allomorphs, relying upon formal criteria in addition to semantic criteria in our analysis. (Aronson 1968:22).

This author, who claims to be most heavily influenced by the Praguian and Neopraguian positions of Trubetzkoy and Stankiewicz, continues to maintain a rather strict variety of the formalist position.

2. The Functionalist Position.

The polar opposite from the formalist position described above is what we may call the FUNCTIONALIST position. A linguist of this persuasion approaching the material which we have been considering would tend to emphasize functional identities over identities of form. He would consider the genitive singular forms

    silvæ   *oculī*   *nāvis*

morphemically identical except for their stems, and would account for their differing forms with statements of allomorphy.

In addition to combining endings appropriate to different stem classes, the functionalist would at the same time tend to separate endings for case and number into separate components for each category represented, in view of the fact that they are independently variable and seem to depend on mutually independent choices in the grammar. This reduces the schema of Table II (a) to that of II (b). Another variant of the same general approach is to consider the singular unmarked rather than a separate morpheme, giving us the schema of Table II (c), with optional plural along with the various cases.

a.	b.	c.
silva + NoSg	silva + No + Sg	silva + No
silva + GeSg	silva + Ge + Sg	silva + Ge
silva + DaSg	silva + Da + Sg	silva + Da
silva + AcSg	silva + Ac + Sg	silva + Ac
silva + AbSg	silva + Ab + Sg	silva + Ab
silva + NoPl	silva + No + Pl	silva + No + Pl
silva + GePl	silva + Ge + Pl	silva + Ge + Pl
silva + DaPl	silva + Da + Pl	silva + Da + Pl
silva + AcPl	silva + Ac + Pl	silva + Ac + Pl
silva + AbPl	silva + Ab + Pl	silva + Ab + Pl

Table II. Three functionalist morphemic analyses of *silva*. (The corresponding analysis of any other noun may be obtained by substituting this noun for *silva* in the appropriate schema.)

This type of morphemic analysis ties in much more readily with the description of the syntax, since it allows such phenomena as case and number concord to be easily described. In view of the fact that it does tie in so well with the syntax, it should not be surprising that the position of the followers of the transformational-generative school has generally been a functionalist one. Koutsoudas, for example, defines the morpheme as 'that unit of grammar the arrangement of which is specified by the syntax and the resulting sequences of which are used to predict the physical form of utterances.' (1963:169).

Despite these advantages, this view is not without its difficulties. The foremost of these involves the ordering of elements. If Latin *silvārum* 'of forests', for example, is to be analyzed as containing the morphemes {silv}, {Ge}, {Pl}, in what order should these three be said to occur? If *ārum* is somehow a combination of {Ge} and {Pl}, it seems clear that, all other things being equal, these two morphemes should be said to follow the stem. But which of the two should come first, case or number? If this and all other expressions of case and number are simultaneous, i.e. portmanteau (Hockett 1947a), there seems to be no basis for establishing an order among them. If one combination should turn out to have separate realizations for case and number, of course, this occurrence could serve as a basis for deciding the problem on the grounds of simplicity, but otherwise any choice of order would be arbitrary. This is undoubtedly one reason why advocates of a position closer to that of the formalist would reject this type of analysis, particularly in the absence of a nonportmanteau occurrence of such combinations.

Another disadvantage of the functionalist view of the morpheme is that it does not allow the maximally general statement of a very frequent type of allomorphy. It does permit any possible variety of allomorphy, from one constant allomorph to many suppletive allomorphs, to be handled. It can treat each of these extremes reasonably, but when it comes to non-suppletive allomorphy, it is forced to treat this in the same way as suppletion, thereby missing many morphophonemic generalizations. In Latin, for example, it would be forced to treat the stem alternation that we see in *rēx* 'king' vs. *rēgis* 'of a king' and that in *lēx* 'law' vs. *lēgis* 'of law'—involving the regular alternation of /k/ and /g/—as if it were as irregular as that of *ferō, tulī, lātus,* and to treat the two stems and any others where a similar alternation occurs as if they were completely separate instances.[5]

A good example of the functional approach is provided by Trager's analysis of the Russian declension (Trager 1953). Here the cases and plural number are regarded as separate morphemes, while singular is considered the unmarked number. Portmanteau interpretations are avoided in this analysis by a seemingly arbitrary assignment of zero morphs to one or the other morpheme in the examples in which both are taken to occur. On the basis of such examples as (Trager's transcription)

rukam	'to hands' (dative)
rukamji	'by hands' (instrumental)
rukax	'hands' (locative)

Trager considers the suffixal morphemes to be {Plural} plus one of the cases. He considers the /a/ to represent plural in these examples, but this morph is absent in *ruk* 'of hands' (genitive) and *ruki* 'hands' (nominative).

He further analyzes *tjotjey* 'of aunts' (genitive) as tjotj-O-ey, with a zero allomorph of the plural morpheme, while *ruki* 'hands' (nominative) is ruk-i-O, with a zero allomorph of the nominative morpheme, and *ruk* 'of hands' (genitive) is said to show zero allomorphs of both suffixal morphemes. Examples such as the dative, instrumental, and locative plural forms mentioned above are then left with overt allomorphs of both plural and the case morpheme, e.g. ruk-a-m.

This analysis is clearly convenient for the integration of the morphology with the syntax, but in order to avoid portmanteau analysis, Trager makes some quite arbitrary decisions with regard to segmentation with zeroes. Still this is a good example of a morphemic analysis with a heavy functional orientation.

3. Intermediate Positions.

It is, of course, possible for a linguist to take positions intermediate between the extremes just described, and a number of such compromise positions have been taken.[6] A common type of compromise in reference to data such as that we have been considering involves adopting the functionalist position with regard to uniting diverse forms, but the formalist position on the question of the divisibility of the components of case and number. Such an approach would set up a morpheme for each combination of case and number which occurs in such an example, as shown in Table II(a).

This approach has the advantage of avoiding the problem concerning the order of separate case and number morphemes which would always have a portmanteau realization. At the same time, it does not allow the separation of the case and number categories that would be most convenient for treating syntactic phenomena.

An example of such a compromise position is seen in Hill 1958, Appendix B, which contains a short sketch of Latin structure. In the analysis of the noun declension, Hill sets up case-number morphemes. He also tries to recognize consistent occurrences of syncretism, however, so he is led to recognize a single morpheme for ablative-dative plural, in view of the fact that these two cases are never differentiated formally in the plural. This is a further compromise with an extreme version of the formalist position, and it has the effect of rendering it still more difficult to relate the morphemes to syntactic phenomena.[7] Since the ablative and dative have functional differences and show some formal distinction as categories, it would be far more convenient for syntactic purposes to consider them always separate, rather than separate in the singular, but not in the plural, as Hill does. But Hill has clearly allowed formal considerations to be dominant in this instance, as well as in the matter of the non-separation of number and case. So on the whole, Hill's analysis is closer to a formal than to a functional one. It can be considered typical of the approach of many later Post-Bloomfieldians to this matter.

4. The Stratificational Position.

Having considered these extreme positions and having pointed out the possibility of various compromises between them, let us now consider the position of stratificational theory. In a sense it is a type of compromise position, but one of a different sort from those considered in 3, above. Instead of trying to decide which of the extreme positions on the morpheme is correct, or whether some other view between the extremes might be better, stratificational theory is willing to consider the possibility that both the functionalist and the formalist positions might be correct, each on its own layer of linguistic structure. According to the position it has arrived at, there are two types of units of morpheme 'size' on different strata. One of these, like the functionalist morpheme, is directly relevant to syntactic structure and would treat the data we have been considering with separate case and number 'morphemes' regardless of the nature of their ultimate realization. The other unit is like the morpheme of the formalist: It cannot have wide variations in form despite identities of function, and would not allow case and number to be separated in languages such as Latin. This view is more useful in treating the formal rather than the functional aspects of the morphology.

Terminologically, the name LEXON is given to the functionally defined 'morpheme', while MORPHEME is reserved for its formal counterpart, which is on a lower stratum.[8] These terms are a part of a consistent set of terminology set forth in Lamb 1966d.

Viewed in terms of one of the classic distinctions in American linguistics, the lexon subsumes both morphologically conditioned and phonologically conditioned allomorphy, while the morpheme subsumes only the latter. (This is true only if phonological conditioning is rather broadly defined to include certain morphophonemic phenomena, such as English *knife* vs. *knives,* which have been regarded as morphologically conditioned in some treatments.)

In essence, then, the stratificational view would accept the extreme functional analysis represented in Table II (b) or (c) for its lexons, and the extreme formalist position of Table I for its morphemes. It would then have the task of relating these two strata.

Some may wish to argue that such a 'multiplication' of units is unnecessary, that it would be far better to accept either one of the extreme positions or some compromise between them, but in any case require only one type of 'morpheme'. Those of such an opinion would select the alternative which gives the least overall difficulty, and accept any consequences of this decision for the treatment of any particular phenomenon. But in stratificational theory, it must be remembered, the simplicity of a solution is not measured in the number of different units or different types of units postulated alone, but rather in the simplicity provided in the treatment of the whole set of facts under consideration. The very 'simplest' kind of theory in terms of units would result in exceedingly complicated descriptions. I am speaking of the 'man-on-the-street' theory, which allows only one primary linguistic unit, the word, related to sound on the one hand and to meaning on the other. Surely a linguistic description of any large body of data would be much more difficult and complex with such a simplistic theory than with one in which more fundamental units, such as phonemes and morphemes, are recognized. So up to a certain point the postulation of more strata or layers of linguistic structure can result in a simpler total description despite the superficial complication of its conceptual apparatus. It can be considered one of the goals of stratificational theory to determine at just what point this multiplication of strata ceases to be fruitful. The answer may be different for different languages (Lamb 1966d:1).

For languages exhibiting phenomena similar to those used here from Latin, it is the contention of the theory that a descriptive format involving both lexons and morphemes will be able to treat the various facts more simply and generally than any system with only one type of 'morpheme'.

4.1 TACTIC PHENOMENA.

In stratificational theory one of the most important components of the system of any given stratum is the TACTICS of that stratum. It is the function of the tactics to specify which combinations of units on its stratum are well-formed. Instead of using one 'syntax' to take care of all features of arrangement, a stratificational system has a separate tactics for each stratum. Each such tactics (except the highest) may be thought of as operating under the control of the stratum above. The lexons are on the LEXEMIC stratum, whose tactics is called the lexotactics. The morpheme is on the MORPHEMIC stratum, and here the tactics is termed the MORPHOTACTICS. The phoneme is on the PHONEMIC stratum, and here the tactics is termed the PHONOTACTICS.

The lexotactics is concerned primarily with the structure of clauses and phrases, so it corresponds most closely to the traditional syntax. Here lex-emes are classified with respect to their syntactic behavior and the various syntactic constructions which the linguistic system allows are specified. The lexeme is a unit composed of one or more lexons. In the data as it is analyzed here, however, each lexeme happens to consist of only one lexon, so the difference is not brought out. So for this data, but not in general, we can think of the lexotactics dealing with lexons.[9]

In the morphotactics, on the other hand, focus is on constructions of word size, and morphemes are classified according to the other morphemes they can combine with on the word level, and relevant constructions are enumerated. It is here that classes such as the traditional declensions and conjugations of Latin and similar inflected languages will be relevant. These classes will be completely irrelevant in the lexotactics.

For the data under consideration, we would want the lexotactics to specify that nouns such as *silva, oculus, nāvis,* and many others can be followed by lexons for case and number. Following the conventions of Lamb 1966d, I will symbolize the noun stems as ^{LN}/silva/, ^{LN}/oculus/ and ^{LN}/nāvis/ using the full nominative in traditional orthography enclosed in slant lines labelled with the superscript LN for 'lexon'. The suffixal lexons include ^{LN}/Ge/ 'genitive', ^{LN}/Da/ 'dative', ^{LN}/Ac/ 'accusative', ^{LN}/Ab/ 'ablative', and ^{LN}/Pl/ 'plural'. I will consider nominative to be the unmarked case, and singular to be the unmarked number. So for the lexotactics these categories are to be considered equivalent to no case or number at all.

Concerning these lexons, we would want the lexotactics to make the statement that the three stems (along with many others, of course) can be followed by any of the case lexons (or by none of them, which is equivalent to nominative case) and optionally by the lexon ^{LN}/Pl/, whose absence sig-nifies singular. The fuller tactics would also specify under what conditions each case is selected, since this choice depends essentially upon syntactic function in larger constructions. This aspect is beyond the scope of the present treatment.

Now we must return to the problem of the order of case and number elements, which was referred to in §2. as one of the difficulties of a functional treatment. In stratificational theory, when it turns out that we can make nothing except an arbitrary decision about the order of such elements, we are not forced to make any statement about their order at all. We may leave them unordered. So the case-number complex would be specified as following the noun stem, but the two elements, case and number, would be unordered with respect to one another. This situation is shown in Table III. In this scheme the Arabic numerals indicate the ordering of columns, while accompanying lower case letters indicate a lack of ordering. So the items of columns 2a and 2b are ordered following those of column 1, but unordered with respect to each other. The optionality of a column is indicated by the use of square brackets around its symbol. So both case and number are optional if we consider nominative and singular to be unmarked. The precise stratificational formalization of this situation will be given in §4.3.

1	[2a]	[2b]
LN/silva/	LN/Ge/	LN/Pl/
LN/oculus/	LN/Da/	
LN/navis/	LN/Ac/	
	LN/Ab/	

Table III. Lexotactics of Some Latin Nouns in Tabular Form.

On the morphemic stratum, the morphemic noun stems corresponding to the lexons LN/silva/, LN/oculus/, LN/nāvis/, etc. will be in different classes in view of their differing inflections. The situation on this stratum could be presented in terms of the formalist analysis given in Table I. With such an analysis the morphotactics would show that stems of these classes combine with the appropriate endings in accordance with the specifications of the lexemic stratum. If we were to follow this analysis, we would find that the endings would have to be treated as distinct for the three classes, except for the dative-ablative plural of the *silva* and *oculus* classes, which would have the same ending, *īs*. This analysis, however, is based directly on the phonemes, and in this case such an analysis leaves many obvious similarities seemingly unrelated. The analysis of such data can be more revealing if it is based on morphophonemic units, which are called MORPHONS in stratificational theory, rather than actual phonemes. Morphons are the components of morphemes. The *nāvis* class presents some morphophonemic problems too complex to be handled in this treatment, but the *silva* and *oculus* classes seem to be morphonically analyzable in the manner shown in Table IV (a) and (b). I have also added the class of neuter nouns of the type of *templum* 'temple', in IV (c), in order to show an example of a third class having a great deal in common with both *silva* class and *oculus* class, yet distinct from both.

This morphonic analysis represents a hypothesis offered for purposes of illustration only. I will not attempt to justify it in detail here, since this aspect is beyond the scope of this paper.[10]

In this analysis the final endings are the realizations of the corresponding lexons, e.g. M/i/ for LN/Ge/ in all three classes, M/i/ or M/a/ for LN/Pl/, or of combinations of lexons, as in the marked plural cases, e.g. M/:rum/ for the combination of LN/Ge/ and LN/Pl/. The stem preceding these endings is broken down into the BASE, e.g. M/silv/, M/ocul/, etc., and the element /a/ or /o/. The latter are stem vowels automatically inserted by the morphotactics when a base of the appropriate class precedes. These stem vowels correspond to what are termed EMPTY MORPHS in Hockett 1947a, in that they realize no lexon, but are predictable on the basis of the morphemes which occur. The overt nominative singular endings /s/ and /m/ are also to be considered empty morphs in this analysis, since there is no lexon for either of these categories.

(No)	silv-a-Ø	ocul-o-s	templ-o-m
Ge	silv-a-i	ocul-o-i	templ-o-i
Da	silv-a-i	ocul-o-:	templ-o-:
Ac	silv-a-m	ocul-o-m	templ-o-m
Ab	silv-a-:	ocul-o-:	templ-o-:
(No) Pl	silv-a-i	ocul-o-i	templ-o-a
Ge Pl	silv-a-:rum	ocul-o-:rum	templ-o-:rum
Da Pl	silv-a-i:s	ocul-o-i:s	templ-o-i:s
Ac Pl	silv-a-:s	ocul-o-:s	templ-o-a
Ab Pl	silv-a-i:s	ocul-o-i:s	templ-o-i:s

Table IV. Stratificational Morphemic Analysis Based on Morphonic Representations.

4.2 DISCREPANCY.

Lamb 1964a introduced the term DISCREPANCY in reference to several types of significant differences which can occur between two given adjacent strata. The existence of such discrepancies helps to establish the separateness of two such strata. To illustrate this point, we will examine the proposed lexonic and morphemic treatments of our data to see what types of discrepancy are to be found between them.

This material clearly shows examples of DIVERSIFICATION and NEUTRALIZATION. By diversification we mean the situation in which one element on the upper stratum is realized sometimes by one, sometimes by another element on the lower stratum. This is illustrated by LN/Da/, which is realized as M/i/ for the class of *silva,* but as M/:/ for the other two classes. Neutralization is the opposite situation, in which two or more different elements have the same realization on the lower stratum. In connection with the *silva* class, for example, LN/Ge/, LN/Da/, and LN/Pl/, when occurring alone with the stem, all have the same realization M/i/.[11]

PORTMANTEAU realization, referred to earlier, is also well represented in this material, since LN/Pl/ in combination with any of the case lexons always shows this phenomenon.

We also find EMPTY realization, the occurrence of 'empty morphs' (in stratificational terminology, DETERMINED MORPHEMIC SIGNS), which realize no lexon. These include the stem vowels and the overt nominative singular endings mentioned previously. The Ø shown in Table IV (a) in the nominative singular of *silva* is actually not such an empty morph, since it is a zero which 'realizes' a zero. If we had a zero realizing an overt lexon, however, we would have a case of ZERO realization, the converse of empty realization, in which an element on the upper stratum is realized by nothing on the lower stratum. This situation can be illustrated in Latin by such nouns as *mare* 'sea' (and all neuters of the third or fourth declension) where LN/Ac/ is realized by zero.

If we consider the relation from lexon to morphon instead of from lexon to morpheme, we can also see examples of COMPOSITE, as opposed to SIMPLE, realization. All the bases in this material are good examples. In the plural, we get composite portmanteau realizations of the various case lexons in combination with LN/Pl/, as sequences of morphons: M/:rum/, M/i:s/, etc. Technically speaking, no example of simple realization—absolute one-to-one correspondence—is shown here. But if we consider, for example, LN/Ab/ occurring alone, unaccompanied by LN/Pl/, we may say that it always has a single morphon M/:/ as its realization, within this limited data. If this were always so, it would be an example of true simple realization.

ANATACTIC realization, in which the order of elements differs between adjacent strata, is completely absent in this material.

4.3 FORMALIZED TREATMENT.

In this section we will seek to put the stratificational treatment of the classes *silva, oculus,* and *templum,* as discussed above, into the formal system presented in Lamb 1966d. As is explained in that work, Lamb considers a language to be a system of relationships. The most fundamental of these relationships are the AND and the OR connections. ANDs express combinations, and ORs express choice or alternation. The relationships may be most readily symbolized in a system of graphic notation such as that presented in the *Outline of stratificational grammar.* It is our task in this section to state in these terms the relations implicit in the analysis already presented.

Figure 1 presents in graphic notation the lexotactic statement already given in Table III. Here the lines connect relational symbols of three different types. An AND relation is expressed by a triangular node. The items entering into such a combination may be either ORDERED, as in the AND at the top, or UNORDERED, as in the lower one. This corresponds to the distinction between ordered and unordered combination referred to in §4.1 The other nodes are ORs, expressing the possible choices. In the operation of the full linguistic system, these choices will be controlled; those ORs for stem selection and for number selection will be controlled by the upper stratum, those for case will be controlled from other parts of the lexotactics, according to the function of the noun in question. The lines leading to a small circle mean that the OR may lead to nothing at all. The circle symbolizes, in other words, a zero element which is useful, among other places, in situations of optionality.

Figure 1. Noun Lexotactics (equivalent to Table III).

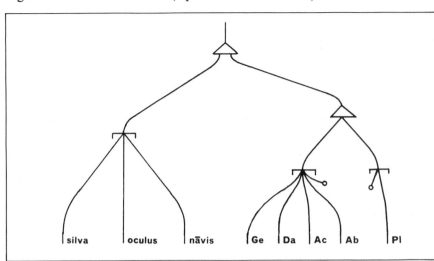

The lexons then have to be related to the morphemes. This relation is expressed by the interaction of the morphotactics, which will be formalized below, and another pattern of relationships, which serves as a bridge, so to speak, between the two strata. This pattern may be termed the LEXOMORPHEMIC (or LEXONIC) ALTERNATION PATTERN, since it specifies the alternate morphemic realizations of lexons or combinations thereof.

Figure 2. Alternation Pattern for Inflectional Lexons.

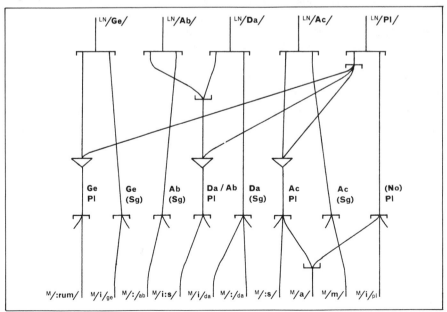

Figure 2 gives the relevant parts of this pattern for Latin, in the same graphic notation. Only the realizations of the suffixal lexons are accounted for. The lines at the top of this diagram lead upward to the lexons, which ultimately come out of the lexotactics of Figure 1. The lines at the bottom lead downward to the suffixal morphemes. This diagram includes several types of nodes not in Figure 1. These include upward unordered ANDS and ORS, the downward counterparts of which were shown previously. Also shown are downward ordered ORS, which indicate the priority of one choice over another: when tracing through the pattern, one must take the leftmost possible branch. If we take the first such OR in the figure, that for LN/Ge/, as an example, the ordered OR means that if the given occurrence of LN/Ge/ is accompanied by a simultaneous occurrence of LN/Pl/, we must use the leftmost line, which leads to the genitive plural endings. The upward AND with lines leading to both LN/Ge/ and LN/Pl/ shows the portmanteau realization. If LN/Pl/ does not accompany LN/Ge/, however, the upward AND will be unsatisfied, so this path will be blocked. In such a case it will be necessary to take the other branch, which leads to the genitive singular endings. The same applies to other combinations of case lexons and LN/Pl/. Note that LN/Ab/ and LN/Da/ lead downward to the same line when in combination with LN/Pl/. This indicates the fact that these two case-number combinations are never formally distinct in the Latin declension.[12] The ordered OR below LN/Pl/ has an unordered OR below its leftmost branch, leading to the various combinations with case lexons. None of these branches has any priority over the others of the set, so they are joined at this unordered OR, but any one of the three will take precedence over the line for nominative plural, the unmarked plural case, which can be taken only if no case lexon has been selected. The unordered downward ORS near the bottom of the diagram indicate the various alternate realizations of the lexons or lexon combinations. The incomplete branches indicate that a fuller treatment of the language would have to recognize additional alternatives. Finally, the upward OR joining lines from accusative plural and (nominative) plural indicates that the two are realized by the same morpheme under certain circumstances. This neutralization can be indicated in the alternation pattern only if the homophonous endings have the same morphotactic distribution—if they occur with precisely the same morphotactic stem classes. This is the case here, since all Latin nouns with accusative plural in /a/ also have the same form in the nominative. The same cannot be said of other homophonous endings in our data, such as M/i/ge, M/i/da, and M/i/pl, of M/:/da and M/:/ab.[13] These can be joined only lower down.

The manner in which stem morphemes combine with these endings will be expressed in the morphotactics, which is presented in Figure 3. The downward OR at the top of this diagram shows that the class of nouns is divided into several subclasses, labelled N_1, N_2, etc. A downward AND for each of these shows the division into BASE, STEM VOWEL, and ENDING. Each of the branches for bases, labelled NB, goes to a downward OR, which will lead to all members of the class. Since lines to the bottom of the diagram

Figure 3. Morphotactics.

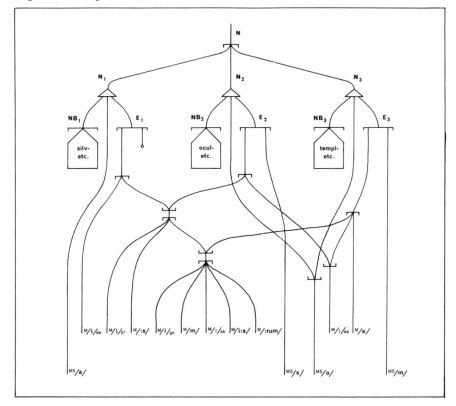

for even a small selection of these bases would make the diagram unwieldy, a pentagonal figure is substituted for them, and in each pentagon an example of the class is given with an *etc.*, meaning all similarly declined bases. The second line from each downward AND leads to the stem vowel: /a/ for the *silva* class and /o/ for the other two. These vowels are not morphemes, since they realize no lexon. This fact is indicated in the diagram by their being shown lower and by the superscript MS, for MORPHEMIC SIGN, a determined morphemic element,[14] instead of M for morpheme.

The final branch of each AND leads downward to the various endings appropriate to the given class. Endings from the left branch of each downward ordered OR are marked—specified from the lexemic stratum via the lexomorphemic alternation pattern. The right branch leads to the maximally unmarked ending, that for the nominative singular. For the *silva* class this ending is zero; for the others it is a morphemic sign, as indicated. The remaining endings pair off exactly with those at the bottom of the alternation pattern of Figure 2 (though not in the same order, for the convenience of representing the separate diagrams). The pattern of upward and downward ORs attempts to state these endings in relation to their classes in the simplest fashion possible, stating each formally and functionally identical ending only once, and making explicit the fact that certain of the classes have endings in common. So it is shown that five endings are common to all three classes, while two are common to *silva* and *oculus* only. Others apply only to *silva* ($^{M}/i/_{da}$), or only to *templum* ($^{M}/a/$).

The endings which occur, and their arrangements, are determined by two factors: (1) the control by the lexons through the alternation pattern, and (2) the arrangements and distribution specified by the morphotactics. In the model set forth in the *Outline* (also in Lamb 1966b), this dual control of the morphemes is expressed by upward ANDs in a KNOT PATTERN. One branch of each such AND leads to the bottom of the alternation pattern, while the other leads to the bottom of the morphotactics. More recently, it has been found that the relation here is not quite the same as that of the upward AND, and therefore a different, diamond symbol has been used for it (D. Bennett 1968).

Below the knot or diamond pattern, the morphonic composition of each morpheme will be explicitly given, and the phonology will handle other types of alternation, mapping the specifications of the morphology into articulatory movements.

5. Conclusion.

The analysis just presented brings out some interesting conclusions about the nature of the distinction between morphology and syntax. This distinction was of considerable importance in traditional grammar. As is well-known, the distinction has most commonly been defined in connection with the concept of the word: morphology deals with the internal structure of the word, while syntax deals with its external distribution in larger structures. This definition has caused many structural linguists to view the distinction between morphology and syntax as something of relatively minor importance. It has been felt that the word is no more natural a point of division within the hierarchy of ranks (size levels) within the grammar than is the phrase or the clause. So some linguists have preferred the compound term MORPHOSYNTAX, which emphasizes the unity of the two rather than their diversity. The present study shows that, from the stratificational point of view, this difference is more than just a matter of rank within a single hierarchy of grammar. It is seen, rather, as a difference of stratum—level of abstraction—as well. All of this seems to offer confirmation of the apparent intuition of the traditional grammarians with respect to the importance of this distinction, though it does not confirm its most usual definition.

It should be further pointed out that the use of two separate but interrelated grammatical strata helps to solve a number of problems in morphology in general. These problems are badly treated by models employing only one type of 'morpheme', due to the inherent limitations of such models. So the morpheme-allomorph model can treat all kinds of alternation, but if strictly followed, it must treat all these types like suppletion. The morpheme-morphophoneme model, on the other hand, cannot by itself handle suppletion reasonably (without postulating *ad hoc* 'morphophonemes' for each suppletive alternation, which no linguist has ever seriously proposed). With the two strata, however, grammatically conditioned, suppletive alternations can be handled in terms of alternate morphemic realization of lexons, and regular morphophonemic allomorphy can be handled by the phonology, as a matter of the realization of morphons by phonological entities.

Finally, we see that by adopting a stratificational view of inflection such as that outlined here, we can allow a clear integration of the units representing inflectional endings with their syntactic functions on the lexemic stratum, while concentrating on the formally different expressions of these, and their distribution, on the morphemic stratum. Earlier points of view, as I have tried to show, were forced by the need to posit only one type of morphemic unit to either vastly complicate the syntax by adopting a formalist viewpoint, to treat the morphology in something short of the most general fashion by adopting a functionalist approach, or to treat neither very well by adopting a compromise.

Whether it is necessary to postulate the two grammatical strata for every language remains to be seen. It seems altogether conceivable that the distinct morphemic stratum may not be necessary in languages which show no inflection. It seems clear, however, that the division is necessary in a heavily inflected language, and Newell 1966 presents evidence for the distinction in English, a less heavily inflected language.

NOTES

1. I am indebted to Sydney M. Lamb, Ilah Fleming, Adam Makkai, and Helen Ullrich for a number of useful suggestions leading to improvements in earlier versions of this paper.

2. Also Chafe 1962 presents a view in which the semantic unity of the morpheme is emphasized over either its formal unity or its functional unity. This could therefore be taken as a view emphasizing assumption (3).

3. The position of the formalist is well described as the 'present treatment of morphemes' in Harris 1942.

4. This is the case unless it is considered that they do contrast in such examples as *magistrī* 'of the master' and *magistræ* 'of the mistress'. It is possible to consider these stems morphemically distinct, however. They may be considered either two homophonous morphemes or a single morpheme in the masculine form and that same morpheme plus a zero derivational suffix in the feminine.

5. A mixed system without this disadvantage is used in Trager 1955. It regards allomorphs (at least some of them) as composed of morphophonemes rather than of phonemes. This view will be outlined in section 4. Other linguists, of course, compromised theory with reality to the extent of allowing themselves to treat morphophonemic alternations in a more regular way than is implied here. But this was generally viewed as a short-cut and a purely practical matter, which was not, therefore, integrated into morphemic theory.

6. This is not to imply, of course, that the linguists mentioned necessarily have made a CONSCIOUS compromise between extreme positions.

7. In this aspect, Hill's analysis is even more formally oriented than the formalist position spoken of in section 1, which I described as allowing the separation of such homophonous morphemes on the basis of their functional differences.

8. Following Lamb 1966d, I am using the convention that a 'higher' stratum is closer to experience, a 'lower' one closer to speech sound.

9. Examples of complex lexemes in English are *undergo, withstand, understand,* etc. They behave as units syntactically, but must be separated below the lexotactics if the morphological facts are to be economically handled. «See also the preceding article by V. B. Makkai»

10. This is a strictly synchronic analysis based on the application of the stratificational simplicity principle. In certain respects, e.g. the use of MN/o/ in the determined suffix of MN/oculos/ and MN/templom/, it further corresponds to a diachronically earlier form. This correspondence merely bears out the observation often made by linguists that a careful morphophonemic (stratificational morphonic) analysis will to a great extent recapture an earlier stage of the language in the same way as the methodologically parallel technique of internal reconstruction. Synchronic morphonic analysis, at the same time, NEED NOT and indeed MUST NOT be approached diachronically.

11. It is the same when viewed as a sequence of morphons, but when viewed in terms of morphemes there are three homophonous units, differing both in their distribution among the same classes, shown by their connections to the morphotactics, and in their connections to the lexons.

12. I have handled this phenomenon in the alternation pattern. In Lamb 1966b it is handled in the SIGN PATTERN of the lexemic stratum. This would introduce a distinction between lexeme and lexon not otherwise present in this analysis. It has also been suggested in as yet unpublished research that portmanteau realization can be handled in the morphotactics with the aid of the new diamond notation (D. Bennett 1968).

13. The subscripts ge, da, pl, ab are used to indicate the functional differences between homophonous morphemes.

14. Actually, every non-zero morpheme leads down to a morphemic sign of some sort. A morphemic sign may be defined as a sequence of one or more morphons which realizes one or more morphemes or determined morphemic elements. Thus zero morphemes are morphemes corresponding to no morphemic sign. Overt morphemes correspond to some morphemic sign, though two or more may correspond to the same one in cases of homophony. Determined morphemic elements (empty morphs) are morphemic signs corresponding to no morpheme, though again they may be homophonous with one or more morphemes.

CHAPTER ELEVEN

The Sememic Approach
to Structural Semantics*

SYDNEY M. LAMB

Introduction

AS PART of the justification for their existence, languages have an intimate but only partially understood relationship to a vague entity which we call meaning.[1] There is no general agreement as to just how intimate this relationship is: that is, as to whether meaning is or is not included within language, partly or wholly, in one of its aspects or levels or more than one (if indeed there are more than one). But many linguists have thought it would be very desirable, and perhaps also possible, to set up or discover some structural units which would either be units of meaning itself or in some other way would help us to systematize our treatment of that vague entity.

A name for such a unit, SEMEME, has been available for a long time. It was provided by Bloomfield (1926). We are not constrained, of course, to use his definition in order to use the term. Just as with the morpheme and other concepts of his and others, we may refine our understanding of the unit without adding a new name to an already formidable collection of terminology. For Bloomfield, the sememe was the meaning of a morpheme. This concept would seem to put sememes and morphemes in a one-to-one correspondence with each other—that is, a sememe for every morpheme and a morpheme for every sememe. Such a view of the relationship ought to make it unnecessary for there to be two kinds of units, and one is led to wonder why, in this case, Bloomfield bothered to have sememes in his

*From *American Anthropologist* 66, No. 3, Pt. 2.57–78 (1964). (= *Transcultural Studies in Cognition,* A. Kimball Romney, and Roy G. D'Andrade, eds.) Reprinted by permission. In the original version the terms *represent* and *representation* were used in place of *realize,* and *realization,* which have been adopted here in conformity with more recent practice. This work was supported in part by the National Science Foundation.

system at all. But the reason becomes clear when we recall that for Bloomfield a morpheme was composed of phonemes. Certainly, sequences of phonemes could not themselves be units of meaning as well; so it was necessary to adopt an alternative, namely that these sequences, the morphemes, HAVE meanings; and these meanings were the sememes. Nowadays, on the other hand, many linguists view morphemes not as COMPOSED of phonemes but as REALIZED by phonemes and combinations of phonemes. For those of us who hold this view, morphemes are not units of expression so the notion of a one-to-one correspondence between morphemes and sememes would amount to the same thing as making the sememes quite useless, except for those who take pleasure in multiplying entities *praeter necessitatem*.

Now, of course, the fact that a name exists, even one given by Bloomfield, does not compel us to go out and find something to use it for. Nor should we be unduly influenced by its suffix, so that we suppose we must find an 'emic' type of entity in the area of content, having those same important properties as other 'emes' we have come to know. Of course, there is no objection to anyone's setting out to look for such an entity, provided he maintains the proper degree of caution. On the other hand, this was not the approach that I used. It was rather the case that I stumbled into the sememe in the process of studying relationships existing among lexemic units of languages. And it turned out that this unit, if not a unit of meaning itself (whatever that would mean), is at least closer to meaning than any other well-defined linguistic unit; and, moreover, that it has the properties required to justify the use of the suffix -EME.

Now the point of this paper is simply this: Just as phonetic material can be 'emicized' to give phonemic material which, in turn, can be 'emicized' to give morphemic, so lexemic material can be emicized to give units of the SEMEMIC STRATUM. To establish this point, I shall explain and elucidate the nature of the linguistic relationship with which emicization is concerned, and then I shall attempt to demonstrate the presence of this same relationship between the lexemic and sememic strata of language.

Strata

The relationship of realization is one of the most important properties of linguistic structure. It is present between each of the pairs of STRATA which may be set up to give recognition to it. The stratum is a type of level, but it differs from other types of levels which linguists frequently talk about. It is not the same as the combinatory or tactic level—the type which is usually involved in discussions of a syntactic level as opposed to morphology, or the level of clauses as opposed to that of phrases. Nor are strata the same as those levels which are really different kinds of activity performed by linguists during the process of linguistic analysis (e.g. phonemics, morphemics; these may be called LEVELS OF ANALYSIS). Instead, strata are the levels of the linguistic structure which are concerned with realization, as that concept is characterized below. Classes and combinations of linguistic units always exist on the same stratum as those units. Thus levels of the tactic or combinatory type also have their existence within a single stratum. For example, phonemes, classes of phonemes (such as the class of vowel phonemes of a language) and combinations of phonemes (such as syllables) all exist on the same stratum, the phonemic. The syllable is on a higher combinatory or tactic level than the phoneme, but on the same stratum. Similarly, lexemes, classes of lexemes (e.g. that of nouns of a given language) and combinations of lexemes (such as phrases) are all on the lexemic stratum. Some of the greatest difficulties in linguistic thinking over the past few decades have arisen from confusion between combinatory levels and realizational levels (i.e. STRATA), and it is essential to keep them distinct (cf. Hockett 1961).

The concept of stratification is not yet well established in linguistics, and the terminology that is appropriate to it is in a state of confusion, flux, and general disarray. The terms PHONEME, PHONEMIC, ALLOPHONE, MORPHEME, MORPHEMIC, ALLOMORPH are well established but their meanings still vary widely from linguist to linguist and sometimes even from page to page within the works of the same linguist. In this paper I use the terms PHONEMIC, MORPHEMIC, LEXEMIC, and SEMEMIC for the four strata which apparently need to be recognized within linguistic structure.[2] (In addition, there are two peripheral strata which relate to the structure but are outside it: the PHONETIC and the SEMANTIC.)

The term MORPHEME is perhaps the most confused technical term in all of linguistic science. If one translates, so far as is possible, other linguistic theories into stratificational terms, one finds the term MORPHEME applied to units ranging throughout the structure of language from the phonemic stratum to the sememic. Bloomfield (1933) describes the morpheme as a unit of the phonemic stratum (if we translate into stratificational terms), but in later pages uses the term to apply also to both morphemic and lexemic entities. Nida's well-known textbook (1949) defines the morpheme first as a phonemic unit (Principle 1), then as a morphemic unit (Principle 2), and finally as a lexemic unit (Principle 3), all in the same chapter. And Chafe (1962) uses the term MORPHEME for some entities which are on the sememic stratum according to the system described here. My use of the terms MORPHEME and MORPHEMIC here is more or less consistent with that of some other linguists, and it would clearly be impossible to use the term at all if one wanted to be consistent with ALL linguists. It conforms essentially to Principle 2 of Nida's textbook (1949).

The differences among the strata are perhaps best grasped through some examples. If we consider the *t* in *eighth* in relation to the *t* of *water* we can see that from one point of view they are quite different. The former is dental, tense, and voiceless; the latter is post-alveolar, lax, and voiced. These are phonetically two different entities, but phonemically the same, since the phonetic differences are nondistinctive. A rule can be given to account for the various nondistinctive phonetic features that are present in different environments, and those features, thus accounted for, no longer need be considered at any higher stratum. Similarly, but one level higher, if we compare *wife* and *wives* we note the contrast indicated in the orthography as a difference between *f* and *v,* a variation between two entities which are phonemically different. But in some other sense these are one and the same unit, just as there is in some sense a single unit *wife* related to the two phonemic units *wife* and *wive-.* (The phonemic difference, by the way, is best analyzed not as between ^{P}/f/ and ^{P}/v/ but between ^{P}/hv/ and ^{P}/v/, the former appearing in ^{P}/wayhv/ *wife* as opposed to ^{P}/wayvz/ *wives.*) Similarly, but differently, the forms which we represent orthographically as *good* and *better* are morphemically altogether different, but lexemically they are partially the same. That is, the latter, from the lexemic point of view, consists of the former followed by the comparative suffix. It can be symbolized lexemically as ^{L}/good er/. Finally, *can,* as in *he can go,* is lexemically different from *be able to,* as in *he will be able to go,* but sememically these are one and the same unit. The examples given here are all concerned with diversification, one of the several properties of linguistic realization defined below.

The names of some principal structural units, with those of the strata on which they exist, are shown in Table I below.

Table I. Principal Structural Units.

STRATUM	ELEMENTARY UNIT	UNIT RELATING TO NEXT HIGHER STRATUM
Sememic	Semon	Sememe
Lexemic	Lexon	Lexeme
Morphemic	Morphon	Morpheme
Phonemic	Phonon	Phoneme

As it happens, linguistic terminology has developed in such a way that the celebrated suffix -EME has been used in the names not of elementary units of the various strata but of units just large enough to have a relation to the stratum above. The phoneme is not an elementary unit but is composed of phonemic components, which are therefore the elementary units of the phonemic stratum. Nor is the morpheme, if taken to be composed of morphophonemes, elementary. And those linguists who have used the term lexeme have generally meant by it a unit composed of smaller entities. Strangely enough, the terminology has developed this far without there having been provided any suffix or other general device to be used in designating the elementary units. The reason is doubtless the confusion which has existed between realizational and combinatory levels, which has led people to think that morphemes are composed of phonemes and lexemes of morphemes. At any rate, the problem is easily solved by borrowing the suffix -ON from the physicists, who use it for elementary particles (e.g. ELECTRON, PROTON, MESON). Thus the elementary units of which the phoneme, the morpheme, the lexeme, and the sememe are composed may be called the PHONON, the MORPHON, the LEXON, and the SEMON respectively. The morphon is pretty much the same as what many linguists call the morphophoneme, and the lexon is about the same as what some linguists (at least some of the time) call the morpheme. Except where portmanteau realization or empty realization is present (see below), a phoneme is a realization of a morphon and a morpheme is a realization of a lexon. (And the morpheme differs from the lexon in that it is usually complex while the latter is elementary and in that a lexon can have alternate morphemic realizations and in that a morpheme may ambiguously realize more than one lexon.)

We can now state more precisely, by reference to diversification, the conditions which differentiate the strata. When alternate realizations are conditioned by phonemic environment, they are alternate phonetic realizations of a phonemic unit. When alternate realizations are describable by morphophonemic rules (which define realizations of morphons in terms of other morphons as conditioning environments), they are realizations of morphemic units. And, in general, the type of rule, as determined by the conditions defining the alternation, determines the stratum at which the unit with alternate realizations exists. For those familiar with Nida's principles (1948, 1949), referred to above, it may be explained (by translation into stratificational terms) that his Principle 1 ('... identical phonemic form in all their occurrences...') defines the MORPH, i.e. phonemic realization of a morpheme, Principle 2 ('... distribution of sound differences is phonologically definable.') defines the MORPHEME, and Principle 3 (which deals with 'morphologically conditioned' alternation) defines the lexon, approximately.

While the table above may appear at first glance to show twelve technical terms, there are really only seven nomenclatural elements present, namely PHON(E), MORPH, LEX, SEM(E), -ON, -EM(E), and -IC (four stems and three suffixes). If we let X stand for any of the four stems, an X$_O$N is a minimal unit of the XEMIC STRATUM, and an XEME is a unit of the XEMIC STRATUM which occurs as the realization of a unit of the next higher stratum such that its components, if any, are not the realizations of the components of that higher-stratum unit.[3] In addition, the realization of an Xeme on the next lower stratum is an X, and if an Xeme has more than one realization they may be called its ALLOXs (e.g. allomorphs). The terminology for levels of analysis and for stratificational rules is also quite simple: if X$_2$ follows X$_1$ in the ordering phone(e), morph, lex, sem(e) (from low to high), the analysis and/or description of the realization of X$_2$emic units on the X$_1$emic stratum is X$_2$OX$_1$EMICS (e.g. morphophonemics); a set of stratificational rules relating the X$_2$emic stratum to the X$_1$emic is an X$_2$OX$_1$EMIC DESCRIPTION; these rules may be called X$_2$OX$_1$EMIC RULES. In X$_2$OX$_1$emic rules the realizates (i.e. the X$_2$emic units—those which are realized) and conditioning environments are expressed in terms of X$_2$ons and the realizations are X$_1$emes. Thus stratificational phenomena in languages are sorted out among the strata according to the type of rule required to account for them. And since we find that three kinds of rules are needed to get from the sememic stratum to the phonemic (i.e. the semolexemic, lexomorphemic, and morphophonemic), we conclude that languages have four structural strata. An attempt to bypass any of the strata (e.g., by trying to combine the lexomorphemic and morphophonemic rules into one set of rules) would result in enormous complexity and lack of generality.

Figure 1 shows a tentative analysis of an English declarative clause on each of the four structural strata. This figure is intended to be merely illustrative of various features of the differences among the strata. A full explanation of it would require detailed discussion that would go beyond the scope of this paper. Further, it should be understood that the analysis shown is subject to revision. In this example, a very short and simple clause, each of the lexemes is composed of a single lexon, but in *the man will be able to catch a red-headed woodpecker,* two of the lexemes are composite, namely *be able to* and *red-headed woodpecker.* On the morphemic stratum M/ m æ n/ is a morpheme composed of three morphons. As the figure shows, the phonons of a phoneme occur simultaneously (written vertically in the notation, with two letters for each phonon), while morphons and morphemes

Figure 1

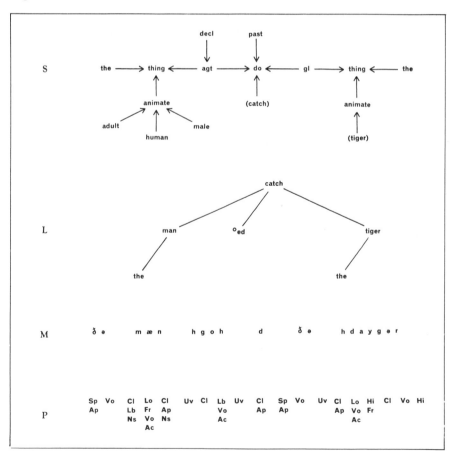

occur in strings, lexemes in trees, and semons in networks. (The analysis shown is oversimplified in that pitch, stress, and juncture are not accounted for.)

Realizational Analysis

The set of rules defining the realization of elements of one stratum by those of the next lower one may be likened to a code, but it is more complicated than familiar codes. We can define a SIMPLE CODE as one in which all realization is one-for-one, as in cryptograms of the Sunday puzzle page. The additional complexities of linguistic realization can be grouped under two headings, which we may call VERTICAL DISCREPANCY and HORIZONTAL DISCREPANCY.

In Figures 2, 3, and 4, the boxes represent linguistic units; the higher stratum is at the upper left, the lower at the lower right of the diagonal line. Where two boxes are present on a stratum, they stand for any number greater than one. The diagram for SIMPLE REALIZATION is given in Figure 2.

Figure 2. Simple Realization

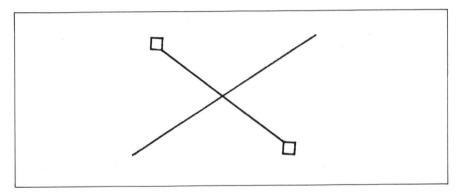

The condition which we may call DIVERSIFICATION is present whenever an item has alternate realizations. This condition is the most characteristic and important property of linguistic realization. The alternate realizations are always in free variation or in complementary distribution in terms of environments on the higher stratum. That is, the differences between them are predictable and therefore nondistinctive. These differences are therefore eliminated (by the analyst) at the higher stratum, which is thereby simpler. Examples are the phoneme P/d/ with its various allophones and the lexon L/good/. with its realizations M/gud/, M/behd/, M/be/.

As Figure 3 shows, neutralization is, in part, just the opposite situation; that is, two or more units have the same realization. For example, M/behd/ is a realization not only of L/good/ but also of a verb meaning 'to wager'. But the diagram does not show the whole story. Different items having the same realization need not be in noncontrastive distribution with respect to the lower stratum, and, in fact, they usually are not. The conditions of neutralization and diversification define relative height of strata. Given a properly formulated set of realization rules, it is always possible to convert correctly to the next lower stratum but not vice-versa. Where realizations are determined by the environment of the realizate it is possible to convert uniquely, since for each environment there is only one possibility. In the case of free variation in a given environment there is more than one possibility, but any of them is correct. But when going in the opposite direction, that is upward, there is often more than one possibility, and this situation is one of ambiguity, not free variation. This matter of relative height and the determination of which are the realizates and which the realizations will be important when we consider the relationship between the lexemic and sememic strata below.

Figure 3. Vertical Discrepancy

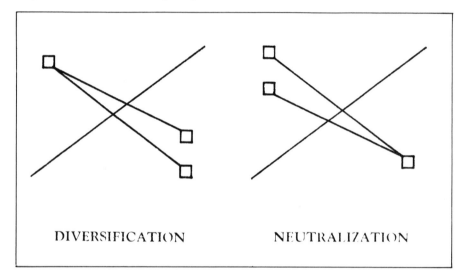

DIVERSIFICATION   NEUTRALIZATION

We may use the term COMPOSITE REALIZATION to describe the situation in which an element is realized by a combination of elements of the next lower stratum. For example, the lexon ^{L}/boy/, a single and indivisible element on the lexemic stratum, is realized by a combination of morphons ^{M}/b/, ^{M}/o/, ^{M}/y/. That is, of course, the usual situation in the realization of lexons and of morphons (i.e. morphemes are generally segmentable into morphons), and the suffix *-eme* provides standard terms for such composites. Because it is usual, many linguists have been misled into thinking that the essential difference between phonemes and morphemes is that the latter are larger; that is, that the morphemic level is of the tactic or combinatory type as compared to the phonemic, rather than a stratum. It is perhaps for this reason that so many linguists mistakenly think of language in terms of the levels phonemic, morphemic, and syntactic as if these were in some kind of linear progressive relationship. But the difference in size between phonemes and morphemes—that is, strictly speaking, the widespread ocurrence of composite realization of lexons—is of secondary importance. It is, of course, an interesting fact about language, and is, in fact, the property which makes it possible for language to realize thousands of lexons with only a small number of phonemes.

PORTMANTEAU REALIZATION is the opposite of composite realization (see Figure 4). The name is a generalization from the term PORTMANTEAU MORPH. which was introduced by Hockett in his classic 'Problems of Morphemic Analysis' (1947). As examples, we have the combination of the lexon ^L/bad/ and the comparative lexon, with the realization M/wərhz/; the by now classical example from French in which ^L/à le/ is realized by ^M/o/; and, from a morphophonemic rule of Korean, the sequence of morphons ^M/wï/ realized by the phoneme ^P/u/.

Figure 4. Horizontal Discrepancy

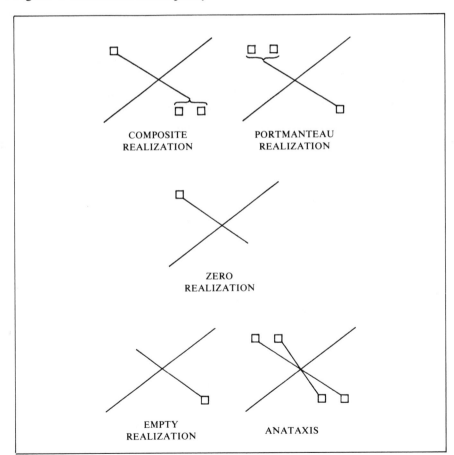

COMPOSITE
REALIZATION

PORTMANTEAU
REALIZATION

ZERO
REALIZATION

EMPTY
REALIZATION

ANATAXIS

In ZERO REALIZATION a unit is realized by zero (i.e. by nothing) on the next lower stratum. This situation always involves neutralization, since zero also occurs as the realization of zero. An example is the plural lexon when occurring with ᴸ/sheep/. A morphophonemic example is provided by Sanskrit, in which ᴹ/s/ is realized by zero when occurring between stop morphons.

EMPTY REALIZATION is the opposite situation. As with PORTMANTEAU the name is a generalization from Hockett's EMPTY MORPH (1947). Hockett's example is the phoneme ᴾ/i/ of Fox occurring between two morphs when the first ends in a consonant and the second begins in a consonant, as in ᴾ/poonimeewa/. Morphemic word juncture ᴹ/+/ in English and many other languages, is empty in many or most of its occurrences, since it realizes no lexon. That is, its presence is predictable, as required between the realizations of certain lexemic units. Empty realization always involves diversification, since zero is realized by zero in other environments. In other words, empty realizations are always in complementary distribution with zero.

Anataxis, which means 'rearrangement', is the term I use for situations in which the order of units of one stratum differs from that of their corresponding realizations on the lower stratum. The best known examples occur in relationships between the morphemic and phonemic strata, where they have usually been referred to as metathesis. An example is provided by a morphophonemic rule from Korean, in which morphophonemic ᴹ/hk/ is realized by phonemic ᴾ/kh/, as in ᴾ/alkho/ 'ailing', realizing ᴹ/alh ko/.

This catalogue of realizational situations may be summarized as follows: (1) a realizate may have more than one realization and a realization may have more than one realizate; (2) realizates and realizations may consist of elements, combinations of elements, or zero; (3) realizations do not always occur in the same order as their corresponding realizates.

The Sememic Stratum

I have said that it is necessary to recognize a sememic stratum, and I am now ready to provide the evidence. By giving examples for each of the various realizational situations which I have described, I will show that the relationship of realization is present between the lexemic stratum and something which can only be another stratum higher than the lexemic.

Considering first diversification, we have a sememic unit ˢ/can/ in *he can go*. But the future of *he can go* is *he will be able to go,* in which ˢ/can/ is realized by *be able to*. Another example is ˢ/agt./, the agent sememe, which occurs with noun phrases and identifies them as agents of verbal action. It is realized by at least three different lexemic entities in different environments: by ᴸ/of/ in such forms as *the growling of the lion,* and *the singing of the farmer;* by ᴸ/by/ in forms like *the duckling was killed by the farmer* and *the killing of the duckling by the farmer;* and by ᴸ/Ø/, i.e. no lexeme, in *the farmer killed the duckling.* In this last example there is also a feature of arrangement involved, but let us go into that later. As one more case of semolexemic diversification, we may consider the sememe which may be symbolized as ˢ/also/ and which has realizations

L/also/ and L/too/, as in *that one also works* and *that one works too*. But if the environment is negative S/also/ is realized by L/either/, as in *that one doesn't work either*. In each of these examples, as with diversification elsewhere, the differences between the alternate realizations are nondistinctive.

Let us now consider neutralization. The lexeme L/of/ occurs as the realization of several different sememic units. We have already seen it realizing the agent sememe in *the singing of the farmer*. But it can also realize the goal sememe S/gl./ as in *the killing of the duckling*. Because it can, we have such ambiguities as *the shooting of the hunters,* in which L/of/ could indicate either S/agt./ or S/gl./. But *of* also can realize the possessive sememe, the partitive sememe, as in *a leg of the table,* and several others.

These sememes are relatively 'grammatical' in meaning. But sememic analysis, like morphemic and lexemic analysis, must also be applied to relatively nongrammatical material. For example, we can recognize in the lexeme L/big/ a neutralization of at least four sememic units, occurring in the expressions *big rock, big sister, big fool,* and *he's a big man in our town.*

On what basis do we make this differentiation? It may appear that I am simply making various distinctions based on semantic considerations, in the manner of lexicographers. But to do so would clearly be a futile and meaningless effort. We would soon find that it is possible to make indefinitely many semantic distinctions, just as we can make indefinitely many distinctions at the phonetic stratum; and in neither case are we speaking about the structure of the language. It is rather between the sememic and the semantic strata that these indefinitely many fine distinctions exist. That is, each of the four sememes *big* has indefinitely many semantic realizates, just as a phoneme has indefinitely many phonetic realizations. But between the sememic stratum and the lexemic we are concerned only with those distinctions which are structurally significant in the language. Structural evidence for the recognition of these four sememes is given below.

We have now seen evidence which leads to an important conclusion. As I mentioned above, the presence of diversification and neutralization in linguistic realization defines the relative height of strata, determining which units are the realizates and which are the realizations. The examples show that THE SEMEMIC STRATUM IS ABOVE THE LEXEMIC, and that it is on the lexemic stratum that we find the allos of the sememes, that is, the ALLOSEMES. For example, given *the shooting of the hunters,* we cannot uniquely convert to the sememic stratum. There are two possibilities, and they are definitely not in free variation. But given the agent sememe in a sememic network, we can always convert to the lexemic stratum correctly. This conclusion may come as something of a shock to some linguists who may have been inclined to suppose that allosemes are on the other side of sememes, as it were, from where I place them (i.e., that the term ALLOSEME should be used for variant meanings). Since the form-substance dichotomy in Hjelmslev's (1961) expression plane fits quite well with the concepts of phoneme and allophone worked out in this country, one is understandably tempted to try to find it meaningful to use the terms SEMEME and ALLOSEME with reference to the form and substance, respectively, of content. But it turns out not to be. Sememes have their realizations, their allosemes, on the lexemic stratum, not on the semantic. It is true, on the other hand, that a partial parallelism exists between content and expression, in that for both there is a form-substance dichotomy with some similar characteristics. Thus the phonetic and semantic strata correspond to Hjelmslev's expression substance and content substance respectively. But whereas the basic relationship between the phonemic and phonetic strata is INDEFINITE DIVERSIFICATION (that is, diversification to indefinitely many isolable realizations in the phonetic substance), that which exists between the sememic and semantic strata is INDEFINITE NEUTRALIZATION (of indefinitely many semantic realizates).

Let us now look at a few examples of horizontal discrepancy in the realization of sememic units. Good examples of composite realization are furnished by some of the 'prepositional' sememes of English which are realized by strings of lexons. Thus we have *with regard to, concerning,* and *insofar as . . . is/are concerned.* We have already seen (above) L/be able to/ as a realization of S/can/. Among the nominalizing sememes of English, some are realized by suffixes, like the *-ing* in *the killing of the duckling by the farmer;* but one of them is realized by the string *the fact that,* as in *the fact that the farmer killed the duckling.* Other examples of composite lexemes include *look up* (words in a dictionary), *red-headed woodpecker* (cf. *yellow-headed canary,* which is polylexemic), *poison oak, computer* (as the name of a type of machine), *Human Relations Area Files,* and many of the strings of lexons which are commonly called idioms. «On the latter see A. Makkai 1965, 1969b, 1972.»

For portmanteau realization, we may adapt an example provided by Hjelmslev (1961:70). In Table II (to which many additional animal names could be added) the members of every row, viewed sememically, share certain semons (that is, sememic components) and there is a semon in common among the members of each of the second, third, and fourth columns.

Table II. Portmanteau Realization

sheep	ram	ewe	lamb
horse	stallion	mare	colt
chicken	rooster	hen	chick

This analysis is supported by such forms as *she-wolf* and *tigress,* both of which belong in the third column, in each of which the female semon is realized by a separate lexon.

Another example is furnished by the set of adjectives which occur with concrete nouns, and their related nominal forms. A few of these are shown in Table III.

Table III. Portmanteau Realization.

size	big	little
length	long	short
width	wide	narrow
depth	deep	shallow

Here the first and third columns may be analyzed as complex, and *length, width,* and *depth* are also complex also on the lexemic stratum and so are not portmanteaus as is *size*. Their complexity, with the separate nominalizing lexon *-th,* furnishes support for the portmanteau analysis of *size* (rather than **bigth*). As for the adjectives, we may take those of the second column as simple with relation to those of the third because the lexons *long, wide,* and *deep* are present in the nominalized forms of column one, and because these adjectives are more neutral or general in meaning than those of column three, as shown by such frames as 'How _____ is it?' Here, if we don't know whether 'it' is big or little, we use *big* in this frame. We do not use *little* unless we already know that it is little. The reader may verify that the same situation holds for the other adjectives in the table and for others which can be added to it. Thus if we set about to place *near* and *far* in the table, intuitive semantic judgements will not tell us which to put in which column, but testing with the frame will show that *far* belongs in the second, *near* in the third. In other words, the sememic realizate of *near* has as components the realizate of *far* plus another which we may symbolize as ^{S}/un/.

Kinship terms are also readily subjected to portmanteau sememic analysis, and the work of Lounsbury, Goodenough, Romney, and others in this area is directly applicable to the present formulation of semology. And it is becoming more and more apparent to those few linguists and anthropologists working in this area that kinship terms are by no means unusual in this respect, except in that componential analysis for them is perhaps easier. In fact, portmanteau realization is such a widespread phenomenon between the sememic and lexemic strata of languages that it is useful to have a term for that combination of semons which is a sememic realizate of a lexeme. For this entity I use the term SEMOLEXEME. Many semolexemes are composed of single semons, while many others are complex. Semolexemes are apparently often also sememes (which are, by definition of the suffix -EME, the realizations of semantic units or denotata), but we should not expect these units to coincide generally.

As an example of the zero alloseme, we may take the USITATIVE sememe, which with the past tense sememe has the realization *used to* as in *he used to walk to campus every day.* But the present tense string which corresponds to this is *he walks to campus every day,* in which the usitative sememe is realized by no lexeme at all. An excellent example of the zero alloseme is provided by the Russian verb 'to be,' which is realized as zero in the present.

Examples of empty lexemes (that is, lexemes which realize no sememic unit) are furnished by *do* in *John didn't call* and *did John call?* (cf. *John called*) and by *it* in such expressions as *it is evening, it's cold here, it's time to go.* In both cases, the empty lexemes are nonsignificant and are present only because they are required by the presence of certain combinations of sememes. Similarly, case-number-gender suffixes occurring with adjective stems in languages such as Latin and Russian to show agreement with nouns realize no sememe but are predictable.

It is only in the area of tactic phenomena that we find something in sememics which is different in kind from what occurs at lower levels. Attributive adjectivals in English precede nouns if they are tactically simple, as in *an easy job,* but follow when complex, as with relative clauses, participial phrases, adjectives modified by prepositional phrases, and in *a job easy to do.* (Some complex adjectivals can also be discontinuous, as in *an easy job to do.*) The position of the adjectival relative to the noun, then, is predictable and nondistinctive, and therefore subsememic. What we have would appear to be not merely anataxis, since the items of the sememic stratum do not appear to have a linear order at all. That is, we may have the adjectival occurring simply WITH what it modifies, rather than BEFORE or AFTER it.

But in some situations difference in order is significant. For example, in those enviornments where the goal sememe is realized by lexemic zero, as in simple indicative expressions such as *the farmer killed the duckling,* its presence is made known by a feature of arrangement, namely the position of the goal phrase after the verb phrase. A more clear-cut instance of this phenomenon is the device used in Russian to indicate approximation with regard to numerical quantities. *Pjat' rublej* means 'five rubles' but *rublej pjat'* means 'approximately five rubles.' Here we have a clear-cut case of a sememe (i.e. 'approximately') realized not by a lexeme or combination of lexemes, but by a feature of arrangement.

Thus some features of lexemic arrangement are significant; they therefore realize sememic units. Others are nonsignificant and therefore empty, just like empty lexemes. In still other instances, although not as commonly, there are alternate arrangements in free variation. These too are usually empty. Thus it is seen that the set of semolexemic rules for a language yields both the lexemes and their arrangement. And since all features of linear arrangement of morphemes are accounted for in lexemic and sememic analysis, they are no longer present in the sememic stratum. In other words, semons do not occur in a linear order relative to one another, and it is not to be unexpected that this should be so. Linearity is appropriate to the lower strata since speech is produced and heard in the time continuum. But thought patterns, relationships, concepts, and the things about which people talk are not linear, so we should not expect semological systems to be.[4] There are, on the other hand, certain nonlinear arrangement patterns present on the sememic stratum, since it is not the case that sememes simply occur in amorphous clumps. These patterns may be described by SEMOTACTIC RULES, which characterize the (infinite) set of well-formed networks of semons.

Sememic Analysis

Since the relationship between the sememic and lexemic strata is essentially the same as that already dealt with by linguists among lower strata, the same general techniques used in analysis at these levels will apply in sememic analysis. Stratificational analysis, whose proper result is a set of rules relating each pair of neighboring strata, is concerned with recognizing all cases of horizontal and vertical discrepancy. This process of analysis may itself be analyzed into distinct types of operations in accordance with the different types of discrepancy. We may isolate three basic types of operations, which may be SEGMENTATION, DIFFERENTIATION, and GROUPING.

SEGMENTATION is necessitated by horizontal discrepancy. In general, it involves the establishment of boundaries in strings of a given stratum to yield substrings having a direct relation to a neighboring stratum. It is most familiar as applied in the determination of morphemes, where the grammarian must discover what substrings of phonemes must be recognized as morphs, i.e., realizations of morphemes. For example, P/pets/ must be segmented into P/pet s/. In examining material of the lexemic stratum for purposes of sememic analysis, it must be recognized that strings like *with regard to, look up* (words in a dictionary) and *give up* must be treated as units (rather than in terms of their component parts) in order to be related to the sememic stratum.

Another kind of segmentation is the analysis of higher-stratum units into their components. This type of segmentation is necessitated by the occurrence of portmanteau realization. Thus in lexemic analysis it is necessary to recognize that the lexemic realizate of *worse* is a combination of two elements. Similarly, a part of sememic analysis is the componential segmentation of semolexemes like the realizates of *ram* and *ewe*, or *uncle* and *aunt*, into their constituent semons.

DIFFERENTIATION is needed because of neutralization. It involves the recognition of different instances of identical units as structurally different from one another from the point of view of the higher stratum. For example, in lexemic analysis the English morpheme which we represent orthographically as -ed must be differentiated as realizing both the past tense lexeme and the past passive participle lexeme. Differentiation is perhaps the most difficult part of sememic analysis; it is discussed further below.

GROUPING, the third basic type of operation, is necessary because of diversification. It involves the recognition that two or more differentiated segments of the lower stratum (e.g., –ed, –en) realize a single unit of the higher stratum (e.g., past participle). Grouping is done on the basis of noncontrastive distribution; that is, the units grouped as alternate realizations of a realizate must be in complementary distribution (as defined in terms of the upper stratum) or in free variation (or partly one, partly the other).

Thus, for example, one may view the process of establishing morphemes by starting from phonemic material as consisting first of segmentation to convert a corpus from strings of phonemes to strings of morphs; then differentiation to convert from morphs to allomorphs (cf. the definition of ALLO-, above); and grouping to convert from allomorphs to morphemes. By this statement I do not mean to suggest that it is necessary or even desirable to use a step-by-step procedure in stratificational analysis. The procedure-oriented statement is only a means of clarifying the explanation of the concepts. Actually, all three types of operations have to be performed with reference to one another, since they are interdependent.

Of these basic operations, it is differentiation which will give the most trouble in sememic analysis. Linguists have not had to work out criteria for differentiation in phonemic analysis since neutralization of phonemes is not allowed. In morphemic and lexemic analysis rigorous criteria for differentiation have not been spelled out completely. Neutralization of sememic units on a large scale is doubtless a device universally employed in languages, which enables them to provide for discourse on everything in the range of human experience, while at the same time being simple enough for children to learn.

(Neutralization A revealed by diversification B)
Figure 5. Interlocking Diversification

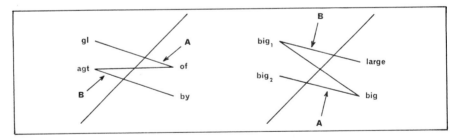

We may identify three types of criteria for differentiation. Perhaps the most important is that in which the presence of neutralization is revealed by its being 'interlocked' with an instance of diversification (see Figure 5). Accordingly, this type of situation may be referred to as INTERLOCKING DIVERSIFICATION. As an example we may consider the lexon [L]/of/, which as noted above is a neutralized realization of the agent sememe and the goal sememe, among others. Ambiguities provide important clues to the possibility that a neutralization has to be recognized, particularly when they are as striking as *the shooting of the hunters*. But ambiguity alone is not a sufficient criterion for differentiation, because one could go on making indefinitely many finer and finer distinctions if one were analyzing on the basis of difference in meaning only. What establishes that we are dealing here with a real case of neutralization is that for each of the interpretations there is an alternate realization not shared by the other. For example, in *the shooting of the ducklings by the hunters* L/by/ has the same function as *one* of the functions of L/of/ in *the shooting of the hunters.* In addition we have already observed that still another realization of S/agt./ is the feature of arrangement whereby *the hunters* precedes *shoot* in *the hunters shoot,* while S/gl./ has as one of its realizations the feature of ordering present in, e.g., *they shot the hunters.* Interlocking diversification is the same criterion as that by which we analyze the suffix *-ed*, a single unit on the morphemic stratum, as a neutralized realization of both the past tense lexon and the past participle lexon, since, for example, the latter but not the former also has the realization *-en*, while the past tense lexon in turn has realizations not shared by the past participle lexon. This differentiation is made despite the fact that for the great preponderance of English verbs, the past tense form and the past participle both have the same suffix *-ed*.

As another example of interlocking diversification in sememic analysis we may consider the lexeme L/big/, referred to above. In many of its occurrences, e.g. with *rock, big* is interchangeable with *large: big rock, large rock; big house, large house.* But if we try *big sister, large sister,* we see that they are by no means interchangeable. This fact establishes a different sememe for *big* as in *big sister.* Again it is because one of the sememic realizates, in this case S/big$_1$/ as in *big rock*, has alternate realizations, only one of which is shared by the other, that we are able to perform the differentiation.

Another situation which makes differentiation possible is the presence of different portmanteau analyses. With reference to the set of adjectives given in Table III, if we continued the tabulation we would find *soft* appearing in the third column of two different rows: *loudness, loud, soft* and *hardness, hard, soft.* In this case, *soft* realizes two different sememic units in a vertical discrepancy, for each of which it realizes two units in a horizontal discrepancy (Figure 6). And it is the presence of the latter which allows us to differentiate.

Figure 6. Neutralized Portmanteau Realization.

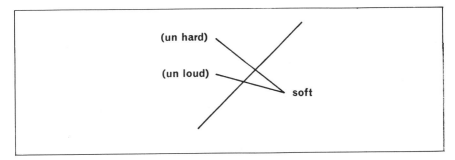

To illustrate the use of distributional criteria, let us continue our analysis of *big.* We find it possible to differentiate three sememes on the basis of differences in distribution, as shown in the table below. We may call them $S/big_1/$, as in *big rock*, $S/big_2/$, as in *big sister*, and $S/big_3/$, as in *he's a big fool*. (See Table IV.)

Table IV. Distribution of Semons.

	big__	__is big	very big how big? bigger
big_1 (rock)	+	+	+
big_2 (sister)	+	–	∟
big_3 (fool)	+	–	+
big_4 (man)	+	+	+

All three occur attributively with their appropriate nominals, as in *big rock, big sister,* and *big fool.* But predicatively we find only $S/big_1/$. That is, we can have *the rock is big* but not *my sister is big* or *the fool is big* (except by a shift of sememe to $S/big_1/$.) In the third column we have a set of environments which are alike for our purposes, and we may note incidentally that their similarity as distributional environments correlates with a semantic feature which they share, since they are all concerned with whether degrees of bigness are possible. We have without difficulty *how big a rock is it, it's a very big rock, it's a bigger rock than this;* and also *how big a fool is he? he's a very big fool,* and *he's a bigger fool than I am;* but not so for *big sister.* Referentially, in the outside world, there is no reason why $S/big_2/$ should not have the same privilege of occurrence. Suppose that I have a sister Elizabeth two years older than I and a sister Jean four years older than I. Then I ought to be able to say that Elizabeth is my big sister and that Jean is my bigger sister; moreover, it would also be correct that Jean is a bigger sister than Elizabeth. But the language does not allow it. That is simply a fact of the structure of English.

Thus we have three different sememes, as shown by three different distributions. Both $S/big_2/$ and $S/big_3/$ can also be differentiated from $S/big_1/$ by use of the principle of interlocking diversification (cf. Figure 4); and the distributional differences differentiate them one from the other. Furthermore, there is a fourth sememe, $S/big_4/$, as in *he's a big man in our town,* which cannot be differentiated from $S/big_1/$ by the use of the distributional tests illustrated here, since $S/big_4/$ can be used predicatively and has degrees. But it can be distinguished from $S/big_1/$ on the basis of interlocking diversification.

Some Additional Observations

In this paper I have proposed an approach to the attack of semantic problems in language which is based on the premise that in order to get anywhere in this kind of study one must be aware of the structuralization of meaning which is present within languages. It would seem that much of the difficulty, vagueness, and inconclusiveness of semantic studies and speculations in the past has been the result of a lack of awareness of this structuring. People have attempted to relate 'words,' whose nature has been variously conceived in terms of one or more of the lower strata of language, directly to denotata, bypassing the intervening sememic stratum. The result has been such complexity in the observations made that to some the task of dealing systematically with meaning has seemed hopeless. Bloomfield (1933, 1939), for example, thought that the proper study of the meanings of linguistic forms could not be undertaken in advance of the attainment by science of considerably more detailed knowledge of the world than we now have. In other words, like many others, he was looking at the problem (if we translate into stratificational terms) as one of relating the lexemic stratum directly to the semantic, and in his case the reaction to the prospect of undertaking such studies was almost one of despair. The situation is parallel to that which used to confront students of language in the area of phonology back in the days when phonemes were not known. The development of phonetics led to the ability to make finer and finer distinctions in the study of the expression side of language, and it was apparent that one could go on and on indefinitely making more and more precise phonetic descriptions of linguistic data, and that one never would get to the end of such a task. Yet it seemed clear that not all of the fine distinctions which were physically observable were linguistically significant. On the other hand one did not know where to draw the line, where to stop making distinctions. The answer, of course, was phonemics; and I suggest that the answer to the problem of determining what is linguistically significant in the study of meaning is sememics.

The phonemic stratum is at the 'bottom' of the structure of a spoken language and the sememic at the 'top.' In other words the phonemic stratum of a language is as closely related to actual sound as possible while retaining the discrete structured properties of a linguistic stratum. And the sememic stratum has a similar position in the area of content. Thus the criteria for determining the phonemic and sememic structures of language also determine the boundaries of linguistic structure. «According to the latest still unpublished insights of Lamb (personal communication), it now seems possible (May, 1972) that much of the conceptual system of a speaker of a language referred to in Stage IV as HYPERSEMEMIC and in the article 'The crooked path of progress in cognitive linguistics' as the GNOSTEMIC SYSTEM could, in fact, be collapsed into one large system with the sememic, where the formalization of linguistic meaning occurs. This has become possible because Lamb found that the highly adaptable relational network notation developed largely during Stage IV can accommodate not only the structural facts of language, but the structural inter-relationships of person's KNOWLEDGE and LOGICAL ASSUMPTIONS as well. Initial steps in this direction were already taken in the essay 'Linguistic and Cognitive Networks' (reprinted in this volume), where the reader can find a relational network description of the structure of a baseball game, the classical syllogism, and a portion of the family of mammals. Lamb's latest research is moving in the direction of describing in network notation the kind of assumptions about the world a speaker makes before committing such knowledge to encoding in a grammatical sentence. Eight years ago when the present article was first published, going as far as the SEMEME seemed sufficiently ambitious, and thus for 1964 Lamb found it sufficient to define the limits of linguistic structure as the PHONEMIC SYSTEM (bottom) and the SEMEMIC SYSTEM (top). There is now, more than ever, increasing evidence that no theory of linguistics can get along without building presupposition and general knowledge into what PRECEDES the uttering of a sentence. Far from being unrealistic, therefore, Lamb's recent attempts at building GENERAL COGNITION and SEMOLOGY together, hopelessly ambitious as this may have seemed to Bloomfield, are moving in a direction that the whole of linguistics is inevitably moving: in the direction of GENERAL SEMIOTICS and PSYCHO-SEMANTICS. Rather than being relegated to the United States alone, this (to our mind healthy) trend in linguistics is internationally spread and includes such countries as the Soviet Union, Czechoslovakia, Hungary, France, Italy, and many others.»

In this connection, one of the cardinal principles of phonemic analysis is that it be done so that there will be no neutralization between the phonemic and phonetic strata. In other words, (assuming an idealized phonetic representation which is free from noise) it must always be possible to convert uniquely from the phonetic to the phonemic stratum (but this is the only place where conversion to an upper stratum is unique). If in a provisional solution there are any cases of neutralization, it means that the level of the putative phonemic stratum has been set, as it were, too high, and that it must therefore be pushed down to the point at which the neutralization will have been eliminated; that is, the instances of neutralization must be treated instead as morphophonemic phenomena. The level would also be set too high if there is a failure to recognize some contrast, i.e., a phonetic distinction that is correlated with a difference in content. On the other hand, the level would be set too low if there were too many putative phonemes recognized in the system, some of them still in mutually noncontrastive distribution. This would mean that not enough grouping had been done, i.e., that distinctions lacking structural significance had been made. When the phonemic stratum is correctly established, then, there will be as much diversification between it and the phonetic stratum as possible (without ignoring contrast), but no neutralization. For illustration we may consider the analysis of stops in Russian, for which, as in some other languages, there is no voiced: voiceless contrast in final position. That is, many morphemes have final voiced stop alternating with final voiceless stop, depending on what follows, while others have voiceless stop everywhere. One might be tempted to eliminate this alternation at the phonemic stratum by setting up phonemic voiced stops in the forms with alternation and a phonemic rule accounting for the voiceless phonetic realization in final position. But such an analysis would violate the principle that neutralization between the phonemic stratum and the phonetic is not allowable. This rule must therefore be made a morphophonemic rule. An attempt to group all occurrences of corresponding voiced and voiceless stops (including those which do not alternate) into single phonemes would be an example of failure to recognize a contrast, since the difference in voicing of stops correlates with meaning differences in intervocalic position. On the other hand, to distinguish phonetically different varieties of (what we know to be) P/d/ at the phonemic stratum would be unacceptable on the grounds that not enough grouping had been done; such phonetic distinctions are phonetic and not phonemic because they do not correlate with a difference in meaning.

It appears that the above principles apply equally, *mutatis mutandis,* in determining the upper boundary of linguistic structure. Here the peripheral stratum, the semantic, is above the structural one, whereas the phonetic is below the phonemic. This means that when the sememic stratum is correctly established there will be the condition of indefinite neutralization between it and the semantic stratum, and as much neutralization as possible, but that there will be no diversification. This principle is a very important guide in sememic analysis and is, in fact, the basis for the criterion of interlocking diversification. If a provisional sememic formulation is such that there are instances of diversification (that is, if there is any choice at all allowed in going from the semantic to the sememic stratum), then it has been set too low, i.e. not enough sememic distinctions have been made. The requirement that there be no diversification means that there can be no choices in the conversion from the semantic stratum to the sememic. On the other hand, the level would have been set too high (that is, distinctions lacking structural significance would have been made) if it were the case that the number of sememes could be reduced by bringing more semantic area into the scope of certain sememes without incurring any diversification or loss of contrast. Loss of contrast, or more precisely, failure to recognize contrast, in this context means ignoring semantic distinctions which correlate with differences in expression (while failure to recognize contrast in phonemic analysis means ignoring phonetic distinctions which correlate with differences in meaning). Thus a failure to recognize L/big/ and L/large/ as alternate realizations of one sememic unit, (i.e., leaving a S/large$_1$/ as a separate sememe from S/big$_1$/) would be allowing diversification between the semantic stratum and the sememic, since L/big/ and L/large/ are interchangeable (i.e., freely varying realizations) as lexemic forms associated with the meaning of S/big$_1$/, so that a choice between them must be made. The diversification must therefore be handled as a semolexemic phenomenon.

On the other hand, an attempt to combine S/big$_1$/ with S/big$_2$/ (of *big sister*) must be ruled out on the grounds of failure to recognize a contrast, since there is a correlated difference in expression in that S/big$_1$/ but not S/big$_2$/ may be realized by L/large/ (which in turn is realized phonetically as something quite different from the phonetic realization of L/big/). But to distinguish, say, the *big* of *eyes big with tears* from S/big$_1$/ (as is done by the American College Dictionary) would be unacceptable on the grounds that not enough semantic area had been assigned to the sememe; whatever difference in meaning there may be here is semantic and not sememic since it does not correlate with a difference in expression.

NOTES

1. At various times when I have been working on the concepts treated here I have been aided and stimulated by discussion with Harold C. Conklin, H. A. Gleason, Jr., David G. Hays, Charles F. Hockett, C. Douglas Johnson, Floyd G. Lounsbury, Samuel E. Martin, E. D. Pendergraft, A. Kimball Romney, William F. Shipley, David S. Shwayder, Robert P. Stockwell, John H. Wahlgren, and others, none of whom necessarily agree with everything I say in this paper.

2. Here I am departing from my own earlier terminology in using the terms MORPHEMIC and LEXEMIC for what I used to call MORPHOPHONEMIC and MORPHEMIC respectively. «In Stage I.»

3. An alternative definition of XEME, which defines a similar but not identical unit, would be that an XEME is the basic tactic unit of the Xemic stratum (i.e. the basic unit of the XOTACTICS), in the sense that the combinations of such Xemes may be efficiently accounted for by general construction rules whereas combinations of Xons up to the tactic level of the Xemes must be listed individually for each Xeme. Thus lexemes, according to this definition, would be the minimum productive units of the lexemic stratum, whose combinations are describable by general lexotactic construction rules. *Width* represents two lexemes according to the definition in the text, one according to this alternative. Both types of Xeme are important, they usually coincide, and the decision as to which type of unit is more usefully called the Xeme is a matter of terminological policy. This alternative has the possible advantage that it allows the Xeme to be defined in terms of structuring on its own stratum rather than by reference to the one above.

4. Furthermore, if one does attempt to have a linear ordering at the highest level of the structure, then it is necessary to have transformational rules in a grammar (cf. Chomsky 1957) to 'transform' strings from one order to another, in dealing with related structures such as corresponding active and passive clauses or declarative and interrogative clauses; and such rules are very complicated.

CHAPTER TWELVE

Kinship Terminology and Linguistic Structure*

SYDNEY M. LAMB

'Mommy, what are girl nephews called?'
CHRISTIE *(age 6)*

THIS PAPER is an attempt to elucidate the relationship of kinship terminology to the rest of linguistic structure. Various anthropologists have shown (e.g., Hammel 1965a) that kinship terminologies are neatly structured. They can be described in terms of certain elements and certain relationships among these elements, as can phonological and grammatical systems. But as a kinship terminology is a terminology, it must be part of a language; so these elements must be linguistic elements, and these relationships must be linguistic relationships. Thus their proper description must in some form belong in the overall description of a linguistic structure. To understand fully the nature of kinship systems it is necessary to understand what kind of linguistic elements these are, and what kind of linguistic relationships. Are the relationships found in kinship terminologies (and similar systems) different from those found in other parts of linguistic structure, or not? Where does their description fit into the overall description of a language? Where do the elements (of various kinds) fit into the overall structure? The answers are not already available, since anthropologists have tended not to work on integrated linguistic theories, and since linguists have not yet done very much systematic work on lexological and semological structures. Moreover, there is not even any general agreement among linguists on what the elements and relationships are among those areas of linguistic

*From *American Anthropologist* 67, No. 5, Pt.2.37–78(1965) (=*Formal Semantic Analysis,* E.A. Hammel, ed.) Reprinted by permission.

structure that have been more intensively investigated, nor on how they may best be described. In this absence of agreement, a structural interpretation of kinship terminology can be valuable for general linguistic theory as well as for social anthropologists, since the data provided by kinship systems (along with various other kinds of data) can serve to 'separate the men from the boys,' i.e. the linguistic theories that can neatly account for them from those that cannot.

Linguistic Structure

The lack of general agreement among linguists and the variety of available linguistic theories just alluded to are actually of lesser proportions than might be apparent from a first glance at the diverse notational systems, linguistic terminologies, and professed aims that have been put forth during the past several years, for it is more a variety in the means of talking about linguistic structure than in what is actually being said. Moreover, the range of real (as opposed to mere terminological) disagreement with regard to some of the more basic issues is becoming progressively narrower. A few years ago the assertion that linguistic structure is stratified was generally considered controversial, despite the long history of renowned scholars who have provided precedent for it, including in this century Saussure (1916), Noreen (1903–18), and Hjelmslev (1943). But it is much less controversial today, and most of what controversy remains is only terminological, since some prefer to refer to the strata by other names. The real opposition of a few years ago was mainly from two different sides. On the one hand there were those of the Sapir and Bloomfield traditions who held that, for example, morphemes were combinations of phonemes (even if sometimes they were different combinations of phonemes in different environments).[1] On the other hand there was the new school of generative-transformationalism (cf. Chomsky 1957), which compared three 'models for the structure of language' all of which were actually single-stratum systems, and concluded that a proper linguistic description was a long sequence of rewrite rules, including a special very complicated kind of rewrite rule called the transformation, that it was all right to mix levels, and so forth. The model that was proposed, with regard to both its morphophonemic component[2] and its transformations, failed to distinguish between elements and their realizations.

But both of these schools, the one traditional and conservative, the other young and militant, have gradually been breaking away from their single-stratum orientation. Those of the Bloomfield-Sapir tradition (it can be called a single tradition, because the differences are less important than the similarities, and the current senior generation of linguists got its orientation from both men) came to the view first that the morpheme is a CLASS of combinations of phonemes, still only a quasi-stratificational view;[3] and many have gone on, under the influence of such arguments as that presented by Hockett (1961), to the view that phonemes and morphemes must be considered to be on entirely different strata from each other. And the transformational school has meanwhile begun to make a clear-cut separation between its 'deep structure' and its 'surface structure' (cf. Chomsky 1966), which correspond, respectively, to the lexemic stratum and the morphemic stratum of the scheme outlined in Lamb 1964a and elsewhere.[4] This separation of strata resulted from elimination of the conflation of elements with their realizations which had necessitated the former optional transformations and from the recognition that the generation of sentences of more than one clause does not require transformations. The only transformations remaining in this increasingly nontransformational system are obligatory, and they are actually conversion rules for converting from the stratum of 'deep structure' to that of 'surface structure.'

Meanwhile, across the Atlantic, the glossematic school (cf. Hjelmslev 1943) has been stratified from its outset, as has the 'scale and category' theory of M.A.K. Halliday (1961), which separates its 'levels' on roughly the same kind of basis that leads different stratal systems to be distinguished in the scheme outlined below. And in Russia the 'applicational generative model' proposed by Šaumjan and Soboleva (1963) distinguishes two strata called the genotype level and the phenotype level, which seem to have a rough correspondence to the deep and surface levels of Chomsky.

Thus the real differences of opinion among linguists, if one separates them from mere terminological differences exaggerated by sectarian disputation, are concerned not with whether or not linguistic structure is stratified but only with how many strata there are and the related questions of what type of system is associated with each and what the relationship is between neighboring strata. In the one of these various modern stratificational schools that has actually come to be called 'stratificational' (cf. Gleason 1964, Lamb 1964a,b), the following strata, listed in order from lowest to highest, are recognized for spoken languages: PHONETIC, PHONEMIC, MORPHEMIC, LEXEMIC, SEMEMIC, SEMANTIC. Of these the two outside ones, i.e. phonetic and semantic, are concerned with substance (in the sense of Hjelmslev 1943) while the inner, or structural, strata consist solely of relationships. On the phonetic stratum are the speech sounds, on the semantic are reference and communicative intent. The linguistic structure relates the semantic stratum to the phonetic. It can be described by means of five systems, each of which relates two neighboring strata and is associated particularly with the lower of the two. These five stratal systems may be called PHONETICS, PHONOLOGY, MORPHOLOGY, LEXOLOGY, and SEMOLOGY. Thus (as an introductory approximation) the relationship between the strata and their associated stratal systems is as shown in Table I.

Each of the stratal systems of a language has certain basic structural features in common with the others and numerous features of detail which differentiate it from the others. The fundamental structural relationships of which the systems are constructed are the same in each of them. These may be referred to by the terms SET (or CLASS) and COMBINATION, or more precisely they may be called the OR relation and the AND relation.[5] Both of these types of relation occur in either of two directions, which may

Semantic	
	Semology
Sememic	
	Lexology
Lexemic	
	Morphology
Morphemic	
	Phonology
Phonemic	
	Phonetics
Phonetic	

Table I
Strata and Stratal Systems

be referred to as UPWARD (towards meaning) and DOWNWARD (towards expression). These matters are discussed further below. The terms COMBINATION, COMPONENT, and COMPOSED OF are used in the following paragraphs with reference to the 'downward and' relation, and the downward class is referred to simply as a class.

The stratal systems also resemble each other in that each may be divided into two parts, which may be called the REALIZATIONAL portion and the TACTIC portion or TACTICS. The tactics of any of the stratal systems specifies how the BASIC UNITS of the system are arranged in larger units, and the realizational part specifies the relationships between the basic units and the 'realized' or 'actual' units, i.e. their realizations. These REALIZED UNITS, except in the phonetics, are composed of ELEMENTARY UNITS, whose function is to control the tactics of the next lower system. In the phonetics, the realized units are speech sounds. The realized units of a stratal system and their components may be said to exist on the stratum associated with that stratal system. For example, sememes and semons are on the sememic stratum. The names of these various units for the phonology, morphology, lexology, and semology are given in Table II.

STRATAL SYSTEM	BASIC UNIT	REALIZED UNIT	ELEMENTARY UNIT
Semology	Basic Sememe	Sememe	Semon
Lexology	Basic Lexeme	Lexeme	Lexon
Morphology	Basic Morpheme	Morpheme	Morphon
Phonology	Basic Phoneme	Phoneme	Phonon

Table II
Linguistic Units

It is to be emphasized that any of the stratal systems has its own tactics, and may accordingly be viewed as a device for generating combinations of elements. Thus a single stratal system has a type of structure like that which earlier linguistic theories attributed to language as a whole. For example, both the transformational system and the so-called 'phrase structure' model to which it opposed itself were like single stratal systems in having tactics followed by rules which operated on the combinations generated by the tactics. The real basis of the inadequacy of the 'phrase structure' model was not that it lacked transformations but that it consisted of only one stratal system. The actual schemes that the partly straw 'phrase structure' model was intended to portray were primarily morphologies, with admixtures of some lexological and phonological information. The transformationalists attempted to deal with the observed inadequacy not by realizing that lexology and morphology are separate systems, each with its own tactics, but by setting up an expanded single stratal system with lexological tactics followed by transformations to transform lexological combinations to appropriate morphological arrangements.

The stratum is called STRATUM to distinguish it from other types of levels with which it has often been confused, such as combinatory or size levels and classificatory or taxonomic levels. The combinatory level is that which is concerned with combinations of linguistic units, the type of which one is speaking when one says that the word is at a higher level than the morpheme or that the sentence is at a higher level than the clause. Such levels exist WITHIN strata. They can be kept distinct from other types of levels by being called RANKS, as is done by Halliday (1961). Combinations of linguistic units exist on the same stratum as those units. Thus each stratum has a series of ranks. For example, the word is at a higher rank than the morpheme, but on the same stratum. Similarly, lexemes and combinations of lexemes such as clauses and sentences are all on the lexemic stratum. It is important to realize that a unit of type A (say a word) which is at a higher rank than a unit of type B (say a morpheme) is not necessarily larger. One may say that if an A is of higher rank than a B, then an A is a combination of ONE OR MORE B's, i.e. it may in some instances consist of a single B. Thus many words consist of single morphemes; in English a syllable can consist of a single vowel, a sentence can consist of a single clause or of more than one. But the unit *man* considered as a word is of higher rank than the unit *man* considered as a morpheme, because of the different relationships which it has to other units at these two ranks.

The stratificational hierarchy also is to be distinguished from taxonomic or classificatory hierarchies. The relationship between one stratum and an adjacent one is NOT that units of the one are classes whose members are units of the other. That is, the stratificational view is not the same as that which holds that a morpheme is a class of allomorphs and that a phoneme is a class of allophones. That view is too simple to fit the empirical data. The actual relationship between units of neighboring strata is considerably more complicated than the class-member relationship. There are classes to be recognized in a linguistic structure, but, like combinations, they exist on the same stratum as their members. For example, the class of nominal lexemes is on the lexemic stratum, and the class of verb root morphemes is on the morphemic.

There are seven types of relationship which collectively characterize the way in which elementary units of one structural stratum differ from those of neighboring ones. These are described and illustrated in Lamb 1964a[6] and may be called DIVERSIFICATION, NEUTRALIZATION, COMPOSITE REALIZATION, PORTMANTEAU REALIZATION, ZERO REALIZATION, EMPTY REALIZATION, and ANATAXIS. If one compares, say, lexemic material (composed of lexons) with morphemic (composed of morphons) for a given language, one may rarely find a one-to-one correspondence between a lexon and a morphon (in English, the third person singular nonpast verbal suffix and the morphon $M/z/$ come close to qualifying, but this $M/z/$ is a neutralized realization of other lexons as well); but in general one finds discrepancies from such simple correspondence of one or more of these seven types.

The difference between lexons and morphons (like that between semons and lexons or morphons and phonons) is a 'full stratum' of difference and is mediated by the basic morpheme and the morpheme. Composite realization may be localized as a relation of morphemes to morphons. That is, a typical lexon is realized as a combination of morphons in that its realization is a morpheme, which is a combination of morphons. Differences between lexons and morphemes may be divided into two kinds, (1) those which contribute to the simplicity or 'neatness' of the morphotactics (i.e. the tactics of the morphology), and (2) those which do not. Those of the first type may be localized as differences between lexons and basic morphemes, while those of the second type are differences between basic morphemes and morphemes.

Differences between lexons and basic morphemes usually involve empty realization, zero realization, or anataxis. Of these, anataxis is often controlled directly by a specific lexon, while empty realization and zero realization may be thought of as automatic adjustments of what is specified by lexon combinations so that the resulting basic morphemes will fit the morphotactics. An example of anataxis is provided by the clause of Figure 1, where it is represented in terms of lexemes (one lexeme at each node) and their constituent lexons (separated by spaces), in comparison with the morphological order, which is the same as that shown in the ordinary orthography: *the cabinetmaker has been looking for his brace and bit.* A transcription in terms of basic morphemes (where spaces separate basic morphemes) is: BM/the + cabinet make r + have z + be n + look ing + for + he 's + brace + and + bit/. In this representation, the BM/+/ is the basic morpheme of word boundary, which is supplied as an empty basic morpheme by the morphotactics. It thus provides an example of empty realization between lexons and basic morphemes. The lexon $L/>/$ specifies to the morphotactics that whatever it accompanies is to be delayed one word. For the interrogative version of this clause, the interrogative semon is realized as the lexeme $L/>/$ occurring with the subject phrase, so that the whole subject phrase is delayed one word, and the order is that seen in *has the cabinetmaker been looking for his brace and bit?* When this interrogative lexeme occurs, the morphotactics goes (as it were) to the position in the tactic structure following that of the noun phrase, delaying the noun phrase until one word has been generated by it. When it gets to the verbal auxilary position there is an element BM/do/ which will be supplied if no specific auxiliary has been called for by the lexology, so that BM/do/ (realized as M/di/ when followed by the past tense basic morpheme) is an example of empty realization in a question like *Did the cabinetmaker find his brace and bit?*

Several examples of differences between basic morphemes and actual morphemes are provided by basic morphemes in the clauses discussed above. The basic morpheme BM/do/ is realized as M/di/ in *did*, M/də/ in *done*, and M/duw/ elsewhere. These three realizations are actual morphemes, written in terms of their constituent morphons. BM/have/ is realized as M/ha/ in *has* and *had* (the latter being a neutralization of both the past tense form and the past participle form), M/hav/ elsewhere. Notice that the morphotactics is more easily stated in terms of basic morphemes than realized morphemes. The relationships among basic morphemes, morphemes, and morphons may be stated by means of a set of realization rules, which specify for each basic morpheme its realization (i.e. realized morphemes) in terms of their constituent morphons, and the conditions for the occurrence of each realization (cf. Lamb 1964b).[7] Of the seven types of discrepancies, diversification and neutralization are the primary ones which differentiate basic morphemes from morphemes, but portmanteau and zero realization also are found, as accompaniments of diversification.

Figure 1. The cabinetmaker has been looking for his brace and bit (Lexemic stratum).

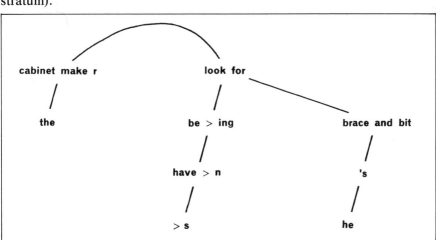

A diagram showing certain relationships among morphological units is given as Figure 2. Both this figure and, in broad general terms, the relationships exemplified above, are to be taken as illustrative of stratal systems

Figure 2. Morphological Units and their Relations.

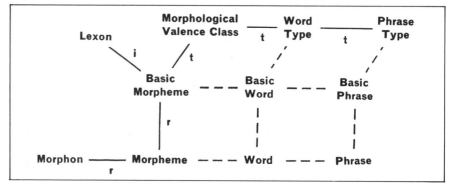

in general. The lines connecting names of different units represent types of relationship, and lines of different slope indicate relationships of different kinds. Horizontal lines connect units of lower rank (at left) to units of higher rank (at right). (The type of relationship involved here is the 'downward and' relation or downward combination.) The vertical line connects items related primarily by diversification (a 'downward or' relation) and neutralization (an 'upward or' relation). The diagonal from lower left to upper right connects valence classes (upper right) to their members (lower left), and the other diagonal is for the interstratal relationship. Solid lines stand for relations which must be directly described by the grammarian whereas the dotted-line relations follow automatically from the solid-line ones. For example, a basic word is a member of a word type, as defined by the (solid line) relations between word type and morphological valence class and between morphological valence class and basic morpheme. A word type *ABC* . . . is the class of all words *abc* . . . such that basic morpheme *a* is a member of valence class *A*, basic morpheme *b* is a member of valence class *B,* and so on. Similarly, a word is a realization of a basic word, namely the combination of morphemes which are realizations of the basic morphemes whose combination is that basic word. The solid lines are labeled *r, t,* or *i* to indicate to what part of the structure the relationships represented by them belong; that is, realizational, tactics, or interstratal (between lexology and morphology), respectively.

A series of examples and informal definitions is given below to provide an indication of how various structural units differ from one another,[8] from phonon to basic sememe, and a diagram which portrays the relationships is given as Figure 3, which is an expansion to four stratal systems (semology, lexology, morphology, and phonology) of a less detailed version of Figure 2.

The English phoneme P/b/ may be analyzed as composed of the phonons (unary distinctive features) P/Cl/ 'closed' and P/Lb/ 'labial'. The syllable P/bad/ may be transcribed phonically as

Cl   Vo   Cl
Lb   Fr   Ap
     Lo

(where the phononic symbols stand for, respectively, CLOSED, LABIAL, VOCALIC, FRONT, LOW, CLOSED, APICAL). The basic phoneme is the basic unit of the phonotactics (i.e. tactics of the phonology). The basic phonemes of a structural description are so set up by the grammarian that the tactic description will be as simple as possible (without being incorrect or incomplete). Basic phonemes may differ from realized phonemes in that a given basic phoneme may be realized as different actual phonemes in different environments (diversification) and in that a given actual phoneme may be the realization of different basic phonemes in different occurrences (neutralization). The combination of basic phonemes BP/e:/ of English is realized as P/iy/, as in *meter* (first syllable), but BP/e/ without following BP/:/ is realized generally as P/e/ when stressed, as in *metrical,* and as P/ɨ/ when unstressed, as in *kilometer.* A basic syllable is a combination of basic phonemes, as defined by the tactics of the phonology, and it appears that in some languages there is another important tactic unit of higher rank than the syllable which is related to stress. It may be called the FOOT. The realization of a basic syllable, which is the combination of the realizations of its components, is a syllable. In addition there are of course larger units than the syllable and the foot on the phonemic stratum, namely combinations which are the phonological realizations of higher-stratum units, such as phrases, clauses, etc.

The differences to be found between basic phonemes and morphons are similar to those between basic morphemes and lexons. In English there is anataxis at this level specified by the morphon M/</, which occurs in such morphemes as M/<u/, the realization of the past tense basic morpheme which occurs with BM/take/. Whereas L/>/ specifies a DELAY of one WORD to the MORPHOLOGY, M/</ specifies to the PHONOLOGY an ANTICIPATION of one SYLLABLE. Note that the word is a fundamental unit for the morphotactics, while the syllable is a fundamental unit for the phonotactics. Since BP/u/ is a vowel, it goes into the vowel position of the preceding syllable (in place of that which would go there otherwise), so that the past tense of *take* is (what we write as) *took.* An example of empty realization is provided by the empty basic phoneme BP/ɨ/ which is supplied by the phonotactics when a vowel is required but no other vowel is specified by any morphon. When the past tense morpheme M/d/ occurs with a verb with final apical stop like *wait,* the empty BP/ɨ/ appears before the BP/d/ (cf. *rubbed,* which does not have the BP/ɨ/). Similarly, when the suffix M/z/ occurs after M/z/, the empty BP/ɨ/ appears, as in *loses* (cf. *loves*).

The morphon is a component of a morpheme, which is a realization of a basic morpheme, as described and illustrated above along with other relationships of the morphology. An example of a portmanteau realization in morphology is English *worse,* for BM/bad er/. The fundamental construction type in the morphology of at least many languages is that which defines the word, and an important higher ranking unit in some languages is the phrase. Of course still higher-ranking units, such as morphological realizations of sentences and texts, also exist. For a typical language of the Indo-

European type, valence classes of the morphotactics would have such labels as 'verbal prefixes,' 'noun bases,' 'deverbative nominalizing suffixes,' 'case suffixes,' and the like.

In the lexology, a lexon is an elementary unit and is a component of a lexeme. Many lexemes are composed of single lexons, such as English L/bird/, L/find/, L/in/, L/nurse/, but many others are complex, such as L/black head ed gros beak/, L/look for/, L/on account of/, and L/bar tend er/. Differences between basic lexemes and realized lexemes involve diversification and neutralization. The verbal auxiliary BL/can/ is realized by the lexeme L/can/ in the present tense, as in *he can swim,* but is realized as L/be able to/ in the future, as in *he will be able to swim.* Similarly, there is a nominalizing basic lexeme BL/-th/ which is realized as L/th/, L/ness/ or in a portmanteau realization (i.e. L/size/), depending on the environment, as seen in the first column of Table III; but both L/th/ and L/ness/ also occur as realizations of other basic lexemes, as in *fifth* and *well-roundedness,* respectively. The table also shows some instances of neutralization, e.g. *short, soft;* and all of the forms in the third column are portmanteau realizations. Thus L/low/ is a portmanteau realization of L/un high/, and L/soft/ is a neutralized portmanteau realization of both BL/un loud/ and BL/un hard/. Evidence for considering forms of the column three complex with relation to those of the middle column is given in Lamb 1964a:69. Evidence for the choice of the proper form for the lefthand column is provided by such frames as the following (in which BL/long/ is used as an example): 'There is a long one and a short one; they are of varying length.' Important constructions which are basic to the lexotactics (of at least some languages) are those which define clause types and sentence types. A clause is a combination of one or more lexemes and a sentence is a combination of one or more clauses.

NOMINALIZED	SIMPLE	NEGATED
length	long	short
height	tall	short
height	high	low
size	big	little
size	large	small
width	wide	narrow
thickness	thick	thin
depth	deep	shallow
loudness	loud	soft
strength	strong	weak
roughness	rough	smooth

Table III

Examples of Lexological Diversification, Neutralization, and Portmanteau Realization

Figure 3. Linguistic Units and their Relations.

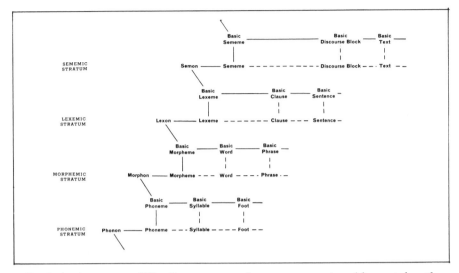

Basic lexemes can differ from semons in arrangement and in certain other ways involving adjustments to the lexotactics of combinations from the semology. An example of empty realization is the BL/it/ in English expressions like *it's cold* and *it's time to go,* which is supplied by the lexotactics since it requires a subject for every nonimperative clause. An example of anataxis may be seen in the lexemic realization shown above in Figure 1 as compared with the sememic network diagrammed in Figure 4. In the sememic network, *the cabinetmaker* is both the agent of *look for* and the possessor of *brace and bit,* but the lexotactics does not allow closed loops, so it provides two separate lexemic units corresponding to S/cabinetmaker/, the second a pronoun.

Turning now to semology, the elementary unit is the semon, and a sememe is a unit composed of one or more semons. In a clause such as *he found his brace and bit* all the sememes are simple, but the following expressions contain or are complex sememes, that is, sememes composed of multiple semons: *she put all her eggs in one basket* (as said of someone who has not put any eggs in any basket), *don't give up the ship* (except when said to someone about to give up some actual ship), *he's got two strikes against him already* (except when said at a particular point in a baseball game), *I'll see you later* (meaning 'goodbye').[9] An illustration of neutralization is available from each of the above examples since, e.g., the expression *he's got two strikes against him* can be used of a player in a baseball game who has two strikes against him. Another type of example is furnished by the so-called present progressive tense of English, as in *he is going to New York,* which can be used either for an action in progress or of one still in the future. As an example of diversification, *I'll be seeing you* and *I'll see you later* are alternative ways of saying goodbye. Also, *break* and *violate* are alternate realizations in *he broke/violated the law,* but *break* is a neutralized realization of a different basic sememe in *he broke his arm*, and *violate* is a realization of a different basic sememe, and one which also can be realized as *desecrate*, in *he violated the temple*. Basic sememes combine with one another in accordance with the semotactics into basic texts (i.e. units whose realizations are texts), and it appears likely that at least one important rank smaller than the text should be recognized for at least most languages. Units of such a rank may be called discourse blocks.

Figure 4. 'The cabinetmaker has been looking for his brace and bit' (Sememic stratum).

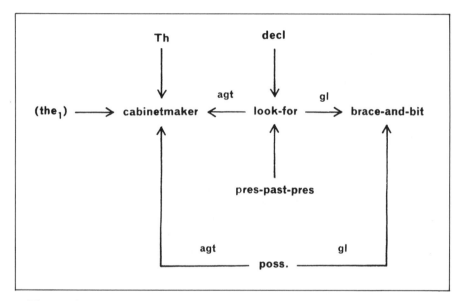

Those who are accustomed to looking at linguistic structure as if it consisted of just one or two stratal systems may wonder how it is that the analyst determines where to deal with a given phenomenon. How does one know whether a given instance of diversification or neutralization belongs in the lexology or in the semology? Indeed the skeptical may well wonder whether lexology and semology are really two different systems, or, more generally, whether linguistic structure can be neatly divided into a small number of stratal systems at all. Perhaps the best type of evidence of distinguishing the stratal systems and assigning linguistic relationships to one or another of them is that furnished by tactic relationships. In this connection it must be kept in mind that each stratal system has its own tactics, which differs from that of every other (cf. Figures 1 and 4 for an example of the type of difference in arrangement to be found between semology and lexology as well as between lexology and morphology). And it is not just the types of combination but also the types of valence classes that differ from one tactics to another. For example, it is a concern of the semotactics that certain types of 'action' basic sememes require certain types of agents (e.g.

human or animate) and/or goals. But the types of category that are relevant for the lexotactics are, for English, those which, among other things, distinguish mass nouns from count nouns, intransitive verbs from transitive verbs (of various types of transitivity), and the like.

Given a particular instance of diversification or neutralization or portmanteau realization in a language, then, if the analyst wants to determine what stratal system to assign it to, he may determine what its relation is to the tactics. (The reader will recall that the basic units of a stratal system are the basic units of its tactics.) For example, English *good* is realized as *bett* when occurring with *-er*, the comparative suffix. One may know that this case of diversification belongs to the morphology rather than the lexology since assignment of it to the morphology simplifies the description of the morphotactics. Failure to assign it to the morphology would mean analyzing *good* and *bett* as separate basic morphemes and complicating the morphotactic description in that *good* would not be allowed to occur with *-er*, while *bett* would be allowed to occur only with *-er*.

As another example, consider the neutralization and diversification involving *break, violate,* and *desecrate* mentioned above and assigned to the semology of English (rather than to the lexology). This example is typical of many found in semology involving interlocking polysemy (that is, different 'senses' or 'meaning'; for example, the different senses of *break* in *break an arm* and *break the law*) and synonymy (that is, *break* and *violate* are synonymous if the goal is *law, rule,* etc.), or neutralization and diversification, respectively. Such matters are to be ascribed to the semology because sorting out the different meanings (e.g. *break$_1$* and *break$_2$*) contributes to the accuracy of the semotactic description, whereas such distinctions are irrelevant to the lexotactics.

	big__	__is big	very big how big bigger
big$_1$ (rock)	+	+	+
big$_2$ (sister)	+	−	−
big$_3$ (fool)	+	−	+
big$_4$ (man)	+	+	+

Table IV
Distribution of *Big*

Applying this principle to the analysis of meanings of *big* in Lamb 1964a:73f, «p. 223f in this volume» it is apparent that the four-way separation given there can be broken down into two steps, one of which is in the lexology, the other in the semology. The four meanings treated there are called *big$_1$*, as in *big rock, big$_2$*, as in *big sister, big$_3$*, as in *he's a big fool,* and *big$_4$*, as in *he's a big man in our town.* The distributional criteria shown in that paper p. 74, «p. 224 in this volume» repeated here as Table IV, distinguish only three types of *big* (as was noted there), but the additional distinction was possible on the basis of interlocking diversification. Now the different types of environment shown in the table are different in terms of lexotactic constructions, so the three kinds of *big* distinguished by them are to be analyzed as lexologically different. But the distinction between *big*$_1$ and *big*$_4$ is to be assigned to the semology. That is, these are two different basic sememes which are realized by the same actual sememe.

Kinship Terminology

Turning now to the question of how kinship terminologies and methods of their analysis fit into the general picture, perhaps the first observation to make is that these matters are semological. That is, what is known as componential analysis of kin terms is a process whose results apparently contribute to the simplicity of the tactic description of the semology of a language but not that of the lexology.

The activity which in anthropological circles has come to be called componential analysis seems to have two primary areas of concern. The division into these two areas is perhaps not always made in exactly the way specified here, but I take certain differences of practice to be minor variations on the same theme, approaching the same conception of the structure involved, particularly since the two-way split is expectable from and fits neatly into the type of linguistic structure outlined above. A division which corresponds approximately to the one made here is referred to by Romney (1965:129) in terms of two stages in the analysis, as follows: (1) 'Reduce the *range* of each term to a single notational expression.... This step is the logical equivalent of reducing allophones to a phoneme, i.e., it reduces the redundancy among the kin types within a range and retains only the unique and distinctive kernel.' (2) '... define components in terms of significant and minimal differences among reduced ranges or kernels.' In the terminology of the linguistic theory sketched above, these two stages are concerned, respectively, with the following linguistic relationships: (1) that of semantic units (i.e. entities of the semantic stratum) to basic sememes; (2) that of basic sememes to sememes, a relationship which for kinship terms generally involves portmanteau realization. This statement will doubtless fail to fill the heart of the reader with excitement, especially at first glance. It is, however, more than any other single sentence, the punch line of this paper, for it is in summary form a characterization of the relationship of those phenomena which the componential analysts have analyzed to linguistic structure as a whole. I therefore indulge in several paragraphs of elaboration upon it.

According to this interpretation the kin types are on the semantic stratum, and the components in a componential definition of kin terms are basic sememes. To say that the definitions are componential is to say that these basic sememes are realized in portmanteau realizations. What Romney calls the RANGE of a kin term is the set of semantic realizates of a sememe, and his rules for reduction of the range of a term constitute a means of getting from the semantic stratum to the semological structure, specifically to approximations of basic sememes. He is quite correct in pointing out the analogy of this process to phonemic analysis, in which one goes from the phonetic stratum to the phonological structure. There are, however, some important differences between these two processes discussed below. Romney also quite appropriately compares his rules for reducing ranges to the reduction rules of Lounsbury (e.g. 1964a). Lounsbury's rules are of course different from Romney's in one very important way, namely in that Romney's are rules to be used in the process of analysis of a kinship terminology, whereas Lounsbury's constitute a means of stating the results of the analysis. But both are treating the relationship between the semantic stratum and the semological structure.

For a clearer understanding of this relationship and of the nature of the componency involved in componential definitions of kinship terms, it is important to distinguish clearly the two directions of the fundamental relations of linguistic structure, i.e. 'upward' and 'downward.' In brief, the situation is simply this: first, as stated earlier, there are two fundamental relations in linguistic structure, namely the 'or' relation (or that which is present among members of a set) and the 'and' relation (or that which is present among components of a combination); and each of these relations exists in each of two directions, which may be called UPWARD and DOWNWARD. In fact neither exists separately from these directions. Thus one might well say that there are really four fundamental relations, i.e. 'upward or,' 'downward or,' 'upward and,' and 'downward and.' The terms UPWARD and DOWNWARD for the two directions are in keeping with locutions whereby one refers to one stratum as being higher or lower than another. A language relates sound (or other expression) to meaning, i.e. it has two sides or ends, and it is a matter of convention for diagrams and terminology to conceive of these two ends as top (for meaning) and bottom (for expression). Thus the semology is said to be higher than the lexology, and UPWARD means toward the meaning end or away from the expression end, while DOWNWARD means towards expression. A morpheme is a downward combination of morphons, because the morphons are a step closer to sound than the morpheme (cf. Figure 3). And in general the relation of realized units to elementary units of a stratal system is a 'downward and' relation. Also, a word is a downward combination of (one or more) morphemes; a clause is a downward combination of lexemes; and in general the horizontal lines of Figure 3 connect downward combinations (at right) to their components (at left). On the other hand, portmanteau realization involves an 'upward and' relation. English *worse* is an upward composite whose components are BM/bad er/ (two basic morphemes) and is simultaneously a downward composite whose components are M/wᵻrhz/ (five morphons). Diversification is a 'downward or' relation, and neutralization is an 'upward or' relation. A valence class (e.g. the class of verb roots in a morphology) is a downward class, whereas the class of syntactic functions of a nominal in a lexology is an upward class.

The term componential analysis has been used in connection with both directions of componency. A componential analysis of phonemes is an analysis into downward components, whereas Harris' 'Componential Analysis of a Hebrew Paradigm' (1948) was an analysis into upward components. The components in a componential definition of a kin term are also upward components. That is, they are in an 'upward and' relation. This is another way of saying that the kin term sememe is a portmanteau realization of basic sememes (which in this case are the components). This type of componency in semology must be distinguished from the downward componency relation which is also found; for example, the components of *will never get to first base,* or *to have all one's eggs in one basket.* Since in semology more attention has been directed to upward than to downward components, one is tempted to use the term SEMON for them (as was done in Lamb 1964a), but it is better to use it for downward components, in order to keep the terminology for semology uniform with that for other stratal systems, and (also for the sake of such uniformity) the upward components of the semology should be called BASIC SEMEMES.[10]

With regard to the different directions of 'or' relations, the set of allophones of a phoneme is a downward set, while the set of kin types corresponding to a kin term is an upward set. To put this thought into other words, the realtionship between phonemic and phonetic units involves diversification whereas that between semantic and basic sememic units involves neutralization. Now basic sememes enter into 'downward or' relations (diversification) as well as the 'upward or' relations to semantic units; for example, the basic sememe (or combination of basic sememes if it is a combination) which can be realized as either *violate* or *desecrate* (see above). Thus, again for the sake of uniformity in terminology, it would be inappropriate to use a term like SEME or ALLOSEME for units ABOVE sememes, as has been suggested by, for example, Lounsbury (1956:192), Goodenough (1956:197), and Joos (1958). Instead the term SEME (by analogy with PHONE and MORPH) should be used for the realization of a sememe, which is a lexological entity, not a semantic one, just as a morph is a phonological realization of a morpheme.

At each end of linguistic structure there must be a bridge between that structure and the 'outside world,' and in both of these areas the analyst is faced with the problem of distinguishing form from substance. Thus there are similarities between the two areas even though the relationships involved are of opposite direction. The similarities have been pointed out often; for example, by Lounsbury (1956:190ff), Goodenough (1956:195ff), and Romney, in the passage quoted above. The differences are also important, and they probably deserve more attention than has been devoted to them so far.

The practice of making too much of the analogy between the form-substance relation at the 'bottom' and that at the 'top' of language is possibly traceable to Hjelmslev's otherwise generally excellent (for its time) 'Prolegomena to a Theory of Language' (1943). To be sure, probably only a minority of linguists have read this work, and even fewer have managed to penetrate its turgid, intricate prose to the point of understanding, but some of its ideas have nevertheless gradually spread from one linguist to another and have become part of the general background of linguistic thinking; and there have more than once occurred in recent linguistic history purportedly original pronouncements which in fact were made years earlier by Hjelmslev (not to mention others still earlier).

One of the important ideas of Hjelmslev, but one of those which carries the analogy between expression and content too far if not carefully qualified, is his commutation test, the basic notion of which has been stated later in different terms by Lounsbury (1956:191), Lamb (1964a:76f), and others. To paraphrase Lounsbury's version, in phonological analysis identification of contrast (distinctive difference) requires not a knowledge of what forms mean but only of whether the meanings of forms are the same or different. Similarly in semological analysis, contrast is defined on the basis of whether linguistic FORMS are the same or different (but it doesn't matter what the forms are). In short, the principle is that a difference in expression which can[11] correlate with a difference in meaning is distinctive, whereas differences which cannot are nondistinctive. Conversely, a difference in meaning which can correlate with a difference in expression is semologically distinctive, whereas differences which cannot are nondistinctive.

Now there is only one problem about this principle, namely that unless it is properly qualified THE SECOND HALF OF IT IS WRONG. It won't do to say that a difference in meaning which can correlate with a difference in expression (that is, which can be expressed) is distinctive and any other is nondistinctive, because ANY difference of meaning, even a very fine one, CAN be expressed, if in no other way just by adding enough sememes to provide a precise specification.[12] For example, even such a subtle distinction as that between a male's patrilateral parallel cousin's wife's paternal grandfather and a male's patrilateral parallel cousin's wife's maternal grandfather CAN be expressed, and in fact I have just expressed it. But these expressions, it might be objected, are several lexemes long. Hence an alternative formulation might be attempted as follows: that only those differences in meaning are distinctive which can correlate with a difference in expression which is a realization of a single basic sememe. This attempt fails also, because in fact the difference in the two expressions above IS a difference of only one basic sememe. In general the most subtle distinctions are those in which there is only one basic sememe of difference.

The next attempt might be to say that any semantic distinction which can be IGNORED, i.e. which does not REQUIRE a corresponding difference of expression, is nondistinctive, whereas only those differences are distinctive which MUST be expressed. This will not do either, for even so gross a semantic distinction as that between a slide trombone and a tiddlywink CAN be ignored in the expression, since either can be referred to as a thing.[13]

Note that this situation is quite unlike that found at the expression end of language, where some phonetic differences NEVER correlate with a difference in meaning whereas all others always do except when conditioned by environment or in occasional instances like the first syllable of *economics*. On the content side, there is no difference so small that it cannot be expressed (that is, be correlated with a difference in expression) and at the same time even very great semantic differences can be ignored. This property is actually essential to the nature of language, since a language is a system that allows men to talk about virtually anything at all, real or imaginary. It would be too cumbersome on the other hand if it required its users to make all possible semantic distinctions in order to say anything. Therefore it must allow both for indefinitely fine distinctions to be expressed and for most distinctions unnecessary to the specific occasion to be ignored.

Thus there IS NO GENERAL DIFFERENCE BETWEEN DISTINCTIVE AND NONDISTINCTIVE SEMANTIC FEATURES as there is in the case of phonetic features. Instead the difference between distinctive and nondistinctive is relative to individual basic sememes, combinations of basic sememes, and semotactic constructions. Any INDIVIDUAL basic sememe has a semantic range, and differences within that range are nondistinctive, RELATIVE TO THAT BASIC SEMEME. The same can be said for any occurring combination of basic sememes. But those same differences are distinctive relative to other basic sememes or combinations of basic sememes, since ANY semantic distinction CAN be expressed. It IS appropriate to use a commutation test to determine the borderline between the distinctive and the nondistinctive RELATIVE TO AN INDIVIDUAL BASIC SEMEME (cf. Lamb 1964a:77 for an example), but what is nondistinctive for that element may be distinctive for another and vice versa.

Now for certain semological subsystems, such as those concerned with kinship, there is apparently more to the situation. Here it isn't just the case that certain differences are nondistinctive for individual basic sememes or even for individual kin terms. It is rather the case that certain differences are in a sense nondistinctive for the system of kinship terminology as a whole (e.g. sex of linking relatives in English), notwithstanding that any such differences CAN be expressed. And it is of course this situation which is responsible for the various assertions of the kinship analysts about differentiating the distinctive from the nondistinctive, and the comparisons to phonemic analysis. But how, in view of the above observations, can this situation be accounted for? How can it be said that some semantic differences are nondistinctive for a system of kinship terminology as a whole if (1) distinctiveness is relative to the individual basic sememe or combination of basic sememes, and (2) any semantic distinction CAN be expressed with any kinship terminology? A possible answer is that there is in every natural language (or at least in every one investigated in this connection so far) A SEMOTACTIC CONSTRUCTION FOR KINSHIP RELATIONS,WHICH ALLOWS CERTAIN COMBINATIONS OF BASIC SEMEMES AND DISALLOWS OTHERS. Thus in English the kinship relation construction does not allow either BS/male/

or ᴮˢ/female/ between two kinship relation links. As a result sex of linking relative cannot be expressed and is therefore nondistinctive relative to any combination generated by this construction. On the other hand, it is of course possible, as indicated above, to express virtually any distinction if the need arises. For example, it is possible to say *my father's brother's daughter* in English, expressing the sex of each linking relative. But this form is to be accounted for as resulting from THREE SUCCESSIVE APPLICATIONS of the kinship relation construction.

Thus semantic distinctiveness is relative to the individual basic sememe, combination of basic sememes, or semotactic construction.

The reader will recall from the sketch of linguistic structure presented above that the tactics of each stratal system imposes certain limitations upon allowable combinations of elements, with the result that such combinations tend to differ in certain respects from combinations of the elementary units of the stratum above. Such differences may be thought of loosely as 'adjustments' of the combinations of elementary units of the upper stratal system (e.g. morphons) to fit the tactics of the lower stratal system (e.g. phonotactics). For example, various morphemes of classical Greek end in ᴹ/... ph/, ᴹ/... th/, or ᴹ/... kh/, e.g. ᴹ/graph/ 'to write.' But the first person singular aorist of this verb is, in terms of basic phonemes, ᴮᴾ/egrapsa/, without the *h*. This absence of a phonological realization of *h* is to be accounted for by the phonotactics, which cannot accommodate it since it does not allow sequences of ᴮᴾ/phs/. Similarly, it can be expected that the semotactics of a language has restrictions upon what it allows and that as a result various semantic features will fail to be realized semologically, simply because they cannot be accommodated by the semotactics (except by such means as repeated use of a construction, as suggested above).

These matters may be looked into more closely with reference to a concrete example, and the penetrating analysis of Crow-Omaha systems by Lounsbury (1964a) provides some excellent material for this purpose. In order to keep matters simple, let us consider just one of the various types which Lounsbury distinguishes, namely Omaha Type III. Lounsbury's reduction rules for Omaha III are as follows (1964a:360,372):

SKEWING RULE: ♂S ... → ♂d ...
I.e., let a man's sister, as linking relative, be regarded as equivalent to that man's daughter as linking relative.
COROLLARY: ... ♀B→ ... ♀F
I.e., let any female linking relative's brother be regarded as equivalent to that female linking relative's father.
MERGING RULE: ♂B ...→ ♂ ... ; and ♀S ... → ♀ ...
Let any person's sibling of the same sex as himself (or herself), when a link to some other relative, be regarded as equivalent to that person himself (or herself) directly linked to said relative.
COROLLARY: ... ♂B→ ... ♂ ; and ... ♀S→ ... ♀
HALF-SIBLING RULE: Fs→ B; Ms → B; Fd → S; Md → S
Let one's parent's child be considered to be one's sibling

With regard to the notation, Lounsbury makes the following comment in a footnote: 'Cover symbols would make for more compact symbolization of some of the rules. However, collections of raw data are generally given in a notation based on maximum differentiation, and there is a certain practical advantage to having the rules symbolized in the same notation.' On the other hand, reduction of notational redundancy can result in an increased understanding of the structural relations involved, so it will serve the purposes of this paper to delete as much unessential surface information from Lounsbury's rules as possible.

The means of eliminating excess surface information (i.e., surface information which does not add to effective information) is to isolate recurrent partial similarities and state them once instead of repeatedly, an operation basically like that of factoring polynomials in ordinary high-school algebra,[14] e.g. the reduction of

$$a^2b + abc + abd + abe$$

to

$$ab(a + c + d + e).$$

In some cases the recurrent partial similarities are not overtly present, so the notation must be revised to make their presence explicit. Then the reduction can proceed as a purely mechanical matter. In the present case it will be profitable to revise the notation so that the sex elements are separately symbolized wherever they occur. For example, F and M may be replaced by P♂ and P♀, respectively. The replacements (at right) for Lounsbury's symbols (at left) are shown below. (For typographical ease I use *m* and *f* for the sex elements; note that these are the only lower case symbols in the revised notation, which has a smaller inventory of symbols.)

♂	m
♀	f
F	P m
M	P f
B	S m
S	S f
s	C m
d	C f

Substitution of the new symbols in the rules as stated by Lounsbury gives the following formulation:

SKEWING RULE: m S f ... → m C f...
COROLLARY: ... f S m → ... f P m
MERGING RULE: m S m ... → m ...; and ... f S f → ... f
COROLLARY: ... m S m → ...m; and ... f S f → ... f
HALF-SIBLING RULE: P m C m → S m; P f C m → S m;
                   P m C f → S f; P f C f → S f

The reduction of surface information by a mechanical 'factoring' operation may be illustrated for the first two parts of the half-sibling rule as follows:

$$P\ m\ C\ m \rightarrow S\ m;\ P\ f\ C\ m \rightarrow S\ m$$
$$(P\ m\ C\ m\ \text{OR}\ P\ f\ C\ m) \rightarrow S\ m$$
$$P(m\ \text{OR}\ f)\ C\ m \rightarrow S\ m$$

Similarly, the other two parts reduce to P(m OR f) C f → S f. The notation may be simplified (and the analogy with familiar algebraic manipulation enhanced) by using '+' instead of 'or.' In the present kind of algebra, the reduction may be allowed to continue as follows:

$$P\ (m+f)\ C\ m \rightarrow S\ m;\ P\ (m+f)\ C\ f \rightarrow S\ f$$
$$(P\ (m+f)\ C \rightarrow S)\ m;\ (P\ (m+f)\ C \rightarrow S)\ f$$
$$(P\ (m+f)\ C \rightarrow S)\ (m+f)$$
$$P\ (m+f)\ C \rightarrow S$$

This last step, in which the final superfluous '(m+f)' is simply dropped, may look a little unlike high-school algebra, although it is clearly justified in terms of the meaning of the rule. A somewhat less intuitive justification is that: (1) m and f are the only two possibilities here (i.e. there is no other sex); (2) hence to write '(m+f)' is equivalent to indicating that sex, at this point in the rule, is irrelevant; (3) thus this term is superfluous, and superfluous terms are to be eliminated. But the other '(m+f),' which remains in the rules as written above, looks irrelevant too, in terms of its meaning. Here also sex is irrelevant, in that either of the only two possibilities, m or f, can be present, and the result is unaffected by which it is. So one is tempted to find it justifiable to eliminate '(m+f)' here also. But this looks more like an integral part of the rule, which is affected by it, rather than just a superfluous bystander like the other; so it is not quite so easily disposed of. The matter is taken up again below, and for the time being this '(m+f)' will be allowed to remain.

But first, notice that in the new notation, with sex elements separately symbolized, the relationship between the skewing rule and its corollary is more explicit than before. The left side of the corollary is identical to that of the rule except that the order of symbols is opposite. And the same is true of the right side except for the symbols P and C. But P and C, although different symbols, stand for what are in some sense quite closely related entities, so perhaps the notation should be revised further to make that relationship explicit. Of course what is involved is not just a matter of playing with notation; rather it concerns directly the structure of the system under investigation.

The closeness of the relationship between the rules and their corollaries is also reflected in the fact that they are, as Lounsbury points out, corollaries, not independent rules. Now he calls them corollaries because they follow from the rules. They do not, however, follow directly from the rules alone; rather they follow from the rules plus an underlying principle, namely a law of consistency of reciprocals. As Lounsbury introduces his first corollary (p. 360) he states, 'If this rule be specified as operative, then it follows as a corollary that a similar equivalence must exist between the reciprocals of the types covered by the rule.' That is, it follows because he assumes such a law. Now if this law is assumed (in one form or another—the exact statement need not concern us here); that is, if a reduction as specified by a rule also applies to the reciprocals of the types covered by the rule, as stated in the corollary, then there is evidently just one reduction 'taking place,' of which the rule and the corollary are describing complementary aspects. This means that THE REDUCTION IS REALLY APPLYING NOT TO KIN TYPES BUT TO KINSHIP RELATIONS; that is, to the relationships which exist between those kin types and their reciprocals.

Now if that is so and if the reductions are to be interpreted in terms of what combinations are allowed and disallowed by the kinship construction in the semotactics, then such a construction must generate designations of kinship RELATIONS, rather than of kin types. The basic sememes which are components of these relations, aside from the sex elements, must likewise be designations of relations. (This suggestion applies of course to languages generally, not just to those with Crow and Omaha systems.) Thus it would appear that in at least most languages there is not a basic sememe 'father' not even the combination 'male parent,' which would mean having 'parent' and 'child' as separate elements. Instead there is a basic sememe 'parent-child relationship.' Thus the basic sememic realizate of *John's father,* if represented in detail without the use of the usual portmanteau realizations, would be 'he (i.e. a male) who is at the parent end of a parent-child relation relative to John (at the child end).' Or, less pedantically, 'he who is parent to John,' but NOT 'John's male parent.' That is, the basic sememic realizate of *John's father* has the PARENT-CHILD RELATIONSHIP basic sememe, with *John* at one end and the MALE element at the other. If the positions of these two terminals are reversed, then the realization is *John's son.*

It is a tactic property of the PARENT-CHILD RELATIONSHIP element that it presupposes two other elements. Of course it makes a difference which is which; *John's father* and *John's son* are two different things. In other words this is not a symmetrical relationship. In this respect it is not an unusual element but is like many other basic sememes in a typical language. For example ᴮˢ/poss./ 'possessive,' which occurs in (the realizate of) *John's hat* presupposes two elements, which must be distinguished from each other; i.e. its two ends are different, and must be distinguished in a semological notation, since *John's hat* is different from **hat's John*. Note that in Figure 4 the valences are separately labelled *agt.* ('agent') and *gl.* ('goal'). For ᴮˢ/parent-child-relationship/ one could use some symbol like ᴮˢ/par./ and label the two valences *p* and *c,* but for purposes of kinship terminology analysis it is more convenient simply to write PC or CP both to identify the element and to distinguish its two sides from each other, it being understood that CP and PC are two ways of writing the same element, just as a < b and b > a are two ways of writing the same inequality.

On the other hand, the sibling relationship is symmetrical, so its symbol need not have distinguishable sides; hence the symbol S may be used for it, with the understanding that it signifies 'sibling relationship,' not 'sibling.'

Substitution of the new symbol in the rules gives the following formulation:

SKEWING RULE: m S f... → m PC f...
COROLLARY: ...f S m → ...f CP m
MERGING RULE: m S m ... → m ...; and f S f ... → f ...
COROLLARY: ... m S m → ... m; and ...f S f → ...f
HALF-SIBLING RULE: CP (m+f) PC → S

The equivalence of each corollary with the rule of which it is a corollary is not entirely explicit. Formally speaking we need only allow a sequence of kinship symbols to be read in either direction, and then the corollaries become altogether redundant and may be dropped. In terms of the meanings of the symbols and their sequences it is of course quite appropriate to allow them to be read either way since they now stand for relationships rather than kin types. Reading left to right gives a kin type, right to left the reciprocal of that kin type. The skewing rule may now be verbalized as follows: a sibling relationship between a male and a linking female is treated like a parent-child relationship with the male at the parent end, the female at the child end; or less pedantically, a brother-sister relationship is treated as a father-daughter relationship, unless the sister is terminal.

Returning now to the irrelevant sex elements in the half-sibling rule, notice first that simply eliminating them without further ado, easy as that would be, would be giving up something, because as they stand, the rules (together with the accompanying explanation of their meaning) are fully explicit in their account of the 'reductions' of kinship relations to fit the kinship relation construction. It would be obvious that m or f in the position indicated is dropped even if '(m+f)' weren't written in the rule, but with it written in it is not only obvious but also explicit. Yet the evident irrelevance of sex in this position agitates one's sense of economy, and there is good reason why it should. For a different treatment of sex will have important structural implications and will make clear the way for still further steps. It is to be noted that in all three of the rules the position of m and f is somehow peripheral to that of the other elements, which may be called link elements. The reduction rules really specify operations on the link elements primarily, and what happens to the sex elements seems to follow along automatically. It is significant also that the obviously relevant condition for the applicability of the half-sibling rule is the presence together of CP and PC, while '(m+f)' is somehow only in the way. These considerations, and others, lead to a revised conception of the arrangement of these elements to one another. Linearity of arrangement is convenient to a notation, and is structurally appropriate as applied to phonemic or morphemic material. But semological and semantic units are not restricted to linear arrangements. The semantic arrangement of link elements and sex elements might better be represented using a two-dimensional notation, with lines indicating what is connected to what, as in the following example, a representation of the relationship between a man and his mother's brother's daughter:

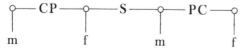

The unlabeled nodes may be taken as representing human beings, i.e. the terminal and linking relatives; and the sex elements are their modifiers. This arrangement treats the link elements and the sex elements as two separate classes, which they are; makes the position of the sex elements subordinate to that of the link elements, which it is; and allows the link elements to be effectively contiguous to each other, which the half-sibling rule (and other considerations) suggests is appropriate.

To call the sex elements subordinate to the link elements is to say that the presence of the former depends upon that of the latter. The former are modifiers that are present only when the latter are present. That is, a sex element (within the present system) presupposes at least one link element, and if its accompanying link elements drop, it also must drop automatically. The reduction process may be illustrated with the example cited above:

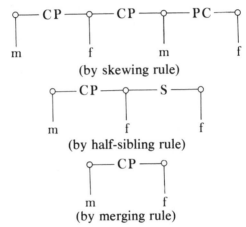

(by skewing rule)

(by half-sibling rule)

(by merging rule)

If the half-sibling rule as last represented above is converted to the new notation, it becomes:

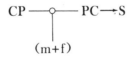

Here the '(m+f)' no longer intervenes between CP and PC. It is just a peripheral and irrelevant part of the environment (since m and f are the only possibilities), like the '(m+f)' which was discarded earlier. If it is dropped from the rule, then when the specified reduction takes place there is no longer anything for the sex element which hung between them to attach to, so it also drops automatically. To get rid of something overtly—by rule—which can't possibly be there anyway would be unnecessary.[15] It can now be said properly that the reduction rules apply only to link elements, and sex elements are written only where needed as significant environment. When not significant, they are no more appropriate to write in the rule than the age or height or hair-color of the linking relative in question (all of which also automatically remain unaccommodated by the kinship relation construction). It may be noted in this connection that Lounsbury did not include in his reduction rules any specification that sex of linking relative of intermediate generation is dropped for the grandparent-grandchild relationship although that appears to be the case for each of the example systems in his Crow-Omaha paper for which he provides sufficient information to make a determination.

As typographically simpler shorthand for the new notation, one can write (for the example given above before reduction):

$$\text{CP} \quad \text{S} \quad \text{PC}$$
$$\text{m} \quad \text{f} \quad \text{m} \quad \text{f}$$

Or, it is even more convenient simply to let the symbols m and f stand for ꝋ and ꝋ, respectively, so that the notation can continue as before (i.e.

m f

m CP f S m PC f), but with a new meaning.

Another possibility for notational manipulation with structural implications is presented by S, the sibling relationship. In fact it lends itself to two possibilities, one of which is to replace it by CP PC, with the result that the half-sibling rule is eliminated and the skewing rule becomes simply a matter of 'dropping' an occurrence of CP. (This treatment would correspond to that employed by Hammel in his Crow-Omaha paper, 1965b.) But the other possibility, which is actually quite closely related, is pursued here. It involves treating CP and PC as canceling each other out when contiguous in that order, and S as a concatenative identity element (within a Crow-Omaha kinship relation system), which may accordingly be symbolized as 1 rather than S. (Technically, this amounts to calling CP a concatenative left inverse of PC. The possibility of occurrence in the order PC CP is ignored here since it is neither accepted nor reduced by a Crow-Omaha kinship relation construction. One's child's parent is either one's spouse, and there is a separate element for the husband-wife relationship, or oneself, who is not one's kin.) Such a formal device fits well with the semotactic kinship relation construction for an Omaha III system and (what amounts to the same thing) is readily rationalizable in terms of its interpretation in such a system. Its meaning in nonformal terms, together with the rationalization, is simply this: CP, for an Omaha III system, means not so much a specifically child-parent relationship in our sense as it does just 'next higher generation'; whereas PC means going down one generation, so CP and PC (actually opposite directions of the same element) reverse each other. In some kinship systems of course this is not the case, but in Omaha III it is in that, because of the skewing and merging rules, different degrees of collaterality are not distinguished; that is, are not accommodated by the semotactics.

In English if you go up two generations and then down two you get a cousin, but in an Omaha III system you are right back where you started.

(Within such a system, of course, going up two and down two—or more or less—means going up or down either in accordance with the actual biological relationship or because of skewing, as the case may be.) Thus, aside from affines, kinsmen of the same terminological generation are the same in the Omaha III system—differentiable only by their sex, except in the special case of the terminal (nonlinking) female (for example, father's sister). So CP and PC cancel each other, resulting in 'no change'; that is, their composite is identity. Now the point that a man does not call his brother by the same term that he uses for himself is no objection to this conception, because a man's brother is his kinsman. That is, the 'brother' term is applied to a male who is in the 'identity' KINSHIP RELATION to a person, but not to a male who is identical to that person. The 'identity' or neutral or unmarked kinship relation is the minimal one, that which involves identity of generation and no marriage link.

In other words S is to be interpreted as 'same generation,' which is taken as the minimal or unmarked kinship relation, and it may be symbolized 1. Of course, $1X=X=X1$, where X is any element of the system, just as in ordinary algebra. Different degrees of generation distance may be written CP^3, CP^2, $CP^1=CP$, $CP^0=1$, $CP^{-1}=PC+PC^1$, and so forth. With this revision, the half-sibling rule, which would be $CP\ PC \rightarrow 1$, is now unnecessary since it merely repeats the definition of CP as left inverse of PC. The merging rule, which would say

$$m\ m \ldots \rightarrow m \ldots; \text{ and } f\ f \ldots \rightarrow f \ldots$$

is also unnecessary, by the earlier considerations which allow the unwanted sex elements to drop away automatically, as shown in the example below. So all that is left is the

SKEWING RULE: $m\ f \ldots \rightarrow m\ PC\ f \ldots$

As an example, the relationship between a man and his mother's father's sister's daughter is reduced as follows (recall that the writings $1X$ and X are optional variants):

$$
\begin{array}{ccccc}
CP & CP & 1 & PC & \\
m & f & m & f & f
\end{array}
$$

$$
\begin{array}{ccccc}
CP & CP & PC & PC & \\
m & f & m & f & f
\end{array}
$$
(by skewing rule)

whereupon the link elements cancel one another out, leaving $_m1f$, that is, the minimal kinship relation, with male and female as terminals. This will be realized as the 'brother' term or the 'sister' term, depending on how it fits into whatever text is being constructed.

There is little left to do; but one final notational manipulation, like that used in the initial reduction of the half-sibling rule, will remove redundancy in the specification of the environment, leaving only:

SKEWING RULE: m(1→ PC) f ...

The above exercises with notation and interpretation have pointed the way to an increased understanding of the underlying structural relations. The resulting simplified notation, and the concepts that go with it, are useful not just for the remaining reduction rule itself but also for writing the kinship relation construction. This, after all, is the really significant rule, for the reductions are not the linguistic structure, but only the results of the structure. They are like the symptoms rather than the disease. The disease is the Omaha III kinship relation construction. It may be written for consanguineal relatives something like this:

[[fm] PC *]

Square brackets enclose optional items. That is, technically, [X] = X+1, where X is any element or combination of elements. The '*' means that the preceding element, i.e. PC, may be repeated one or more times. This construction is stated only for the kinship relations themselves and does not include the sex of the terminals. Sex elements can be attached at either end, except at the left if 'fm' is present. To illustrate, some sample relationships generated by the construction are:

f m PC LEFT TO RIGHT, woman's brother's child
PC RIGHT TO LEFT, father's sister
PC² LEFT TO RIGHT, grandchild
RIGHT TO LEFT, grandparent
1 sibling

Because of the outer square brackets it is possible to 'go through' the construction without picking up any elements, in which case we get the minimal or unmarked kinship relation, as in the last example.

The skewing rule as stated above, together with the definition of CP as left inverse of PC, indicates how semantic kinship relations may be adjusted if necessary so that they will fit this construction. As the construction indicates by implication, sex of all linking relatives except terminal female's brother is dropped.

NOTES

1. There was a strange lack of consistency in the thinking of a whole group of linguists during a period of over 20 years, which allowed them to assert on the one hand that morphemes are composed of phonemes and on the other hand that they can have different phonemic shapes in different environments. This contradiction appeared in such generally excellent works for their time as Bloomfield's *Language* (1933:161–164) and Nida's *Morphology* (1949:Chap. 2 and elsewhere), as well as in numerous other places, particularly classrooms; and it persisted in the minds of some all the way through the 1950's and even into the early 1960's.

2. The assertion that mixing of levels was all right in morphophonemics seems to have stemmed largely from a failure to distinguish grammatical elements from their phonological realizations.

3. The CLASS concept of the morpheme was put forth by Harris in 1942 and was commonly repeated by others in later years. Although it was generally known and accepted, many linguists failed to digest it properly, in that they persisted in thinking of the morpheme as composed of phonemes. Perhaps even more peculiar than this type of thinking, on the other hand, is

the modern transformational view according to which not only morphemes but apparently also even lexemes are held to be composed of phonological distinctive features.

4. The correspondence is only a rough one, since Chomsky's deep structure is still heavily laden with morphological (and even phonological) features, and has a certain admixture of semological material as well.

5. Cf. Hjelmslev's 'either-or function' and 'both-and function' (1943), which occupy a basic position in his system.

6. In the original version of that paper the term REPRESENTATION was used for what is here called REALIZATION.

7. In that paper the realization rule was described as a means of stating a 'full stratum' of difference, e.g. all the way from the lexon to the morphon, whereas in the present scheme it is intended only to account for the relationships from, e. g., basic morpheme to morphon, since differences between lexons and basic morphemes can be accounted for in terms of morphotactics.

8. Note that as linguistic structure is a system of relationships, the only way to specify what a structural unit is is to specify what its relationships are to other units related to it.

9. This distinction between sememes and semons is not the same as that for which these two terms were used in Lamb 1964a. In that paper the term semon was used for the 'upward component' in the semology, i.e. the type of component which is involved in portmanteau realization. But to keep the terminology in semology consistent with that of other stratal systems, SEMON should be used for downward components of sememes.

10. To some, this term may be lacking in esthetic appeal or may be awkward in that it consists of (strickly speaking, is realized by) two words. So I am prepared to offer an alternative, inasmuch as the unit in question must be referred to so often in discussions of semological analysis, namely SEMAD, formed with a Greek nominal suffix -AD (cf. *gonad, nomad, Iliad*). Similarly, the terms LEXAD, MORᶠHAD, and PHONAD are available as alternatives for BASIC LEXEME, BASIC MORPHEME, and BASIC PHONEME, respectively.

11. I say 'CAN correlate' rather than 'correlates' since distinctive differences in expression (i.e., phonemic differences, for a spoken language) do not always correlate with differences in meaning. Some instances of phonemic differences result from different conditioning environments and sometimes they involve 'free variation,' as in the first syllable of *economics*.

12. My thinking on this point has benefited from a discussion with E.N. Adams. On various other points I have been aided and stimulated by discussions with Floyd Lounsbury and others.

13. Cf. Conklin's discussion of levels of contrast (1962:127ff).

14. This same type of 'factoring' operation, in the same algebraic system, underlies Romney's rules for reducing the range of a kin term to a single expression (1965:129). By introducing a few definitions and conventions, one can in fact make Romney's individual rules unnecessary, since there is only one operation involved, namely 'factoring' in accordance with a distributive law (cf. note 15).

15. These considerations apply also to the operations treated in Romney's paper (cf. note 14), since Romney's reduction of the range of a kin term is also concerned with the relationship of semantic material to basic sememic. With regard to Romney's Rule 1 (minimum difference within range), one may apply the same two-dimensional arrangement of link elements and sex elements, and the practice of dropping superfluous elements. Thus Romney's example may be treated in the present system as follows:

$$\text{CP m CP m} + \text{CP f CP m}$$
$$\text{CP (m CP m} + \text{f CP m)}$$
$$\text{CP (m+f) CP m}$$
$$\text{CP CP m}$$

In connection with Romney's Rule 2 (sequence difference within range), a notational device used also at the end of this paper is helpful, namely square brackets, defined as follows: $[X]=X+1$, where X is any element or combination of elements, and 1 is the concatenative identity element (i.e., the element such that $1X = X = X1$). It is also to be noted that in the present algebra $X+X = X$ (recall that '+' means 'or'). Thus $[X]^2 = (X+1)^2 = X+X^2+X$

+1 = X^2+X+1. Thus Romney's example reduces to m CP f S [m PC]^{2}m. For Romney's Rule 3 (paired sequence difference) I prefer not to adopt a special device like that suggested by Romney, but instead to allow S to be rewritten as CP PC wherever simplification can result. Thus Romney's example may be treated as follows:

$$CP \; m \; S \; m \; PC + CP \; f \; S \; f \; PC + S$$
$$CP \; (m \; S \; m + f \; S \; f) \; PC + S$$
$$CP \; (a \; S \; a) \; PC + CP \; PC$$
$$CP \; [a \; S \; a] \; PC$$

Here 'a' is a variable having the values m and f, and the convention is followed that if a variable occurs more than once in the same formula it has the same value in each occurrence.

Thus in general the analytical process of reducing ranges may be treated as a simple 'factoring' operation. Romney's Rule 4 (reciprocals) belongs in a separate category according to the present system, which deals with kinship relations rather than kin types as such. Rule 4 is concerned not with a relationship of semantic material to basic sememes but rather with the circumstance in which the two directions of a kinship relation have a single (i.e. neutralized) realization.

CHAPTER THIRTEEN

Contrastive Analysis
in Discourse Structure*

H. A. GLEASON, JR.

A FULLY ACCEPTABLE SENTENCE impresses a native speaker as fundamentally different from a randomly selected sequence of words. The linguist accounts for this by ascribing to the sentence a number of properties, one of which, grammatical structure, he considers his special province. An acceptable longer discourse also differs fundamentally from a randomly selected series of sentences. In the recent past few linguists have been willing to accept any responsibility for accounting for this fact, but now an increasing number believe that here too a linguistic dimension can be segregated from the others, and we are beginning to see studies appearing under some such rubric as 'discourse structure'.

The phenomena to be accounted for in contrastive linguistics come most forcibly to attention in the course of careful translation. Many of the most crucial problems lie in attaining connectivity between successive sentences while conveying the intended message, that is, in achieving proper discourse structure. Experience with other translational problems, as well as with second language teaching, has shown the utility for precise interlingual work of detailed contrastive study of the patterns involved. We may assume, therefore, that discourse structure may profitably be subjected to contrastive analysis.

The most extensively cultivated area within contrastive analysis is bilingual lexicography. But like all lexicography, it has not been deeply theory-informed work.[1] Traditional grammars intended for non-natives follow close behind. Such grammars do not, in general, distinguish between contrastive

---

*From *Monograph Series on Languages and Linguistics* 21.39–63. Reprinted by permission.

and descriptive statements, and this is clearly a major methodological weakness. More 'modern' work has insisted on the distinction, but usually by rigorous exclusion of the contrastive. In this way linguists have thought to justify the title 'descriptive' for their work. Indeed, contrastive linguistics is having a hard struggle to live down the disparagement of the Bloomfieldians while suffering trivialization from the current fad of free-and-easy appeal to universals. The friends of contrastive analysis have seemed to assume always that this work should follow and be based on purely descriptive work. But pure descriptive work has seldom provided a useful base, and good contrastive studies have not been numerous.

Sequential development may not be an efficient program. I would like, therefore, to suggest that both should receive attention from the beginning, though of course they should not be commingled or confused. Perhaps we linguists owe this to our fellows, for the fact of the matter is that for almost all practical applications in bilingual situations only contrastive grammars have real value. The pure descriptive grammar is important and valuable, but for the most part only to linguists.

Discourse analysis is really just getting underway. There are as yet very few firm substantive results, either descriptive or contrastive. But the course of future development is beginning to take shape, and it is well to look ahead and ask what direction we ought to take. I hope we can redress the balance between descriptive and contrastive, allowing each to make its maximum contribution to the other. This may, incidentally, provide the profession with some much needed immunity to extremism on the question of language universals.

This paper[2] is frankly programmatic. I hope it will indicate some of the questions worth investigating in the immediate future, suggest a few features of a framework within which they are profitably to be approached, and recruit additional interest in them. I make no apology either for this or for my 1964 Georgetown paper, severely criticized for being 'merely programmatic'. In 1957, I would remind you, *Syntactic Structures* was a programmatic paper; that fact does not in any way alter its value. And no lesser paper need be scorned for this reason either.

For simplicity, I will restrict myself to a single form of discourse, narrative. More comprehensive coverage would complicate the statement, but scarcely alter the basic principles. The features of a narrative which must be accounted for in a full description fall under five convenient heads, only two of which can receive more than passing mention here:

(1) The chain of events which forms the back-bone of a narrative and whose structure controls its overall organization.

(2) The identification of the participants and the indication of their roles in the several events.

(3) The detailing of the attendant circumstances and the indication of the scope of their application. The setting in time is the most frequently specified.

(4) The relation of the observers to the unfolding narrative. 'Observer' is to be taken as including both the narrator and the audience, since a narrative

is a device to make the audience in some way observers. Halliday's work (especially in 1967–8) on theme and rheme, and given and new in English is a germinal contribution on one aspect of this.

(5) Certain dimensions of the text as text—register, style, and level of redundancy among them. These lie not within the domain of linguistics as such, but astride the boundaries, so that linguists must be joined by others in attacking them.

A narrative is a language representation of a happening, real or imagined—that is, typically of a continuous stream of activity, only rarely broken into distinct parts. The narrative describes this in terms of a sequence of discrete actions related into a structure. A language provides at the minimum some guidance in mapping the stream into an articulated sequence. Some features of the operation are common to all or many languages. Others are peculiar to one or a few. A full language description must cover all the aspects which are linguistically controlled, and a contrastive analysis must indicate which features are unique and which shared.

Benjamin Lee Whorf has, of all recent linguists, been the most insistent in propounding the notion that languages map the same reality in various ways.[3] His examples show this dramatically. He points to the differences both in vocabulary and in grammatical structure between the English sentences: *I push his head back,* and *I drop it in the water and it floats.* But in Shawnee, according to Whorf (1941:235), both are expressed by single verb forms built on the same verb root—a root referring to one force being met by an opposing force—and constructed according to the same basic pattern. Like so many of his illustrations, however, this one is too complex to show clearly what is involved. Several kinds of differences are exhibited at once. It will be helpful for our purposes to separate these, giving some simpler examples which more nearly illustrate minimal differences of various types.

The two English verbs *break* and *tear* may describe much the same phonomenon, but are discriminated on the basis of the kind of object affected. Carib (Guatemala) makes no such distinction using only a single verb where English uses two. Yom (Dahomey), like many others, makes more distinctions than does English. English is not alone in dividing the territory into two, but other languages cut in different ways (Table I).

Table I

	stick	*rope*	*cloth*
English	break	break	tear
Carib	baú-	baú-	baú-
Yom	kaal-	tós-	tɔt-
Cashinawa	baxne-	tese-	baxne-
Thai	hàk	khà:t	khà:t

There can also be differences in the way pieces are cut out from the stream of observed reality. We may illustrate this first in English. The activity suggested by the picture to the left in Figure 1 can be described in two ways: one with a sequence of verbs, and one with a single verb. That is, there is a choice open to us, though generally we speakers of English prefer the second in most instances. But now consider the very similar situation pictured at the right in Figure 1. English here allows no comparable choice. There is no verb analogous to *drop,* though there is little reason other than the arbitrariness of language why there should not be. There seem to be many languages in which the equivalent statements in both situations require two verbs, often reasonably close translations of the longer English form. In such a language, of course, *he dropped the stone* must be drastically restructured in translation. I have not yet found a language in which the situation to the right can be expressed by a single verb, but I am fairly confident that one might exist. In such a language, the best translation of *he let go of the balloon and it rose* would be drastically restructured. A comparable restructuring is involved in the Shawnee translation of *I dropped it in the water and it floats.* Now consider the first of the two situations in Gbeya. The verb glossable 'let go' is not used unless it has been explicitly stated that the affected item has been held. Moreover, the verb meaning 'fall' is not used in such a situation without further specification. In certain circumstances the briefest possible translation of *he dropped the stone* is ã kā́sí ta gã̄ã́ é rá go ték nũ̄ 'he held the stone in his hand; he let go of it; and it fell to the ground'.

Figure 1

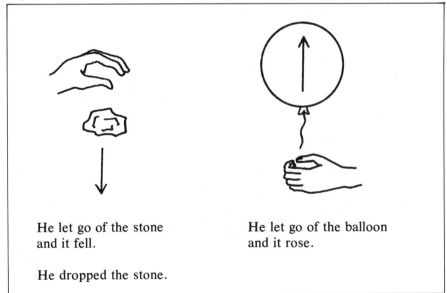

He let go of the stone
and it fell.

He let go of the balloon
and it rose.

He dropped the stone.

Languages differ, then, in how they cut up the stream of activity into a sequence of actions, some languages requiring more successive specifications in certain places than do others. The differences come primarily in the minima allowed. There does not seem to be any upper limit on possible detail in any language. This is demonstrated, for example, by the fact that English imposes no difficulty, in this matter, in a literal translation of the Gbeya sentence with three verbs where English would normally use only one. Secondarily, when two languages both allow the same alternative articulations, their speakers may show different preferences. The briefest permissible statement is not always the preferred one.

You have, perhaps, been a little uneasy about *he let go of the balloon and it rose*. You might prefer a different verb, say, *flew away*. This does not alter the principle illustrated. Rather it suggests alternative vocabulary possibilities within the structure, one of the ingredients of style.[4] Or you may have asked, why not just say *he released the balloon* with a single verb? Indeed, this is a quite normal description of the situation. But it is not at all parallel to *he dropped the stone*. The latter states explicitly which way the stone went, but *released* tells nothing of the kind. We can guess, but this rests on our fund of information about balloons. And this brings up a third dimension of differences in the narrative mapping of the real-life stream of activity. Not everything has to be said. There is more than simply articulation; there is also selection.

Perhaps you would rather say that this feature is non-linguistic. Gravity displacing the lighter balloon by the heavier air is a concept of physics, not linguistics. Bloomfield (1933:74) denied the responsibility of the linguist to define meanings because this required full knowledge of the entire universe. His simplistic view discarded far too much. We must not repeat the same mistake. Exploring the proper limits of the linguist's professional concern with the mapping of reality must be done with care and responsibility, and with courage to skirt the impossible.

From one point of view we face the problem of how much and what sort of things can be omitted. But it is better thought of in another way: Activity is a continuous stream. What points, and how many, must be specified to convey, adequately, the course of that stream? The word 'adequately' suggests that the answer must be relative to some purpose. Again, there is no upper limit to the possible detail and precision attainable in description, though the cost may mount rapidly. By analogy, we may describe a curve by stating a limited number of points along it. The Xs in Figure 2 do the job as well as the almost wholly different Os, but the Vs are badly chosen and do not specify a major feature of the shape. The speaker of a natural language picks out points to specify and thus suggest the shape of the whole. He has considerable freedom, and how he uses that may be a major difference between a good narrator and a poor one, but he does not have complete freedom; the language—and his culture—must impose certain constraints.[5]

A fourth difference may be seen by an example from a Kâte reader: *Rorâ râreckerâ ŋenuc mumbiŋ*. 'Then they sat around it and said,' (Flierl 1958:44). What I have translated 'sat around' is expressed by two verbs, 'encircle' and 'sit'. (Incidentally, all four Kâte words above are verbs!)

Figure 2

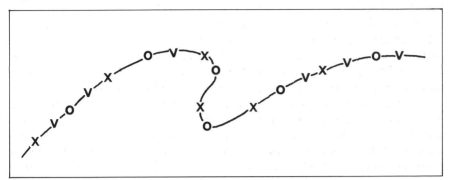

Much of the meaning of one of these is embodied in an English preposition. One feature of the 'reality' is given a place in the main sequence of verbs in Kâte, whereas English puts it outside the main sequence as an adjunct.

If you return to Whorf's example, you will see all four of these differences intertwined. Shawnee differs from English in what is selected to mention, how it is articulated into parts, where some of these parts are placed (in the central structure or the periphery), and how the delimited parts are classified. All this occurs in the compass of a very short utterance. This makes such an example quite unusual. But in a longer passage all of these phenomena can be expected, even in rather ordinary cases. It would be more appropriate to my topic to have chosen illustrations on a grander scale, but they would have been more difficult to present and expound. And they would have illustrated no better. A discourse is a long sequence of actions; a sentence is, at its most complex, merely a shorter portion of such a sequence. The phenomena are the same. Discourse analysis cannot reach down to the sentence and stop.[6] When discourse organization extends into the sentence, it must be treated as part and parcel of the wider structure. Sentences will never be fully described apart from the discourses in which they occur, and by which they are moulded.

The skeleton of a narrative is by no means simply a set of actions merely juxtaposed. They are related in some specifiable way into a structure. Four aspects of this must be noted:

First, they are ordered into a sequence. Usually, but not always, this reflects something best described as the 'natural' order of occurrence. Of course, the mass of activity in the real world is not so simply linear, not even that small eddy that one narrative will describe. But observers of any one language background seem to agree, more closely than physical facts require, in tidying things up. So what a linguist might think of as a 'natural' order is itself partly fictive, perhaps already strongly affected by linguistic constraints. Even so, languages seem to differ in the closeness with which they must adhere to this order. English even allows us to tell a short narrative completely in reverse, though it takes some ingenuity to reorder more than three or four clauses without serious discomfort. Some languages allow nothing of the kind. Even a simple inversion may be disallowed. *Before he left, he telephoned home* may have to be translated into something of the general form 'He telephoned home, and then he left.' Bible translators are often made painfully conscious of such constraints, since a division of the text into serially numbered verses has become so well established that it is often demanded in the version. All too often they find they cannot preserve both the order and the sense.

Second, each action in the narrative is related, directly or indirectly to the others. The most common pattern is for each to be related to the preceding and the following. The result is not, then, simply a linear sequence but a chain. Some languages seem to allow only rare and special departures from this structure. English narrative, however, is not infrequently organized in a more complex fashion, perhaps with short branch chains tied onto a main chain. Here again, the translator may face a problem.

Third, each connection between two actions is made by means of one of a small set of contrasting relations. These may mark sequence in time, causality, closeness of association, or various other matters. For example, between pairs of actions in Kâte there is usually indicated one of the following sets:

IMM Action B follows immediately after Action A. (The meaning of 'immediately' is a referential problem that I cannot go into here. Suffice it to say that it is not simple.)

LAP Action B follows after Action A with an appreciable lapse of time. (And again, not all the instances seem to be the same from a non-Kâte point of view.)

SIM Action B starts while Action A is still underway, and is at least partly simultaneous.

There is at least one other cross-cutting set of components. All-in-all, this seems to be a rather simple and symmetrical system. I will not attempt to describe English at this point.[7] A native speaker can see immediately that it is much different, and, presumably, more complex and less symmetrical or both. We have as yet so little information on this aspect of discourse structure that I can say little more, but my general impression is that there is considerable range of pattern. This is the place where I find it most frequently impossible to make a 'literal' translation of a Kâte passage into English.[8] All this suggests that here is, perhaps, one of the key questions in the contrastive analysis of discourse structure.

Fourth, there may be widely varying amounts of repetition. Sometimes this is stylistic, as Jones and Carter assert of the Tonga narrative they translate literally:

We lived in the village of Munakasaka, near the farm of chief Jojo. When we had lived there for some time, we heard that the Matebele were coming. When we had heard the Matebele coming, we ran away, we ran away into the forest, and the Kalanga had also entered the country. When we had finished running, the Matebele entered all the forest. (Jones and Carter 1967:99)

But sometimes the repetition is at least partially the manifestation of linguistic structure, required under certain definable circumstances by the grammar. This happens frequently in Kâte. A little larger part of the same passage quoted before reads: *Eku hâpic sâko moc bâfuarâ rombiŋ. Rorâ râreckerâ ŋehuc mumbiŋ.* 'Finally, they found a large grasshopper and caught it. Having caught it, they sat down around it and said,' Note the stem of a sentence final word *(ro-)* repeated in the initial word of the next sentence. I have carried this into my gloss, but the best English translation seldom shows this feature by more than a connective, say, 'then'.

No such repetition introduces new information into the narrative—though the bare fact of repetition may, and the attached and invariably unlike desinences (here *-mbi* and *-râ)* may have some important signalling function. The second occurrence of the stem is simply required by the grammar—that is, by a part of the grammar controlling relatively shallow structures. Our understanding of the discourse structure will be advanced if we overlook such required repetition. To do so in any principled way, we must set up a deeper underlying structure without these features. This should, of course, omit any other shallow structure features that we cannot account for otherwise. This deeper structure is best labeled 'semologic'.

May I suggest a model? We postulate, first, a class of ACTIONS. (Up to this point I have used 'action' loosely; hereafter I will be more precise.) An Action will be a member of a class of linguistic units behaving in the structure of discourse in the way I am now describing.[9] We postulate also a second class of linguistic units; I have called them here CONNECTIONS. The tactics—and there will be minor differences in tactics from one language to another—provide for the arrangement of these units in long chains, generally with members of these two classes alternating. We will call such a chain of Actions joined by appropriate Connections in the way required by the tactics of the language an EVENT-LINE. Abstractly, a common type of Event-Line appears in Figure 3.

Figure 3

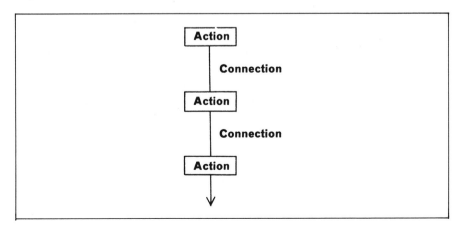

I have suggested one way in which the Event-Line may differ from the procession of verbs through a text. There are certainly many others. The order may not be the same: Displacement of single clauses from 'normal' order may be anatactic. Sometimes an Action in the Event-Line may be realized outside the verb, as in English *he took a walk* where the Action is certainly what is realized as *walk,* a noun complement, rather than as *took.* Indeed, *take* has no place whatever in the semologic structure, being supplied by a grammatical rule whenever a certain situation arises.

There is a more fundamental difference between the Event-Line and the sequence of verbs. That lies in the nature of the units I have called Actions, as different from morphemes as morphemes are from phonemes.

Consider again the pair of English verbs *break* and *tear,* now in some minimum context: *The stick broke. The cloth tore.* There is heavy redundancy here. Given *stick,* everything that differentiates *break* from *tear* is redundant, and conversely given *cloth.* Our underlying structure ought to have neither *break* nor *tear* but something in some sense common to the two.

Or consider a simple discourse like the following:

Father: Go to mother.
Child: What did he say?
Mother: He said, come to me.

The mother is using a colloquial kind of indirect discourse. To describe this, one might at first sight seem to have an option. The linguist might set up the underlying structure as containing *go* and provide a rule that changes *go* to *come.* Or he might set up a different unit *X,* and describe *X* as realized in one place as *go* and in another as *come.* But again, notice that much of the meaning of either *go* or *come* is redundant with its context and need not be specified.

I gave an example from Kâte where the verb stem at the end of one sentence is repeated at the opening of the next. If you examine a text such as that from which this is taken, you will find many instances of the same kind. But you will also find a great number in which the verb stem is paraphrased in the opening of the next sentence. One or the other of these patterns occurs at almost every sentence break, and the mechanisms must be described in an adequate grammar.

This and other forms of paraphrase figure prominently in the structure of discourse in many languages. Southworth (1967) has recently suggested that a componential semologic structure is required to account for various paraphrase relations. I concur. He does not, however, indicate as strongly as he should why paraphrase is of such great interest. One reason is that it is fundamental to various mechanisms of discourse cohesion.

But morphemes like *break, tear, go,* or *come* cannot consist of such semological components. The Actions related to these morphemes can, and indeed must, and for this to be possible, they must be of fundamentally different character. That is one of the things implied by labeling the units in the Event-Line 'Actions' not 'verbs'.[10]

The model I am presenting is one within the stratificational family of models. It differs in only relatively minor ways from that described by Lamb (1966d) who gives much further detail and a bibliography of other sources. I believe that this framework, or one much like it, is a suitable one for either descriptive or contrastive work on discourse structure. It seems to provide a rational place for most, if not all, of the linguistic features of textual connectivity.

We started out by classifying possible differences in the skeletal structure of narratives under a number of heads. We can now see another quite different classification opening to us, in terms of the three kinds of linguistic apparatus that must figure in their specification. First, there may be differences in the organization of the Event-Line; that is, in the inventory of semologic units or in the tactics controlling their arrangements. Second, there may be differences in the grammatical organization of the sentences; that is, in the lexical units employed or in the tactic patterns. Third, there may be differences in the way semologic Event-Lines are realized in grammatical sentences; that is, in the complex mapping relations between the two strata.[11]

Of course the Event-Line or the series of verbs is only the backbone of a narrative. While much more might be said about it, we must now turn to a second sector of discourse structure, the PARTICIPANTS.

Participants are semologic constituents of narratives related to some or all of the Actions by Roles. There is in any language a small set of such Roles, perhaps a dozen. 'Agent', 'goal', 'beneficiary', 'affected', 'causer' are appropriate labels. We must distinguish semologic roles from grammatic functions within clauses, such as subject, direct object, or indirect object. The Roles join totally different units, and they do not relate in any simple way to grammatic functions. In English, for example, a clause subject may represent almost any one of the Roles that the language distinguishes. The passive construction is used to indicate some of the less central possibilities, but even in active clauses a great deal of variety may be encountered.

A single Participant may be related to several Actions. The most direct way of diagramming this is simply to join a spot representing a Participant by a line to each Action concerned. But, when the discourse is long, this poses difficulties of a purely practical sort. And therefore, the difficulties may be met by a purely practical convention. We will represent Participants by lines parallel to the Event-Line, dashed to distinguish them from VALENCES.[12] Remember, however, that this dashed line has the topologic properties of a point, regardless of how we draw it. Taking account of only the Event-Line and the Participants, a semologic structure may be diagrammed as in Figure 4.

Actions differ as to how many and what Roles they permit or require. Those underlying meteorological verbs in English, for example, require none. English grammar, however, requires a subject, and there being no Role of any sort connecting a Participant which might be realized in the subject,

Figure 4

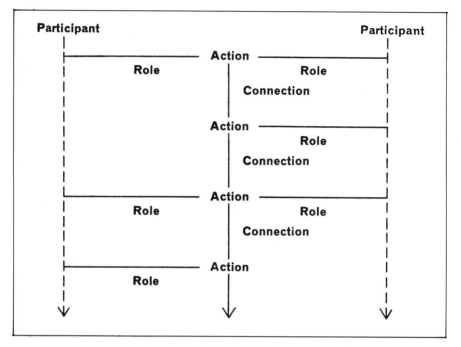

an empty subject is inserted, giving, say, *it rained*. Other Actions require one or two or three, and in various assortments. All this must be specified for the use of the semologic tactics. The realizational relations of these Roles are, of course, complex. For instance, the Role realized by the object of *please* is realized as the subject of *like*, while the subject of *please* and the object of *like* realize the same Role. The two verbs, themselves, realize either the identical Action, or two that are very similar—that is, sharing most components. This accounts for the fact that *John likes opera*, and *opera pleases John* are in some sense paraphrases.

But I need say no more here about this element of the structure. It falls within the now more-or-less classical notions of syntax since it is describable within single sentences and the fragments of semology realized in such sentences.[13]

The Event-Line and the Participants of the Kâte text we have mentioned before can be diagrammed as in Figure 5. Other features—for example, time—are omitted. The embedded quotation is not here analyzed. From this diagram, given interpretation of the valences *imm, lap, sim, ag, gl*, one can not only get the drift of the story, but also see something of the Kâte way of organizing it as its deepest structural stratum. Of course, in some cases the English glosses put in to represent Kâte semologic units are very imprecise equivalents, since the two languages do not classify actions and, in this instance, animals in the same way, but this causes only occasional difficulty.

Figure 5

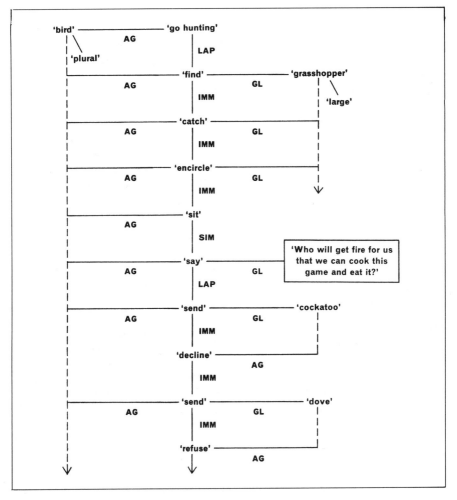

While Roles and their realizations can in most instances be adequately described within a sentence-limited grammar, the identification of the Participants cannot be. The latter is a true discourse feature, usually operating over stretches much longer than a single sentence. There are sometimes profound differences in the patterns of Participant identification from language to language.

A semi-literal translation of the Kâte text is given in Figure 6, with, to the left, an indication of the realization of each Participant. Each of the Participants is realized once by a noun phrase, and thereafter by 'zero anaphora', the absence of a clause constituent in a circumstance that points to a Participant in the previous clause, and by a complex scheme of Participant identification in the verb desinences.

Contrast this with the pattern in the Adamawa Fulani story in Figure 7.

Figure 6

'bird'	'grasshopper', etc.	
wipe jaŋe		(One day) the birds went hunting.
Ø		When they had hunted a long time
Ø	hâpic sâko moc	they found a large grasshopper
Ø	Ø	they caught it.
Ø	Ø	When they had caught it
Ø	Ø	they encircled it
Ø		they sat
Ø		they said, 'Who will get fire for us so that we can cook this game and eat it?
Ø		When they had asked this for a long time
Ø	qaŋ	they sent the cockatoo
	Ø	but he declined.
	Ø	When he had declined
Ø	hâpa	they sent the dove
	Ø	but he refused.

Figure 7

'hyena'	'anteater'	
fowru	yeendu	Hyena strove with Anteater.
ɓe		They both survived.
fowru	yeendu	Hyena wanted to catch Anteater.
ndu	yeendu	But he saw Anteater's claws,
ndu	yeendu	and thought Anteater had teeth like them.
ndu		He was afraid.
ndu		He planned how
ndu		he would know
	yeendu	whether Anteater does or doesn't.
ndu	yeendu	He said to Anteater...
	yeendu	Anteater scowled because
	Ø	knew there were no teeth.
ndu		Later he returned
ndu		and he said again...
	yeendu	Anteater smiled
	Ø	and laughed.
ndu		Then he saw no teeth, just claws.
ndu		He arose
ndu	yeendu	and he examined Anteater.
ndu	yeendu	When he examined Anteater
ndu		he found no teeth.
ndu	yeendu	He caught Anteater
Ø		and ate.

Here the two Participants show very different patterns. 'Hyena' is realized twice by a noun, fourteen times by a pronoun, *ndu,*[14] and once by zero anaphora. 'Anteater' is, however, realized eleven times by the noun, and twice by zero anaphora.

The two languages cited are not only very different one from the other, but equally from English. A translation of either text into English requires a total restructuring of the system of Participant identification. This was not altered in the translation of the Fulani, but reading the translation will indicate immediately that adjustment would be necessary to make proper English. And the adjustment would run in different directions for the two Participants: more nouns for 'hyena', less for 'anteater'.

This set of devices is one of the features of discourse structure most frequently mentioned in subrecent work. Bloomfield, for example, (1933:247–263) devotes a chapter to 'Substitution' in which he discusses, among other things, the use of pronouns, though he does not attempt to define in any specific way when a pronoun is used rather than a noun phrase.[15] This cannot be done without crossing the sentence boundary.

The model of semologic structure I have presented gives a basis for the systematic examination of anaphora. We posit a SEMOLOGIC RETICULUM[16] generated by its proper tactics. In a text-producing application, this keeps ahead of sentence generation, though not necessarily far ahead. The semotactics are such that an Event-Line (and other structures built around it) is generated by continuous accretion at the end. Successive clauses are generated in a way that conforms to the requirements of the semologic structure. The grammatical tactics allow an option, say, between an overt subject and none. In terms of possible structures of single clauses, this is a free option. But for a clause within a discourse the choice is determined and can be specified in terms of certain configurations in the semologic reticulum. Thus, in the first clause to be produced to realize the structure partially diagrammed above, a subject is required, and *wipe jaŋe* 'the birds' must be that subject. In a subsequent clause built around a realization of 'find', there can be no subject because the configuration in the semology is one realized by omission, but a direct object must be put in to realize 'large grasshopper'. Notice that as here described, two tactics are involved. Structures produced by one are realized in those produced by the other through control over choice of options.[17]

Translators are aware of the differences, occasionally crucial, in the ways that languages require selection of nominal, pronominal, or zero realization for Participants. Some such scheme as that proposed here provides the required basis for precise statement, that is, for significant contrastive analysis. It also relates this question to another one which has received far less attention—given that a noun phrase must be used at a particular point, what noun phrase will it be?[18] Consider the following opening of a narrative:

> A tall, lanky high-school basketball star folded himself into the little foreign car with his short, pudgy father beside him. The son drove carefully down

the busy highway, obviously restrained by the older man's presence. He watched the other traffic intently. He signalled before each turn and came to a full stop at the blinker. Classmates stared in amazement, but the driver took no notice of them. The athlete's strange behavior seemed totally inexplicable. The poor boy was obviously in some trouble.

This passage has been contrived to include a range of phenomena usually requiring a longer text for exemplification, and to give some of them slight exaggeration.

There are two Participants. On introduction each is given a certain amount of description. Aside from whatever literary function such description may have, it serves also to define initially the set of contrasts which will be used, from place to place, to identify these Participants. For example, one is described as a *basketball star;* toward the end of the paragraph, he can, therefore, be indentified by *athlete.* It is not the description, as such, that counts but the contrasts that are set up. For example, *the son* serves as an identification in the second sentence because the other Participant has been described as *father,* and in a somewhat more complex manner *older man* exploits the same contrast. These potential identifications may be set up by the mention of just one term, as in the examples just mentioned, or by explicit specification of both, as *tall, lanky* versus *short, pudgy.* In either case, it is only the network of contrast and componency that makes the system operable. Subsequent identifications use selections of the available features and so take on much of the aspect of paraphrase.

Not only so, the corpus of usable identifications is cumulative. Thus the Action 'drive' in the second sentence is added in such a way that *driver* becomes a possible label several sentences later.[19] The opposite phenomenon is not illustrated here: a feature may cease to be distinctive when the development of the narrative associates it with a second Participant.

In this system pronouns have a special place. They may operate like any other paraphrase, conveying a selected subset of the contrastive features already assigned to one of the Participants. In English *he* carries the feature 'male', *they* either 'plural' or 'animate, sex unknown'. Or, pronouns may be used in ways that provide precise identification by anaphoric rules.[20] The one fully precise case in English is that of the reflexive uses of *-self* pronouns. These always signal coreference with a precisely definable constituent in the same sentence. Thus, in *John shaved himself,* the Participant identified by *himself* must be the same as that identified by *John.*[21] Or, pronouns may just fill grammatical slots leaving Participant identification to other clues. In most instances some combination of these is involved.

For example, our sample text has two occurrences of *he.* Neither identifies by specifying one of the contrasting features, since both Participants are male. In the first occurrence, *he* must be anaphoric to some Participant mentioned in the preceding sentence. English patterns of anaphora suggest *the son* as more likely than *the older man,* but the latter is not impossible.[22] In the second occurrence, 'common sense' tells us that *he* must refer to the Participant known to be driving. We cannot be sure what is involved in this appeal to 'common sense' until we have examined the whole system in detail; it might cover any combination of linguistic and non-linguistic clues. But in any case, the two occurrences of *he* must by normal grammatical patterns identify the same Participant.

Adjectives[23] have three broad classes of functions. Taking examples from this text: some are descriptive, as *tall;* some are identifying, as *older;* and some are affective—indicating the observer's attitude, evaluation, or involvement—as *poor.* There are differences in the grammatical treatment of these. For example, superlative adjectives in affective function are always elative, and comparative do not occur. Only descriptive adjectives occur in predicate position or as non-restrictive modifiers. Some of the puzzling problems of adjective position within noun phrases seem likely to be correlates of the fundamental distinction. All this is important to discourse analysis because these adjective functions are definable only relative to discourse. Descriptive adjectives function in some ways just like elements on the Event-Line. They add to the stock of known characteristics of the Participant, altering in some way the available contrasting features. Identifying adjectives are those functioning within the Participant-identification system itself. Affective adjectives are wholly outside. They tell us nothing about the Participant —only about the observer's reaction to a Participant—and they cannot serve to identify.

Description, identification, and affect are functions of adjectives, not classes. To be sure not all adjectives can function in all three ways. Affective uses are restricted to a relatively small class of adjectives, but most of these can also be used in other functions.[24] But in English, at least, there is a special organization of adjectives associated with the discrimination of these functions. If one Participant is described as *little,* then *big* automatically becomes identifying. If one is *small,* subsequent use of *large* is identifying. But after *little, large* preserves at least some of its descriptive function, as does *big* after *small.* A significant difference between these pairs of synonyms is that they operate in different sets of formal contrasts, and thus differently in the Participant-identification system.

I have been able to discuss only two of the systems of structure that hold together a discourse—the organization of the Event-Line and the identification of the Participants. I have only hinted at their richness and intricacy and have hardly mentioned the interaction of these systems with each other and with other systems. I might plead in my defense the necessary restriction in length on a paper of this kind. But the more honest course is to admit that I know little more than I have presented, and even much of that is based on superficial and random observation. The fact is that the whole area of discourse analysis is just at the beginning of its development.

But while there is much to learn, I think we can say that we do now have a framework within which the next round of work can be done, a framework which permits relating the various phenomena of discourse structure to one another and each of them to the better known facts of sentence syntax. And not only so, we now have a framework that provides a better starting point than any we have had before for systematic contrastive work. It allows us to focus on what may well prove to be the most interesting of all contrastive problems, the differences in the way connected discourse is organized and the way that organization is signalled to the hearer or reader.

NOTES

1. This is not to condemn lexicography, an activity to which I am personally deeply committed, but to point out a probably inescapable fact. It is highly doubtful that a dictionary in anything like the familiar form can be given any reasonable theoretic base. Language is simply not organized in such a way that all the features we expect in a dictionary can be brought together at any one place. It is of some possible interest that those linguists who have recently proposed a prominent central place for the dictionary in their linguistic theory have so far produced neither any dictionary nor any reasonable fragment of one to exemplify their ideas.

2. This paper has grown out of several years of discussion with students and colleagues at the Hartford Seminary Foundation and elsewhere. Specific help (including examples cited and many other examples not used) has been received from: Priscilla Baptista, Gordon Beacham, Randy Brock, Ilah Fleming, Michael Manickham, Roland Pickering, Peter Reich, William J. Samarin, Leslie H. Stennes, Charles R. Taber.

3. Criticism of Whorf has recently been popular. While some of his conclusions may have been controverted, his examples remain for the most part. With regard to them, all that we can say is that by selection of dramatic instances he has overstated the case for difference in modes of expression.

4. Linguists have tended to discount the extent of unconditioned variation. But there is a great deal in every language, in particular in the grammatical or lexical realization of semologic structures, not conditioned within the linguistic system. Style—or one aspect of style—is based on the patterned choices among the options so presented. Style is an important variable in language, one that linguists will continue to neglect at their peril.

5. Anyone working extensively with texts from a different culture will observe differences that are apparently patterned and suggest that something, linguistic or cultural, does exert some control on selection. We have, however, almost no carefully controlled experimental evidence. This is certainly a fruitful field for ethnolinguistic work.

6. Neither can grammatical analysis (in a narrow sense) go up to the sentence and stop. There are larger structures composed of sentences and having structural features worth describing. For example, in Adamawa Fulani a sentence is marked intonationally by a lowering of pitch on the last few syllables. A certain kind of discourse is marked by the overall lowering of pitch on the last few sentences (with, of course, further lowering on their last syllables). Such a discourse unit it, therefore, marked intonationally. It is my conviction, however, that only a relatively small part of the structure of longer discourses is effectively described in such a framework. The failures of constituency structure models at the 'syntactic' level are real, but often exaggerated. I would, however, expect them to become more severe as the work progresses upward into lengthy connected discourse. Attempts to patch up a basically constituency approach by adding a transformational component will also fail when attempted on the discourse level. Short trips with an old car patched up with baling wire and chewing gum are one thing; long trips under grueling conditions are another.

7. This is the kind of feature where the insight of the non-native investigator is needed. The native speaker-linguist has some special competences in elaborating details, but some special liabilities in breaking into hitherto unanalyzed portions of the structure. Native competence in a language is designed in exactly the way best suited to keeping structural details implicit, for which non-linguist native speakers should be most grateful. That introspective linguistics is producing so extensively today is the consequence of a great deal of ground breaking by external observation in the recent past. The younger son has taken his inheritance into a far country and is, currently, living high.

8. Pilhofer (1933) translates many of his Kâte examples 'literally' into 'German'. To do

so he had to create, by misusing various German particles, a system of connection-markers partially conformable to the Kâte system. I found many of his glosses totally incomprehensible until I learned enough of the system not to need them anymore. Otherwise an excellent traditional grammar, this book is my chief source of information on Kâte.

9. As always, technical terms seeming to have an etymology must be understood to apply to a group in which the etymology is not necessarily appropriate in other typical instances.

10. If I say that semologic units are fundamentally different from morphemes, I do not mean that they are 'abstract' while morphemes are 'concrete', or that there is any difference in the degree of abstractness. One of the most misleading notions in recent linguistic discussion is that the 'deep structure' is in some special sense 'abstract', implying that the 'surface structure' is not 'abstract'. Linguistic units have linguistic reality, and no other kind, though they relate in various ways with physical reality, psychological reality, etc. In going from grammar to semology we do not take one more step along a continuum away from physical reality, for no linguistic unit has physical reality, and we have departed explicitly from physical reality when we have entered language.

11. There is currently much debate and experimentation concerning the number of strata. I write this paper against the assumption that there are just three: phonology, morphology, and semology. I do not want to prejudge the case. I suspect that three are enough. But the argument is not changed, merely elaborated if there are more.

12. I use 'Valence' for any of the relations indicated on semologic structure diagrams by labeled lines. Alternatively, of course, these labels could be assigned to nodes and these nodes connected by two unlabeled lines. And there are other possibilities. But the device shown suffices at this stage of development, and seems to be suggestive.

13. Important treatments within different frameworks are those of Halliday (1967–8) and Fillmore (1969).

14. Fulani has an elaborate system of noun classes. The reference of a pronoun is commonly identifiable on this basis. However, both *fowru* and *yeendu* belong to the same class, so *ndu* might be coreferent with either. There seems to be a structural pattern, however, which makes it, in this text, only interpretable as coreferent with *fowru*.

15. The very chapter title 'Substitution' suggests a major difficulty with Bloomfield's treatment. He is taking another step toward the transformational-generative technique of introducing a noun-phrase into a sentence and then substituting a pronoun for it. At best, the notion that the noun-phrase (that is, a construction of morphemes) is in any sense there, is an artifact of describing sentences out of discourse context and in a process framework. It is preferable to consider noun-phrase and pronoun as alternative realizations of some semologic unit. The large number of different noun-phrases that may serve as realizations of a single Participant (see below) is a major reason for the superiority of a realizational over a transformational description.

16. Since it has become common to speak of 'networks of rules' it is desirable to avoid confusion by speaking of a 'reticulum' of semologic units rather than a 'network'. No change of theory is implied in the change of terminology.

17. Realization is a linkage between two tactics such that they produce matched structures. In practice the relation between the grammar and the semology can be described in either of two ways: as conditions attached to alternatives in the morphotactics such that they allow the production of a morphologic structure matched to a given semologic structure, and as conditions attached to alternatives in the semotactics with the opposite outcome. Thus the relation can be applied in either direction. Anything short of this misses important facts about language, facts necessary either to explain human behavior or to facilitate practical applications.

18. For an account of some features of this system and for an exemplification of stratificational treatment of narrative, see Taber (1966).

19. At the 1967 Annual meeting of the Linguistic Society of America Paul Postal criticized stratificational theory on the ground that it assumed that coreferent elements are always identical in meaning. He advanced a sentence similar to the following as a counterexample: *Mary married a confirmed bachelor, but after two years divorced him. Him* certainly does not 'mean' the same as *confirmed bachelor*. Actually the stratificationalist makes the opposite assumption,

namely that there is a cumulation through a text, so that the case where the meaning remains the same would be the exception.

20. That is, by a certain set of realizational rules determining such morphologic choices as that between a pronoun and a noun phrase in certain structures. Moreover, 'anaphoric' is too narrow here. Pronouns may also be cataphoric: *he who steals my purse steals trash. He* refers forward to *who steals my purse*.

21. Because reflexives always operate within single sentences in English, they have been extensively examined by transformational-generative linguists. They are, however, minimally involved in the full system of paraphrasal realization of Participants mentioned above, and hence taking reflexives as the paradigm of pronominalization has resulted in missing much of the richness of the system.

22. Notice that *son* is marked as anaphoric (in the broad sense) by the presence of *the*. The function of the article in such a situation is simply to indicate that the reference of the noun can be determined from the context but not to specify what context. The relevant context here is *father* in the first sentence.

23. The same thing is true of any other specification within a noun-phrase. The component 'female' realized in *woman* may be either descriptive or identifying. *Bum* and *vagrant* differ, among other things in the greater openness of one to affective use, just as do *poor* and *poverty-stricken*.

24. The only possible exceptions are the 'cuss words'. For most speakers *damn* seems only to be used affectively. This is one, but only one of the characteristics of this group. In addition, *damn* and *hell* (in each case with its more innocent surrogates, *darn, heck,* etc.) have peculiarities of grammatical construction that should be investigated.

CHAPTER FOURTEEN

English Prepositions*

DAVID C. BENNETT

1. Introduction

IN A PAPER READ at the Tenth International Congress of Linguists, Bucharest, 1967 (Bennett 1970), I discussed the question of synonymy within the framework of the stratificational theory of language, taking examples from the area of English prepositions.[1] The present paper has two aims. On the one hand, it incorporates the findings of more recent work on synonymy. Thus whereas, for instance, in the earlier paper two levels of synonymy were distinguished, it now seems necessary to recognize four or possibly five levels. On the other hand, the paper will attempt to set the discussion of synonymy in a wider framework by sketching the outlines of a semological description of English prepositions. To present such a description would be beyond the scope of the paper. I hope merely to indicate the general shape that the description might take. In addition to the remarks on synonymy there will be some discussion of polysemy, componential analysis and idioms. In particular it is hoped that a clear picture will emerge of the relationship between these various areas.

2. Stratificational Grammar

The view of the overall structure of language subscribed to here is that described in Lamb (1966d).[2] The graphic notation employed in Figures 1, 3 and 4 is also that of Lamb (1966d).[3] Reduced to its bare essentials, the stratificational view of language is characterized in the following few sentences. There are two ends to language: a meaning end (by convention

---

*From *Journal of Linguistics* 4.153–172. (1968), under the title 'English prepositions: a stratificational approach.' Reprinted by permission.

the top) and a sound end (by convention the bottom). At either end is a set of discrete elements, components of meaning (hypersememes) and components of sound (hypophonemes). A language is the network of relations that exist between the components of meaning and the components of sound. All discrepancies from a simple one-to-one relationship can be described in terms of the basic relations AND and OR, each of which can be either ordered or unordered, and upward or downward. Certain recurrent configurations of these relations are known as patterns, e.g. alternation pattern, sign pattern. Certain recurrent configurations of patterns are known as stratal systems. In addition to the patterns in the vertical or realizational dimension, each stratal system has a tactic pattern which can be thought of as being in a horizontal plane and which specifies the permitted combinations of the elements at that particular level of the realization chain.

3. The Lexemic and Sememic Strata

For a more detailed account of the model than that given above the reader should consult Lamb (1966d). Since, however, the present discussion will center around the lexemic and sememic stratal systems, it will perhaps be helpful to begin with a characterization of some of the differences between the lexemic and the sememic stratum. The following example should clarify the need for a distinct lexotactics and semotactics. If we consider the relative distribution of *before* and *in front of,* it will be apparent that there are two distinct senses in which the set of environments of *in front of* is a subset of the set of environments of *before*. On the one hand, *in front of* has the distribution of a preposition whereas *before* has the combined distribution of a preposition, a conjunction and an adverb. This fact is shown in the lexotactics, which is roughly equivalent to syntax in the traditional sense. On the other hand, if we think of *in front of* and *before* as binary relations,[4] each relates things to things or events to things, but in addition *before* relates events or points in time to other events or points in time. This is a matter of 'collocability' or 'selectional restrictions' and as such belongs in the semotactics of a stratificational grammar.

The main difference between lexemes and sememes depends on the fact that the lexemic alternation pattern is situated between them. Sometimes there is a one-to-one correspondence between a sememe and its lexemic realization, but in many cases a sememe has more than one lexemic realization (i.e. there is a downward OR below it) and a lexeme is the realization of two or more distinct sememes (i.e. there is an upward OR above it). For instance, the relational sememe 'cause' can be realized as the noun/verb *cause;* the conjunction *because;* the prepositions *because of, on account of, owing to;* the abverbs *therefore, so,* etc.; the adjective *due (to);* etc. And the preposition *on* has a spatio-temporal sense (cf. section 4); a sense that means 'on the subject of'; etc. Consequently, the distribution of a given lexeme can be at the same time both smaller than and greater than that of a sememe which it realizes.

A discrepancy of a different kind between lexemes and sememes results from the fact that there is also a sign pattern, the sememic sign pattern, between them. Some sememes are complex, i.e. consist of two or more semons, each of which is realized as a separate lexeme. Consider the sentences:

(1) He was standing at the door
(2) He was looking at the door

These exhibit the same structure on the lexemic stratum: in each case *at the door* is a constituent. On the sememic stratum, however, *at* in (1) is a separate sememe, whereas *at* in (2) is part of the complex sememe *look at,* which functions as a unit in the semotactics.

4. Polysemy

As indicated in the previous section polysemy is represented in a stratificational description by means of upward ORs at the bottom of the lexemic alternation pattern. In other words, a polysemous lexeme is connected to two or more different points on the sememic stratum rather than to a single point. At present I see no need for distinguishing between polysemy and homonymy in the area of English prepositions. As these terms are often used, polysemy results from a content-split, whereas homonymy results from an expression-merger. Often homonymy is recognizable as such from the fact that members of two different parts of speech have merged, but in many cases the two items belong to the same part of speech, so that this criterion will work for identifying only a subset of all cases of homonymy. In cases where the two or more meanings are associated with the same part of speech, it becomes progressively more difficult with time to see whether a split or a merger has taken place. Conceivably one might distinguish polysemy and homonymy synchronically on the basis of whether or not the two or more distinct meanings share any component of meaning. Alternatively it might be the case that accepted examples of homonymy involve neutralization below a particular point in the realization chain, whereas examples of polysemy involve neutralization above that point. At all events, only the term polysemy will be used in what follows.

At first sight it might seem that the facts of the polysemy of English prepositions are already well described both in reputable dictionaries and in numerous articles and theses devoted to the subject. In most cases, however, no consistent policy is followed for deciding whether two occurrences of a given preposition are instances of the same sense or of a different sense. On the whole, far too many senses are recognized. Thus Lindkvist (1950), discussing only local senses of four prepositions, claims that *in* has seven local senses. Three of them are as follows:

1. Enclosure within a body, e.g. *in the cupboard*
2. Enclosure within an area, e.g. *in a field*
3. Location along a line, e.g. *in a line*

Now these three so-called senses of *in* are in complementary distribution. Thus the preposition has the first 'sense' only when the accompanying noun designates a three-dimensional object. Similarly 'senses' 2 and 3 depend on the occurrence of a noun designation a two-dimensional and a one-dimensional object respectively. It is preferable, therefore, to recognize only one general sense of the preposition occurring in 1, 2 and 3. The specific meaning that the preposition seems to have in each of the three examples is determined by the context. Notice also that the so-called temporal sense of *in* that occurs in the phrase *in the morning* is in complementary distribution with the other three specific meanings. Consequently it would seem that we need to set up a general spatio-temporal sense of *in* (in^{s-t}) that can be characterized as meaning simply 'inclusion'.

Up to this point our approach has been that of Jakobson (1932, 1936). As items of 'langue' lexemes need to be attributed general meanings (Gesamtbedeutungen) rather than large sets of specific but related meanings. We depart from Jakobson, however, in allowing the possibility that a lexeme may have two or more distinct general meanings. This is necessary for two reasons. In the first place, one can find many examples where two meanings of a lexeme contrast, e.g.:

(3) He wrote a book *on* the Queen Mary

which can mean either 'while he was on the Queen Mary' or 'a book about the Queen Mary'. The first of the two senses is the general spatio-temporal sense (on^{s-t}), of which *on October 1* provides another instance. The second sense has the meaning 'on the subject of'. Thus there is one lexeme but two underlying sememes. Secondly, in many cases where two meanings do not actually contrast, they are so dissimilar that it would be a distortion of the synchronic facts to try to unite them in a single Gesamtbedeutung. Thus, for instance, *in* in *light in color* is in complementary distribution with in^{s-t} but meaning ('in respect of') is quite distinct from that of 'inclusion'. There is a parallel here with traditional phonemics. The specific meanings that an item has in particular contexts are like allophones (Joos 1958 employs the term 'allosemes' for them). They are grouped into Gesamtbedeutungen provided (1) that they do not contrast; and (2) that they exhibit semantic similarity. To say that *in* in *light in color* is a different sense of the preposition from in^{s-t} is comparable to assigning English [h] and [ŋ] to different phonemes even though they are in complementary distribution.

5. Synonymy

It requires no great insight to observe that the term synonymy has been used in a variety of ways in the past. Sometimes it has been explicitly defined, but more often it has remained undefined. However, each usage can be reduced to the form of a definition and the various definitions can then be ranged along a scale according to the number of synonyms that they permit one to recognize. A conservative definition would be one that recognized a relatively small set of synonyms in a given language. A liberal definition would be one according to which there were relatively many synonyms in the language. Definitions of so-called true or complete synonymy, such as definition 1, are ultra-conservative in that they force one to the conclusion that there are no synonyms in natural languages.

DEFINITION 1: Any two lexemes which are substitutable for each other in all their environments without any change of meaning are synonymous.

To propose this as the only conceivable or permissible definition of snyonymy is unrealistic. More often, however, a definition of so-called partial synonymy is proposed in addition to or instead of a definition of complete synonymy. This is to be welcomed since it reflects a desire to show how the term synonymy has been used in the past. After all, the existence of dictionaries of synonyms for numerous languages speaks against the view that there is no such thing as synonymy in natural languages.

Definition 2 represents one attempt at a definition of partial synonymy.

DEFINITION 2: If there are one or more environments in which two lexemes are substitutable for each other without any change of meaning, then they are synonymous in that environment or those environments.

At first sight this would appear to be a more liberal definition than definition 1. However, it can be claimed that there is always SOME difference in meaning when one lexeme is substituted for another. For instance, many native speakers of English feel that there is a difference in meaning between *because of* and *on account of*. If it is true that the substitution of one lexeme for another is always accompanied by some change of meaning, then definition 2 as well as definition 1 will yield no pairs of synonymous lexemes. Definition 2 is therefore in need of some modification before it will work as a definition of partial synonymy. If we accept that there is a difference in meaning between *because of* and *on account of,* at least it is not comparable to the difference between, say, *chair* and *table*. The latter differ in cognitive meaning, whereas *because of* and *on account of* seem to differ only stylistically and have the same cognitive meaning. What we are saying is that the total meaning of a lexeme can be broken down into a number of constituents, of which two are the cognitive and stylistic constituents. In section 6 five constituents of meaning will be discussed. For the time being only one need be illustrated in addition to the cognitive and stylistic constituents. This is a particular kind of suggested or implied meaning that will be referred to below as 'reflected' meaning. For instance, the prepositions *on* and *about* can both mean 'on the subject of' and yet there is a difference in meaning between *a book on astronomy* and *a book about astronomy*. The former suggests a more serious, scholarly work than the latter.

I would now like to propose a third definition of synonymy, which it seems to me corresponds to a fairly widespread use of the term.

DEFINITION 3. If there is one or more environment in which two lexemes are substitutable for each other without any change in COGNITIVE meaning, then they are synonymous in that environment or those environments.

According to this definition both *because of* and *on account of*, and *on* and *about* (in the environment *a book... astronomy*) are synonymous, because the difference in meaning is stylistic in the one case and 'reflected' in the other.

Now it would be possible to give more liberal definitions of synonymy than definition 3. For instance, one could remove the condition of substitutability, in which case members of different parts of speech would be considered synonyms if they had the same cognitive meaning. Thus *in spite of*, *although* and *nevertheless*, which all signal the failure of an expected cause-and-effect sequence, e.g. in (4), would be regarded as synonyms.

(4) I went *in spite of* the rain
   I went *although* it was raining
   I went *nevertheless*

There are doubtless some linguists who see no objection to describing *in spite of* and *although* as synonyms, but it seems to me that there are more linguists for whom synonyms always belong to the same part of speech. Consequently we prefer definition 3 to a definition that does not include the requirement of substitutability.

Another direction in which definition 3 could be liberalized would be to allow synonymy to apply not only to pairs of lexemes (or words, for those who make no distinction between words and lexemes) but also to pairs of sentences. There are in fact many linguists who use the word 'synonymous' of pairs of sentences. Notice, however, that there are probably no linguists who would say that a particular sentence is a 'synonym' of some other sentence. For this reason we have preferred a definition of synonymy that applies only to lexemes. For the relation of meaning-equivalence between sentences there is in any case another term, namely 'paraphrase' ('sentence 1 is a paraphrase of sentence 2').

What we have done so far is try to find a definition of synonymy that corresponds to the most widespread use of the term. In the remainder of this section we will first indicate how this view of synonymy fits into the framework of the stratificational theory of language, and then present a classification of some examples of synonymy by distinguishing a number of levels of synonymy.

In section 2 we spoke of the two ends of language as the sound end and the meaning end. It is not the case, however, that the whole of meaning is located at the top of language. In fact, some constituents of meaning have their origin relatively low down and at least one constituent of meaning is best accounted for by reference to a separate subsystem of a grammar rather than the main system. These questions will be discussed in section 6. The main network of a stratificational description should be thought of as primarily as relating cognitive meanings to sound.

Any two lexemes that are synonymous in the sense of the preferred definition of synonymy, i.e. which have the same cognitive meaning in some context, are shown in the description as being dominated at some point higher up the realization chain by a downward OR node. In other words, synonymy depends on the realizational phenomenon known as 'diversification' (Lamb, 1964a, 1966d), the same phenomenon that is involved in the alternations *sleep:slep-* (as in *slept*) and *good:be(tt)-* (as in *better, best*). However, not all instances of diversification are examples of synonymy. In the first place, diversification below the lexemic stratum does not involve meaning directly and is not regarded as synonymy. Secondly, we have decided that substitutability is an essential feature of the notion of synonymy, and in order for two items to be substitutable for each other, they must share at least one lexemic and sememic environment. Now, the relative distribution of two items on any stratum can be coincident, incorporating, overlapping or complementary (cf. Bloch 1953). In the case of the first three there is at least one shared environment, but in the case of complementary distribution there is no common environment. Thus if two items with the same cognitive meaning are in complementary distribution on the lexemic or sememic stratum, they are not substitutable for each other and are not regarded as synonyms.

Lexemic complementary distribution has already been illustrated by *in spite of, although,* and *nevertheless*. An example of sememic complementary distribution is provided by *after* and *behind*, which have the cognitive meaning 'posteriority' (to be interpreted as meaning 'further along some dimension'). On the lexemic stratum their relative distribution is incorporating: the set of environments of *behind* is a subset of the set of environments of *after*, since both function as prepositions or adverbs but *after* has in addition the distribution of a conjunction. However, they are not substitutable for each other, because their sememic environments are mutually exclusive: *after* relates events or points in time to other events or points in time, while *behind* relates things to things or events to things. On the other hand, *before* and *in front of* are substitutable for each other (cf. (5)) since their relative sememic distribution is incorporating—the set of sememic environments of *in front of* is a subset of the set of environments of *before*—and they are regarded as synonyms.

(5) He was standing *before* the crowd
    He was standing *in front of* the crowd

The claim that *after* and *behind* do not contrast would appear to be contradicted by examples such as (6) since the environment is apparently identical and the meaning of (6a) and (6b) is different.

(6a) the street *behind* the church
(6b) the street *after* the church[5]

It would seem, however, that the best way of describing this example is by recognizing distinct sememic environments in (6a) and (6b), and regarding only the lexemic environments as identical. *The church* in (6a) is a thing, but *the church* in (6b) is elliptical and stands for an event.[6] It is our knowledge of the semotactic properties of *after* that leads us to interpret (6b) as meaning 'the street (that you get to) after you have passed the church'.

It was said above that the alternations *sleep:slep-* and *good:be(tt)-* involve diversification. We can, however, be more precise. In the alternation *sleep:slep-* we have a case of morphophonemic diversification: a morphon of vowel length is realized as phonemic zero in the environment of a following consonant cluster and as a phoneme of vowel length elsewhere. (In fact, this example also illustrates diversification between the level of the phonons and that of the hypophonemes, since the vowel quality alternation—as opposed to the vowel length alternation—involves feature-sized rather than segment-sized units.) On the other hand, the diversification exhibited by *good:be(tt)-* is lexomorphemic: the lexeme /good/ is realized as the morpheme /be^T/ in the environment of a following comparative or superlative suffix and as ^{M}/gud/ elsewhere. (The morphon /^{T}/ then participates also in morphophonemic alternation, being realized as ^{P}/t/ in *better* and as ^{P}/ø/ in *best*, cf. *late, latter, last*.) Thus the downward ORs representing these two examples belong at different points in the realization chain. Similar considerations higher up the realization chain lead us to distinguish different levels of synonymy. In Bennett (1970) two such levels of synonymy were recognized. They were said to depend on semolexemic and hypersemo-sememic diversification. Thus in the one case the downward OR was below the level of the sememes and in the other case it was above. The downward OR is placed below the level of the sememes wherever the synonyms are not distinct semotactically, i.e. with regard to collocability. Thus the synonymy of *because of* and *on account of*, which—apart from stylistic considerations—can always be substituted for each other, was assigned to the lower level. On the other hand, wherever the synonyms have a different semotactic distribution, as in the case of *before* and *in front of*, it is necessary to set up distinct underlying sememes, and the downward OR belongs above the level of the sememes.

Now one of the revisions that Lamb has made in stratificational theory since the appearance of his *Outline of Stratificational Grammar* is the recognition of an additional alternation pattern below the tactics of each stratum for cases of non-conditioned alternation, i.e. cases where—apart from stylistic considerations—the alternants are in free variation (exhibit coincident relative distribution). This revision was called for on grounds of simplicity, as will be apparent from consideration of the two diagrams of Figure 1. Both diagrams contain the same effective information, but diagram (b), which lowers the diversification to below the lexotactics, is simpler than diagram (a). The point is that *because of* and *on account of* are not only not distinct semotactically—they are not even distinct lexotactically. Thus they constitute two 'lexemic signs' (Lamb 1966) which realize a single lexeme. This necessitates a minor change in our definition of synonymy: instead of '... two lexemes...' it should now read '... two lexemes/lexemic signs...'.

Figure 2 shows the current hypothesis concerning the structure of the sememic and lexemic stratal systems in terms of patterns.[7] Conditioned alternation (where the relative distribution of the alternants is incorporating, overlapping or complementary) is represented in the upper alternation pattern

Figure 1. Two Ways of Describing an Instance of Diversification.

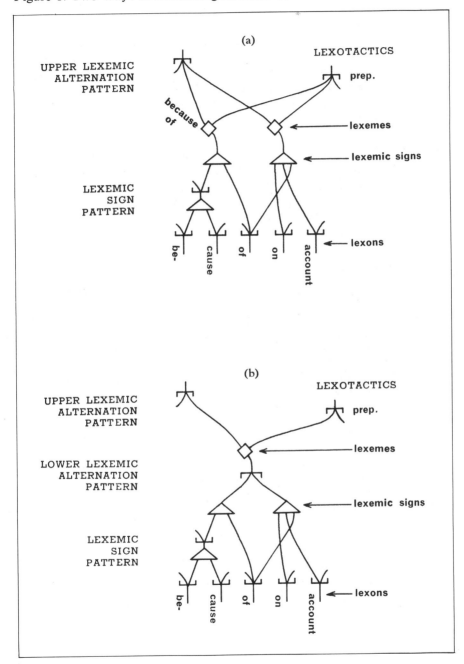

of each stratal system, the environments of each realization being specified in the tactics. Non-conditioned alternation, as stated above, belongs in the lower alternation pattern.

Where previously two levels of synonymy were distinguished, there are now four, dependent on diversification in the lower and upper lexemic and sememic alternation patterns. The example of *because of* and *on account of* belongs in the lower lexemic alternation pattern (cf. Figure 1b). That of *before* and *in front of* belongs in the upper sememic alternation pattern: a hypersemon 'anteriority' is realized as the sememe underlying *before* in one set of sememic environments and as the sememe underlying *in front of* in another set of environments (which happens to be a subset of the environments of *before*).

Figure 2. The Structure of the Sememic and Lexemic Stratal Systems. (U.A.P. = upper alternation pattern; L.A.P. = lower alternation pattern; S.P. = sign pattern.)

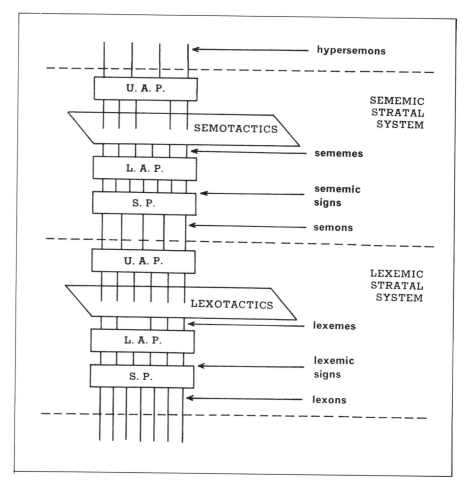

As an example of diversification in the upper lexemic alternation pattern, we can consider *because of* and *on account of* in those varieties of (colloquial)

American English where *on account of* functions not only as a preposition but also as a conjunction, cf.:

(7) I didn't go *on account of* I didn't have any money

Here *because of* and *on account of* exhibit incorporating lexotactic distribution, since *because of* functions only as a preposition. Thus it is necessary to recognize two distinct lexemes and the diversification belongs above the lexotactics.

The synonymy of *encounter* and *come across* provides an example of diversification in the lower sememic alternation pattern. The verbs are lexotactically distinct since *come across* consists of two lexemes whereas *encounter* is only one, but semotactically non-distinct. (There is, of course, a stylistic difference.) Therefore the downward OR belongs between the level of the sememes and that of the lexemes, i.e. in either the upper lexemic or the lower sememic alternation pattern. Two considerations indicate that the latter is the correct place. First, the alternation is not lexemically conditioned, i.e. there is no lexotactic environment that requires a verb plus particle rather than a simple verb, or vice versa. Secondly, the downward OR must be above the sememic sign pattern since it is there that *come across* is shown to be a complex sememe consisting of two semons (cf. section 8).[8]

All the examples of synonymy discussed above involve meaning in the narrow sense, i.e. intension, as opposed to reference, or extension. That is to say, in each case it seems legitimate to postulate some higher-level linguistic unit of which the synonyms are alternate realizations. Consider now example (8):

(8a) At this moment he's *on* a train going to London
(8b) At this moment he's *in* a train going to London

Setting aside the possibility that *on a train* might conceivably mean *on top of a train*, (8a) and (8b) would normally describe the same situation, but it would be counter-intuitive to postulate some higher-level linguistic unit that can be realized alternately as *on* or *in*, since *on*-ness and *in*-ness are essentially different notions, i.e. on^{s-t} and in^{s-t} differ in cognitive meaning. What we have, rather, is a case of coextensiveness. There are certain situations in reality that can be perceived by a speaker of English as involving either *on*-ness or *in*-ness. One such situation is the boarding of a train, which can be perceived as getting *onto* it or getting *into* it. Thus whether one uses *on* or *in* in (8), the situation described is the same.

It is probably preferable to restrict the term synonymy to the first four levels and use the term coextensiveness, as I have done in the preceding paragraph, for the phenomenon illustrated by example (8). On the other hand, if it were the case that the majority of linguists were in the habit of using the term synonymy also of examples such as (8), we could easily decide to speak of five levels of synonymy rather than four. Four of these levels would then be purely linguistic, while the highest would involve the relationship between language and non-language. Our definition of synonymy would have to be modified somewhat to reflect this wider usage, namely by stating that synonyms have either the same cognitive meaning or the same reference (extension) in some environment. However, as stated above, it is probably preferable to use the term synonymy of the first four levels and coextensiveness of the highest level.

For the final example of this section we return to a consideration of *after* and *behind*. In (9) as in (6) the two prepositions appear to occur in the same environment.

(9a) John is dragging a chair *behind* him
(9b) John is dragging a chair *after* him

However, there is clearly a difference in meaning in (6) between *the street behind the church* and *the street after the church,* but (9a) and (9b), on the other hand, do not contrast. An explanation of this fact suggests itself within the existing theoretical framework. The choice of *after* or *behind* in (9), as in (6), can be attributed to a difference in the sememic environment of the relational 'posteriority'. But whereas the difference in sememic environment in (6) results in a difference in meaning, in (9) there is no accompanying difference in meaning.[9] The reason for this is that we have in (9) an instance of coextensiveness. Since John and the chair are engaged in forward motion, it amounts to the same thing whether we describe the chair as being spatially or temporally related to him. The same situation can be perceived in either way. Hence (9a) and (9b) do not contrast.

It should be stressed, in conclusion, that 'synonymy' is not a technical term of stratificational theory. Consequently a stratificational description is not altered in any way by the particular definition of synonymy we decide to use. Thus *before* and *in front of* exhibit hypersemo-sememic diversification and complementary lexotactic distribution—irrespective of whether one, both, or neither example is regarded as an instance of synonymy.

6. More on Meaning

When a polysemous lexeme occurs in context, the context as it were selects one from among its alternative possible meanings (except where the utterance containing the lexeme is ambiguous). However, the meaning that a lexeme has in a context (and this applies also to non-polysemous lexemes) is not monolithic. Rather, it can be broken down into a number of simultaneous constituents (where 'constituent' has a somewhat wider sense than the 'component' of componential analysis, cf. section 7). It is not surprising that there are various separate constituents to the meaning of a lexeme, once we realize that there is considerable linguistic structure above the level of the lexemes and that a given lexeme has connections to various parts of this structure. Five constituents of meaning will be discussed briefly here: cognitive, connotative, stylistic, reflected and semotactic meaning. It is not the case that all five are present in the meaning of all lexemes. In fact connotative meaning may well never be present in the meaning of a preposition or of relationals generally. It is included in the discussion merely because it is an important constituent of meaning that has long been recognized. On the other hand, a more extensive treatment of English semology would certainly need to distinguish more than five constituents of meaning.

Cognitive and connotative meaning can be considered together. The distinction would seem to depend on a division of the features of extralinguistic experience into distinctive and non-distinctive features. Lamb has pointed out (1965b:51–53) that one cannot speak in any GENERAL sense of non-distinctive features of meaning, since any semantic difference, however small, can be expressed. Distinctive and non-distinctive can only be understood relative to a particular sememe. Whenever a given sememe occurs, certain features of the speaker's extralinguistic experience are obligatorily present. Otherwise a different sememe would have to be used. These features are the distinctive features, which together constitute the cognitive meaning of the sememe. In addition there is a set of non-distinctive features associated with each sememe and these constitute its connotative meaning. Sometimes there is a good measure of agreement between different speakers of a language as to the connotative meaning of a particular item, for example, 'tropics' connotes heat for most, if not all, speakers of English. Often, however, there is considerable discrepancy. Thus, for instance, the connotations of 'dog' may be quite different for two speakers of English, depending on their experience with dogs. Emotive meaning, or emotive connotation, is not a separate constituent of meaning but merely a special case of connotative meaning, namely where the connotation involves some emotional reaction.

The features of meaning on which cognitive and connotative meaning depend are all elements on the hypersememic stratum, viz. hypersememes. However, the nature of the hypersememic stratum is not very clearly understood at present and it is not obvious, to the present writer at least, how the distinction between cognitive and connotative meaning should be represented in a stratificational description.

Stylistic questions—more specifically questions of 'register' (Halliday et al. 1964:87–98)—such as the fact that a given lexeme may be restricted to colloquial, literary, scientific, etc., varieties of the language, are probably best handled by setting up a separate subsystem of the grammar to account for choices of register. This would be connected to the main network at a number of points, in such a way that the choice between two items represented in the main network as being in free variation could be shown to be determined by the choice of register.

The constituent of meaning that we are referring to as 'reflected' meaning is restricted to lexemes (or sememic signs, cf. fn. 8) that are polysemous. When such an item occurs in a context (as the realization of one particular sememe) it may have, in addition to its cognitive meaning, a secondary constituent of meaning that is as it were a reflection of the meaning of some other sense of the lexeme (or sememic sign). The difference in meaning between *a book on astronomy* and *a book about astronomy* seems to be of this kind. The spatiotemporal sense of *on* and *about* describe a precise or an approximate relationship respectively, cf. *on or about October 1*. Now it would appear that when *on* and *about* are used with the (cognitive) meaning 'on the subject of', they carry with them something of the preciseness or approximateness of the spatiotemporal sense, and that it is for this reason that *a book on astronomy* suggests a more serious, scholarly work. To provide a stratificational account of what is involved here, we need to consider the decoding process. This can be visualized in terms of impulses passing upwards through the network of the grammar from sound towards meaning. Whenever an impulse encounters an upward OR—and we are particularly interested here in the upward ORs in the upper lexemic and lower sememic alternation patterns—there is more than one path that it can take. In the case of an unambiguous utterance all paths but one are blocked because the next higher tactics—in this case the semotactics—shows the utterance to be deviant for all but one of the possible readings of the lexeme/sememic sign in question. Now before an impulse succeeds in getting through to the level of the sememes along the one available path, it is as though all the possible paths were at first tentatively activated, and it is the tentative activation of unused paths leading out of the upward OR on which 'reflected' meaning depends. In more familiar terms, this amounts to saying that the hearer is subconsciously aware of other senses of the item in question than the one that constitutes its cognitive meaning in a particular utterance. It seems likely, however, that reflected meaning is only carried over from a more concrete sense to a less concrete sense.

The semotactic meaning of a lexeme depends, as the name implies, on the tactic properties of its underlying sememe, of which speakers of the language are also subconsciously aware. It will be recalled that we attributed the same cognitive meaning to *after* and *behind*. Yet most speakers of English would regard these two lexemes as having different meanings. What we are suggesting now is that the difference in meaning resides in the collocability of the two items, i.e. in their semotactic distribution.

7. Componential Analysis

Componential analysis of meaning (cf. Goodenough 1956; Lounsbury 1956, 1964b, etc.) consists in identifying the features of extralinguistic experience that are distinctive for a particular sememe or class of sememes. Together the components of a sememe constitute its cognitive meaning. This last statement, while true, is not the complete picture. There is namely an intermediate level between that of the sememes and that of the components of meaning: the level of the hypersemons. This level owes its existence to the fact that there is an alternation pattern above the level of the sememes. As we have seen, two sememes—for example, *after* and *behind*—may be alternate realizations of a single hypersemon. Now if the cognitive meaning corresponding to this hypersemon is complex, there are two or more hyper-sememes (components) present in it and we have an instance of portmanteau realization (Lamb 1964a, 1966d). Thus components of meaning are (upward) components of hypersemons,[10] and only indirectly components of sememes. The hypersemon 'posteriority' is, as it happens, not susceptible to componential analysis, so that in this case there is a one-to-one relationship between the level of the hypersemons and that of the hypersememes. However, other examples can be found where two or more hypersememes (components) are simultaneously present in a hypersemon. Thus, for instance, to^{s-t} and *till* are distinct at the level of sememes (since they differ in collocability) but they realize a single hypersemon (i.e. have the same cognitive meaning), and this hypersemon has two components of meaning: a locational component, present also in at^{s-t}, and a directional component.

On the whole, however, comparatively little componential analysis as such needs to be performed on the semological elements underlying English prepositions. Concepts such as 'inclusion' (realized lexemically as *in, during, while, include, inclusion, contain,* etc.) and 'posteriority' (realized lexemically as *after, since, behind, follow,* etc.) are indivisible from the point of view of meaning. The same is true of grammatical relations such as 'agent', 'goal', 'beneficiary', 'instrument', etc., which can also be realized lexemically as prepositions. On the other hand, there would be a need for far more componential analysis if we were to attempt to state the meaning of lexemes directly. Thus we would have to recognize components of meaning such as 'time' and 'place' in order to distinguish *after* and *behind,* and then further components to distinguish *after* and *since.* The reduction in actual componential analysis that the present approach entails is a consequence of recognizing a considerable amount of linguistic structure above the level of the lexemes. Furthermore, it seems more correct intuitively to explain the difference in meaning between *after* and *since* by reference to their semotactic distribution (*since* occurs with one set of tenses, *after* with another set) and therefore as residing within their environments, than to regard the difference as residing within the items themselves.

8. Idioms

An idiom is a grammatically complex string whose meaning is not deducible from that of its constituent parts. Wherever a preposition occurs as a constituent of an idiom, it is sufficient merely to state this fact. The preposition as such has no connection to the higher levels of linguistic structure. Thus whatever components of meaning are present in the idiom *take to* ('conceive a liking for'), they do not include the directional component that is realized in the preposition *to* in a sentence such as *he's gone to London.* In a stratificational description an idiom is represented by a downward AND. If the idiom contains a preposition, one of the lines from the plural side (the bottom) of the AND is connected, lower down in the description, to the preposition in question.

The main problem with regard to idioms stems from the fact that they do not come into being abruptly, but only after a long process of synthesis. Examples can readily be found of sequences that are on the way to becoming idioms but have not yet arrived. This is particularly obvious in the area of verb + particle sequences, where a moment's reflection will yield examples that exhibit varying degrees of cohesion between the verb and the particle. *Look for* belongs somewhere in the middle of the continuum separating idioms from nonidiomatic sequences. In certain respects it seems to function as a unit, and yet the meaning of the whole can be deduced from that of its constituent parts, since it is necessary in any case to recognize a sense of *for* that can be labelled 'aim or purpose'. The way to handle such a case within a stratificational description is to allow two possible encodings and decodings: as a unit or as a sequence, cf. Figure 3.

Now if a sequence such as *look for* eventually becomes a full-fledged idiom, there are theoretically two possibilities with regard to its interpretation as a sequence: either this remains also possible, in which case there is both an idiomatic and a literal interpretation (cf. *stand by,* which can mean 'support, be loyal to' or merely 'stand near'); or, on the other hand, the literal interpretation is no longer possible. (In either case the facts would be reflected in the semotactics, which would either permit or not permit the sememes in question—e.g. ^{S}/look/ and ^{S}/for^{aim}/, cf. Figure 3—to enter into a construction with one another.)

Figure 3. Two Coexistent Interpretations of *look for.*

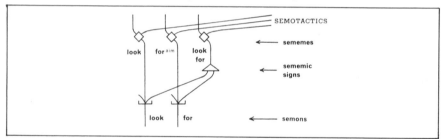

Figure 4. Two Interpretations of *in spite of.*

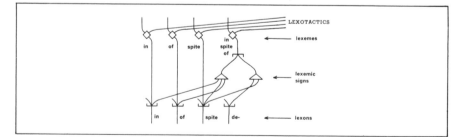

The complex preposition *in spite of* might appear initially to be a good example of a sequence that has only an idiomatic interpretation. This view would be supported by the fact that from the grammatical point of view *in spite of* seems to function in all respects as a unit (cf. Quirk & Mulholland 1964). Thus, for instance, there is no determiner preceding the noun *spite,* nor can the noun be modified by any adjective, nor does the noun show number contrast, etc. However, examples such as (10) indicate that a literal interpretation of *in spite of* is still possible.

(10a) She is taking dancing lessons *in spite of* her mother
(10b) *She is taking dancing lessons *despite* her mother[11]

Figure 4 clarifies the situation. There are two possible interpretations of *in spite of:* an idiomatic (or unit) interpretation and a literal (or sequence) interpretation—of which, admittedly, the unit interpretation is by far the more common. *Despite,* on the other hand, has only one possible interpretation. The idiom *in spite of* can always be replaced by *despite,* but where *in spite of* is meant literally, as in (10a), *despite* cannot be substituted for it. It should be pointed out that there is an alternative explanation of the facts of example (10), namely that the inappropriateness of *despite* is merely a stylistic matter. Perhaps the ideal approach is one which regards the choice of *in spite of* in (10) as being determined by the combined effect of a number of factors, of which two are the ones given above.

It will be noticed that the downward AND in Figure 3 is labelled a sememic sign, whereas the downward ANDs in Figure 4 are labelled lexemic signs. There are namely two levels of idiomaticity (cf. A. Makkai 1965, 1969c, 1972). An important criterion for differentiating between lexemic and sememic idioms is the possibility of interrupting the string in question. The idioms *by heart* and *in spite of* cannot be interrupted and therefore seem to function as units in the lexotactics. Consequently they are best regarded as complex lexemes. The verb and particle of a phrasal verb such as *take to* ('conceive a liking for') also normally stand side by side. However, sentences such as (11) are by no means deviant:

(11) I *took* immediately *to* him

Consequently in our lexemic representation of the utterance it is preferable to regard *take* and *to* as filling separate slots. It is only on the sememic stratum that *take to* is a single unit. Phrasal verbs in general are single sememes which are realized as sequences of two (or more) lexemes. An important consequence of this approach is that intrastratal discontinuity can be dispensed with. In a lexemic representation of (11) there is no discontinuity since *take* and *to* are separate lexemes, and in the sememic representation there is no discontinuity either, since—as stated above—*take to* is a single unit on the sememic stratum. Discontinuity exists only when we try to place a deep interpretation on what is in fact a more surface representation.

Finally it should be noted that the tendency for certain prep+NP+prep sequences to become complex prepositions constitutes one of the respects in which the class of prepositions is open-ended. Other respects in which the class can be augmented are illustrated by the relatively new prepositions: *near, concerning* and *due to.* In the first case an adjective has taken on the function of a preposition after the disappearance of the following preposition *to* (cf. also, *opposite* and *like*). In the case of *concerning* a transitive verb *(concern)* has been adjectivalized by the addition of the suffix *ing,* and then this 'adjective' has come to function like a preposition—although the transitional nature of *concerning* is clear from the unacceptability of (12d):

    (12a) an article *about* the financial situation
    (12b) what is the article *about?*
    (12c) an article *concerning* the financial situation
    (12d) *what is the article *concerning?*

It is clear that there are certain similarities between transitive verbs and prepositions, but the nature of the relationship between the two categories requires considerable further examination. *Due to* probably has even less claim to membership of the class of prepositions than *concerning.* What is involved here is an extension of the lexotactic distribution of *due to,* presumably by analogy with *owing to* and possibly also *because of* and *on account of,* which have the same cognitive meaning but a different lexotactic distribution. Unlike most linguistic change, this particular kind does not go unnoticed. As a result it tends to be resisted by a fairly substantial section of the speech-community. Other similar examples come readily to mind.

9. Concluding Remarks

As was pointed out in the introductory section, it was one of the aims of this paper to sketch the outlines of a semological description of English prepositions. We have seen that, as soon as one considers the strata above the lexemic, one is forced to examine relationals in general rather than prepositions in particular. It is hoped that in the course of the preceding discussion we have succeeded in giving some idea of the general nature of semological description, as conceived within the framework of one view of the structure of language.

NOTES

1. I am indebted to Roger Higgins, Yoshihiko Ikegami, Sydney M. Lamb, N.V. Smith and Rulon S. Wells for many helpful comments on earlier versions of this paper. In addition, I have profited considerably from discussions with the following: Katharine A. Davies, Ilah Fleming, M. A. K. Halliday, Peter A. Reich and J. Michael Young. The main debt, however, is to Sydney Lamb, the influence of whose teaching should be evident throughout the paper. The responsibility for the shortcomings of the paper is, of course, entirely my own.

2. One respect in which Lamb has modified the theory since Lamb 1966d, is in the recognition of an alternation pattern below the tactics of each stratal system in addition to the one above the tactics. The question is discussed at greater length in section 5. «See Chapter 2 of this volume for a more recent discussion of such changes».

3. The graphic notation has been modified by the introduction of a 'diamond' node to replace the upward ANDs of the knot pattern. The four sides of the diamond allow connections (from top left, clockwise) to the higher stratum, higher in the tactics, the lower stratum and lower in the tactics. No more than three lines come out of any one diamond, but it enables one to distinguish more clearly between units of one stratum that have an overt realization on the next lower stratum and those that are realized as a tactic construction, e.g. the semon /Q/ (question). In the former case the diamond is at the bottom of the tactics. There is a

connection to the higher stratum, the lower stratum and higher in the tactics. In the latter case the diamond is in the middle of the tactics. There is a connection to the higher stratum, higher in the tactics and lower in the tactics. In addition, the diamond is more appropriate for a model that is edging its way towards the performance end of the competence-performance scale. It is ordered clockwise for encoding and counter-clockwise for decoding. Thus, for instance, in decoding, an impulse from a lower stratum passes through the knot pattern and on towards the higher stratum only AFTER the necessary tactic requirements have been satisfied. In a competence model, on the other hand, it would be sufficient to state that a given unit has (simultaneously) a particular tactic property and a connection to the higher stratum.

4. The parts of speech are lexeme-classes. On the sememic stratum it would seem that we need to recognize at least the following distribution classes: things, actions (or processes), properties (which subdivide into properties of things, e.g. *tall, height,* etc., and properties of actions, e.g. *quick, speed,* etc.), and relationals. The latter are realized particularly frequently, but not exclusively, as prepositions, conjunctions and adverbs on the lexemic stratum. 'Event' is used below to designate a semotactic construction involving an action and any other sememes that are directly associated with it. Basically this is the scheme proposed by Nida (1964:62–69), although with somewhat different terminology. It should be kept in mind that wherever in the following an English word is used as a label for a sememe, we are nevertheless talking about a rather abstract unit, which may have several other surface realizations than the one used to refer to it. It would be inconvenient to have to invent labels such as 'cause-effect failure' (realized lexemically as *in spite of, although, nevertheless,* etc.) for each individual sememe.

5. I am indebted to Roger Higgins for drawing my attention to this and similar examples.

6. It is now apparent that the statement of the sememic distribution of *after* given in the preceding paragraph was incomplete.

7. The same structure is attributed also to the morphemic and phonemic systems. The hypophonemic (and possibly also the hypersememic) stratal system would appear to lack one or more patterns.

8. I am well aware that the classification of examples of synonymy proposed above is dictated by the stratificational view of language and that adherents of other theories will not necessarily welcome it with open arms. Similarly there are no doubt linguists who would say there is little or no justification for assigning the alternations *sleep:slep-* and *good:be(tt)-* to different levels. Providing they can made out a reasonable case in favor of their position, this is fine. Permit me, however, to indicate the significance within the stratificational framework of distinguishing various levels of synonymy, idiomaticity (cf. section 8), etc. They are a consequence of assigning considerable importance to one particular kind of order that can be recognized in language, namely the order associated with the phenomenon known as realization. A stratificational description of a language aims at relating meanings to sounds in a fully explicit way. In proceeding from meaning towards sound (or in the reverse direction) it is essential to show certain instances of the various realizational relations (diversification, neutralization, composite and portmanteau realization, etc.) as occurring BEFORE certain other instances of these relations. This point was illustrated in the discussion of the *encounter-come across* example. In providing further illustration of the point we can at the same time supply a necessary amendment to the remarks contained in section 4. The view of polysemy presented there was somewhat simplified—in order not to confuse the reader unduly at the outset—in so far as only one level of polysemy was mentioned. Certainly two levels of polysemy need to be differentiated. The one already discussed involves neutralization in the upper lexemic alternation pattern. The second level involves neutralization in the lower sememic alternation pattern. Consider, for instance, the phrasal verb *give up,* which can mean 'stop', e.g. *give up smoking,* or 'surrender'. This polysemy involves the whole phrasal verb rather than *give* or *up* alone. Consequently the upward OR representing the polysemy must be above the downward AND that represents the composite realization. Moreover, *give up* is a complex sememe rather than a complex lexeme (cf. section 8). Therefore the downward AND belongs in the sememic sign pattern and the upward OR in the lower sememic alternation pattern. This is a simple example, but it is essentially this kind of reasoning that determines where a particular

AND or OR belongs. Incidentally, the terminology of stratificational theory, which may at first appear somewhat formidable but is really very straightforward (!), serves the purpose of permitting one to specify at what point in the realization chain any instance of diversification, neutralization, etc., is situated.

9. If we employ 'intension' and 'extension' for the meaning-reference distinction, this allows us to use 'meaning' in its very general everyday sense. It is in this way that it is intended in the present paragraph.

10. If there is any composite realization in the hypersememic stratal system, there will not always be a one-to-one correspondence between hypersememic signs and hypersemons. Strictly speaking, components of meaning would then be components of hypersememic signs. At any rate, the point is that they are not directly components of sememes.

11. I am indebted to Katharine Davies for this example.

CHAPTER FIFTEEN

A Stratificational View of Polysemy*

DAVID C. BENNETT

IN STRATIFICATIONAL TERMS polysemy, or multiple meaning, is a specific instance of the general phenomenon known as neutralization (Lamb 1964a, 1966d), which is represented in graphic notation (Lamb 1966d) by means of an UPWARD OR node in the realizational part of a grammar.[1] Moreover, the UPWARD OR representing a case of polysemy is situated above the level of lexemes. The aim of this paper is to present a few general observations on polysemy, illustrated mainly by reference to the meaning of the preposition *over*.

If we look up *over* in a dictionary, we may find up to 20 different senses listed. However, it is well known that, no matter now useful dictionaries are for practical purposes, they recognize far more polysemy than is appropriate for a strictly linguistic description. Weinreich (1963:162) states this point as follows:

> Most dictionaries vastly exaggerate the incidence of polysemy at the expense of vagueness or generality, e.g. in listing separate meanings for *fair* as in *fair chance* and *fair* as in *fair health*.

It is advisable therefore in making use of the information given in a dictionary to subject it first to close examination rather than merely to incorporate it as it stands into a description of a language, e.g. by drawing an UPWARD

*Read at the December 1968 annual meeting of the Linguistic Society of America, this paper was reproduced as a report of the Yale University Linguistic Automation Project. Reprinted by permission. Bennett 1972 provides a revised discussion of these problems in a broader context.

OR corresponding to the lexeme *over* with 20 lines coming out of it, each connecting to a separate sememe.

Eight of the senses of *over* that one might find in a dictionary[2] are listed, together with one example of each, as (1)–(8) below.

(1) Directly above
   The airplane flew over the town
(2) Above and covering
   She spread a cloth over the table
(3) Before and covering
   They hung a curtain over the picture
(4) Above in status or position
   He has two people over him in the office
(5) Above and onto the other side of
   We climbed over the gate
(6) Across, from one side to the other
   The bridge over the river is closed
(7) Downwards from the edge of
   John fell over a cliff
(8) As the result of collision with
   John fell over a stone

Two things need to be said about these eight senses. First, they all overlap—in the same way that the allophones of a phoneme overlap. The situation can be represented diagrammatically by means of intersecting circles, as in Figure 1. (For the sake of simplicity only three circles are shown. To facilitate reference to the diagram, the area of overlap of the circles is shaded, and the total area covered by the three circles, the union of the circles, is enclosed by a dotted line.)

Figure 1. Three Overlapping 'Senses' of a Lexeme (a, b, and c).

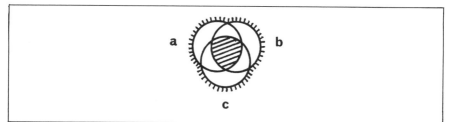

Common to each of the above senses of over is a feature of meaning which I will refer to as 'superiority'. It involves the relationship between two things in a vertical dimension, stated from the point of view of the higher one. This feature is present even in sense (3), despite the gloss 'before and covering', in that in the example given *(they hung a curtain over the picture),* some part of the curtain would be higher than the picture.

Secondly, the features of meaning by which the eight senses are distinguished are determined in some way by the context. Thus the notion of 'covering' which is stated as part of the meaning of sense (2), as in *she spread a cloth over the table,* is determined partly by the meaning of the lexeme *spread* and partly by our knowledge of what cloths and tables are like. The difference between sense (7), 'downwards from the edge of' as in *John fell over a cliff,* and sense (8), 'as the result of collision with' as in *John fell over a stone,* depends on our assumptions as to the relative size of John and cliffs, on the one hand, and John and stones, on the other. The only way that a normal-sized man may fall over a normal-sized cliff is downwards from the edge of it. He could also fall as a result of colliding with a cliff, but this would not involve falling *over* a cliff. However, we should not overlook the possibility that *John* might be the name of a giant in some fairy tale. In this case the average-sized cliff might reach no further than John's knee and he could fall over it in much the same way as a normal-sized man might fall over a chair, or even a large stone.

If it is true that the features of meaning by which the various senses of *over* are distinguished are determined by the context, then there is little justification for regarding them as inherent in the meaning of *over* itself. In other words, with reference to Figure 1, it seems preferable to regard only the shaded area as the meaning of the lexeme, rather than the whole of the area inside the dotted line.

It may be helpful at this point to draw a parallel between semology and phonology. The diagram of Figure 1 could also represent a phoneme, the three circles corresponding in this case to perceptually distinct manifestations of the phoneme, i.e. allophones. The question 'what exactly is the phoneme?' can be answered in two distinct ways: either we consider the whole of the area inside the dotted line to be the phoneme, or we regard the phoneme merely as the shaded area. The former view corresponds to the class-of-allophones view of the phoneme, while the latter view corresponds to the bundle-of-distinctive-features view of the phoneme. That is to say, an obvious way of defining the area enclosed by the dotted line is by listing the various manifestations of the phoneme; whereas the shaded area can be defined by specifying the features that are shared by all manifestations of the phoneme. These two approaches to the phoneme may also be characterized as the 'extensional' approach (the class-of-allophones view) and the 'intensional' approach (the bundle-of-distinctive-features view). Notice that the possibility of these two approaches is really independent of how abstract one's particular phoneme happens to be. It would be possible to define a generative-transformational 'systematic phoneme' by listing its various manifestations, rather than specifying its distinctive features. I hasten to add, however, that I am not recommending anyone to do this, because it is clear that the intensional approach is far more profitable than the extensional approach.

Returning now to semology, the last point we made (although at that stage the distinction between extension and intension had not yet been introduced) was that an intensional approach to meaning is preferable to an extensional approach. We have seen that the dictionary approach to describing the meaning of a preposition such as *over* is an extensional approach. The alternative approach, the intensional approach, has been advocated in the past notably by Jakobson, and is often referred to as the *Gesamtbedeutung* approach (see, for instance, Jakobson 1932, 1936). The *Gesamtbedeutung* of a lexeme is a conjunctive definition of its meaning in terms of a bundle of distinctive semantic features. Thus the dative case in Russian, according to Jakobson (1936), contains features that distinguish it from the accusative and the instrumental with reference to the 'Stellungskorrelation' and 'Bezugskorrelation' respectively. More recently this approach has been adopted by anthropological linguists working in areas such as kinship (see, for instance, Lounsbury 1956, 1964a).

Now a special case of a bundle of distinctive features is the case where there is only one distinctive feature, and I would suggest that the meaning of *over* in all the examples considered so far can be specified by means of a single feature, namely the feature 'superiority'. A consequence of adopting an intensional view of meaning, rather than an extensional one, is that the meaning of *over* is the same in (1)–(8). Thus according to a somewhat different use of the term 'sense' than the customary one, we may say that the same sense of the preposition occurs in each of the eight examples.

The question now arises whether an intensional view of meaning forces us to regard all lexemes as having only one sense. The answer to this question is no. Wherever there is no overlap whatsoever between two senses of a lexeme given by a dictionary, it IS necessary to recognize separate senses. There seems to me to be nothing in common to the meaning of the preposition *by* in (9) and (10):

(9) He is standing *by* the door
(10) It was painted *by* a professional

In such cases the facts would be represented in a stratificational description by means of an UPWARD OR, showing the lexeme in question as being connected to two separate sememes.

We saw from the quotation given above that Weinreich did not approve of the policy on polysemy adopted by most dictionaries. But the discussion of polysemy in Weinreich (1966:411–412) suggests that he was prepared to recognize more polysemy than, as it now seems to me, is appropriate. The remainder of the paper is devoted to an elaboration of this last observation.

Weinreich was prepared to recognize polysemy wherever a lexeme seemed genuinely ambiguous, as opposed to merely vague. Obviously there are problems associated with drawing the line between genuine ambiguity and vagueness, but sentence (11) would appear to be genuinely ambiguous.

(11) The helicopter is *over* the hill

The ambiguity can be resolved by replacing *over* by either *above* or *on the other side of*. Let us assume for the time being (although this view will be revised later) that this is proof that *over* has at least two senses, and let us represent the polysemy by means of an UPWARD OR, as in Figure 2.

Notice, however, that one may substitute *over* for *on the other side of* only in certain cases. Corresponding to (12) we may say (13):

Figure 2. First Approximation to Accounting for the Ambiguity of Sentence (11).

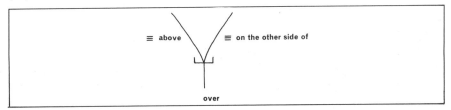

(12) He lives *on the other side of* the hill
(13) He lives *over* the hill

but many speakers of English would not accept (15) as a paraphrase of (14):

(14) He lives *on the other side of* the valley
(15) ?He lives *over* the valley

And it seems reasonable to assert that no-one would accept (17) as a paraphrase of (16):

(16) He is standing *on the other side of* the bus
(17) *He is standing *over* the bus

Figure 3. Second Approximation to Accounting for the Ambiguity of Sentence (11).

Figure 4. Third Approximation to Accounting for the Ambiguity of Sentence 11.

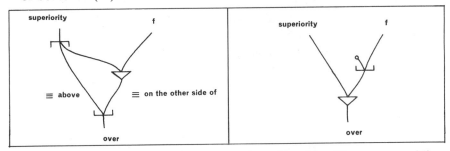

It would appear that we may replace *on the other side of* by *over* providing that the normal route for getting to the other side involves going over something in the 'above' sense of *over*. In other words, the feature of meaning 'superiority' is present in *over* even when it appears to mean *on the other side of*. Figure 3 incorporates this additional information. It shows *over* as having two senses, one of which means 'superiority', while the other contains the feature 'superiority' together with—the little triangle is an UPWARD AND node—some further feature or features that we can refer to temporarily as 'f'. But this diagram can be simplified, because we arrive at the feature 'superiority' whichever path we take out of the UPWARD OR. In Figure 4 this generalization is stated explicitly by making the lowest node an UPWARD AND rather than an UPWARD OR and allowing one line out of it to connect directly to the feature 'superiority'. *Over* is thus shown as always containing 'superiority' and, in addition, optionally containing 'f'. (Optionality may be symbolized by means of an UPWARD OR with one line going to zero: one may take either the line leading to 'f' or the line leading nowhere.)

At this point we may interrupt the discussion of *over* to show that we are dealing here with a quite general phenomenon. The prepositions *across, along, around* and a few others also seem to behave like *over,* i.e. each seems to be ambiguous in a similar way. Consider, in addition to (11), examples (18)–(20):

(18) There's a tree *across* the road
(19) There are some trees *along* the road
(20) There's a white line *around* the corner

Figure 5 gives a pictorial representation of the two interpretations of each of these four sentences. In each of the (b) pictures (the ones on the right) the X marks a reference point. The (b) interpretation can be stated unambiguously by adding 'from X' to each of the original sentences. Thus:

(11b) The helicopter is *over* the hill from X
(18b) There's a tree *across* the road from X
(19b) There are some trees *along* the road from X
(20b) There's a white line *around* the corner from X

Figure 5. Four Ambiguous Sentences.

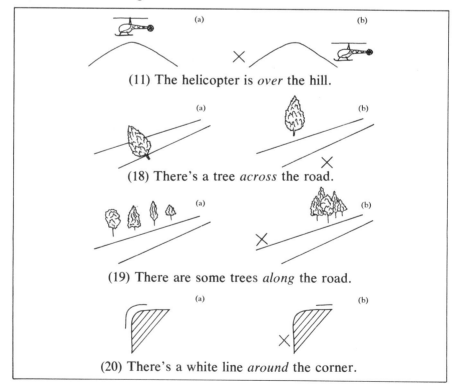

(11) The helicopter is *over* the hill.

(18) There's a tree *across* the road.

(19) There are some trees *along* the road.

(20) There's a white line *around* the corner.

The (b) interpretations may therefore be said to contain a deictic component; the (a) interpretations, on the other hand, contain no such deictic component.

If we consider now sentence (21) and its accompanying pictorial representation, Figure 6, it will be apparent that progression through space can be broken down into three phases: a source, a path and a goal.

(21) John walked from behind the house over the hill to the river

Imagine now the situation where John is at the river and someone else back at the house is informing a third person of John's location. There are essentially two ways of specifying John's position, one non-deictic and the other deictic. The nondeictic possibility is:

(22) John is *at* the river

The deictic possibility (which is admittedly less precise) is:

(23) John is *over* the hill

The meaning of (23) is, of course, 'John is over the hill with relation to the house', which is clearly distinct from being over the hill with relation to the river.

Now in (21) and Figure 6 we saw that *over the hill* was a path-expression.

Figure 6. Three Phases of Progression through Space.

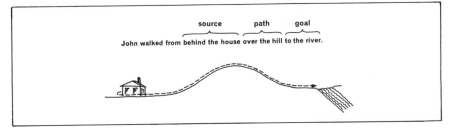

This suggests that (23) (in its deictic interpretation of course, since it is potentially ambiguous) 'really means': 'John is at the end of a path leading over the hill'.

Returning to sentences (11) and (18)–(20), and Figure 5, it would now seem that the deictic interpretation in each case, the (b) interpretation, involves a path-expression. Furthermore, the X in each of the drawings on the right of Figure 5 marks the beginning of the path, which one needs to know before one can work out where the end of the path is.

Let us now consult Figure 4 once again. It is still necessary to identify the feature or features labelled 'f'. An obvious candidate is the feature 'path'. In this case Figure 4 would state that *over* always contains the feature 'superiority' and may in addition contain the feature 'path'. This seems reasonable in the light of sentence (21), where it will be noticed that there is an overt marker of the source and goal (*from* and *to* respectively), but no overt marker of the path. *Over* in this sentence thus appears to be a portmanteau realization of 'superiority' and 'path'.

There is, however, a further complication. The sentence

(24) The helicopter is flying *over* the hill

is three-ways ambiguous.[3] It can mean

(24a) The helicopter is hovering directly above the hill
(24b) The helicopter is in the process of traversing the hill
                                    or
(24c) The helicopter is flying on the other side of the hill

As a first and highly tentative suggestion for handling this three-way ambiguity, one might invoke an aspectual feature 'completion'. Version (a) contains neither 'path' nor 'completion'; version (b) contains the feature 'path', but not 'completion'; and version (c) may be said to contain both 'path' and 'completion', thereby indicating that something is happening at the end of a path leading over the hill. If this analysis is correct, then the feature 'completion' is present also in the (b) version of (11) and (18)–(20).

In Figure 7, therefore, the feature 'completion', as well as the feature 'path', is allowed to be realized together with the feature 'superiority' in the lexeme *over*. A parallel analysis is shown for *across,* and we could have added *along, around* and a few other prepositions. But this analysis as it stands states separately for each of these prepositions that they may contain the features 'path' and 'completion'. There is an alternative analysis which avoids this duplication of information. This is shown in Figure 8. Here the features 'path' and 'completion' (which are in fact sememes, in stratificational terms) are allowed to be realized lexically as zero. There is a considerable amount of information that is not included in the diagram because I have yet to work out the details (such as stating when the sememe 'path' may be realized as zero and when it is realized as the lexeme *via*). But, assuming that this information could be incorporated into a larger diagram, Figure 8 has the same effective information (Lamb, 1966d) as Figure 7, in that it is supposed to show that when 'superiority', 'path' and 'completion' co-occur,[4] they are realized simply as *over*. However, the surface

Figure 7. Fourth Approximation to Accounting for the Ambiguity of Sentence (11).

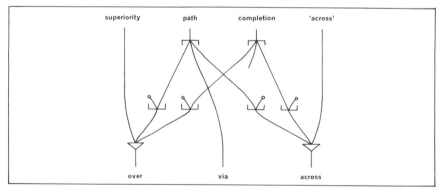

information (Lamb, 1966d) of Figure 8 is considerably less than that of Figure 7. The portmanteau realization of Figure 7 (the UPWARD ANDS) is eliminated from Figure 8. However, more important for the present discussion, the polysemy of *over* is also eliminated. In Figures 2, 3, 4, and 7 *over* was represented as being polysemous in that there was at least one UPWARD OR above it. (An OR node represents a choice between two or more alternatives; thus we were saying that the meaning of *over* involved such alternatives.) In Figure 8, on the other hand, there is no UPWARD OR and *over* is consequently not shown as polysemous.

Figure 8. Final Solution to the Ambiguity of Sentence (11).

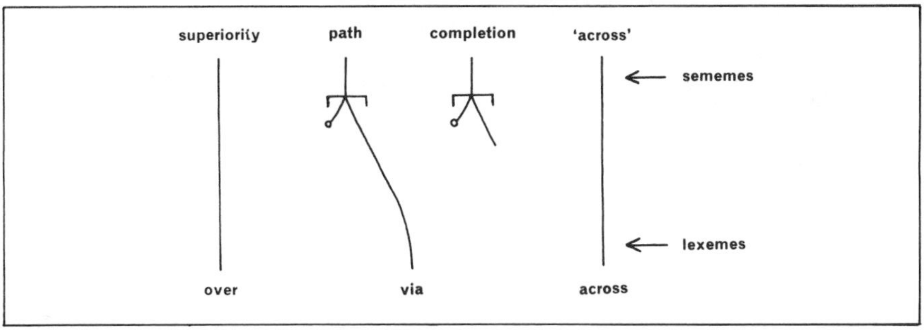

According to the previous analyses, the ambiguity of sentence (11) *(the helicopter is over the hill)* depended on the polysemy of the preposition *over*. According to the preferred analysis, the ambiguity depends on the presence or absence of the sememes 'path' and 'completion'. When the latter are present, they have no overt realization in the surface structure. However, their meaning combines with the 'superiority' of *over*, with the result that the preposition appears to mean 'on the other side of'.

From the discussion of the second half of the paper the following conclusion may be drawn: wherever an ambiguous sentence can be 'disambiguated' by substituting for one of its lexemes, this does not necessarily prove that the original lexeme was polysemous.[5]

NOTES

1. During the preparation of this paper I benefitted considerably from discussions with Edward N. Adams III, Jorge Hankamer, Sydney M. Lamb, Samuel E. Martin, Geoffrey R. Sampson and Alexander M. Schenker. I am grateful also to all those who contributed to the discussion following the paper in New York.

2. These 8 senses were taken actually, with some modification of the examples, from among the 15 senses of over given in Wood 1967:67–69.

3. I am aware that it is possible to distinguish at least two of the three interpretations phonologically, but of course this does not affect the fact that three distinct semological structures need to be postulated.

4. It was pointed out quite correctly by James D. McCawley during the discussion following the oral presentation of this paper that it is not adequate to state merely that 'superiority', 'path', and 'completion' may 'cooccur'. It is necessary to specify what kinds of constructions these elements may (and, by implication, may not) enter into. Such information about the

combinatory possibilities of semological elements belongs in the semotactics of a stratificational description. In preparing this paper I concentrated on realizational phenomena, to the exclusion of tactics. Recently I have begun to tackle the relevant parts of semotactics, but the results obtained so far are at too preliminary a stage to be reported here.

5. Some evidence was provided in this paper in support of the view that the preposition *over* has only one sense rather than the large number of senses that are listed in dictionaries. In the discussion following the oral presentation of the paper it was suggested by James E. Redden that in a sentence such as

(25) I've got mud all *over* the bottom of my boots the meaning of *over* is not 'superiority' but 'covering'. It is now clear to me that Dr. Redden's observation is correct and that it is necessary to recognize at least two senses of *over*. I would still maintain, however, that the semantic feature 'covering' that can be identified in (2) (*she spread a cloth over the table* is determined by the context of *over* rather than a distinctive feature of its meaning. Thus 'covering' is in some instances a distinctive feature of the meaning of *over* and in others a determined feature.

With regard to the more general question of the optimal approach to polysemy, it should be stressed that the present paper is very much in the nature of a progress report. Considerable work remains to be done.

CHAPTER SIXTEEN

The Transformation of
A Turkish Pasha
into a Big Fat Dummy*

ADAM MAKKAI

THE PRESENT PAPER deals with the process of creating a verse translation of a didactic-performative nursery rhyme from Hungarian to English,
and evaluates the adequacy of contemporary linguistic theories in coping
with translation problems in general.

I intend to show, with a simple concrete example involving two unrelated
languages, that, among familiar theories, transformational-generative grammar is hard put, if at all able, to handle translation, and that the most
reliable scientific hypothesis of the nature of translation will in all likelihood
be a stratificational model if that theory manages to incorporate in its hypersememic system the cultural taxonomy of Pike's behavioremes.

By way of illustration I shall present a brief text in a foreign language:

Pont, pont, vesszőcske,
Készen van a fejecske.
Kurta nyaka, nagy a hasa,
Készen van a Török Pasa.

The text is in Hungarian, and consists of two sentences: (1) *Pont, pont,
vesszőcske, készen van a fejecske,* and (2) *Kurta nyaka, nagy a hasa, készen
van a Török pasa.* A raw, undoctored morpheme-for-morpheme translation
yields the following in English:

*The paper appeared originally in *Working papers in linguistics,* Department of Linguistics,
The University of Hawaii, 3: 4:267–73 (The 'PCCLLU' Papers) and was presented orally
at the Pacific Conference of Contrastive Linguistics and Language Universals in Honolulu
(January 1971). The present version contains some minor revisions. Reprinted by permission.

period, period, comma, diminutive suffix,
ready, adverbial suffix, is, the, head, diminutive suffix.
short, neck, possessive suffix, large, the, belly, possessive suffix,
ready, adverbial suffix, is, the, Turkish, pasha.

Rearranging the content units of the text in accordance with their usual appearance in English, we get the following literal translation:

Period, period, little comma,
The little head is ready.
His neck is short, his belly is big,
The Turkish pasha is ready.

This is a completely accurate literal translation of the original yet it somehow fails to communicate.

If I tell you that I last heard it uttered by my twenty-seven month old daughter Sylvia, otherwise a developing native speaker of English, you will have little difficulty in guessing that it must be some kind of nursery rhyme. Now nursery rhymes are known to be flimsy in the well-formedness of their semological progression, which they usually counterbalance with catchy imagery and sound patterns. What is significant about *this* piece is that it is not a simple nursery rhyme, but what we may call a didactic-performative one. Sylvia was last heard saying it while attempting to draw a human figure with a crayon on a sheet of paper. It is important to observe here that the saying of the various portions of the nursery rhyme is designed to coincide in time with the various drawing motions. Thus during the uttering of *pont, pont, vesszőcske* (i.e., 'period, period, little comma'), the child draws two eyes and a nose, and perhaps also a mouth, depending on her degree of skill and coordination of verbal rhythm with manual rhythm:

Figure 1

During the pronunciation of the seven syllables *Készen van a fejecske* ("the little head is ready"), the child draws a circle around the eyes and nose, and we have the abstract representation of a human head:

Figure 2

During the next four syllables, *kurta nyaka,* meaning "his neck is short", the child draws two vertical strokes stemming downward from the circle:

Figure 3

while *nagy a hasa* ("his belly is big") coincides with the drawing of a large circle below, representing the belly:

Figure 4

The next eight syllables, *készen van a Török Pasa,* 'the Turkish pasha is ready', with their rhythmical breaks into four pairs of two syllables each, provide the child with the exterior stimulus to draw two stick arms and two stick legs:

Figure 5

We now know a fair amount about the nursery rhyme, what it is used for and what it means literally, but we haven't really TRANSLATED it.

The problem became a very real one when Sylvia approached me and requested, 'Daddy, I want to draw the Török Pasa in mommy language' (that is English).

The task is really more complicated than it appears, because a great deal of cultural substitution must take place. Turkish pashas are meaningless for American children. This aspect of the translation problem may seem linguistically irrelevant, but it cannot be ignored if one is interested in obtaining the best possible translation.

At this point we must, by necessity, enter the suspicious world of poetic license. We must make value judgments. What is more important? The rhyming and the number of syllables, or the exact cultural connotations a Hungarian child would have when drawing his Turkish pasha in Hungarian? Having discovered that we are concerned with the rendition in English of a Hungarian nursery rhyme of the didactic-performative type, the translator must decide in favor of the rhymes, the rhythm, and the completion of the human figure, over the preservation of the exact, if at all available, cultural connotations of the lexemes involved.

Briefly, and to start with the second line first, the translation *ready is the little head* covers *Készen van a fejecske* rather well; as a matter of fact even the word order corresponds. The translator is now committed, however, to the word *head* being at the end of the line; thus whatever the translation of the line above, it must end with a word that rhymes with *head*. The word *thread* appears to fill the bill, and thus we get:

Dot, dot, tiny thread,
Ready is the tiny head.

Through essentially similar calculations, resulting in the omission of *Turkish pasha,* and aided by the discovery that *tummy,* a fair synonym for *belly,* rhymes reassuringly with *dummy,* we come up with the following English version:

Dot, dot, tiny thread,
Ready is the tiny head.
Short his neck, and huge his tummy,
Ready is the big fat dummy.

It may not be great poetry, but then neither was the original. Once in pronounceable and meaningful shape, Sylvia was confronted with the English version. Delighted, she went through the same drawing motions as with the Hungarian, and completed the drawing, on schedule, on the twenty-eighth syllable.

It is my contention that transformational-generative grammar, in its present shape, is unable to account, not only for how the present translation was accomplished, but for translation in general. If we believe, as Chomsky asserts, that the syntactic component is creative, and the semantic and phonological components interpret what the syntax generates, translation could only be accomplished under one of the following procedures:

(1) The phonological output of Hungarian is algorithmically mapped onto an English phonological output. But this is absurd. Phonologies, being interpretive of the syntaxes that generate them, cannot be mapped onto one another without control from the syntactic components.

(2) The second possibility is that the surface structure of the Hungarian is mapped onto the surface structure of the English, after the appropriate dictionary look-ups have been made. But that is exactly what we got when we substituted literally morpheme for morpheme. We must abandon this approach also, since it does not yield comprehensible English.

(3) Thirdly, if we try to map deep structure onto deep structure we might come up with the adjusted literal translation:[1]

Period, period, little comma,
The little head is ready.
His neck is short, his belly is big,
The Turkish pasha is ready.

The problem is that the rhymes are lost, as is also the knowledge of the fact that the nursery rhyme is a didactic-performative game in the source language. These are the most obvious objections to the transformational-generative approach. But there are more basic ones as well. If the syntax generates and the semantic component interprets, what exactly happens in translating into the target language? The translator does not interpret anything. He in fact takes the semantic interpretation of the source language and re-encodes it in the target language. Furthermore, he must re-encode it with discretion, as the case of our omission of *Turkish pasha* shows. One might argue that what happens in the target language is not the same as what happens in the source language; that in the source language one starts with syntax and then interprets it, whereas in the target language the semantic interpretation comes over ready-made from the source language, and the syntax must follow suit. The problem with such a view is that it supposes a double standard: we describe a person's COMPETENCE in the source language, whereas the only way his ability to translate into the target language can be handled is by ascribing it to PERFORMANCE. The transformationalist would, in fact, have to say that translation belongs to performance, not to competence. But it is a logical contradiction to suppose that a person can out-perform his own competence. (See A. Makkai 1971b) And yet the mappings attempted above, of phonology onto phonology, etc., do not produce an adequate result.

If one cannot go directly from the phonology of language A to the phonology of language B, or from the surface structure of A to the surface structure of B, or from the deep structure of A to the deep structure of B, the only recourse is to go from the phonology of A to the surface structure of A, then to the deep structure of A, and then to the semantic component of A; and *only then* can one transfer to B. This obviously must be on the semantic or cognitive level. Thus from the semantic component of A we go to the semantic component of B, then to its deep structure, its surface structure, and down to its phonological component. But at this point we have really abandoned transformational-generative grammar.

In fact, this amounts to a recognition of the stratification of language. The translator actually procedes as is illustrated in the following diagram:

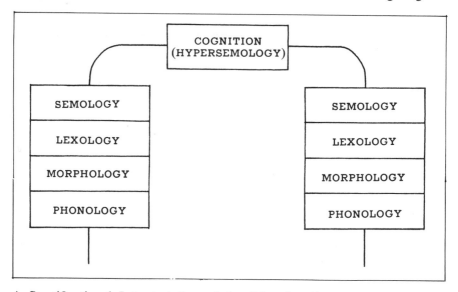

A Stratificational Interpretation of the Directionality of the Translation Process

The knowledge that the source text is a traditional nursery rhyme is stored in the hypersemology, as is the awareness that it is a didactic-performative rhyme, and that Turkish pashas are not meaningful for English speaking children. This knowledge causes the translator to adjust, correspondingly, the semology and the lexology of the text in the target language. In terms of tagmemics, such a nursery rhyme would be a behavioreme in the source culture, with its feature and manifestation modes.

Rhyming is essentially a phonological matter. In most instances of verse translation it so happens that the translator, upon some concentration and effort, finds a pair of words in the target language that make sense in the context set up by the source language and which ACCIDENTALLY HAPPEN TO RHYME. In our case this was the discovery that *tummy* and *dummy* were such words in English, suitable both phonologically and semantically. But as most verse translators will testify, such discoveries usually occur BEFORE one commits the discovered, semantically available target-language rhymes to perform any task in the emerging target-language sentence-syntax at all. Far from being INTERPRETIVE, then, it is precisely the phonology of the target language that will 'co-generate', by the power of suggestion as it were, the sentence that will result. Or alternatively, the finding of the acceptable target-language rhyme pair may occur just about the same time one is building the sentence structure that must carry the rhymes. This allows us to choose between two alternatives only: (1) Either the rhyme (a phonological matter of the target language) can have a delimiting and determining effect on the outcome of the sentence, or (2) the finding of the appropriate rhyme is co-synchronous with the building of the sentence. What in fact NEVER HAPPENS is the third alternative, namely (3) whereby the sentence structure *qua* syntax, would determine the outcome of the rhyme. THAT IS, HOWEVER, PRECISELY WHAT TRANSFORMATIONAL THEORY CLAIMS! Thus we see transformational theory claiming the absurd while not being able to account for the obvious, i.e., the commonly observed fact that rhymes can 'dominate' sentence production or be co-synchronous with it. The reason why transformational theory cannot account for cosynchronicity and/or the possible occasional supremacy of phonological criteria over syntactical ones is the central fixation of rule ordering. What happens in verse translation is that the independent features of various levels (rhyme : phonology; number of syllables : phonotactics; available words per meaningful form classes : morphology; available lexemes per context-defined sense and their tactics : syntax; availability of cross-cultural contex-defined sememes : semology AND cognition) are amalgamated by the translator into ONE COHERENT TEXT. Hence the only theory that can account for verse translation is one that can account for SYSTEMS OF SIMULTANEOUS AWARENESS. Pending further details of elaboration, this problem has been solved, at least in PRINCIPLE, by stratificational theory in which we have both ordered and unordered nodes. In the translator's cognitive system there is an 'unordered AND' node which allows him to explore the rhyming possibilities and the sentence building in any order, or simultaneously, as many times as necessary. This is also the only sensible way to explain how a child actually uses such a rhyming didactism: In the child's consciousness there is, again, an unordered AND node one line from which activates the speech mechanism (i.e., the child says the verse out loud), while the other activates the muscular co-ordination center of the central nervous system resulting in the drawing motions. The pedagogical value of such didactisms rests precisely in the fact that they reinforce drawing ability by the mnemonic aid of the verse, and verbal memorization by the aid of the drawing. Note, however, that this varies with age. For Sylvia at 27–28 months it was far easier to say the words in two languages than to draw a half-way decent Pasha, whereas at the age of three and a half the drawing skill got much better co-ordinated. This difference in verbal versus manual skill in the very young, however, does not invalidate my suggestion that at the actual time of performing a drawing-rhyming didactism the person so doing must, by necessity, use a mental ability whose abstract representation is, as far as analogies go, adequately captured by the notion of the UNORDERED AND node.

Note also that this process of translation, as illustrated above, does not apply only to poetry. Consider English *How do you do?*, whose French equivalent is *enchanté* (literally 'enchanted'), while in Indonesian it is *apa kabar* 'What is the news?'. In the case of greetings we lexicalize the entire form and simply utter the corresponding form in the target language, since the cognitive adjustments have been made for us by the social situation in which the greeting occurs. In the translation of new texts however, we must determine by cognitive means what the situation is, and then recreate its proper expression in the target language.

A stratificational grammar, in fact, handles all types of translation: literal prose, slightly idiomatic texts, traditional sayings, and poetry, with the same directionality illustrated on the diagram. If the text is straightforward, as in *dogs bark,* the cognitive system does not signal to the speaker that additional cultural material needs to be added or suppressed. The cognitive system functions as a flexible monitoring device: without it we can translate only as if we were incompletely programmed computers; with it we are able to translate straightforward prose, if that is our task, but also complicated texts which would not otherwise reach the target language in a contextually adequate format.

POSTWORD: Since the presentation of this paper, Mr. Igor Miletić of the University of Illinois at Chicago Circle brought to my attention the fact that in Serbo-Croatian there exists a similar didactic-performative nursery rhyme. The text is as follows:

Točka, točka, točkica,
Gotova je glavica.
Male uši, dugi vrat,
Trbuh mu ko crkven sat.
Male noge ko u miša
Gotovi je čika Gliša.

Literally it means:

Period, period, little period,
Ready is the little head.
Little ears, long neck,
His belly is like the church clock.
Small legs like a mouse,
Ready is Uncle Glisha.

The reader is invited to create his own verse translation. The author would sincerely appreciate word of similar nursery rhymes in other languages.[2]

NOTES

1. The 'deep structures' of both the Hungarian original and the 'adjusted English prose translation' can be worked out in several ways by lexicalist-interpretivist, and generativist transformational readers depending on their vintage of graduation and personal preferences. Labeled trees, bracketed strings, Katzian semi-sentences, deep word order mapped onto surface word order by transformations can all be used as well as pre-lexical predicate raising and semantic feature syntax. Whatever the outcome, you will find that given the ideally 'best' deep structure for the Hungarian version and the 'best' version for the English, the translator has still not fulfilled his goal of translating the given didactism AS VERSE.

2. In addition to the Hungarian, Serbo-Croatian and English (translated) versions, I now have a Danish, two Austrian German, and one Bavarian German version in addition to a native Midwestern American rhyming-drawing didactism involving a fish. (May, 1972)

Bibliography

THE PURPOSE of this bibliography is twofold. In the first place, all references from papers within this volume have been consolidated into this single bibliography. Secondly, we have tried to provide as complete a list as possible of available works on stratificational linguistics, whether included or referred to elsewhere in the volume or not. For properly stratificational works, those written under the influence of Lamb and/or Gleason, we have adopted the device of placing the year designation (or its substitute, such as **in press, forthcoming**) in **boldface type.** Listed works not highlighted in this manner serve solely as references for one or more papers in the volume. Fleming 1969 contains further information in the form of annotations to many of the stratificational works.

ABELSON, ROBERT P.
  1963 'Computer Simulation of "hot" Cognition'. In *Computer Simulation of Personality.* (Silvan S. Tomkins and Samuel Messick, eds.), pp. 277–298. New York: Wiley.
ABELSON, ROBERT P. & CARROLL, J. DOUGLAS
  1965 'Computer Simulation of Individual Belief Systems'. *American Behavioral Scientist* 8:9.24–30.
ABELSON, ROBERT P. & KANOUSE, DAVID E.
  1966 'The subjective acceptance of verbal generalization'. In *Cognitive Consistency.* (Shel Feldman, ed.), pp. 171–197. New York: Academic Press.
  1967 'Language Variables Affecting the Persuasiveness of Simple Communications'. *Journal of Personality and Social Psychology* 7.158–163.
ALGEO, JOHN
  1969 'Stratificational Grammar'. *Journal of English Linguistics* 3.1–7. Earlier version published in *South Atlantic Bulletin* 33:2.1–4 (1968). Reprinted in this volume, pp. 4–11.
ARONSON, HOWARD I.
  1968 *Bulgarian Inflectional Morphophonology.* The Hague: Mouton.
AUSTIN, VIRGINIA M.
  1966 *Attention, Emphasis, and Focus in Ata Manobo.* Hartford Studies in Linguistics, No. 20. Hartford, Ct.: Hartford Seminary Foundation.
BACH, EMMON
  1964 *An Introduction to Transformational Grammars.* New York: Holt, Rinehart, & Winston.
BAR-HILLEL, YEHOSHUA
  1967 Review of: Fodor & Katz 1964. *Language* 43.526–550.
BARKER, M. A. R.
  1964 *Klamath Grammar.* University of California Publications in Linguistics, 32. Berkeley & Los Angeles: University of California Press. (Stage I).
BENNETT, CHARLES E.
  1942 *New Latin Grammar.* New York: Allyn & Bacon. (Earlier editions 1895, 1908, 1918.)

BENNETT, DAVID C.
   1968 'English Prepositions: a Stratificational Approach'. *Journal of Linguistics* 4.153–172. Reprinted in this volume, pp. 277–296. (Stage IV)
   1969 'A Stratificational View of Polysemy'. *Linguistic Automation Project Report*. New Haven: Yale University. (Originally presented at the annual meeting of the Linguistic Society of America, New York, December 1968.) Reprinted in this volume, pp. 297–306. (Stage IV)
   1970 'English Prepositions and Synonymy; a Stratificational View' in *Actes du Xᵉ Congrès Internationale des Linguistes*, Vol 2, pp. 527–535. Bucharest: Éditions de l'Académie de la Républic Socialiste de Roumanie.
   1972 'Some Observations Concerning the Locative-Directional Distinction' *Semiotica*. 5. 58–88.
BEVER, THOMAS G., FODOR, JERRY A., & GARRETT, MERRILL
   1968 'A Formal Limitation of Associationism'. In *Verbal Behavior and General Behavior Theory*. (Theodore R. Dixon & David L. Horton, eds.), pp. 582–585. Englewood Cliffs, N.J.: Prentice-Hall.
BEVER, THOMAS G., FODOR, JERRY A., GARRETT, MERRILL, & MEHLER, JACQUES
   1966 'Transformational Operations and Stimulus Complexity'. (Mimeographed, M.I.T.)
BIDWELL, CHARLES E.
   1963 *Slavic Historical Phonology in Tabular Form*. The Hague: Mouton.
BIERCE, AMBROSE
   1958 *The Devil's Dictionary*. Mt. Vernon, N. Y.: Peter Pauper.
BILIGIRI, H. S.
   1959 'Kannada Verb: Two Models'. *Indian Linguistics* 2.66–89. (Stage I)
BLOCH, BERNARD
   1947 'English Verb Inflection'. *Language* 23.399–418. Reprinted in Joos 1957.
   1948 'A Set of Postulates for Phonemic Analysis'. *Language* 24.3–46.
   1950 'Studies in Colloquial Japanese IV: Phonemics'. *Language* 26.86–125. Reprinted in Joos 1957.
   1953 'Contrast'. *Language* 29.59–61.
BLOOMFIELD, LEONARD
   1926 'A Set of Postulates for the Science of Language'. *Language* 2.153–164. Reprinted in Joos 1957.
   1933 *Language*. New York: Holt.
   1939 *Linguistic Aspects of Science*. Chicago: University of Chicago Press.
BROWN, R. & HONLON, C.
   1968 'Derivational Complexity and the Order of Acquisition in Child Speech'. Paper presented at the 1968 Carnegie-Mellon Symposium on Cognitive Psychology.
CARTERETTE, EDWARD C. (ed.)
   1966 *Brain Function III: Speech, Language, and Communication*. (UCLA Forum in Medical Sciences 4) Berkeley & Los Angeles: University of California Press.
CHAFE, WALLACE L.
   1962 'Phonetics, Semantics, and Language'. *Language* 37.335–344.
   1967 'Language as Symbolization'. *Language* 43.57–91.
   1968a 'Idiomaticity as an Anomaly in the Chomskyan Paradigm'. *Foundations of Language* 4.109–127.

1968b Review of: Lamb 1966d. *Language* 44.593–603.

1968c 'English Noun Inflection and Related Matters from a Generative Semantic Point of View'. *Project on Linguistic Analysis Reports, Second Series, No. 6.* Berkeley: Department of linguistics, University of California.

CHAO, YUEN-REN

1934 'The Non-uniqueness of Phonemic Solutions of Phonetic systems'. *Bulletin of the Institute of History and Philology, Academia Sinica* 4:4.363–397. Reprinted in Joos 1957.

CHOMSKY, NOAM

1956 'Three Models for the Description of Language'. *IRE Transactions on Information Theory.* Vol. IT–2. Reprinted in Luce, Bush, and Galanter 1965, Vol. II.

1957 *Syntactic Structures.* The Hague: Mouton.

1959 Review of: Skinner, B. F. *Verbal Behavior. Language* 35.26–58. Reprinted in Fodor & Katz 1964.

1963 'Formal Properties of Grammars'. In Luce, Bush, & Gallanter 1963, pp. 323–418.

1964 *Current Issues in Linguistic Theory.* The Hague: Mouton. Reprinted in Fodor & Katz 1964.

1965 *Aspects of the Theory of Syntax.* Cambridge, Mass.: M.I.T. Press.

1966 *Topics in the Theory of Generative Grammar.* The Hague: Mouton. Also in Sebeok 1966.

1967a 'Some General Properties of Phonological Rules'. *Language* 43.102–128.

1967b 'The Formal Nature of Language'. Appendix to Lenneberg 1967, pp. 397–442.

CHOMSKY, NOAM & HALLE, MORRIS

1965 'Some Controversial Questions in Phonological Theory'. *Journal of linguistics* 1.97–138.

1968 *The Sound Pattern of English.* New York: Harper & Row.

CHOMSKY, NOAM & MILLER, GEORGE A.

1963 'Introduction to the Formal Analysis of Natural Languages'. In Luce, Bush, & Galanter 1963, pp. 269–322.

CHOMSKY, NOAM & SCHUTZENBERGER, M. P.

1963 'The Algebraic Theory of Context-Free Languages'. In *Computer programming and formal systems.* (P. Braffort & D. Hirschberg, ed.), pp. 118–161. Amsterdam: North Holland.

CONKLIN, HAROLD C.

1962 'Lexicographical Treatment of Folk Taxonomies'. In *Problems in Lexicography* (Fred W. Householder & Sol Saporta, eds.), pp. 119–141. Indiana University Research Center in Anthropology, Folklore, and Linguistics, Pulication 21.

CROMACK, ROBERT E.

1968 'Language Systems and Discourse Structure in Cashinawa'. Unpublished doctoral dissertation, Hartford Seminary Foundation.

DIXSON, ROBERT J.

1951 *Essential Idioms in English for the Foreign Born.* New York: Regents.

EDMUNDSON, H. P. (ed.)

1961 *Proceedings of the National Symposium on Machine Translation.* Englewood Cliffs, N. J.: Prentice-Hall.

FEIGENBAUM, EDWARD A. & FELDMAN, JULIAN (eds.)
1963 *Computers and Thought.* New York: McGraw-Hill.

FERGUSON, CHARLES A.
1966 'Linguistic Theory as Behavioral Theory'. In Carterette 1966, pp. 249–261.

FICKEN, F. A.
1964 'Mathematics and the Layman'. *American Scientist.* 52.419–430.

FILLMORE, CHARLES J.
1969 'The Case for Case'. In *Universals in Linguistic Theory.* (Emmon Bach & Robert T. Harms, eds.), pp. 1–90.

FLEMING, ILAH
1967 'Omission of the determined elements: a type of aphasic error'. Paper read at the summer meeting of the Linguistic Society of America, Ann Arbor.
1969 'Stratificational Theory: an Annotated Bibliography'. *Journal of English Linguistics* 3.37–65.

FLIERL, W.
1958 *Wowosere Tikihata, Buk I.* Madang: Lutheran Mission Press.

FODOR, JERRY A. & GARRETT, MERRILL
1966 'Some reflections on Competence and Performance'. In *Psycholinguistic Papers.* (John Lyons & R. J. Wales, eds.), pp. 135–179. Edinburgh: Edinburgh University Press & Chicago: Aldine.

FODOR, JERRY A., JENKINS, JAMES, & SAPORTA, SOL
undated 'Some Tests on Implications from Transformational Grammar'. (Mimeographed) Palo Alto: Center for Advanced Study.

FODOR, JERRY A. & KATZ, JERROLD J. (eds.)
1964 *The Structure of Language: Readings in the Philosophy of Language.* Englewood Cliffs, N.J.: Prentice-Hall.

FRASER, BRUCE
1970 'Idioms within a Transformational Grammar'. *Foundations of Language.* 6. 22–42.

GEACH, PETER
1957 *Mental Acts.* London: Routledge & Kegan Paul.

GLEASON, H. A., JR.
1964 'The Organization of Language: a Stratificational View'. *Monograph Series on Languages and Linguisitcs* 17.75–95. Georgetown University Institute of Languages and Linguistics.
1968 'Contrastive Analysis in Discourse Structure'. *Monograph Series on Languages and Linguistics* 21.39–63. Georgetown University Institute of Languages and Linguistics. Reprinted in this volume, pp. 258–276.

GOODENOUGH, WARD H.
1956 'Componential Analysis and the Study of Meaning'. *Language* 32.195–216.

HALLE, MORRIS
1959 *The Sound Pattern of Russian.* The Hague: Mouton
1962 'Phonology in Generative Grammar'. *Word* 18.54–72.

HALLIDAY, M. A. K.
1961 'Categories of the Theory of Grammar'. *Word* 17.241–292.
1964 'Syntax and the Consumer'. *Monograph Series on Languages and Linguistics* 17.11–24.
1966 'Some Notes on "Deep" Grammar'. *Journal of Linguistics* 2.57–67.
1967–68 'Notes on Transitivity and Theme in English'. *Journal of Linguistics* 3.37–81, 199–244; 4.179–215.

HALLIDAY, M. A. K., McINTOSH, ANGUS, & STREVENS, PETER
  1964 *The Linguistic Sciences and Language Teaching.* London: Longmans, & Bloomington: Indiana University Press.
HAMMEL, EUGENE A.
  1965a (ed.) *Formal Semantic Analysis. American Anthropologist* 67:5, part 2.
  1965b 'An Algorithm for Crow-Omaha Solutions'. In Hammel 1965a, pp. 118–126.
HAMP, ERIC, HOUSEHOLDER, FRED W., & AUSTERLITZ, ROBERT (eds.)
  1966 *Readings in Linguistics II.* Chicago: University of Chicago Press.
HARRIS, ZELLIG S.
  1942 'Morpheme Alternants in Linguistic Analysis'. *Language* 18.169–180. Reprinted in Joos 1957.
  1944 'Simultaneous Components in Phonology'. *Language* 20.181–205. Reprinted in Joos 1957.
  1948 'Componential Analysis of a Hebrew Paradigm'. *Language* 24.87–91. Reprinted in Joos 1957.
  1951 *Methods in Structural Linguistics.* Chicago: University of Chicago Press.
HAYS, DAVID G.
  1961 'Grouping and Dependency Theories'. In Edmundson 1961, pp. 258–266.
  1963 'Research Procedures in Machine Translation'. In *Natural Language and the Computer.* (Paul Garvin, ed.), pp. 183–214. New York & San Francisco: McGraw-Hill.
  1966 (ed.) *Readings in Automatic Language Processing.* New York: Elsevier.
HAYS, DAVID G. & KAY, MARTIN
forthcoming
      'The Failure of Chomskian Theory in Linguistics'. RAND paper. Santa Monica, Calif: The RAND Corp.
HEBB, DONALD O.
  1966 *A Textbook of Psychology.* Philadelphia: Saunders.
HERRICK, EARL M.
  1966 *A Linguistic Description of Roman Alphabets.* Hartford Studies in Linguistics, No. 19. Hartford, Ct.: Hartford Seminary Foundation.
HILL, ARCHIBALD A.
  1958 *Introduction to Linguistic Structures.* New York: Harcourt, Brace.
  1966 'A Re-examination of the English Articles'. *Monograph series on Languages and Linguistics* 19.217–231. Georgetown University Institute of Languages and Linguistics.
HJELMSLEV, LOUIS
  1943 *Omkring Sprogteoriens Grundlaeggelse.* Copenhagen: Munksgaard
  1954 'La stratification du langage'. *Word* 10.163–188.
  1961 *Prolegomena to a Theory of Language.* English translation of Hjelmslev 1943 by Francis J. Whitfield. Second edition. Madison: University of Wisconsin Press.
HOCKETT, CHARLES F.
  1947a 'Problems of Morphemic Analysis'. *Language* 23.321–343. Reprinted in Joos 1957.
  1947b 'Peiping Phonology'. *Journal of the American Oriental Society* 67.253–267. Reprinted in Joos 1957.
  1947c 'Componential Analysis of Sierra Popoluca'. *International Journal of American Linguistics* 13.258–267.

1951   Review of: André Martinet, *Phonology as Functional Phonetics. Language* 27.333–342.

1954   'Two Models of Grammatical Description'. *Word* 10.210–234. Reprinted in Joos 1957.

1955   *A Manual of Phonology. International Journal of American Linguistics*, Memoir 11.

1956   'Idiom Formation'. In *For Roman Jakobson*. (Morris Halle, ed.), pp. 222–229. The Hague: Mouton.

1958   *A Course in Modern Linguistics*. New York: MacMillan.

1961   'Linguistic Units and their Relations'. *Language* 27.29–53.

1967 *Language, Mathematics, and Linguistics*. The Hague: Mouton. Also in Sebeok 1966. (Stage II)

1968a Review of: Lamb 1966d. *International Journal of American Linguistics* 34.145–153.

1968b *The state of the art.* (Janua Linguarum, 73.) The Hague, Mouton.

HOUSEHOLDER, FRED W., JR.

1959   'On Linguistic Primes'. *Word* 15.231–239.

1965   'On some Recent Claims in Phonological Theory'. *Journal of Linguistics* 1.13–34.

IKEGAMI, YOSHIHIKO

1969 'The Semological Structure of the English Verbs of Motion'. *Linguistic Automation Project Report*. New Haven: Yale University.

1970 *The Semological Structure of the English Verbs of Motion: A Stratificational Approach.* Tokyo: Sandeido.

1971 'A Stratificational Analysis of the Hand Gestures in Indian Classical Dancing'. *Semiotica* 4. 365–91.

JAKOBSON, ROMAN

1932   'Zur Struktur des russischen Verbums'. In *Charisteria V. Mathesio oblata*, pp. 74–83. Prague: Cercle linguistique de Prague. Reprinted in Hamp, Householder, & Austerlitz 1966.

1936   'Beitrag zur allgemeinen Kasuslehre: Gesamtbedeutungen der russischen Kasus'. *Travaux du cercle linguistique de Prague* 6.240–288. Reprinted in Hamp, Householder, & Austerlitz 1966.

JAKOBSON, ROMAN, FANT, GUNNAR, & HALLE, MORRIS

1952 *Preliminaries to Speech Analysis*. M.I.T. Acoustics Laboratory Technical Report No. 13. Cambridge, Mass.: M.I.T. Press.

JONES, A. M. & CARTER, H.

1967   'The Style of a Tonge Historical Narrative'. *Australian Literary Studies* 8.93–126.

JOOS, MARTIN

1957   (ed.) *Readings in Linguistics*. Washington, D.C.: American council of learned societies. Republished in 1966 as *Readings in linguistics I*. Chicago: University of Chicago Press.

1958   'Semology: a Linguistic Theory of Meaning'. *Studies in Linguistics* 13.53–70.

JORDEN, ELEANOR HARZ

1955   *The Syntax of Modern Colloquial Japanese. Language Dissertation* No. 52.

KATZ, JERROLD J.

1964   'Mentalism in Linguistics'. *Language* 40.124–137.

KATZ, JERROLD J. & POSTAL, PAUL M.
   1963   'Semantic Interpretation of Idioms and Sentences Containing them'. *Quarterly Progress Report* (M.I.T. research laboratory of electronics) 70.275–282.

KAY, MARTIN
   1967   'From Semantics to Syntax'. RAND paper P–3746. Santa Monica, Calif.: the RAND Corp. Reprinted in *Progress in Linguistics* (M. Bierwisch & K. Heidolf, eds.) The Hague: Mouton, 1970.

KOUTSOUDAS, ANDREAS
   1963   'The Morpheme Reconsidered'. *International Journal of American Linguistics* 29.160–170.

LAMB, SYDNEY M.
   1957   'Northfork Mono Grammar'. Unpublished doctoral dissertation, University of California, Berkeley. (Stage I)

   1961a   'Segmentation'. In Edmundson 1961, pp. 335–342.

   1961b   'MT Research at the University of California, Berkeley'. In Edmundson 1961, pp. 140–154. (Stage I)

   1961c   'On the Nature of the Sememe'. Mimeographed. Paper read at the summer meeting of the Linguistic Society of America, July 1961, and also at a Semantics conference in Cambridge, England, September 1961. (Stage II)

   1962a   *Outline of Stratificational Grammar*. Berkeley: Associated students of the University of California. (Stage II)

   1962b   'On the Mechanization of Syntactic Analysis'. In *1961 International Conference on Machine Translation of Languages and Applied Language Analysis*, pp. 673–684. London: Her Majesty's Stationery Office. Reprinted in an abridged form in Hays 1966, pp. 149–157. (Stage II)

   1963   'On Redefining the Phoneme'. Paper read at the annual meeting of the Linguistic Society of America. (Stage II)

   1964a   'The Sememic Approach to Structural Semantics'. *American Anthropologist* 66:3, Pt. 2.57–78. Reprinted in this volume, pp. 207–228. (Stage II)

   1964b   'On Alternation, Transformation, Realization, and Stratification'. *Monograph Series on Languages and Linguistics* 17.105–122. Georgetown University Institute of Languages and Linguistics. (Stage II)

   1964c   'Stratificational Linguistics as a Basis for Machine Translation'. Paper read at the U.S.–Japan Seminar on Mechanical Translation, Tokyo, 1964. The first published version of this paper appears in the present volume, pp. 34–59. (Stage III)

   1965a   'The Nature of the Machine Translation Problem'. *Journal of Verbal Learning and Verbal Behavior* 4.196–210. (Stage II)

   1965b   'Kinship Terminology and Linguistic Structure'. In Hammel 1965a, pp. 37–64. Reprinted in this volume, pp. 229–257. (Stage III)

   1965c   'On Form and Content'. Paper read at the annual meeting of the Linguistic Society of America.

   1966a   'Epilegomena to a Theory of Language'. *Romance Philology* 19.531–573. (Stage III)

   1966b   'Prolegomena to a Theory of Phonology'. *Language* 42.536–573. Reprinted in this volume, pp. 128–165. (Stage IV)

   1966c   'The Use of Semantic Information for the Resolution of Syntactic Ambiguity'. *Actes du colloque international de linguistique appliquée,*

Faculté des lettres et des sciences humaines, Nancy, pp. 13–36. (Stage II)

1966d *Outline of Stratificational Grammar.* Revised edition. Washington, D.C.: Georgetown University Press. (Stage IV)

1966e 'Linguistic Structure and the Production and Decoding of Discourse'. In Carterette 1966, pp. 173–199. (Stage II)

1967 Review of: Chomsky 1964 & 1965. *American Anthropologist* 69.411–415.

1968 'Lamb's reply to Teeter'. *American Anthropologist* 70.364–365.

1969 'Lexicology and Semantics'. In *Linguistics Today.* (Archibald A. Hill, ed.), pp. 40–49. New York: Basic Books.

1970 'Linguistic and Cognitive Networks'. In *Cognition: a Multiple View.* (Paul Garvin, ed.), pp. 195–222. Reprinted in this volume, pp. 60–83. (Stage IV)

1971 'The Crooked Path of Progress in Cognitive Linguistics' *Monograph Series on Languages and Linguistics.* 24. 99–123. Reprinted in this volume, pp. 12–33.

1972 'Some Types of Ordering.'*Phonological Theory: Evolution and Current Practice,* ed. Valerie Makkai, pp. 670–677. New York, Holt, Rinehart and Winston.

LAMB, SYDNEY M. & JACOBSEN, WILLIAM H., JR.

1961 'A High-Speed Large-Capactiy Dictionary System'. *Mechanical Translation* 6.76–107. Reprinted in Hays 1966, pp. 51–72.

LENNEBERG, ERIC H.

1967 *Biological Foundations of Language.* New York: Wiley.

LIEMAN, S. L.

1967 'The Queens Grammar'. RAND memorandum RM-5209 PR. Santa Monica, Calif.: the RAND Corp.

LINDKVIST, K. G.

1950 *Studies on the Local Sense of the Prepositions IN, AT, ON and TO in Modern English.* (Lund studies in English, No. 20). Lund: Gleerup.

LOCKWOOD, DAVID G.

1967 'Some Morphotactic Properties of the Czech Noun Declension'. Paper read at the summer meeting of the Linguistic Society of America. (Stage IV)

1969 'Markedness in stratificational phonology'. *Language* 45.300–308. Reprinted in V. B. Makkai 1972 (Stage IV)

1972a 'Neutralization, Bi-Uniqueness, and Stratificational Phonology' In V. B. Makkai 1972, pp. 656–669. (Stage IV)

1972b *Introduction to Stratificational Linguistics.* New York: Harcourt Brace Jovanovich.

1972c The Problem of Inflectional Morphemes'. In this volume, pp. 190–206. (Stage IV)

1972d ' "Replacives" without Process'. In this volume, pp. 166–180. (Stage IV)

LOUNSBURY, FLOYD G.

1956 'A Semantic Analysis of the Pawnee Kinship Usage'. *Language* 32.158–194.

1964a 'A Formal Account of the Crow and Omaha-type Kinship Terminologies'. In *Explorations in Cultural Anthropology: Essays in Honor of George Peter Murdock.* (Ward H. Goodenough, ed.), pp. 351–393. New York: McGraw-Hill.

1964b 'The Structural Analysis of Kinship Semantics'. In *Proceedings of the*

Ninth International Congress of Linguists, Cambridge, Mass., 1962. (Horace Lunt, ed.), pp. 1073–1093. The Hague: Mouton.

LOWE, IVAN

Forthcoming
'Formal and Sememic Structures in Nambiquara Independent Verbs'. (Stage II)

LUCE, R. DUNCAN, BUSH, ROBERT R., & GALANTER, EUGENE (eds.)

1963 *Handbook of Mathematical Psychology,* Vol. II. New York: Wiley.

1965 *Readings in Mathematical Psychology.* New York: Wiley.

LJUNG, MAGNUS

1965 'Principles of a Stratificational Analysis of the Plains Indian Sign Language'. *International Journal of American Linguistics* 31.119–127. (Stage II)

MAKKAI, ADAM

1965 *Idiom Structure in English.* Unpublished Yale University Ph.D. dissertation. (Stage III)

1969 'The Two Idiomaticity Areas in English and their Membership: a Stratificational View'. *Linguistics* 30. 44–58. (Stage III)

1970 'Why Language is Stratified'. *KIVUNG* 2:3. 16–51.

1971a 'The Transformation of a Turkish Pasha into a Big Fat Dummy' *Working Papers in Linguistics* (University of Hawaii) 3:4. 267–275. Reprinted in this volume, pp. 307–315.

1971b 'Degrees of Nonsense, or Transformation, Stratification, and the Contextual Adjustability Principle' in *Papers from the Seventh Regional Meeting, Chicago Linguistic Society,* pp. 479–491.

1972 *Idiom Structure in English.* The Hague: Mouton. (Based on Makkai 1965, revised.)

MAKKAI, VALERIE BECKER

1969 'On the Correlation of Morphemes and Lexemes'. In *Papers from the Fifth Regional Meeting, Chicago Linguistic Society.* (Robert L. Binnick, Alice Davison, Georgia M. Green, & Jerry L. Morgan, eds.), pp. 159–166. Reprinted in this volume, pp. 181–189.

1972 *Phonological Theory: Evolution and Current Practice.* New York: Holt, Rinehart, and Winston.

MALKIEL, YAKOV

1959 'Studies in Irreversible Binomials'. *Lingua* 8.113–160.

MARKOV, A. A.

1954 *Theory of algorithms.* (Works of the V. A. Steklov Mathematical Institute, 42) Moscow: Academy of Sciences of the USSR. (Translated by J. J. Schoor-Kon & staff. Jerusalem: Israel program for scientific translation, 1961. Washington, D.C.: Office of Technical Services, U.S. Department of Commerce, OTS 60–51085)

MARKS, LAWRENCE E.

1968 'Scaling of Grammaticalness of Self-Embedded English Sentences'. *Journal of Verbal Learning and Verbal Behavior* 7.965–967.

MARTIN, SAMUEL E.

1951 'Korean Phonemics'. *Language* 27.519–533. Reprinted in Joos 1957.

McGINNIS, ROBERT

1965 *Mathematical Foundations for Social Analysis.* Indianapolis: Bobbs-Merrill.

McNEILL, DAVID
1966 'Developmental Psycholinguistics'. In *The Genesis of Language: a Psycholinguistic Approach*. (Frank Smith and George A. Miller, eds.), pp. 15–84. Cambridge, Mass.: M.I.T. Press.

MEHLER, JACQUES
1963 'Some Effects of Grammatical Transformations on the Recall of English Sentences'. *Journal of Verbal Learning and Verbal Behavior* 2.346–351.

MILLER, GEORGE A.
1956 'The Magical Number Seven, plus or minus Two: Some Limits on our Capacity for Processing Information'. *Psychological Review* 63.81–97. Reprinted in Luce, Bush, & Galanter 1965, Vol. I.
1962 'Some Psychological Studies of Grammar'. *American Psychologist* 17.748–762.

MILLER, GEORGE A., & McKEAN, KATHRYN OJEMANN
1964 'A Chronometric Study of some Relations between Sentences'. *Quarterly Journal of Experimental Psychology* 16.297–308.

MINSKY, MARVIN
1961 'Steps toward Artificial Intelligence'. *Proceedings of the Institute of Radio Engineers* 49.8–30. Reprinted in Feigenbaum & Feldman 1963, pp. 406–450. Page references to this version. Also in Luce, Bush, & Galanter 1965, Vol. II.
1963 'A Selected Descriptor-indexed Bibliography to the Literature on Artificial Intelligence'. In Feigenbaum & Feldman 1963, pp. 453–523.

MURRAY, Sir JAMES H. A. (ed.)
1961 *The Oxford English Dictionary*. Oxford: At the Clarendon Press.

NARASIMHAN, R.
1967 'On the Non-Relevance of Transformational Linguistic Theory to Psycholinguistics'. *Technical Reports 22 & 22a,* Computer Group, Tata Institute of Fundamental Reserch, Colaba, Bombay–5.

NEWELL, LEONARD E.
1966 'Stratificational Analysis of an English Text'. Appendix to Lamb 1966d, pp. 71–106. (Stage IV)

NEWMAN, STANLEY
1954 'Semantic Problems in Grammatical Systems and Lexemes: a Search for Method'. In *Language in Culture*. (Harry Hoijer, ed.), pp. 82–91. Chicago: University of Chicago Press.

NIDA, EUGENE A.
1948 'The Identification of Morphemes'. *Language* 24.414–441. Reprinted in Joos 1957.
1949 *Morphology: the Descriptive Analysis of Words*. Ann Arbor: The University of Michigan Press.
1964 *Toward a Science of Translating*. Leyden: Brill.

NOREEN, A.
1903–18 *Vårt språk*. Lund: Gleerup. (Selections translated into German by H. W. Pollak, 1923.)

OCHS, SIDNEY
1965 *Elements of Neurophysiology*. New York: Wiley.

PALMER, F. R.
1968 Review of: Lamb 1966d. *Journal of Linguistics* 4.287–295.

PILHOFER, G.
1933 *Grammatik der Kâte-Sprache in Neuguinea.* Dietrich Reimer.
POLLAK, H. W.
1923 *Einführung in die wissenschaftliche betrachtung der sprache.* Halle, M. Niemeyer.
POSTAL, PAUL M.
1964 'Limitations of Phrase-Structure Grammars'. In Fodor & Katz 1964, pp. 137–152.
1966 'On So-called "Pronouns" in English'. *Monograph Series on Languages and Linguistics* 19.177–206. Georgetown University Institute of Languages and Linguistics.
1968 *Aspects of Phonological Theory.* New York: Harper & Row.
QUILLIAN, M. R.
1966 *Semantic Memory.* Report AFCRL-66–189. Cambridge, Mass.: Harvard University Press.
QUIRK, RANDOLPH, & MULHOLLAND, JOAN
1964 'Complex Prepositions and Related Sequences'. *English Studies* 45 (Supplement) 64–73.
REICH, PETER A.
1967 'Competence, Performance, and Relational Networks,' Paper read at the annual meeting of the Linguistic Society of America. Published (1968) as a Linguistic Automation Project Report. New Haven: Yale University. Reprinted in this volume, pp. 84–91. (Stage IV)
1968a 'Symbols, Relations, and Structural Complexity'. Linguistic Automation Project Report. New Haven: Yale University. Reprinted in this volume, pp. 92–115. (Stage IV)
1968b 'The Relational Network Simulator'. Linguistic Automation Project Report. New Haven: Yale Universtiy.
1968c 'The English Auxilaries: a Relational Network Description'. Linguistic Automation Project Report. New Haven: Yale University. (Stage IV)
1969 'The Finiteness of Natural Language'. *Language* 45. 831–843. (Stage IV)
1970a 'Relational Networks'. *Canadian Journal of Linguistics* 15.95–110.
1970b 'The English Auxiliaries: a Relational Network Description (Revision of Reich 1968c) *Canadian Journal of Linguistics* 16. 18–50.
1970c *A Relational Network Model of Language Behavior* Unpublished Ph.D. Dissertation. University of Michigan.
Forthcoming
'Toward a Model of Language Acquisition'. Linguistic Automation Project Report. New Haven: Yale University.
REITMAN, WALTER R.
1965 *Cognition and Thought.* New York: Wiley.
1966 'Information Processing Models, Computer Simulation, and the Psychology of Thinking'. Preprint No. 196. Ann Arbor: Mental Health Research Institute.
ROBERTS, THOMAS H.
1968 'Noun Phrase Substitutes and Zero Anaphora in Mandarin Chinese'. Unpublished doctoral dissertation, University of Hawaii.
ROGERS, HENRY E.
1967 'The Phonology and Morphology of Sherbro'. Unpublished doctoral dissertation, Yale University.

ROMNEY, A. KIMBALL
1965 'Kalmuk Mongol and the Classification of Linear Kinship Terminologies'. In Hammel 1965a, pp. 127–141.

SAMPSON, GEOFFREY R.
1967 'A Stratificational Analysis of the English Numeral System'. Paper read at the summer meeting of the Linguistic Society of America. (Stage IV)
1968 'Noun-Phrase Indexing, Pronouns, and the "Definite Article." ' Paper read at the annual meeting of the Linguistic Society of America. Published (1969) as a Linguistic Automation Project Report. New Haven: Yale University. (Stage IV)
1970 *Stratificational Grammar: a Definition and an Example*. The Hague: Mouton. (Stage IV)

SAPIR, EDWARD
1921 *Language*. New York: Harcourt, Brace.

SAUMJAN, S. K., & SOBOLEVA, P. A.
1963 *Applikativnaja porozdajuščaja model' i isčislenie transformacij v russkom jazyke*. Moscow: Academy of Sciences of the USSR.

SAUSSURE, FERDINAND de
1916 *Cours de linguistique générale*. 5th edition. Paris: Payot, 1955. (First edition 1916). (Translated into English by Wade Baskin, *Course in General Linguistics*. New York: Philosophical library, 1959.)

SAVIN, HARRIS B., & PERCHONOCK, ELLEN
1965 'Grammatical Structure and the Immediate Recall of English Sentences'. *Journal of Verbal Learning and Verbal Behavior* 4.348–353.

SEBEOK, THOMAS A. (ed.)
1966 *Current trends in Linguistics III: Theoretical Foundations*. The Hague: Mouton.

SHIPLEY, WILLIAM F.
1964 *Maidu Grammar*. University of California Publications in Linguistics, 41. Berkeley & Los Angeles: University of California Press. (Stage I)

SMITH, CARLOTA S.
1964 'Determiners and Relative Clauses in a Generative Grammar of English'. *Language* 40.37–52.

SOUTHWORTH, FRANKLIN C.
1967 'A Model of Semantic Structure'. *Language* 43.342–361

STIMSON, HUGH M.
1967 'Stress in Peking Phonotactics'. *Monumenta serica* 26.202–212. (Stage IV)
1968 'Peking Tonal Hypophonotactics', In *Papers of the CIC Far Eastern Language Institute: The University of Minnesota, 1966, & The University of Michigan, 1967*. (Joseph K. Yamagiwa, ed.), pp. 29–38. Ann Arbor: Panel of Far Eastern Language Institutes of the Committee on Institutional Cooperation. (Stage IV)
1969 'Peiping Tonal Phonotactics'. *Bulletin of the Institute of History and Philology, Academia Sinica*. 39:2. 197–201 (Stage IV)

SWADESH, MORRIS
1934 'The Phonemic Principle'. *Language* 10.117–129. Reprinted in Joos 1957.
1946 'Chitimacha'. In *Linguistic Structures of Native America*. (Harry Hoijer, et al., eds.), pp. 312–326. New York: Viking Fund Publications in Anthropology.

TABER, CHARLES R.
   1966   *The Structure of Sango Narrative*. Hartford Studies in Linguistics, No. 17, Hartford, Ct.: Hartford Seminary Foundation.
TESNIÈRE, LUCIEN
   1959   *Éléments de syntaxe structurale*. Paris: Klincksieck.
THOMPSON, RICHARD T.
   1967   'Chinese Lexotactics: a Stratificational View'. Unpublished doctoral dissertation, Georgetown University.
TRAGER, GEORGE L.
   1953   'Russian Declensional Morphemes'. *Language* 29.326–338.
   1955   'French Morphology: Verb Inflection'. *Language* 31.511–529.
TRAKHTENBROT, B. A.
   1963   *Algorithms and Automatic Computing Machines*. Boston: Heath.
ULDALL, H. J.
   1949   'On Equivalent Relations'. *Travaux de cercle linguistique de Copenhague* 5.71–76.
VEILLON, GÉRARD
   1963   'Consultation d'un dictionnaire et analyse morphologique en traduction automatique'. Thesis, University of Grenoble. Mimeographed.
WAHLGREN, JOHN H.
   1963   'Derivational Suffixes in Russian General Vocabulary and in Chemical Nomenclature'. Mimeographed. Berkeley: Machine Translation Project, University of California. (Stage II)
WEINREICH, URIEL
   1963   'On the Semantic Structure of Language'. In *Universals of Language*. (Joseph H. Greenberg, ed.), pp. 114–171. Cambridge, Mass.: M.I.T. Press.
   1966   'Explorations in semantic theory'. In Sebeok 1966, pp. 395–477.
   1969   'Problems in the Analysis of Idioms'. In *Substance and Structure of Language*. (Jaan Puhvel, ed.), pp. 23–81. Berkeley & Los Angeles: University of California Press.
WEIZENBAUM, J.
   1963   'Symmetric List Processor'. *Communications of the ACM* (Association for Computing Machinery) 6.524–543.
WELLS, RULON S.
   1947   'Immediate Constituents'. *Language* 23.81–117. Reprinted in Joos 1957, page reference to this version.
WHITE, JAMES H.
   1964   'The Methodology of Sememic Analysis with Special Application to the English Preposition'. *Mechanical Translation* 8.15–31. (Stage II)
WHORF, BENJAMIN LEE
   1938   'Language: Plan and Conception of Arrangement'. In Whorf 1956, pp. 125–133.
   1941   'Languages and Logic'. *Technology Review* 43.250–252, 266, 268, 272. Reprinted in Whorf 1956.
   1956   *Language, Thought, and Reality: Selected Writings of Benjamin Lee Whorf*. (John B. Carroll, ed.) Cambridge, Mass.: M.I.T. Press.
WILLIAMS, GERALD E.
   1966   'Linguistic Reflections of Cultural Systems'. *Anthropological Linguistics* 8.13–21.

WOOD, FREDERICK T.
1967 *English Prepositional Idioms*. London: MacMillan
YNGVE, VICTOR H.
1960 'A Model and an Hypothesis for Language Structure'. *Proceedings of the American Philosophical Society* 104:5.444–466.
1962 'Random Generation of English Sentences'. In *1961 International Conference on Machine Translation of Languages and Applied Language Analysis*, pp. 65–82. London: Her Majesty's Stationery Office.

Index

This index covers all references in the text to various linguists and other writers and researchers or their ideas. Brief credit notes for discussion, advice, or unpublished examples are not included.